A RISING TIDE

to Christine

A RISING TIDE

*Evangelical Christianity
in New Zealand
1930–65*

Stuart M. Lange

First published in New Zealand 2013 by Otago University Press
Level 1, 398 Cumberland St, PO Box 56, Dunedin, New Zealand

Text copyright © Stuart Lange
Volume copyright © Otago University Press

The moral rights of the author have been asserted.
ISBN 978-1-877578-55-7

A catalogue record for this book is available from the National Library of New Zealand. This book is copyright. Except for the purpose of fair review, no part may be stored or transmitted in any form or by any means, electronic or mechanical, including recording or storage in any information retrieval system, without permission in writing from the publishers. No reproduction may be made, whether by photocopying or by any other means, unless a licence has been obtained from the publisher.

Publisher: Rachel Scott
Editor: Gillian Tewsley
Design/layout: Fiona Moffat
Index: Diane Lowther

Printed in New Zealand by PrintStop Ltd, Wellington

Cover photograph by Nushka Lange
Author photograph by René Lange

Contents

Preface 7

Abbreviations 9

Introduction 11

PART ONE: A TURN OF TIDE, 1930–45
1. Thomas Miller and Friends 25
2. The Evangelical Unions 42
3. William Orange and the Orange Pips 57
4. The IVF and a New Evangelical Generation 72

PART TWO: A RISING TIDE, 1945–65
5. Anglican Evangelicals 1945–55 87
6. Presbyterian Evangelicals 1945–55 107
7. EU/IVF and the Postwar Evangelical Resurgence 126
8. Anglican Evangelicalism Expands, 1956–65 150
9. Presbyterian Evangelicalism Expands, 1956–65 176

Conclusion 206

Epilogue: A Glimpse of What Came Next 212

Notes 216

Glossary 272

Select Bibliography 274

Index 289

Preface

We cannot really understand the history of any society without considering its spiritual beliefs and practices. This book takes up part of that task, telling the story of the resurgence of 'evangelical' forms of Protestant Christianity in mid-twentieth century New Zealand. It was a development which cut across denominational boundaries. It involved countless individuals and families, many churches, and universities and schools. It also had many international connections.

'Evangelicalism' – a broad stream of belief and practice within Christianity – consciously looks back to the New Testament, and has strong roots in the Reformation. It took shape as a modern movement in eighteenth-century Britain and America, and in the following century was a dominant influence on the beliefs and values of both societies. Evangelicalism played a pivotal part in the formation of New Zealand, with evangelical Christians crucial to both the Māori acceptance of Christianity and the Treaty of Waitangi. Evangelical expressions of Christianity have been an important aspect of New Zealand society ever since.

The word 'evangelical' is sometimes confused with 'evangelism'. The latter refers to a particular activity (i.e. spreading the Christian message), whereas the former refers to a theological position. Beliefs and practices can be described as 'evangelical', and people themselves can be identified as 'evangelicals'.

In the northern hemisphere, evangelicalism has become the focus of a considerable body of historical scholarship. The New Zealand part of that story has been much less explored. This book is about Protestant evangelicals in twentieth-century New Zealand, from the 1930s to the 1960s and beyond, and especially about evangelicals within the mainline churches, in the universities, and in card-carrying evangelical organisations. It was a period when the influence of a moderate British evangelicalism was paramount, especially through the influence of the university-based Inter-Varsity Fellowship of Evangelical Unions. This book is not about either pentecostalism or fundamentalism as such. Those two movements both overlap with evangelicalism, but in some respects are significantly different, and most of the growth of pentecostalism in New Zealand has been subsequent to the period covered in this book.

Many thanks are due: to the many informants, most of them evangelical leaders in days gone by, who with generosity and extraordinary trust shared with me their memories and reflections; to the leaders of the Tertiary Student Christian Fellowship, Latimer Fellowship and Westminster Fellowship, for granting me unrestricted access to their archives; to the helpful and efficient staff of several libraries and archives, including the Presbyterian Research Centre, Deane Memorial Library and Kinder Library; to all those who generously corresponded, or kindly sent me various historical resources; to those who searched out and posted me old photographs; to Wendy Harrex and particularly Rachel Scott of Otago University Press, who efficiently brought this book through to publication; to editor Gillian Tewsley, for her thoroughness and many helpful suggestions; to those who in earlier years inspired me with their intelligent evangelical faith, including Win Lewis and Professor Murray Harris; to Robert Glen, who first got me studying and teaching church history; to Associate Professors Peter Lineham (Massey) and John Stenhouse (Otago) for their generous input back when I was completing my PhD; to those who have read and commented on parts of this book in its draft form; to all my Laidlaw College colleagues (and particularly Dr John Hitchen, Dr Tim Meadowcroft, Dr Mark Keown and Dr Martin Sutherland) for their various encouragements; to the College for its ongoing support of research and writing; to all the students in my classes for the stimulus and enjoyment they give; to Valerie Tracey and Jenny Mackie for help in some practical matters; to all the wonderful members, leaders and staff of our church, for their constant support and understanding; to many fine friends, in many places; to my parents and wider family; to our four great sons, René, Richard, Christopher and Jonathan (and daughters-in-law Caitrin, Kathy and Emily), and above all to my ever lovely wife, Christine.

Stuart Lange, 2013

Abbreviations

AEF	Anglican Evangelical Fellowship
AU(C)EU	Auckland University (College) Evangelical Union
BC	Bible Class
BCNZ	Bible College of New Zealand
BD	Bachelor of Divinity
BTI	Bible Training Institute
CBHS	Christchurch Boys' High School
CE	Christian Endeavour
CET	Cashmere Evangelical Trust
CGF	Christian Graduates' Fellowship
CICCU	Cambridge Inter-Collegiate Christian Union
CIM	China Inland Mission
CLTC	Christian Leaders Training College
CMS	Church Missionary Society
CSSM	Children's Special Service Mission
CU	Christian Union
CU(C)EU	Canterbury University (College) Evangelical Union
ECF	Evangelical Churchmen's Fellowship
EFAC	Evangelical Fellowship in the Anglican Communion
EMF	Evangelical Ministers' Fellowship
EP	Evangelical Presbyterian
ESF	Evangelical Students' Fellowship
EU	Evangelical Union
FEBC	Far Eastern Broadcasting Company
ICCC	International Council of Christian Churches
IFES	International Fellowship of Evangelical Students

IVCF	Inter-Varsity Christian Fellowship
IVF	Inter-Varsity Fellowship
IVFEU(NZ)	Inter-Varsity Fellowship of Evangelical Unions (New Zealand)
IVP	InterVarsity Press
NAE	National Association of Evangelicals
NCC	National Council of Churches
NLM	New Life Movement
NCF	Nurses' Christian Fellowship
NZBTI	New Zealand Bible Training Institute
NZSCM	New Zealand Student Christian Movement
OMF	Overseas Missionary Fellowship
OUEU	Otago University Evangelical Union
PBCM	Presbyterian Bible Class Movement
PCANZ	Presbyterian Church of Aotearoa New Zealand
PCNZ	Presbyterian Church of New Zealand
SCM	Student Christian Movement
SU	Scripture Union
TPU	Teachers' Prayer Union
TSCF	Tertiary Students Christian Fellowship
TSF	Theological Students' Fellowship
TSPU	Theological Students' Prayer Union
UMM	United Māori Mission
VU(C)EU	Victoria University (College) Evangelical Union
WBT	Wycliffe Bible Translators
WCC	World Council of Churches
WEC	Worldwide Evangelisation Crusade
WF	Westminster Fellowship

Introduction

In all the Protestant denominations in New Zealand there exist a large number of those who are called 'evangelicals' ...[1]

New Zealand evangelical Protestantism was part of a worldwide movement. In the last thirty years there has been considerable historical study of evangelicalism in Britain, North America and Australia. The New Zealand part in that story needed to be told much more fully, in relation to both the international context and New Zealand's general history.[2] This book is a contribution towards closing that gap in the writing of New Zealand's history. It examines the resurgence in Protestant evangelicalism in New Zealand after the Second World War, against the backdrop of similar developments in English-speaking countries elsewhere.

A number of questions lay behind this book. What were the main reasons for the postwar evangelical boom? What were the main overseas influences? Who were the crucial personalities? What phases did the movement go through? Were there major denominational variations? Were there different regional characteristics? Was there anything particularly distinctive about New Zealand evangelicalism?

The subject of this book is not the more separatist and fundamentalist forms of evangelicalism, but the moderate, transdenominational, conservative evangelical stream that developed in the universities and in New Zealand's main Protestant denominations from about 1930 to 1965. This book tells the story of how such a self-aware and cohesive evangelicalism developed in New Zealand. It was partly a defensive reaction to liberal and ritualist types of Christianity; but primarily it was a positive reassertion of a Protestant Christianity that was both biblicist and evangelistic. The university Evangelical Unions were a major factor in the reconstruction of evangelical identity and confidence, and in the development of vigorous evangelical movements in New Zealand's two largest

Protestant denominations, the Anglican and Presbyterian churches. The two key church leaders who inspired those denominationally based evangelical movements, Thomas Miller and William Orange, also worked closely with the Evangelical Unions.

Evangelicalism should be understood as both a historical movement and a set of doctrinal commitments. A distinction can also be made between those people and groups who consciously identified themselves as 'evangelical', and those who shared characteristic evangelical beliefs and practices but did not explicitly call themselves evangelical.

Evangelical Christianity is an attempt to recapture the faith of the New Testament. The term derives from the Greek New Testament word *euangelion*, meaning 'gospel'. From the time of the sixteenth-century Reformation, 'evangelical' meant belief in justification by faith and in the primacy of biblical authority and practice. In churches that came out of the Reformation, especially on the Continent, 'evangelical' sometimes meant little more than 'Protestant'.[3] Recent historical writing acknowledges that evangelicalism had its roots in the Reformation, and in the subsequent movements of Puritanism and Pietism. However it sees the modern evangelical movement as a phenomenon which first emerged in the 1730s in Britain and its colonies, with new emphases on revival, religious experience and evangelism.[4]

To define evangelicalism, David Bebbington proposed four recurring characteristics: 'conversionism', 'biblicentrism', 'crucicentrism' and 'activism' (the latter includes such things as evangelism, overseas mission and evangelical humanitarianism).[5] Some historians have offered alternatives, such as Noll's description of evangelicalism as 'culturally adaptive biblical experientialism',[6] but Bebbington's definition is widely accepted. Some evangelical leaders have argued for long lists of defining characteristics.[7] However, John Stott identified evangelicalism with just two markers: Bible and Gospel;[8] and J.I. Packer reduced that to just one: faithfulness to scripture.[9] Historians have shown how evangelicals emphasised different doctrines and practices at different times, and were constantly adapting to new contexts. They have also pointed out how evangelicalism has always been populist, and informally spread by voluntary associations and hymns.[10]

The writing of evangelical history has its own particular challenges. Because evangelicalism is a mindset rather than a closed system, and an unstructured transdenominational movement crossing many ecclesiastical and national boundaries, it has often escaped attention from historians preoccupied with the history of denominations. Evangelicalism has often been inadequately or negatively portrayed by those outside the movement. On the other hand, in-house evangelical histories have sometimes given insufficient attention to shifts and variations within evangelicalism, or have been marred by hagiography.

The International Evangelical Context
The United States

In North America, evangelical Protestantism was influential in shaping religion and culture from the mid-eighteenth century to the end of the nineteenth century, and then resurgent from the mid-twentieth century. There has been extensive historical study of American evangelicalism and all its varieties,[11] with one writer identifying no fewer than fourteen different types of evangelicalism in the United States.[12]

In American evangelicalism since the late nineteenth century, three broad phases can be identified. In the first of these, c.1870–c.1930, evangelicalism became more reactionary. The reasons for that included the challenges of Darwinism and sceptical biblical criticism, the rise of theological liberalism and modernism, and the secularisation of higher education. Many evangelicals became very alarmed. Some came to see liberal Christianity as a new and 'different religion'.[13] Conservative reactions included a stronger and narrower emphasis on biblical authority (including insisting the Bible is 'inerrant' – without error in any respect, even in minor and incidental details), the writing of the anti-modernist series of books entitled The Fundamentals (1910–15), and the battles and schisms of the 1920s.

In the second period of American evangelicalism, c.1930–45, many American conservatives splintered off into separate churches and were often anti-intellectual.[14] They generally identified themselves as 'fundamentalists', not 'evangelicals'.

In the third period, c.1945–70, many theological conservatives moved from relative isolation to become once again a positive, intellectually self-assured and more united movement, determined to regain cultural influence. Reformist leaders such as Carl Henry and Harold Ockenga distanced themselves from fundamentalism and called themselves 'neo-evangelicals', reclaiming a confident mainstream evangelical Protestant tradition. The National Association of Evangelicals (1943) helped differentiate neo-evangelicals from the militant and separatist fundamentalism represented by Carl McIntire and the American Council of Christian Churches.[15] From 1949, the main unifying figure in the recovery was Billy Graham. Other important factors in the neo-evangelical recovery were the establishment of the Inter-Varsity Christian Fellowship (IVCF) in the United States (1939), the building of evangelical publishing houses such as Eerdmans, and the huge influence of British evangelicals such as John Stott.[16]

Britain

In the early twentieth century, British evangelicalism[17] experienced its own form of the conservative–liberal theological divide. A powerful symbol of that divide was the 1910 split of the Cambridge Inter-Collegiate Christian Union (CICCU) from the liberalising Student Christian Movement (SCM).[18] Other indications were the formation of a Modern Churchmen's Union (headed by an expatriate New Zealander, H.D.A. Major), and the growth of a 'liberal evangelical' movement. But the theological divide was less severe in Britain than in the United States, because of various factors. These included the influence of the Keswick movement, which, in its annual Bible-teaching convention in the Lakes District, emphasised spiritual experience and unity rather than doctrine.[19] Another factor was the mediating approach of many British biblical scholars.[20] Conservative evangelical scholars in Britain avoided insisting on describing the Bible as 'inerrant', preferring the term 'trustworthy'. British evangelicals were also less focused on disputing evolution.

Between the wars, British evangelicalism was under pressure on two fronts: theological liberalism dominated the universities, and Anglo-Catholicism was at its peak in the Church of England. Evangelicals were steadily losing young leaders to other streams and were very discouraged.[21] In the 1950s and 60s, however, British evangelicalism experienced a marked renaissance. The reasons for that are many, including the sobering effects of the Second World War and the Cold War, the influence of C.S. Lewis, and a new interest in evangelism. There was also the impact of the Billy Graham campaigns (Haringay 1954; Glasgow 1955), which boosted evangelical profile and confidence, and the dramatic recovery of evangelical scholarship. By the end of the 1950s, evangelicals sensed a much more favourable spiritual and theological atmosphere in Britain.[22]

Bebbington asserts that 'probably the most important single factor behind the advance of conservative Evangelicalism in Britain in the postwar period was the Inter-Varsity Fellowship'. He notes that the Inter-Varsity Fellowship (IVF) deliberately set out to change the perception that conservative evangelicalism was intellectually 'obscurantist'.[23] The principal contributions of the IVF were to train future evangelical leaders and to sponsor the revival of conservative evangelical scholarship. The IVF developed a strong publishing work, and there was a growing influx of evangelical scholars into British university teaching positions. A number of other historians have reached similar assessments on the importance of IVF to the recovery of British evangelicalism.[24] Goodhew, writing on CICCU, asserted that 'the history of the modern Church is incomplete without an understanding of the role of conservative Evangelicalism within student Christianity'. He suggested various reasons for CICCU's vitality, which could equally be applied to IVF as a whole: a 'clear message', the avoidance of unnecessary controversies (on eschatology, evolution and inerrancy), and an emphasis on 'the objective, factual basis of Christianity' that suited the times.[25]

British evangelicals firmly rejected a 'fundamentalist' identity.[26] Various British evangelical leaders, such as Graham Scroggie and Campbell Morgan, returned from visits to America and publicly deplored the extremism of fundamentalism.[27] Historians have similarly rejected attempts to equate British conservative evangelicalism – including IVF – with 'fundamentalism', noting that the fundamentalist hallmarks of strict inerrantism and a denunciatory tone were not commonly found in British evangelicalism.[28] Harris argued that many British evangelicals have at least elements of a 'fundamentalist mentality', with their 'empirical rationalism' (reflecting Scottish Common Sense philosophy) and their strong evidentialist preoccupation with the accuracy of scripture. But she agreed that the IVF was not fundamentalist 'by American standards'.[29]

Comparisons between modern evangelicalism in Britain and America are relevant to the New Zealand story.[30] Historians have suggested that the effect of having dominant state churches in England and Scotland was to make evangelicals more cautious and moderate in Britain than in the United States. In Britain, religion was associated with social conformity and respectability, whereas in the US, religion was populist and boisterous. In Britain, evangelicalism was led by socially conservative clergy, whereas in the US, it had a more 'lay' and entrepreneurial tone. British evangelicals, living in a traditional society, emphasised restraint and prudence, whereas their American counterparts, living in a new, expansive society, emphasised growth and success. In Britain, evangelicals often showed more respect for education. They were also in a much more secularised society, with little access to public media, whereas evangelicals in America had the numbers, freedom and means to gain access to the media. New Zealand evangelicals, who were likewise part of a new society, might have been expected to follow the American pattern, but New Zealand society continued to be strongly British in identity up until at least the end of the 1960s and, as a result, New Zealand evangelicalism more closely followed the British rather than the American model.

Canada and Australia

Canadian evangelicalism similarly reflected strong British influences and showed characteristics such as a moderate tone, doctrinal statements in the British tradition (which avoided taking sides on secondary issues), and a uniting of evangelicals around personal piety, evangelism, student work and overseas mission.[31] Large numbers of evangelicals stayed within the main denominations.[32] The IVF was also very important in shaping twentieth-century evangelicalism in Canada.[33]

Australia, the nearest neighbour to New Zealand and with a similar colonial background, is obviously the country most likely to have similar patterns of evangelical history to New Zealand's.[34] Stuart Piggin noted that, in the early twentieth century, reactions to liberalism made evangelicals defensive and isolated. Piggin argued that in the 1950s there was a fresh synthesis of the three evangelical strands of experientalism, biblicism and activism, and a consequent Australian evangelical 'resurgence'.[35] He and other historians have described much in Australian evangelicalism that parallels developments in New Zealand, such as the strength of revivalism at the turn of the century, and the impact of large numbers of missioners from overseas (including R.A.Torrey, who conducted campaigns in both countries). Australian historians have also noted the closeness of interdenominational evangelical links, which were strengthened by Keswick-type conventions, Bible Institutes, and faith missions like the China Inland Mission. They have written about the spiritual awakening associated with the 1959 Billy Graham Crusade, and have noted the role of the IVF in strengthening evangelical faith among students and introducing new evangelical scholarship from overseas.[36] Another parallel was in the prevailing 'Britishness' of Australia, where a 'British reserve' restrained religious expression. On the other hand, there was no counterpart in New Zealand to the large Anglican Diocese of Sydney, which since the 1930s had been almost exclusively controlled by conservative evangelicals, and which also had its own major theological college.[37]

The New Zealand Context

In around 1930, evangelical confidence, cohesion and identity in New Zealand were generally at a low ebb. The broad societal context was a general moral conservativism, valuing rectitude, self-discipline and domesticity. The identity of New Zealand was still very British.[38] Belich has argued that there was a 'Great Tightening' in New Zealand society, commencing in the 1880s and continuing into the 1960s.[39] But religious conservatives believed that moral and spiritual decadence was worsening. The vast majority of New Zealanders still identified themselves in the Census with some church denomination and were still christened, married and buried by a minister.[40] But church attendance was declining. By 1926 weekly attendance had reduced to 18 per cent of the total population, a decrease of more than a third from the peak of attendance of just under 30 per cent of the population in 1896.[41] The theological context, as in Britain and Australia, was that liberal and modernist tendencies were ascendant in mainline Protestantism.[42] However, at a popular level, revivalist preachers still attracted considerable support.

Among the Anglicans (New Zealand's largest denomination at 40 per cent of census respondents), only 15 per cent regularly attended church by 1926,[43] and an overt evangelicalism was relatively rare. The evangelicalism of many of the earliest settlers, reflecting the dominance of evangelicalism in the Church of England up to about 1850, had later been gradually modified by (and mixed with) more ritualistic tendencies.[44] Among Protestant denominations, the Anglicans had been the least affected by revivalism.[45] There were scattered individual ministers with leanings towards Low Church tradition, and others who had been influenced by the English Keswick tradition, the Church Missionary Society (CMS), or the China Inland Mission (CIM). Such ministers were often imports from Northern Ireland or England, rather than those trained in New Zealand.[46] There was also an enclave of Low Church and evangelically-minded Anglicans in the isolated and largely rural diocese of Nelson, where the bishops were often Australians or Englishmen with CMS connections and many clergy were graduates of Moore College in Sydney. Across New Zealand, however, the prevailing pattern among clergy was a traditional Anglicanism, modified – in varying degrees – by successive High Church movements (Tractarianism, ritualism, Anglo-Catholicism).[47] Many Anglican clergy were 'broad church', defying neat classification.[48] Anglican lay people were often more theologically conservative and Protestant in outlook than the clergy; they preferred a Low Church approach and resisted ritualistic innovations.[49] Ministerial training – mostly conducted in two diocesan colleges in Auckland and Christchurch – tended towards a theological perspective of mild liberalism.[50] A survey of Christchurch's diocesan newspaper in 1930 reveals minimal theological content, an overwhelming preoccupation with the mundane, and no revivalist or evangelistic emphases.[51]

Among the Presbyterians[52] (24 per cent of census respondents in 1926),[53] there were still memories – especially in the far south – of a conservative and generally evangelical heritage.[54] From 1848, Otago and Southland had been settled by serious-minded Free Church settlers, veterans of the 1843 Disruption when large numbers of evangelicals had left the Church of Scotland.[55] For many decades, Bible reading, family prayers and keeping Sunday as the Sabbath, a day of rest, were commonly observed. Ministers serving in nineteenth-century Otago and Southland generally reflected the dominance of evangelicalism in late nineteenth-century Scotland. Many had been influenced by the intense spiritual atmosphere in parts of Scotland during the 1859 'Revival', or by the Scottish preaching campaigns in 1873–75 of the American evangelist D.L. Moody.[56] In the 1880s and 90s, in the Mataura and Clutha districts, there had been indications of local revival.[57] The 1902 campaign in New Zealand by American revivalist R.A. Torrey had attracted strong support from many Presbyterians.[58] Conservatives in the Free Church tradition had been greatly fortified by the Princeton College theologians in the United States, with their sturdy scripturalism, their enthusiasm for the historic Reformed confessions of faith, and their philosophical commitment to the reliability of evidence and logic.[59] There were also frequent infusions into the New Zealand ministry of zealous evangelicals from Scotland, such as J. Kennedy Elliott, Isaac Jolly, P.B. Fraser, A.G. Irvine, C.A. Kennedy – and H.B. Gray, in North East Valley, Dunedin, whose parish prayer meetings had sustained attendances of up to 110, and who wrote of times when 'the fire of God fell'.[60] Before the First World War, organisations such as Christian Endeavour, YMCA and the Presbyterian Bible Class Movement showed considerable spiritual intensity and evangelistic zeal.[61]

After the war, there had been a noticeable shift in New Zealand society's religious and moral climate. Following earlier trends in the northern hemisphere, there had also been a theological swing, and strict doctrine was no longer favoured: the mood became 'mollifying and humanising'.[62] At the Theological Hall (where all Presbyterian ministers in New Zealand were trained), Professor John Dickie had since 1910 been advocating a 'progressive orthodoxy'.[63] An older scholarly evangelicalism was being displaced by a critical view of the Bible and a broader theology. Those ministers with a strong 'confessionalist' emphasis (i.e. they were still strictly committed to the historic Presbyterian doctrinal standards, the Westminster Confession of Faith and the catechisms) felt increasingly marginalised. Some, like P.B. Fraser, vigorously protested.[64] The growing attitude among younger ministers, especially those schooled by the SCM (which was at its height in the interwar period), was that some classic Reformed and evangelical doctrines were no longer tenable in the light of new questions raised by modernity, science and sceptical 'higher criticism' of the Bible, and that theological conservatives had become remnants from a bygone era.[65]

Revivalism still appealed to many Presbyterians, however. It was conspicuously promoted by such Auckland figures as the Revs Evan Harries (St James Presbyterian), Joseph Kemp (Baptist Tabernacle) and Lionel Fletcher (Beresford Street Congregational), by the Bible Training Institute's 'Blind Evangelist' Andrew Johnston, and by the official PCNZ evangelist, Rev. John Bissett. Revivalists shared a conservative approach to doctrine, and would have heartily agreed with Kemp's public denunciation of liberalised theology:

> *I charge modernism with being a menace to the whole work of God. It has attacked our mission stations. It has destroyed faith in the miraculous. It has banished God from the world. It denies worship to Christ. It has smitten the pulpit with a paralysis of unbelief. The churches have withered under its influence. It has lowered the standard of ethics. It has robbed us of the Bible. It has taken away my Lord and I do not know where they have laid him.*[66]

Nationwide, the Presbyterian environment at the beginning of the 1930s was neither clearly evangelical nor clearly liberal. It was broadly evangelical, and mildly liberal. Its leadership had adopted a cautiously liberal theological outlook. But to a considerable extent the PCNZ also preserved, especially at the grassroots, a devotional piety and activism that reflected a more evangelical past. Such elements were combined, often uneasily, in the Presbyterian Bible Class (BC) movement. In 1930 a national BC conference could be found singing songs by Alexander and Sankey, the two great revivalist hymn writers.[67] Easter Bible Class campers might be urged to come forward explicitly to 'confess faith in Christ as their Saviour', or – more often – they were being challenged with a generalised exhortation to 'follow the call of Christ' to a life of heroic Christian service.[68]

A survey of the pages of *The Outlook* ('The Official Organ of the Presbyterian Church in New Zealand') in 1930 reveals a denomination that was theologically mixed. Articles in the *Outlook* could tilt either way, depending on the writer. One the one hand, the editor included pieces on repentance,[69] predestination,[70] the Church's seventy-year captivity to 'the modern Pharaoh and his great falsehood' (evolution),[71] and instructions – lifted from the Salvation Army's *War Cry* – on 'How to be saved'.[72] On the other hand, he accepted pieces on the obsoleteness of mass evangelism[73] and in praise of H.E. Fosdick (the leading American modernist).[74] But there was an overall theological blandness in the *Outlook*, suggesting a deliberate downplaying of theological divisions. Where controversy was reported, it was overseas. In 1930, there appeared to be just one (passing) reference to the debates between modernists and fundamentalists.[75] Letters to the Editor, however, were often adamantly pro-modernist or anti-modernist.[76] The pages of the *Outlook* indicate a denomination that was fretting – along with much of Western mainline Protestantism – about religious nominalism and decline.[77] Its pages did not indicate a denomination closely tied to its confessional heritage: references to the Catechisms were rare, and to Calvin even rarer.[78] A frequent contributor to the *Outlook* was PCNZ missionary J.L. Gray, who clearly believed in conversion and in consecrated prayer.[79] The only weekly column that was invariably 'evangelical' in its concerns was 'Our Evangelistic Page' by Evan R. Harries.[80] His page focused on fervency in prayer, Holy Spirit conversion, the surrendered life and – sixteen times in late 1930 – anticipations of imminent Dominion-wide revival.[81] Reporting many recent all-night interdenominational prayer meetings, he warned the Presbyterian Church not to be left out.[82]

The 1931 *Outlook* fare was similarly mixed. There were conservative items against dancing at BC socials, and one on the saintly character of the typical BC girl (daily 'growing sweeter, purer, kinder …').[83] There was a series of solid doctrinal studies by Isaac Jolly, who emphatically believed in substitutionary atonement.[84] There was an article lauding the SCM.[85] There were also assertions that 'faith cannot be built upon history', that Bultmann (a radical) represented 'present-day' biblical scholarship, and that 'one could say without fear of contradiction that there is no Presbyterian theologian of any standing within the British Empire that would not call himself Liberal'.[86]

The *Outlook*'s use of the term 'evangelical' in 1930–31 shows that the meaning of the word 'evangelical' in New Zealand had become extremely diffuse. Sometimes the term simply meant 'Protestant'.[87] Sometimes it meant 'non-conformist' (i.e. Protestant but not Anglican).[88] Sometimes it meant 'evangelistic',[89] or having a particular 'zeal' for evangelism.[90] A broad interpretation of the word 'evangelical' might mean a 'campaign for the enrolment of men and women in the Kingdom of God'.[91] 'Evangelical' did not necessarily imply biblically conservative: modernist Fosdick could readily be described as leading 'modern evangelical Christianity'.[92] Karl Barth – although he held a critical view of the scriptures – could be acclaimed as 'thoroughly evangelical in the truest sense of that word'.[93]

It was clear that, in the early 1930s, the term 'evangelical' was confusing, and it did not exclusively belong to any particular theological tendency. The term could still be used historically, referring to eighteen-century revivals and nineteenth-century streams within the church. However, since the rise of theological liberalism and modernism (and then neo-orthodoxy), the term 'evangelical' appeared to have lost much of its usefulness as a 'party' label, because adherents of those new approaches could also often call themselves 'evangelical'. In New Zealand churches in the early twentieth century, the term 'evangelical' had yet to be claimed as a distinct mark of identity by those who were both biblically conservative and evangelistically active. It was in that somewhat muddied context that a new type of New Zealand evangelical identity began to develop, from about 1930.

A New Evangelical Movement

Part One of this book traces the 1930s and 40s development of a new type of New Zealand evangelicalism, with a clear identity and a strong sense of purpose. The crucial catalyst was the establishment of the university Evangelical Unions (EUs). In conjunction with Presbyterian minister Thomas Miller in Dunedin and Anglican minister William Orange in Christchurch, the IVF/EU movement raised up a generation of confident, self-aware 'evangelicals', many of whom would later become evangelical leaders. Part Two tracks the flourishing postwar evangelical movement. A brief Epilogue updates what has happened with New Zealand evangelicalism since 1965.

The Anglican and Presbyterian churches, New Zealand's largest two Protestant denominations, provide an obvious window into what was going on in mainstream Protestantism in this country. Those were the two denominations most clearly affected by the rise of the evangelical student movements. There were also numerous evangelicals in most of the smaller denominations. The Brethren and Baptists often made a strong contribution to interdenominational evangelical movements. In this period, the Methodist denomination was generally moving in a more liberal direction. The Pentecostals were still a relatively small movement whose members had negligible involvement in the universities.

The book is not about popular evangelicalism as a whole, but focuses on the evangelical formation of its university-trained leaders, both men and women, and especially future ministers. This was, of course, a period when only men could become ministers, and when the universities were so much more monocultural than they are now. Along the way the role of many evangelical organisations and initiatives is also covered, including the New Zealand Bible Training Institute (BTI), the Crusader Movement, Christian Endeavour, the Keswick-style conventions, the work of various itinerant evangelists, and the 1959 Billy Graham Crusade.

As a study of beliefs, values and identity, this book tells the story of many individuals – people who were representative of the evangelical movement and its various strands, people who were especially influential, and people with all their strengths and foibles. But this is not an all-inclusive family history of New Zealand evangelicalism. It is more an attempt to build up an understanding of the movement, by identifying a range of important beginnings, turning points, ideas and personalities.

Sources and perspective

In researching the New Zealand evangelical movement, I had access to some extensive archives, particularly the records of the Tertiary Students Fellowship, the Westminster Fellowship and the Evangelical Churchmen's Fellowship. These are rich collections. Evangelical periodicals and publications were also fertile sources, along with memoirs, personal papers and diaries. Local church records, often mundane and weak in theological awareness, were less helpful. The minutes of one parish, for instance, record that someone was 'empowered to look at the Church Vacuum Cleaner', but never gave the slightest hint about the parish's emerging evangelical ethos. In the period of William Orange's outstanding evangelical ministry in Christchurch, there was only one reference in the minutes of his Sumner parish to the word 'evangelical'.[94] Parish newsletters, however, were often more revealing of theological flavour. I also conducted over fifty oral history interviews, some of them very extensive. The interviews provided an amazing wealth of knowledge and insights not otherwise available, including invaluable information about theological formation, motivations and emphases.[95] Oral sources were especially strong on recalled emotions, as when two evangelical stalwarts each recounted their own side of a squabble they had had on a Southland cycling trip some seventy years previously.

All writing of history has a perspective. As one Christian historian expressed it, 'Our work is interpretative, but so is everyone else's.'[96] My own perspective could be described as that of an 'observer–participant'[97] in the evangelical movement – but from a period much later than that explored here. On the one hand, profile as a participant enabled me privileged access to sources. On the other hand, time and generational differences gave me some detachment. I write this book with an awareness of evangelicalism's strengths and also its eccentricities. This is an attempt to understand and explain an important twentieth-century movement of New Zealand Protestantism, and to do so in a 'critical yet empathetic manner'.[98]

PART ONE

A TURN OF TIDE
1930-45

CHAPTER ONE

Thomas Miller and Friends

The most influential man in the Church.[1]

The key figure preparing the way for a postwar renaissance of evangelical Presbyterianism in New Zealand was the Rev. Thomas Miller (1875–1948).[2] His Dunedin ministry in the 1930s and 1940s, strategically situated near both the Otago University and the Theological Hall, inspired scores of protégés.

Thomas Miller was a man not easily ignored – confident and articulate, sharp-minded and tenacious, and with very strong convictions. He was a commanding preacher,[3] who modelled his preaching on that of John Wesley and Charles Spurgeon.[4] He preached fluently and with great earnestness, and would sometimes get indignant and hammer the pulpit.[5] His public prayers could last for up to twenty minutes. His admirers regarded him with awe; they felt there was 'an air about the Reverend Thomas Miller, you couldn't help but sense that he lived reverently in the presence of God'.[6] Helmut Rex, a lecturer at the Theological Hall, recalled a 1939 sermon of Miller's as a 'rare combination of devoutness, clarity of thought and beauty of language'.[7]

Thomas Miller had arrived in the North Dunedin parish of St Stephen's in July 1928.[8] There were other evangelicals in Otago pulpits, but Miller stood out as especially gifted and forthright. His ministry began to attract people into his congregation from other parishes and denominations.[9] However, numerous existing parishioners – including the man who referred to Miller as 'that yellow-livered tripe hound' – decided that Miller's ministry was not for them, and left.[10]

Miller had been brought to New Zealand from Scotland when he was two. His family was proudly Scottish in outlook, and devoutly Presbyterian.[11] They had attended First Church, under the ministry of Rev. Dr Gibb.[12] At fifteen,

Miller left school to work in a foundry. Under the gaslights at a revivalist street mission conducted by a Christian Endeavour group, he had a conversion experience.[13] He became very active in the Russell Street Bible Class, a mission outpost of First Church, and was also strongly influenced by the Christian Endeavour movement, with its emphasis on consecration and prayer.[14] Miller had felt a call to ministry. At school, a master had advised him against taking up any work which would require 'any brains',[15] but after conversion Miller became a voracious reader, gaining a university prize in debating and an MA with first-class honours.[16] In 1905–07 he was at the Theological Hall and active in the SCM. Through a spiritual crisis in his final year he developed profound convictions about the substitutionary death of Christ and the work of the Holy Spirit.[17]

In his first three ministries, at Westport (1908–11), Rangiora (1911–15) and Feilding (1915–28), Miller established the patterns of ministry that he later demonstrated in Dunedin: an earnest spiritual emphasis, prayer meetings, Bible exposition, a hunger for conversions, one-to-one evangelism, the use of visiting missioners, and a strenuous development of young men's Bible Classes.[18] In 1909 he married Marion Strang, a high-school teacher with a passion for running Bible Classes for young women.[19] The Millers maintained robust habits of prayer, including rising very early for individual prayer, and a daily half hour of prayer together as a couple.[20] Family devotions – daily after breakfast and dinner – consisted of a hymn from the Sankey hymnbook, a Bible reading, and everyone kneeling in prayer.

Although genial in disposition, Miller did not shrink from controversy. In Westport, a small town with seventeen hotels on the main street, Miller – a strong supporter of the Temperance movement – had tangled with the liquor trade.[21] In Feilding he had been beaten up by Catholics after a rally for Howard Elliott of the Protestant Political Association (the Methodist minister also got beaten up, but the Salvation Army officer fought back).[22] In each parish, Miller made it known that he was opposed to church fundraising (such as cake and produce stalls) and that only direct congregational giving was biblically appropriate.

As Presbyterian theology became more liberal after the First World War, Miller spoke out against it. 'One cannot remain silent', he wrote, without becoming 'in measure a consenting party'.[23] He was in close touch with the editor of the *Biblical Recorder*, P.B. Fraser, who was bitterly critical of the new theological developments.[24] In a 1916 article in the *Outlook,* Miller eloquently deplored the 'airy confidence' and glee with which 'arrogant' and 'destructive' biblical critics were attacking the veracity of Scripture. Such sceptics decried the possibility of either an infallible pope or an infallible Bible, yet loftily assumed the role of 'infallible critic'.[25] Under the tutelage of Dr J. Kennedy Elliott, Miller became a frequent speaker at General Assembly.[26] Miller debated issues forcefully, but without animosity. From 1917 Miller and Elliott collaborated in opposing church union, a cause that was beginning to polarise the Presbyterian denomination. Miller penned the 'Twelve Points against the Grand Betrayal', and the leaflet was posted from Feilding to every Presbyterian parish in New Zealand.[27] Miller's opposition to church union was essentially theological. He regarded ecumenism as doctrinally reductionist. In the 1919 General Assembly Miller argued that Christian unity is spiritual not external, and that by the providence of God every denomination brings a unique testimony to the riches of divine revelation.[28]

Thomas Miller's Evangelicalism

When Miller arrived in Dunedin to begin his most influential ministry, he was fifty-two and at the height of his powers. His theology and methods were well established. In theological self-identity, Miller was unequivocally 'evangelical'. Well read in Protestant history, he clearly identified himself with the historic evangelical tradition of Luther, Calvin, Bunyan, Wesley, Erskine, McCheyne, Chalmers and Spurgeon.[29] He particularly identified with the Scottish evangelical tradition. He was mindful of the historic sufferings of the Scottish faithful – Reformation martyrs, Covenanters, and participants in the 1843 Disruption. He saw the first few decades of the Free Church as the golden age of Scottish theology.[30] He greatly admired the conservative Presbyterian theology of Princeton College scholars A.A. Hodge and B.B. Warfield in the United States, with their strong rational appeals to biblical inspiration and authority, to evidence and logic, and to orthodox Protestant doctrine. The agencies and individuals Miller cooperated with (Christian Endeavour and various missionaries) were all recognisably within the evangelical tradition. They shared its characteristic preoccupations with evangelism, biblicism, personal salvation and consecration, even if they did not always explicitly refer to themselves as 'evangelical' (they might also describe themselves as 'spiritual', 'vital', 'godly', 'Bible-believing' or 'soul-winners'). From 1930, Miller would unhesitatingly embrace the sharp new evangelical identity being fostered by the Evangelical Unions.

A series of four articles by Miller in 1929 offers further insights into the shape of his theological thinking.[31] An all-important principle for him was the authority of the Bible, as inspired and revelatory. He argued that humanity is powerless to know God without revelation, and that the Bible was thus 'the central citadel' of the Christian faith.[32] While he acknowledged that biblical revelation came through the 'prism' of human personality, he believed it was the divine authorship of scripture that really counted.[33] Theological modernism, he declared, was in continuity with unbelief in every age, including that of Celsus (the outspoken second-century pagan critic of Christianity) and the eighteenth-century deists. Miller deplored that some theologians and ministers had 'betrayed what they were appointed to defend'.[34] Modernist ministries proved 'barren', whereas the ministries of those who 'believe and use' the Bible experienced blessing.[35] The four articles also clearly demonstrate that Miller's evangelical identity was that of the British evangelical tradition, not American fundamentalism. His articles twice used the term 'evangelical', but not the term 'fundamentalist'. In 1934 Miller published a book in which he argued that until about fifty years previously, those people who were determined to claim 'errors, discrepancies and deficiencies' in the Bible were all outside the church (infidels such as Voltaire and Thomas Paine), but that now such people had come to dominate both church and academy.[36] His book showed familiarity with scholars on both sides of various debates. It dismissed theories of evolution as unbiblical and unproven, but gave relatively little attention to the issue.[37]

Miller was an avid reader of church history and theology. He subscribed to several international Christian magazines, including the *Evangelical Quarterly*, and closely followed overseas debates over scripture and theology. He was fully aware of the American debates between modernism and fundamentalism.[38] Like many ministers of his time, Miller possessed a set of 'The Fundamentals', the anti-modernist series of books published in the United States between 1910 and 1915. In the 1930s he corresponded with the leading American theological conservative, Machen, who wrote to Miller of 'their fellowship together in the great battle against Modernism'.[39] Miller was naturally drawn to such a warhorse for orthodoxy as Machen, and admired his penetrating intellect and clearcut beliefs. Like Machen, Miller did not identify himself as a 'Fundamentalist'.[40] Miller saw the term as foreign, and as a 'theological swear-word'.[41] He was content to see himself as 'evangelical' – and as 'Reformed', 'conservative' or 'biblical'.[42] Miller also abhorred some of the recurring characteristics of militant fundamentalism. He was indignant about theological modernism, but was very reasoned in his objections; he was anything but anti-intellectual. He disliked acrimony. He had a 'dread' of denominational schisms.[43] He preached the second coming, but rejected premillennialism.[44]

Miller's evangelicalism was expressed in the priority he gave to prayerfulness, to expository preaching and to running Bible Classes. He was mildly revivalist. He was Calvinistic, but not strictly so.[45] Although unswervingly loyal to Presbyterian doctrine and polity,[46] he was also extremely open to interdenominational cooperation with other evangelicals.

An evangelical strategy, the Bible Class

One of Miller's main strategies was to shape youth and young adults through teaching a Bible Class. Miller held the view that a minister who grasped control of his senior young men's Bible Class not only stabilised the youth work but also the future of the congregation – and for the same reason, he appointed himself Sunday School Superintendent.[47] Miller's Bible Class, in a leading New Zealand university and theological centre, was to make a crucial contribution towards growing a new Presbyterian evangelical movement. Every Sunday at 4 p.m., Miller taught a Young Men's BC with a regular attendance of about forty – a rare size even then.[48] His wife taught a similar group of young women, and there were also junior classes. Their three sons and four daughters provided a ready nucleus and an effective means of recruiting others. Classes were followed by the evening service, often preceded by a meal.

Miller's approach to BC was stern: there was minimal interaction, and he insisted on 'absolute reverence'.[49] That did not suit everyone, and there was an early revolt and walk-out. But enthusiastic Christian youth arrived from elsewhere. By 1929 the BC exhibited 'great earnestness', with its members eagerly meeting for prayer.[50] Whenever new recruits to the class showed signs of serious spiritual interest they would be summoned to the manse for a personal evangelistic interview, where Miller would read them various Bible verses and invite them to repeat a prayer for salvation.[51] In the language of that time, Miller was a 'soul winner'.[52]

Unhappy with what he perceived of the theological direction of the wider Presbyterian BC movement, and irritated at having to read out weekly invitations to dances, Miller disaffiliated the St Stephen's BC from the Presbyterian Bible Class Union. Miller was not just reacting against dancing, which he saw as a worldly distraction, but deploring the spiritual and moral laxity which he believed gripped society and church after the First World War.[53] He also saw the national BC movement as having lost the spiritual fervency it had once exhibited.

> The loss of life in the leadership of movements like CE and BC was so horrific … [They] had to grow a new generation in a new climate, [and] they didn't inherit the zeal of the early founders, and the only climate was this postwar

madness, the women smoking, the fellows having an uproarious time ... so there were football tournaments in the BC everywhere.[54]

Others shared similar perceptions.[55] Thomas Miller felt the Presbyterian Bible Class Movement's adoption of a 'four square' approach (spiritual, mental, physical, social) de-emphasised the spiritual.[56] Members of his BC socialised informally, with walks and bike trips (ideal low-cost activities during the Depression); but along with other conservative evangelicals in that era, they spurned dances, Sabbath-breaking, alcohol, cards and cinema. Miller retained the restrictive moral and social code he had grown up with,[57] and zealous youth generally accepted it.[58]

The move to disaffiliate his BC illustrated an interesting set of contradictions in Miller. Although intensely loyal to his denominational heritage, and active in Presbytery and General Assembly, he increasingly resisted contact between his young people and those in other Presbyterian churches. While he was staunchly opposed to church union, he was nevertheless enthusiastically involved in numerous interdenominational organisations and missions: he took prominent regional leadership roles in the Evangelical Bible League of Otago,[59] the annual Pounawea Conventions in the Catlins, Christian Endeavour, the Bible Society of Otago and Southland, the China Inland Mission, and EU/IVF. Miller was also chairman for the Dunedin campaigns of several evangelists, including Lionel Fletcher (1929) and W.P. Nicholson (1933). Miller's approach was characteristic of staunch evangelicals in mainline churches: they intensely distrusted the state of their own denominations, disdained the ecumenical movement, but warmly embraced fellowship and cooperation with those who shared their evangelical beliefs and priorities. In their interdenominationalism, evangelicals were often less cautious than those in other theological streams. Evangelical loyalties were stronger than denominational loyalties: when the Anglican Bishop of Dunedin declined permission for the (evangelical) Bishop of Nelson to preach in Dunedin, Miller was 'delighted' to have him preach at St Stephen's.[60]

The Interdenominational Evangelical Nexus

Miller's ministry was constantly being reinforced by an interlocking mesh of other evangelical ministries and organisations. These included Christain Endeavour, the Pounawea Conventions, missionary societies, Scripture Union, the Bible Training Institute, the Crusader Movement, the Evangelical Union, and itinerant evangelists conducting either parish missions or inter-church campaigns. It was obvious to Miller that such evangelical initiatives usefully strengthened his own ministry, especially among young people. His involvement in them also gives many insights into some of the main features of New Zealand evangelicalism in the 1930s and 40s.

Christian endeavour

From 1929, Miller reinforced the work of the Bible Class by starting a Christian Endeavour (CE) group at St Stephen's.[61] The aim of the CE was not evangelism and basic teaching, but Christian consecration and training.[62] It was a self-consciously 'spiritual' movement, intended for those already converted and committed.[63] As a method of conserving and discipling converts it was similar in principle to the Class Meetings of the early Wesleyans. CE met for ninety minutes every Saturday night, with Miller and his wife always present. The CE gatherings were highly participatory, to train youth in ex tempore prayer, testimony and leading meetings.[64] Bible passages were assigned to members to prepare and speak on. Once a month, the CE pledge was repeated: 'Relying on the Lord Jesus Christ for salvation and trusting in God for strength, I promise Him that I will endeavour to lead a Christian life.' CE members also committed themselves to personal Bible reading and prayer. Unlike Bible Class, CE was co-ed. It was a 'rich and warm and intelligent fellowship' – and 'Saturday night was cornered', usefully keeping young Christians away from the pictures and dances.[65] CE also fostered a lively missionary interest, especially at rallies and conventions where missionary speakers served as exemplars of the consecrated life.

Although the CE had flourished in Otago before the First World War, it had become almost defunct during the war, mainly because of the crippling loss of leaders.[66] It was re-established at St Stephen's after two CE enthusiasts visited Dunedin in 1929 – evangelist Lionel Fletcher, and Miss Jennie Street from Britain.[67] Although Street was a Quaker[68] (and a woman), Miller had her preach at St Stephen's.[69] An Otago CE Union was formed, drawing support from evangelically minded churches of several denominations, and – with Miller as chairman and his daughter Jean as organiser – it became the strongest CE Union in New Zealand.[70]

Christian Endeavour was also growing elsewhere in New Zealand – mainly in Auckland, where Fletcher was based.[71] CE was an expression of popular, pietistic evangelicalism. So long as it was being led by Fletcher or Miller – its two most prominent New Zealand supporters – it was going to stay evangelical.[72] The first Otago CE Convention, in 1930, closed with an altar call and the singing of 'All to Jesus I surrender'. However CE's evangelicalism was implicit rather than explicit: the focus of the movement was consecration, not theology.⁷³ The records of the Otago CE provide a striking example of grassroots interdenominational evangelicalism. At conventions, rallies and executive meetings, Miller and CE members developed strong fellowship across many denominations – Baptist, Methodist, Church of Christ, Congregational, Salvation Army, Brethren and Presbyterian – but never Anglican.

From 1933, the CE began holding Easter Conventions in country schools and churches around Otago and Southland. Miller and his wife were always present at these.⁷⁴ Most Protestant denominations were represented (except Anglicans); Presbyterians usually made up more than half the numbers (reflecting the large evangelical Presbyterian base in Otago and Southland, especially in rural areas). The conventions stressed the 'surrendered life' and devoted much time to worship, teaching and prayer. There were at least three sermons per day, on topics such as 'The Holy Spirit', 'Consecration' and 'Power from on High'.⁷⁵ There were testimony meetings and missionary speakers from faith missions. The CE conventions appeared to be very similar in theology, intensity, hymnology and patterns of piety to any other New Zealand evangelical convention of this period, all of which broadly reflected Keswick traditions and values.⁷⁶

Miller's prominent support of the CE was not welcomed by Presbyterian denominational leaders, and probably strengthened the perception that he was an anti-establishment maverick. They regarded a revived CE as a potential threat to the Bible Class movement. A hostile article in the *Outlook* in 1930 argued that one organisation (the BC) was 'sufficient', that the control of the BC was 'within' the church (whereas control of the CE was 'without'), and that the CE Pledge created a 'spiritual egotism' in pledgers.⁷⁷ Miller was undeterred. In his time at St Stephen's, CE was often the main instrument in the evangelical formation of young people who were not at university and in the Evangelical Union. In many other evangelical settings around New Zealand, however, CE had no presence, and evangelical formation occurred in other ways.

The Keswick-style conventions

The summer Pounawea Convention, held near Owaka in the Catlins in South Otago, was another important interdenominational evangelical involvement by Miller, who was Chairman of the Convention.⁷⁸ Every year he attended Pounawea with his family, along with others from St Stephen's. The Pounawea Convention was in the tradition of Keswick, the annual spiritual life convention held in northern England. The conventions offered a strong dose of biblical exposition, testimony, prayer and fellowship, and were for serious believers thirsty for spiritual refreshment and a deeper Christian life. The Pounawea

Convention was similar to the evangelical conventions held in the North Island, at Cambridge and Ngaruawahia. Pounawea, however, had only about 200 attending, whereas the Ngaruawahia Easter Conventions – run by BTI – could draw up to 1000, and appeared 'very large and impressive'.[79] While the northern conventions were dominated by Baptists and Open Brethren, the majority of Pounawea attendees were Presbyterian, especially from those country districts swept by revival in the 1880s and beyond.[80] Speakers at Pounawea included Miller, John Bissett, Andrew Johnston, Evan Harries and J.O. Sanders.[81] The Keswick themes of consecration and surrender were always evident, but at Pounawea there was no strict adherence to the Keswick theology, and those with a more Reformed theology were, in any case, wary of 'second blessing' theology.[82] The summer conventions at Cambridge (later Rotorua) were closest to the Keswick model and theology, and the Ngaruawhia Easter Conventions were the least so.[83]

At the 1929 Pounawea Convention, Harries spoke on the Holy Spirit, and those present were invited to 'stand and pray for refreshment by the Holy Spirit in a deepened spiritual consecration', to 'yield completely to the Saviour', or to 'testify'.[84] Many did so. One of Miller's sons stood 'in an act of full surrender, imploring the empowering of the Holy Spirit'.[85] It was reported to the *Outlook* that the Convention had experienced 'a deep work of the Holy Spirit' and a 'great outpouring of the spirit of prayer'.[86] The next year, another young member from St Stephen's wrote, 'To-day 27th of Dec 1930 I give myself all to God for the service of Jesus', and the following day, 'I received on this day the filling of the Holy Spirit'.[87]

Harries' glowing reports of Pounawea in the *Outlook* were not appreciated by everyone. They provoked Rev. J.V.T. Steele in 1931 to write a blistering attack on 'Pietism', which he contrasted with 'Calvinism'.[88] The 'worst forms of the Pietistic Movement today', he asserted, 'are seen in the Keswick teaching and similar conventions in NZ, and in what is known as revivalism generally'. Pietism, he claimed, is contrary to the spirit of 'OUR church', it is 'Sectist', it produces 'emotional perversions', it is 'one of the most dangerous and disintegrating of all psychological conditions' (disturbing the 'deep roots' of personality), it is similar to 'primitive religions', it stirs up a 'highly ... artificial sense of sin' – and, moreover, Pietism had been opposed by Jeremiah, Paul, Augustine, Calvin, Forsyth and Barth. Steele's article provoked many responses, including a quietly reasoned letter from Morrison Yule and another from E.M. Blaiklock (lecturer in classics in Auckland, and first-time attendee at Pounawea).[89] Blaiklock defended the 'sanity' of the convention's teaching and reported he had seen 'no extravagance, no emotionalism', but a 'quiet earnestness, a reality of devotion, and a self-effacement that rang true'. Steele's attack on Pounawea would not have changed Miller's thinking, but merely confirmed his assessment of the parlous theological condition of his denomination.

John Bissett and Lionel Fletcher

In 1929 Miller had a parish mission conducted in St Stephen's by John Bissett, the Presbyterian 'Assembly Evangelist'.[90] Bissett was a product of 1890s revivalism in the Scottish Counties.[91] He was no 'hell-fire' preacher, but 'sound and sane and warmly persuasive'.[92] He would conduct about a dozen major parish missions a year, mostly in rural or developing parishes.[93] Missions usually spanned two weeks (taking in three Sundays).[94] During a Bissett mission a young attendee, Rymall Roxburgh, was 'convicted in the Holy Spirit', and anxiously awaited the end of the meeting so he could make a public commitment of faith.[95] Such a response, at an evangelistic meeting, would usually include coming forward at the speaker's invitation and joining in a prayer of commitment to Christ. For those with previous church involvement, such experiences were often more about assurance of salvation than a dramatic change of direction. When Roxburgh reached home he told his mother 'I'm a Christian.' She asked: 'Haven't you always been one?' He replied, 'Now I know I am.' Other future Presbyterian ministers who responded to evangelistic appeals at Bissett meetings included Mervyn Milmine, Jack Smith, Morrison Yule and Jack Somerville.[96] For some parishes, a Bissett mission could have enduring consequences.[97] For ministers like Miller, the missions were a reassuring link with a time when the denomination had seemed more evangelistic and spiritually ardent. For some younger liberal ministers, though, Bissett was an embarrassing relic from the past.[98]

In 1929 Miller also supported the Dunedin meetings of the evangelist Lionel Fletcher.[99] An Australian, Fletcher had previously been minister of the largest Congregational church in Australia, and had become that country's most prominent evangelist.[100] In New Zealand, he became the dynamic minister of Beresford Street Congregational Church in Auckland (1924–32), during which time its membership grew from 224 to 825.[101] In Dunedin, Fletcher's Sunday afternoon meeting for men attracted over 1000, and about 200 responded to the appeal.[102] Fletcher's preaching persuasively appealed to the listeners' will, but some evangelicals wished it had contained more specific doctrinal content.[103]

W.P. Nicholson

When the flamboyant, fiery Irish evangelist W.P. Nicholson conducted his extensive campaigns around New Zealand in 1933–34,[104] Miller chaired and promoted the Dunedin meetings which took place for three weeks in the Town Hall. Miller saw enduring results among his young people.[105] Nicholson, converted after a riotous youth on the crew of windjammers, had developed a deliberately provocative and populist style. He peppered his talks with swearwords such as 'damn' and 'bastard', took potshots at anybody and anything (including most denominations), and sometimes bawled out members of the audience: 'A woman came in late … wearing a yellow coat, and was dithering about where to sit. He said, "When that canary finds a perch, I'll continue."'[106] Nicholson went out of his way to mock fellow Presbyterians as lukewarm, and to blast modernists as traitors. 'The road to hell,' he declared, 'is lined with the skulls of Presbyterian ministers.'[107] Nicholson angered some with his frequent passionate denunciations of Dr John Dickie, the principal of the Theological Hall.[108] At one Dunedin meeting Nicholson announced: 'Your professors at the Theological Hall, [they] don't believe a thing. If I weren't a converted man, I'd go up and shoot them in their beds.'[109] Thomas Miller was uncomfortable with such crude outbursts, but nevertheless praised Nicholson as a godly preacher of rare 'compass and power'.[110] New Zealand's future evangelical Presbyterian leaders were delighted by Nicholson's irreverent humour and emboldened by his rhetoric: 'We youngsters thought it was terrific.'[111] It helped consolidate their 'them and us' outlook, their awareness of theological battle lines, and their own identity as evangelicals.[112] As elsewhere, some took offence at Nicholson;[113] the New Zealand Presbyterian establishment was definitely not amused. Outside of Harries' 'Evangelistic Page', the *Outlook* studiously ignored Nicholson. Nevertheless, Nicholson's known converts included at least seven who would later become ministers in the Presbyterian Church.[114]

The Bible Training Institute and the 'Blind Evangelist'

A byproduct of the Nicholson mission was that he energetically promoted the New Zealand Bible Training Institute, which had sponsored his campaign. Founded in Auckland in 1922 by Joseph Kemp, BTI described itself as 'evangelical' (not 'fundamentalist').[115] While it was 'frankly conservative' in doctrine,[116] BTI valued moderation and avoided conservative extremes.[117] Nicholson praised BTI as a stronghold of orthodoxy – in contrast to the Presbyterian Theological Hall – and as the ideal place to go for training. For many of his young listeners, Nicholson 'put BTI on the map' and helped build its growing status, across a wider denominational base, as a valued custodian of evangelical faith.[118] The Institute's reputation was also being built by its magazine, the *Reaper*, and by the calibre of staff such as J.O. Sanders, who was a strong and incisive speaker.[119] With Miller's encouragement, a number of his parishioners went to study at BTI.

Andrew Johnston, the BTI evangelist, also helped enhance the credibility of BTI and of evangelicalism in general. Blinded in the First World War – on his first day in the trenches – Johnston was an itinerating missioner from 1929–40. Miller used him several times as a parish missioner at St Stephen's. The 'Blind Evangelist' had none of the eccentricities of Nicholson. He was quiet and earnest. He prepared thoroughly, often sending new messages to Blaiklock to be checked.[120] His speaking straightforward and thoughtful and full of scripture. He preached in a logical and convincing manner, avoiding controversy, but with 'liberty and fire'.[121] His blindness, and the fact that it had happened at war, increased interest and respect for him. His impact was primarily in country areas, but his influence was also 'pervasive'.[122] A minister in Invercargill gave a glowing account of Johnston speaking to a packed church of over 1000:

> *The evangelist was very quiet, very simple. A more humble, modest, sincere man never breathed … He was himself so manifestly the embodiment of the Gospel he preached. Andrew Johnston speaks with an authority that silences every criticism. Moreover, he is such a radiant, joyful personality. His amazing command of the English Bible gave great weight to his preaching and teaching … A strong ethical note took the place so often occupied in evangelistic mission by controversial, secondary topics.*[123]

It was characteristic of Miller to recognise such a ministry, and to use it to strengthen his own.

Controversies Renewed

Miller's wider denominational involvements were relatively sparing, but were enough for him to be recognised as a leading evangelical voice within Presbyterianism: someone too strong and eloquent to be ignored; too reasoned and well informed to be easily discredited. At General Assemblies, Miller frequently fought against the prevailing theological current:

> *The other side would raise points of order so as to curtail Thomas Miller's flights of oratory, to break in on the thread of his argument, they just didn't like some of the things he said. He perhaps overstated some things. He was strong, he was battling for the truth in those pretty tough days. He was a lone figure.*[124]

Occasionally, Miller wrote for the *Outlook*. In 1923 he wrote a piece defending the divine inspiration of scripture.[125] In 1926, he wrote expressing concern that theological colleges around the world focused on 'barren negations' and 'unapplied theory', and lacked emphasis on evangelism. Bible Training Institutes, he asserted, were closer to 'the living heart of things'.[126] Miller's words were an implied criticism of the Theological Hall, and were interpreted as such. Principal Dickie decided to put Miller in his place. With deep condescension, he asserted that Miller was defective in both 'knowledge and mentality', and was 'living in an intellectual back-wash' with a 'crude' conception of salvation. He mocked Miller's attachment to the conservative Princeton theology: long before Miller had 'discovered Dr Hodge on the West Coast', Protestantism had left Dr Hodge 'far behind'. Furthermore, the Bible Institutes were intended only for those who were unable to think for themselves.[127]

Miller wrote back deploring Dickie's descent into personal attacks.[128] Dickie responded with a letter containing numerous repetitions of the words 'real scholar', and stating that 'Mr Miller has been talking at large about a number of important and difficult subjects about which he does not know enough to know his own ignorance; when he is old, Miller will thank him for teaching him a painful lesson.'[129] Miller's response noted Dickie's 'self-imposed mantle of omniscience' and his 'wild and whirling' opinions, which all must accept 'purely on his own authority' if they are to escape being 'instantly bludgeoned'.[130] At this point, the editor called a halt. The exchange of letters highlighted the differences between Miller, an uncowering spokesman for an older evangelical and confessional Presbyterianism, and Dickie, the rather prickly defender of the newer, more liberal theological establishment.

In 1931, the publication of Dickie's *Organism of Christian Truth* made public the principal's views on many important doctrines.[131] Isaac Jolly wrote to the *Outlook* that Dickie's explicit denial of substitutionary atonement and his neglect of the Cross was a 'direct contradiction' of scripture, and contrary to the teaching of the Presbyterian Church.[132] At the 1932 Assembly, Miller prepared to move a resolution that substitutionary atonement be taught at the Theological Hall, that James Denney's work on the atonement be prescribed for examination, and that the Assembly reaffirm 'its strong adherence' to the doctrine of substitutionary atonement as 'central and essential to the preaching and reception of the Gospel'.[133] Miller's motivation was not to attack Dickie, but to have orthodoxy upheld in the college responsible for training ministers. Working with Jolly, Miller prepared a careful speech.[134] Without any hint of personal rancour, Miller argued that in Dickie's book there had been 'a radical and serious departure' from historic orthodoxy, with two essential Christian doctrines explicitly compromised: the scriptures as the ground of authority, and substitutionary atonement as the heart of the gospel. At Assembly, however, Miller could not find any minister willing to second his motion.[135] He interpreted that as evidence of liberal dominance over the Assembly and that evangelical ministers were intimidated.[136] In the end, he persuaded an elder from Waiwera South to do so. George Neale uttered just four words ('I second the motion'), returned to his seat, and suffered a collapse.

A reaffirmation of basic doctrine might have been achievable, but anything that could be construed as an attack on the denomination's eminent theological principal was unlikely to succeed.[137] Miller's initiative may have been associated in the minds of many with P.B. Fraser's protracted campaign against Dickie, which could have been perceived as a personal vendetta. Instead of supporting Miller's motion, Assembly pointedly heaped praise on Dickie (including the 'lustre' of his great learning).[138]

Miller's perception that he was part of a beleaguered and browbeaten minority making little headway against a strong tide was strengthened when the *Outlook* failed to give adequate coverage of the Assembly debate or its issues.[139] The *Outlook* had a policy of ignoring Fraser, and in 1932 Miller felt the same cold wind. The *Outlook* refused to print his speech, a decision which greatly annoyed him. Such censorship deepened the feeling among conservative evangelicals that they were the faithful remnant in a corrupted denomination, being deliberately locked out of real voice or influence by the denomination's controlling forces.[140] With all other doors closed to him, Miller took the unusual step of protesting to the Synod of Otago and Southland, but without success.[141] The *Outlook* reported Miller's discomfort in great detail, but did not report any other business from the Synod.[142] A few months later, Assembly further endorsed Dickie by choosing him as moderator-elect. Two years later, it eulogised Dickie at length, noting that 200 of the 250 active ministers in the PCNZ had been 'largely moulded' by him.[143]

In 1940 Miller was back at Assembly, seconding an unpopular amendment against church union.[144] Ironically, the amendment was by Dickie, who had also become opposed to union. The amendment was lost, 11/147. Three individuals asked for their dissent to be recorded: Dickie, Miller and D.N. McKenzie.[147] Over the next few years they joined forces to fight church union. In the face of a strongly pro-union editorial stance,[148] and to the frustration of Dickie's professorial colleagues and ministerial protégés, they were the three signatories to a notable open letter: 'The Case against Church Union: Twelve Reasons'.[147] The *Outlook* received a flood of letters, both pro- and anti-Union: the trio were castigated as 'miserable and mean ... trouble-makers', a 'few intolerant isolationists' who cannot 'discern the times'.[148] Miller was evidently an acceptable personal target, at least for a scathing Professor Hunter, but nobody mentioned Dickie himself. The correspondence shows that the chief objection of evangelical conservatives to church union was the fear of doctrinal indifferentism.[149] Miller believed that church union proposals mistook organisational merger for genuine spiritual unity. He saw it as a human construct, a 'Tower of Babel', an 'illusory thing' devised to 'to hide the facts ... when life within the church runs low'.[150] The union issue ensured Miller remained a prominent dissident, continuing to incur the disdain of the church establishment.

Other evangelicals under fire

Miller was not the only conservative evangelical who felt offside with the denominational leadership. P.B. Fraser had long been banished to the margins. By the 1930s Isaac Jolly, a former moderator once widely respected for his scholarship and churchmanship, found his conservative biblical and doctrinal emphases were no longer smiled upon by those in high places. Bissett, Assembly evangelist, old-style in both theology and practice, was increasingly the target of liberal murmurings.[151]

The 1931 article by Steele against 'Pietism' was not just directed at Keswick.[152] Its main targets were Bissett and especially Harries, his faithful publicist. Week by week, with a content and idiom increasingly in contrast to the rest of the *Outlook*, Harries had been calling for a new 'Pentecost', 'the fire of the Holy Spirit', and a 'quickened Church'.[153] In November 1931, putting aside his normally peaceable tone, Harries had spoken out on behalf of 'the Bible believer' and 'the godly remnant', and denounced the 'mischief' of those theologians who assume a 'patronising attitude ... toward the Bible'. Only a Church which 'trembles at God's word', he declared, is one which God could use.[154]

> It is not surprising to find in dead or dying churches so much hatred of evangelism, so much indifference or antagonism towards the teaching of holiness ... and the Bible is little known by, or it has never conquered the heart of, the average church member.[155]

It was after countless *Outlook* columns from Harries about prayer meetings, conversion, the surrendered life, Bissett's missions and imminent revival, that Steele had launched his red-hot blast against 'Pietism'. With Harries clearly in mind, he railed against 'a certain section of people in our own Church who repeatedly tell us in the Assembly, and in the pages of the *Outlook*, that the salvation of Presbyterianism in NZ depends on a spiritual revival of this kind in our midst'. 'The time has come', Steele announced, 'for ... opposition to be freely and fully vented ...'

The ferocity of Steele's attack on evangelical figures such as Bissett and Harries, and on all they and Miller stood for – and the fact that the *Outlook* printed it – must have seemed a powerful indication to old-style Presbyterian evangelicals that their denomination no longer stood where they did. It would not be lost on them that after Bissett retired, the decision was taken not to replace him, and that the first proposal presented to Assembly by the new Life and Work Committee in 1936 was a motion lavishing praise on Steele.[156]

By the early 1930s, both confessionalist and revivalist elements within the New Zealand Presbyterian Church were on the defensive, and their influence was fading. Jolly and Fraser represented the traditional confessionalist emphasis. Bissett and Harries reflected the revivalist element. Miller reflected something of both. By the time Miller had begun at St Stephen's, both Jolly and Fraser had retired.[157] By 1934, Bissett had retired and Harries had left for overseas.[158] But in 1928 Miller was still at the beginning of his most important ministry, and it was he who would have the greatest long-term impact.

Miller's Evangelical Legacy

Miller's ministry was a bridge between Presbyterian evangelicalism before World War I and that which would emerge after World War II. When he died in 1948, his gravestone carried the inscription 'Valiant for Truth'.[159] His critics would have described him differently. They could not dismiss him as a lightweight, but they had regarded him as outmoded and obscurantist in theology, suspect in his revivalist sympathies, standoffish in his churchmanship, obdurate in his opposition to church union, and treacherous in his support of the Evangelical Union. In one historian's assessment, Miller was seen by other Presbyterian leaders as a 'crank', 'with nothing to contribute to the questions of the day'.[160] But the significance of Miller's ministry was in fact considerable.

That significance did not lie in the size of Miller's congregation: St Stephen's was a relatively small parish, dwarfed by First Church and Knox Church, and struggling against the demographic trends of Dunedin's inner suburbs.[161] Miller's legacy was through his work among the next generation. By 1944, about thirty young people were in full-time Christian work or in training for it.[162] Miller's protégés included around ten future Presbyterian ministers. Among these were his sons Graham and Rob, his sons-in-law Morrison Yule and Bill Wallace (married to Marion and Beatrice respectively), and others such as Rymall Roxburgh.[163] His influence on others such as J.D.S. Moore, Bill Moore, Ian McMillan, Ian Fleming and George McKenzie was perhaps less pronounced, though they were still substantially products of St Stephen's.[164] Because of St Stephen's proximity to the university and the Theological Hall, many other future ministers passed through Miller's congregation – for example David Sage, Roy McKenzie, Bill Milligan, Gordon Reid and John Johnson – but their primary formation had often been elsewhere.[165] Sage, for instance, came from the evangelical Hawera parish, and McKenzie and Reid had trained in BTI. There were also many evangelical lay people who were shaped by the ministry of Thomas Miller.[166] Eight members of St Stephen's became wives of Presbyterian ministers. Others became missionaries.[167]

There was no other evangelical Presbyterian minister in the interwar period who had anything like the influence of Miller. Dr John Laird, who knew the national evangelical scene perhaps better than anyone, wrote to Miller with the assessment, 'I have always felt that your work at St Stephen's has been monumental in the evangelical and student life not only of Dunedin but of the Dominion.'[168] It was presumably because of Miller's effect on so many future ministers that Professor Salmond of the Theological Hall considered him 'the most influential man in the [Presbyterian] Church'.[169]

Miller's many protégés would become the core of a Presbyterian evangelical resurgence. What would most ensure the enduring impact of Miller's ministry, however, was the sharp new identity provided by the the Evangelical Union.

CHAPTER TWO

The Evangelical Unions

More than anything else, it was the university-based Evangelical Unions, established from 1930 onwards, which effectively relaunched evangelicalism in mid-twentieth century New Zealand. In the Evangelical Unions – in their name, ethos and doctrinal basis – was a clear and cohesive new identity for New Zealand evangelicalism, an identity that was understandable and readily communicable. Large numbers of younger New Zealanders first learned the meaning of the term 'evangelical' and adopted it for themselves.[1] The Evangelical Unions shaped a new generation of self-aware 'evangelical' leaders and ministers. From the outset, Thomas Miller and his young people enthusiastically embraced the Evangelical Union and the identity it expressed; William Orange did the same in Christchurch. Their own ministries were reinforced and made much more enduring by the emerging Evangelical Unions.

Evangelical Unions Begin

The Evangelical Unions began in New Zealand in 1930, as a result of the visit of Dr Howard Guinness from the Inter-Varsity Fellowship in Britain.[2] Guinness had already spent time establishing IVF groups in Canada and Australia. He came to New Zealand at the invitation of an Open Brethren leader in Dunedin, Cree Brown.[3] The IVF had arisen out of a major schism in Christian student work in Britain. Following the 1910 disaffiliation of the Cambridge Inter-Collegiate Christian Union from the more liberal Student Christian Movement, conservative evangelicals had established student groups in numerous British universities, and in 1928 formed the Inter-Varsity Fellowship. The IVF was regarded with disdain by the theological and ecclesiastical establishments, but its emergence was a crucial factor in the recovery of an educated evangelicalism in twentieth-century Britain. It offered 'a new kind of intellectually adequate classical evangelicalism', which 'combined evangelistic zeal with doctrinal substance'.[4]

In both Dunedin and Auckland there were already small student groups of disaffected evangelicals who had left the SCM. The New Zealand SCM had become more liberal from about 1912, and markedly so in the late 1920s. Its general secretary, Donald Grant, had denied the divinity and resurrection of Christ, championed modernist views on scripture and the atonement, and blocked the expression of conservative evangelical viewpoints.[5] In 1927, the Student Bible League had begun in Auckland, under the leadership of graduates such as medical doctor William Pettit (who had earlier been a leader in SCM) and E.M. Blaiklock.[6] Bible study and prayer were the chief activities, along with a strong interest in 'evidential' issues.[7] Members, mostly drawn from several large evangelical churches in central Auckland,[8] were required to sign a detailed doctrinal statement.[9] In 1928, against the opposition of SCM, the League had gained recognition as an official student society.[10] In the same year, a similar prayer and Bible study group had been established in Dunedin in the home of Cree Brown.[11]

Guinness was in New Zealand for eight weeks only (September–November 1930). A charming, good-looking Irishman, just twenty-five years old, Guinness was a gifted speaker. His evangelistic appeals provoked large responses.[12] An SCM observer described Guinness as 'a man with a most vital Christian experience, full of power and persuasion and simply radiating personality'.[13] In Dunedin Guinness spoke twice at the SCM's Otago branch (the Christian Union), at eight CU study groups, at two large city churches (Knox and First Church), and at a university meeting where one third of the student body was present.[14] The SCM was unsure about Guinness and his intentions, but – apprehensive about a possible conservative breakaway – felt they had little option but to give him a platform. Evangelicals had already told SCM's Otago president that if the SCM could not be brought back to a 'a real evangelical basis', a new movement might be formed 'to maintain true testimony to evangelical truth'.[15] Evangelicals themselves were in two minds as to whether a separate evangelical student work should be started or whether EUs could be formed as an evangelical wing within SCM. Cree Brown was initially open to the latter approach as there were still some SCM leaders with strong evangelical sympathies, and all the members of his own group were still members of the Otago CU.[16] One of them, Hallam Howie, was on the Christian Union executive, and worked hard for an EU to be affiliated as a group within SCM.[17]

In each main centre, Guinness received the support of leading evangelicals. In Dunedin, sponsors included Cree Brown, Thomas Miller and the Evangelical Bible League.[18] In Christchurch, they included Rev. William Orange (Anglican), botany lecturer Miss Herriot (Brethren) and dentist Howell Fountain (Brethren).[19] In Auckland, key figures included Pettit (Brethren), Blaiklock (Baptist), Harries (Presbyterian), schoolmaster A. Donnell (Presbyterian) and businessman R.A. Laidlaw (Brethren).[20] In Wellington – a city which Guinness saw as 'a great stronghold of the devil'[21] – he had the support of Anglican businessman A.E. Birch.[22] Such cooperation across denominational boundaries would be characteristic of the evangelical movements that Guinness was about to pioneer. In Auckland, the Student Bible League staged a 1600-strong Town Hall meeting to welcome Guinness, chaired by Blaiklock.[23] The League announced a change of name, to the 'Evangelical Students Fellowship', and 'association' with British IVF. Previously accused of being 'fundamentalist', 'sectarian' and 'bible bangers', the group hoped linkage with an Empire-wide university movement might help it become better accepted.

In Dunedin, Cree Brown eventually decided that 'you can't do much in a mixed movement with unsaved and doubting leaders', that a 'half-awakened' SCM would not suffice, and that 'God's purpose is to raise up a new testimony to His truth and saving power'.[24] The nucleus of a future EU already existed, in his study group. Three times it was requested that an Evangelical Union be officially recognised *within* SCM's Otago Christian Union,[25] but with a constitution requiring a clear profession of faith for members, and subscription to the British IVF doctrinal basis for officebearers. The outcome was predictable: it was a non-negotiable policy of the SCM to be doctrinally open and comprehensive (though IVF people questioned how open it really was),[26] and the defining principle of the IVF was to insist on a clear doctrinal position. The two approaches were therefore mutually exclusive.

The IVF Doctrinal Basis was 'resolutely conservative but by no means extreme'.[27] It listed several truths of Christianity that the IVF was committed to upholding:

> (a) *The divine inspiration and infallibility of the Holy Scripture, as originally given, and its supreme authority in all matters of faith and conduct.*
>
> (b) *The unity of the Father, the Son, and the Holy Spirit in the Godhead.*
>
> (c) *The universal sinfulness and guilt of human nature since the Fall, rendering man subject to God's wrath and condemnation.*
>
> (d) *Redemption from the guilt, penalty and power of sin only through the*

sacrificial death (as our Representative and Substitute) of Jesus Christ, the Incarnate Son of God.

(e) The Resurrection of Jesus Christ from the dead.

(f) The necessity of the work of the Holy Spirit to make the Death of Christ effective to the individual sinner, granting him repentance toward God and faith in Jesus Christ.

(g) The indwelling and work of the Holy Spirit in the Believer.

(h) The expectation of the Personal return of the Lord Jesus Christ.

While many individual SCM members may have held similar beliefs, SCM as a movement was unable to accept the theological content of the IVF Doctrinal Basis. Modernist theology rejected verbal inspiration, biblical infallibility and substitutionary atonement, so clauses (a) and (d) gave particular difficulty to those who followed the prevailing theological directions of SCM.

Unsurprisingly, the SCM declined the request for an EU within the SCM, and informed the EU that affiliating it 'would not be in the best interests of the Kingdom'.[28] The EU felt it had no option but to form a separate movement in Otago and elsewhere. When the SCM wished to discuss the matter again, the EU declined.[29] The EU as not about to forgo the righteous status of having been forced to begin a separate work. When, from time to time, the EU was subsequently accused of schism, it was always quick to point out the history of the matter as it perceived it.[30] One of the EU pioneers believed that 'the EU was forced into being by the narrowness & bigotry of those who now strongly oppose it'.[31] Within the CU at Otago, there remained some evangelical members who agitated for reform and for an accommodation with the EU.[32] But the reality was that the EU had gone for good, and was relishing developing a life of its own.

In the early days, friendships and family relationships often bridged the divide: the first OUEU president was brother of the immediate past president of the Otago CU; both lived in the same family home.[33] Cree Brown wrote to the SCM in Wellington promising that the EU's relationship with the SCM would be 'independent but friendly'.[34] The subsequent relations of the two rival movements were certainly independent – but not always friendly; in fact, the prevailing relationship was one of suspicion and coolness. The SCM, which felt it had proprietary rights over Christian witness in the universities, objected to the EU's existence and resented any initiatives that gave the EU profile.[35] SCM members suspected EU members of narrow-mindedness, fanaticism and obscurantism. For its part, as in any schism, the EU probably exaggerated the failings of the movement it had deserted. It saw itself as having originated in a heroic struggle for truth in the face of fierce and unjust opposition. The EU was established, it felt, against 'a very cold blizzard' from the SCM.[36] A decade and a half after the schism, John Deane observed that the EU 'heartily despised the SCM', and the hostility appeared to be reciprocated.[37] The stand-off perhaps also reflected the tendencies of zealous youth – of any stripe – to oversimplification and dismissiveness. Nevertheless, at an official level there were often gestures of friendship, including regular invitations to each other's events.

As a result of Guinness's visit, an EU was also established at Canterbury University College, Christchurch.[38] Guinness was unable to get an EU started in Victoria University College (Wellington), but one began there in 1933.[39] In 1935 Auckland's Evangelical Students' Fellowship renamed itself (again) as the Evangelical Union and altered its membership basis to be the same as that of other EUs.[40] In each context, it was a struggle to persuade the Students' Associations to affiliate the EUs, as SCM supporters argued that the EU was too similar to the SCM.[41] By 1936, EU groups had also been established in the four teacher training colleges and two agricultural colleges (Lincoln and Massey).[42]

SCM and EU Contrasted

The breach between the SCM and the EU was symbolised by different styles of spirituality and mission – often minor, but considered significant at the time. A meeting between the leaders of the Otago SCM and EU finished with a time of prayer. 'All the EU fellows knelt, and all the SCM ones sat bolt upright in their chairs, and this seemed to be a true paradigm for the difference between the two.'[43] The EU – whose members always knelt at their early morning prayer meetings – suspected (probably unfairly) that the SCM members would 'not be used to praying at all, as a group'.[44]

The differences between the two movements were partly theological, partly subcultural. The differences were important, because it was primarily against the SCM that the EU defined itself. The SCM prided itself on being the Christian presence in the university, welcoming all and intelligently exploring new horizons; the EU prided itself on being the true believers. The SCM had discussions; the EU had Bible Study. The SCM had 'socials'; the EU had 'fellowship'. The SCM might entertain itself with secular songs, sometimes bordering on the bawdy or the irreverent;[45] the EU would sing songs from Sankey, Alexander or Keswick for spiritual uplift. The SCM might have a dance; the EU would not dare.[46] The SCM was interested in speculative theology; the EU was interested in biblical doctrine. The SCM valued 'breadth'; the EU valued 'soundness'. The SCM was open to the world, and wanted to study it and change it; the EU was wary of the world, and sometimes tried to avoid it. The SCM embraced modern science and philosophy; the EU was defensive. The SCM believed in evangelism, and sometimes felt guilty about not doing much, but it was nevertheless generally coy about evangelism because it feared 'unsound emotional revivalist methods';[47] the EU, however, claimed evangelism as its primary purpose, and was not averse to a touch of revivalism. The SCM was uncomfortable with religious excitement; the EU – within limits – welcomed spiritual fervour, and loved a good conversion. The SCM – in the eyes of EU members – was 'wishy-washy' and 'ambivalent about everything';[48] the EU was definite about most things.

Ironically, within a few years of the split, the New Zealand SCM was becoming somewhat more conservative in theology, partly because of the influence of neo-orthodox theologians such as Barth and Brunner.[49] But that made little difference: the EU insisted on having a defined doctrinal position, whereas the SCM was committed to avoiding one. Because of its commitment to Christian unity, the SCM regarded the existence of the EU as 'sinful', as a 'calamity'.[50] Reflecting its desire for united witness and mission, the SCM frequently made overtures to an EU for 'cooperation'. The EU almost always declined, thus frustrating and offending the SCM. But the EU had little room to manoeuvre: it was a basic principle, always written into its constitutions, documents and publications, that it could not cooperate with those who did not hold to the same doctrinal position.[51] The EU had arisen out of a reaction to doctrinal looseness, and felt cooperation was potentially 'fatal'.[52] 'To maintain our existence', it insisted, 'we have to stay separate.'[53] Any university missioner sponsored by the SCM was almost certainly theologically unacceptable to an EU.[54] Issues of cooperation were being decided in an atmosphere where the EUs were constantly suspicious of what the SCM was 'up to' and what was behind its latest 'move'.[55] When, in 1941, OUEU allowed the SCM to use its own meeting room (after the SCM venue was commandeered for military use), OUEU was warned 'the whole situation is fraught with danger'. (It was cautioned with a story about a camel that initially put just its nose into an Arab's tent, but then, by moving in slightly further every night, it eventually ended up displacing the Arab.)[56]

The existence of two rival student Christian organisations accentuated the very sharp sense of theological polarisation in the 1930s and 40s. There were two distinct ecclesiastical 'tribes', each loyal to itself and privately dismissive of the other. The SCM was regarded with loyalty by denominational leaders and many ministers, and the EU was regarded as a reactionary intruder.[57] The

SCM promoted itself, in the official church newspapers, as the natural choice for discerning students, with the EU implicitly excluded. It asserted 'there is no place in the student community for division of activity', and 'the SCM needs all the Christians in the University'.[58] The 1931 *Outlook* carried an unabashedly pro-SCM article, condescendingly depicting 'conservatives' as those who showed a 'disconcerting' anxiety for souls, asked people 'direct questions' and gave 'testimonies'. In contrast to conservative 'crudity', the SCM provided 'intellectual leadership'. The 'fresher' at university, being a 'thoughtful chap and backed by the sound advice of minister or BC leader', would join SCM, and start reading SCM books such as Fosdick's *Modern Use of the Bible*.

When students began at university, there was thus a tussle between SCM and EU to recruit them first.[59] Induced to join one or the other group, students were then acculturated into its values, customs and prejudices. Those who tried to retain links with both movements were regarded with suspicion.[60] If graduates went on to theological colleges they continued their participation in SCM or EU, retained the identity they had learned, and associated closely only with their own ilk. Many student leaders in each movement stayed active members for many years and were lifelong supporters.

Regional Distinctives

The four university Evangelical Unions were all distinctive in various ways. Otago EU was an especially important one, because of its relationship with Presbyterian theologues and also with New Zealand's sole medical school. The Otago EU contained a disproportionate number of Presbyterians, because of Otago–Southland's background as a Free Church settlement, and the presence of the Theological Hall. In common with other EUs, OUEU observed the pattern of daily prayer meetings, weekly meetings for Bible teaching, and monthly teas, along with occasional special meetings, missions and weekend houseparties. The EU was supported by a small number of local ministers, including Miller, W.A. Hamblett of St Matthew's (Anglican), and Alan Stevely of First Church.[61] Classics lecturer Dr H.R. Minn was a frequent speaker, and was closely identified with OUEU: a student newspaper referred to 'the E.U. and its Minn-ties'.[62] Student presidents in the 1930s and early 1940s included Hallam Howie, Mervyn Milmine, Harry Thomson, Graham and Rob Miller and Russell Kenward.[63]

The Canterbury University College EU (CUCEU) was characterised by a mix of Open Brethren and evangelical Anglicans. Other denominations (including Baptist and Presbyterian) were rarely present.[64] Almost all of the

Anglican members were associated with the influence of Orange, who spoke frequently at EU. Another influence on CUCEU was Orange's close friend Howell Fountain, whose home was frequently the Christchurch venue for evangelical gatherings and prayer meetings. The EU held its main meeting every Friday night in the 'Catacombs', an underground room that to a visiting Thomas Miller 'seemed to be a conspirators' chamber, a subterranean vault ... surrounded by beams and pipes'.[65] By 1938, CUCEU would eclipse the SCM group as the largest Christian group on campus.[66]

The Auckland EU was numerically strong and reflected the strength of several vigorous evangelical churches in Auckland.[67] It was predominantly Brethren and Baptist in make-up, but it did have some Presbyterians, Congregationalists and Church of Christ (Life and Advent) members.[68] In contrast to Christchurch, AUCEU had very few Anglicans.[69] It enjoyed the strong support of Dr Pettit and, especially, classics lecturer E.M. Blaiklock. For at least three decades, the AUCEU was very strongly associated with the influence and mana of Blaiklock. He was its leading mentor, and cast a 'great benign shadow' over the EU.[70] A magnificent orator and Bible teacher, Blaiklock often spoke at EU. For the AUCEU, and increasingly for the whole evangelical cause in New Zealand, Blaiklock's combination of strong Christian commitment and outstanding erudition and eloquence lent 'respectability as well as substance' to the evangelical position.[71] As an increasingly well known writer, speaker and columnist, Blaiklock in the postwar era arguably did more than any other New Zealander to raise the public profile of evangelical Christianity in New Zealand. In the secular-minded and sometimes hostile university environment, Blaiklock's support was very important. The EU was always anxious to have credibility. Its brochure – presumably alluding to how CICCU had preceded SCM – claimed that EU represented 'the original Christian Movement among Students'.[72]

There were many evangelical ministers and leaders the AUCEU could call on to speak, including the Brethren Robert Laidlaw, and BTI staff J.O. Sanders and H. Yolland.[73] In common with the other EUs, AUCEU liked to have William Orange come and speak at some of its house parties. On the first such occasion some students were deeply impressed by Orange's teaching and spirit and the 'fragrance of a life lived in closest touch with God'.[74] Along with Orange and Blaiklock, Dr John Laird was similarly an inspiration to many young EU members;[75] Laird headed up the new schools-based Crusader movement and related very closely to each of the four Evangelical Unions. An early AUCEU leader was Archie Morton, who was later an Anglican minister in Sydney.

The 1938 president was Colin Becroft, later general secretary of Scripture Union. Many other future evangelical leaders (and leading professionals) were produced by the pre-war AUCEU – such as Ivan Moses (IVF worker, educationist, Presbyterian layman), Ian Kemp (IVF worker, Baptist minister, missionary, lecturer), Arnold Turner (judge, Baptist layman), Francis Foulkes (Anglican minister, missionary, biblical scholar) and Kevin O'Sullivan (lawyer, Anglican layman). During the war years, women such as Mavis Addison and Jean Day found increased opportunities to give leadership.[76]

The weakest EU was in Wellington, reflecting what was often regarded as the especially secular and hostile environment of Victoria University College, and the lack – until the 1950s – of a substantial evangelical base in the Wellington churches. An internal EU report noted:

> *Church life in Wellington lacks, in general, an evangelical element of any strength. This possibly has some connection with the rationalist bias in V.U.C. There is a marked lack of evidence of the evangelical viewpoint among the city's clergy.*[77]

In such a situation, the EU's role in shaping evangelicals was especially important: EU students 'look to the EU for the instruction which they do not get from their church'.[78] Because of the weakness of the city's Crusader groups, many of which were forced to meet after school and off school premises, the annual influx of ex-Crusader members into VUCEU was minimal. For a long time, VUCEU was dependent on the 'fatherly care' of John Laird[79] and of Cliff Cocker, a former VUCEU member who worked in the Treasury Department. Unlike other EUs, VUCEU was denominationally nondescript.[80]

Were the Evangelical Unions 'Fundamentalist'?

Evangelical Union members were often branded 'fundamentalist' by their SCM rivals.[81] It was not an identity EU members welcomed, and 'fundamentalist' was not a word they normally used – in part because it was a foreign, North American term.[82] The assumptions, influences and identity that shaped the Evangelical Unions were overwhelmingly British rather than North American. For EU members, the evangelical glory days were not 1920s America, but eighteenth- and nineteenth-century Britain. The word 'evangelical', long used in the British theological and church scene, seemed sufficient to EU people – and furthermore, it was enshrined in the name of their movement. EU members in the 1930s and 40s saw themselves as simply 'evangelical'.[83] New Zealand evangelicals realised, too, that 'fundamentalist' was becoming a pejorative term.[84] In the 1920s and 1930s, the terms 'fundamentalist' and 'evangelical' were regarded by some people as more or less synonyms;[85] but the terms gradually became less synonymous as EU members, taking their lead from British evangelicals, became increasingly aware of the negative connotations of the American term.[86] In 1939, for example, EU leader Max Wiggins warned that:

> *One of the difficulties under which the Evangelical movement labours is its association in the minds of many with the extremes and extravagances of American Fundamentalism. It is the opportunity of the Evangelical Unions ... to counteract this impression.*[87]

By the 1950s, there was a general awareness in EU circles that 'fundamentalist' was a compromised word.

Nevertheless, members of the prewar EUs were universally prepared to identify with the earlier, more benign sense of the term 'fundamentalist'. They shared in the general evangelical assimilation of the word 'fundamental' (as used in America from 1910) to denote the core orthodox doctrines which all conservatives agreed should be defended. 'I was probably called ... ['fundamentalist'],' recalled one EU stalwart, 'but I did not mind it. I understood that it had a "good" meaning, that you believed in the fundamentals.'[88] Likewise, OUEU stated that one of its three aims was establishing Christian students 'in the fundamentals of the Christian faith'.[89]

Were EU people 'fundamentalist' nevertheless – crypto-fundamentalists who fitted the definition, even if they avoided the terminology? If the word 'fundamentalist' simply means 'biblically and theologically conservative', then EU members certainly were in that category. The EUs expected of their members a strong commitment to the authority of scripture, and an unequivocally orthodox faith commitment. If the term is defined as 'reacting against theological modernism', then that fitted too: the EUs self-consciously perceived themselves as upholding true biblical faith against the inroads of a diluting modernism. But such definitions of the term 'fundamentalist' are not particularly useful. 'Fundamentalism' does entail biblical conservatism, and does entail a reaction against modernism; but there are varying degrees of biblical conservatism, and not all biblical conservatives are 'fundamentalist'. In their reactions against modernism, conservatives displayed a range of different tones and stances.

The EUs' biblical conservatism was not extreme. The IVF Doctrinal Basis shared by the EUs was conservative and firmly held, and avoided ambiguities on points where liberals and conservatives clearly differed. But it was not excessively narrow or prescriptive. It avoided unnecessary precisianism or elaboration. It left some things – such as the nuances of 'inspiration' and 'infallibility' – undefined. The Doctrinal Basis ignored secondary controversies, and avoided such subjects as evolution, the Virgin Birth, or detailed scenarios for the Second Coming.[90] It avoided any hint of stridency or militancy, and was couched positively in the language of classical doctrinal confessions, rather than in language that suggested a direct reaction to modernist positions.

No doubt some individual EU members sometimes exhibited elements of a supposedly 'fundamentalist' mentality, such as arrogant dismissiveness of contrary viewpoints, the rejection of scholarship, excessive literalism, the piling up of proof texts without reference to context, legalistic anxiety about peripheral matters, and clumsy styles of evangelism. EU was, after all, a movement of young students, and some of its members had come from very conservative backgrounds. Nevertheless, especially at leadership level, there was a characteristic moderation about the EUs, in keeping with the firm but nuanced conservatism of the British IVF movement and with educated British culture in general. As the EUs grew in numbers and confidence, and as the intensity of the schism with SCM began to fade, a moderate spirit increasingly prevailed. That moderation was conscious and deliberate: an important value in the EU movement, pervading and restraining everything, was 'sobriety and balance'.[91] Significantly, EU leaders stressed the importance of that 'sobriety and balance' in precisely the context of articulating the contrast between (British) evangelicalism and American fundamentalism.[92]

Evangelical Union meetings were characterised by a temperate, restrained atmosphere. The tone was set by leaders such as Orange, Blaiklock, Minn, Laird and Miller. The most highly valued activity in EU settings – apart from prayer – was the thoughtful devotional exposition of scripture. The pitch of such exposition was 'spiritual'. It was not given to polemics. While Orange's relish for seeing the New Testament foreshadowed in the Old could sometimes border on the whimsical, there was a prevailing attitude in EUs that biblical exposition should be careful and judicious, and based on sound, sensible exegesis.

Prewar EUs were anxious for intellectual and ecclesiastical respectability, and their letterhead and brochures always prominently listed the names of respected academics and clergy on their advisory councils. With their own reputation at stake, those who were listed had a vested interest in guiding the EUs away from anything extremist; Blaiklock in particular was hypersensitive about anything in the EU that might appear ignorant, irrational, fanatical or emotionally excessive. The EUs steered clear of anything eccentric or sectarian. Bible study leaders from the Brethren might occasionally promote elaborate schemes about the end-times, but there was little general enthusiasm for those. It was assumed by most EU members that biological evolution *by chance* was contrary to the teachings of scripture, but in most EUs there was in practice little focus on discussing or opposing evolution, and there was considerable variety (and liberty) in the ways in which EU members correlated science and creation.[93]

If 'fundamentalist' denotes 'anti-intellectual', then that designation did not fit the EU. It is also true that EU members were not encouraged to speculate, to accommodate their faith to the latest winds of contemporary human thought, or to be theologically sophisticated. It is true that spiritually zealous students could be tempted towards anti-intellectualism, especially if they had absorbed the idea that scholarship led to doubt and unbelief. But an unthinking or uninformed approach to faith was definitely not favoured by the EU leadership. The whole movement was premised on the principle that a clear and reasoned understanding of biblical doctrine was an essential foundation for a strong faith. The Evangelical Unions therefore placed a high premium on instructional reading and teaching. The basic EU text – Hammond's *In Understanding Be Men* – was an attempt to have EU students thinking, studying and well informed, at least to the same level as they attained in their university studies.[94] The book revolutionised the outlook of some EU students.[95]

If 'fundamentalist' means a strident, Bible-thumping revivalism (such as that of W.P. Nicholson), or a high-pressure evangelism, the description would not fit the EUs. Such an image would have been anathema to Blaiklock of the Auckland EU. The EUs were anxious to evangelise (with their anxiety often exceeding their action), but there was nevertheless a restraint in the manner in which they went about it. There was usually a consciousness that their Christianity was being articulated in a university setting, and that scepticism had to be countered with rationality rather than hype. The messages in EU missions were often pitched to promote the reasonableness of Christian faith, and excessive emotional intensity or pressure would have undermined that approach.

If 'fundamentalist' means 'separatist', the answer to whether the EUs were fundamentalist must be qualified in at least two directions. The EUs had grown out of a rift with the SCM, and were steadfastly intent on maintaining a separate, 'sound' Christian work among students. In their desire for doctrinal clarity and purity, the EUs were certainly doctrinally 'separatist': they were wholly opposed to any compromise with theological modernism, and firmly resisted rejoining or cooperating with a student movement that seemed to them to be doctrinally indifferent and spiritually lax. But they were never ecclesiastically 'separatist'. They held no brief for ecclesiastical separatism, or for church splits along theological lines. They invariably taught loyalty to one's own denomination. They encouraged EU members to be active in their local churches, and to engage with and reclaim their denominations rather than leave them.

The critical significance of the EUs was not 'fundamentalism', but the formation of an explicit 'evangelical' theology and identity among a generation of New Zealand students. It was the growth of a confident, new, university-based evangelicalism that was the crucial contribution of the Evangelical Unions – a development that would become very important for the postwar Protestant Church.

The Crusader Movement

Guinness was not only interested in university-based EUs: he also developed the clever strategy of creating a feeder movement for EU in New Zealand secondary schools (with EU members helping to run the school groups). While in New Zealand, he spent most of his time visiting secondary schools. His aim was to seed evangelical school groups, meeting – with official permission – in the schools themselves.[96] As in Australia, Guinness called the school groups 'Crusader Unions', in an unauthorised borrowing of the name (and badge) of the English 'Crusader Bible Class' movement.[97] Guinness had himself been converted through such a group and he liked the biblical symbolism of being a 'soldier of Christ'. The constitution of the new movement included the IVF Doctrinal Basis, which committee members were required to accept.

Crusader groups were established in secondary schools around the country. These groups helped nurture young evangelicals, and then handed them on to the EUs. Kevin O'Sullivan attended Crusaders at Auckland Grammar School, and 'suddenly saw personal Christianity – for the first time'. Then, when he went on to university, his Crusader leader strongly urged him to join EU.[98] Three of the four EU presidents in 1940 had been converted through Crusaders.[99] The Crusader groups also often had strong links with evangelical churches: the Crusader Union at Christchurch Boys High, for instance, shared many of its members with Orange's Bible Class at Sumner.

Holiday Crusader Camps became an important adjunct to the school groups. The first such camp was held at Governors Bay in 1931 and included both high-school and university students. The speakers were Orange and Laird. Among the campers were Max Wiggins, Bob Nicholson, Roger Thompson and Basil Williams – all of whom later played a part in the growth of Anglican evangelicalism. In January 1932, the celebrated Ponui Island boys' camps began in the Hauraki Gulf.[100] These hardy camps were held under canvas on the remote island farm of Fred and Gertrude Chamberlin. The formula included beautiful natural surroundings, boisterous activities and robust evangelical piety. The camps modelled a very 'masculine' Christianity; the outdoor 'wide' games at Ponui (such as 'storming the heights') were often more rugged than anything encountered on a rugby field.[101] Leaders at the first two camps included Rowland Harries and Steve Clark (both later Presbyterian ministers), David Burt (a Brethren elder and lawyer) and Vine Martin (later a Crusader staff member). Wyn Fountain, who later became a prominent Auckland layman, recalled a spiritual awakening as he looked out across the bay at the first Ponui camp in 1932:

> *The setting sun was painting the hills a hundred shades of red and orange. The black silhouette of the bushes on the point against the western sky all suddenly came alive. I had not noticed this sort of beauty before, but now I said to myself: 'This didn't happen by chance. God must be real.'*[102]

Ian Kemp, later a BCNZ principal, recalled his first conscious appreciation of expository Bible teaching from a series at Ponui by Becroft and Laird:

> *A hundred or more boys, huddled in the marquee ... or spread out in the grassy glade among the manuka trees up the hill by the old Maori fort, drank in every word. Our teachers were men of God whom we respected beyond their formative teaching for their manly approach to life and their genuine interest in each one of us ... It was foundational for my own ministries ...*[103]

Some other campers, however, may have agreed with the one who summed up his own Ponui experience as 'dreadful', on account of 'to [sic] much religion'.[104]

In 1939 only sixty-four secondary schools in New Zealand had Crusader Unions, with a combined membership of 1100 (out of a total of 226 schools, and 42,000 students).[105] But the significance of Crusaders was not in its numbers; it was in the foundations the movement was laying for the future. An EU annual report in 1941 noted that, 'year by year, the Crusader Unions supply new members reared in an evangelical atmosphere at their respective secondary schools'.[106] Evangelican Union members were also constantly being channelled back into producing more young evangelicals, by serving as leaders at Crusader Camps – and likewise at beach missions run by the Children's Special Service Mission (CSSM). Lists of camp leaders include large numbers of future evangelical leaders.[107] O'Sullivan, for instance, saw leadership at Ponui as his 'launching' into a life-time of Christian leadership.[108]

John Laird

It was Guinness who pioneered the twin evangelical student movements; but John Laird was the one who ensured their survival and growth. The two men were both products of British IVF. Laird arrived in New Zealand in December 1930 as a ship's doctor – a month after Guinness had left – and was recruited by Dr Pettit.[109] Laird's entry to schools was assisted by newspaper publicity about his going ashore and giving medical help in the immediate aftermath of the 1931 Napier earthquake.[110] With the help of co-workers in the girls' schools – Winifred Robertson and Margaret MacGregor – Laird worked hard to consolidate and grow the Crusader Movement. He also watched over the young EUs and for the first few years was effectively their national leader, until Cliff Cocker became IVF general secretary in 1937.[111]

Laird was less flamboyant than the somewhat erratic Guinness. He had an engaging personality, a sparkling wit and a capacity to relate warmly to everyone.[112] A CSSM report noted that Laird had 'drawn together the various evangelical circles in the Dominion'.[113] Under Laird's leadership, the new network of evangelical movements – Crusaders, EUs, IVF, CSSM – created opportunities for evangelicals from across New Zealand, and from across the denominations, to work together in a way that had not previously happened. Laird was no firebrand or separatist, but very much in the moderate evangelical tradition of Britain. He tried to reassure mainline denominations and educational authorities that the Crusader movement was responsible and balanced. Laird was Brethren, but interdenominationalist in spirit.[114] He was wary of extremes.[115] He was uncomfortable with American fundamentalism, and keen to ensure that the evangelical movement in New Zealand should be distinguished from it.[116] He warned a gathering of EU and Crusader supporters in Dunedin about what he had observed of some American evangelicals: they were 'too hard-line', and what was needed was 'fundamentalism plus love'.[117] By the time Laird left New Zealand in 1945 to return to Britain, his leadership style had helped foster a positive tone in New Zealand's evangelical movement.

The formation of the university Evangelical Unions in the early 1930s, and the schism with the Student Christian Movement, were important developments in Protestant Christianity in New Zealand. The EUs offered a clear and intellectually defensible new evangelical identity, based on a coherent set of Christian doctrines and reflecting British evangelical values such as soundness, reasonableness, and 'sobriety and balance'. This was a development that was going to have long-term effects.

CHAPTER THREE

William Orange and the Orange Pips

The pre-eminent prewar Anglican evangelical leader was William Orange (1889–1966), vicar of the seaside Christchurch parish of Sumner from 1930 to 1945.[1] Orange was a Bible teacher of outstanding giftedness. His ministry had an extraordinary spiritual impact, particularly on young men: there were numerous conversions and scores of his protégés later became Anglican ministers. He became the catalyst for a new evangelical Anglican movement in New Zealand.

Orange was passionately spiritual and the heart of his spirituality was devotion to Christ. A bachelor, he poured his energies into prayer, preaching and Bible teaching among youth. Every Sunday afernoon, forty or so young men would cycle out to his Bible Class and listen intently to his hour-long devotional discourses on passages of scripture. At the rate of one chapter per week, Orange worked his way through different books of the Bible. The Bible Class was followed by a prayer meeting, a meal and then a further Bible exposition in the evening service. It was spiritually intense: 'we young ones could not fail to be aware that we were on holy ground'.[2]

Affectionately known as 'Pekoe' (after Orange Pekoe tea), Orange became mentor to many young evangelical admirers, only some of whom were Sumner locals.[3] Many of his BC members were also members (or ex-members) of the Crusader Union at Christchurch Boys High School.[4] A common pattern was for youth to be converted through the CBHS Crusaders and then be nurtured by Orange's BC – and, if they were at university, also to be part of the Evangelical Union.[5] Many of Orange's charges then became leaders themselves, in Crusaders, EU and CSSM. From the late 1940s, those whom Orange had inspired to become ministers were commonly dubbed 'Orange Pips'. While

Orange's ministry was primarily directed towards young men,[6] women also attended his evening service and his mid-week Bible Class.[7]

Orange's preaching and teaching consisted of powerfully evocative meditations on biblical passages. He avoided giving any discernible headings or structure to his exposition; he simply worked through the text section by section. Every word was crafted. His language was 'golden', conveying the 'absolute wonder and beauty' of the Gospel.[8] His teaching was intriguing: he took details in the biblical text, especially in the Old Testament, and developed them into fascinating spiritual allegories.[9] His tone was gentle, not polemical.[10] Although Orange avoided using rhetorical tricks, his talks were enlivened by frequent humorous asides.[11]

Orange had a rare capacity to captivate his listeners. Some observers felt he had 'an anointing' – an unusual spiritual endowment.[12] One of his curates recalled an experience in about 1941:

> *I came back early one Sunday night from taking a service at Redcliffs, and as I arrived at the door of the church ... along the back seat there was a row of people with their eyes glued on the preacher, and leaning forward, neck outreached, to get every word that fell from his lips. It was exciting to watch, to see the interest that was being maintained. And then when they came out of church ... and I saw these people with their radiant faces, they had a tremendous blessing, it was a real work of the Holy Spirit, ministering the Word through his servant Canon Orange.*[13]

A former member of Orange's Bible Class recalled: 'Pekoe ... made the Bible the most interesting book you could possibly want to read ... the Scriptures came alive'.[14] He reflected that most of those who went out to Sumner were 'fairly academic kids', and found Orange's interpretations 'fascinating'. A different Orange Pip remembered Orange's ability to hold 'spellbound' a large group of youths, even on Leviticus.[15] Orange, another asserted, was deeply convincing: 'he could make you believe *anything*!'.[16] Above all, Orange imparted to his hearers 'a sheer delight in the marvels of Scripture'.[17] A member of the group who later became a classical scholar wrote of how he was 'profoundly' influenced by Orange's 'intense respect and interest in every last detail of the text. Every word. That remains with me to this day.'[18] Someone else gained a life-long appreciation of the 'wonderful wholeness of Scripture ... the New Testament was foreshadowed in the Old, and the Old was fulfilled in the New'.[19]

One of Thomas Miller's sons, who often heard Orange at student conferences, observed:

> *At any IVF conference, he had them eating out of his hand. I was one of them. You put your pen down. It was sacrilege to go on scribbling your notes.*[20] *When*

> he spoke to students in Dunedin on the book of Esther, our hearts burned within us. It was the voice of the Lord we heard speaking, and our eyes were opened to behold wondrous things ... [21]

Orange's charisma 'drew you like a magnet'.[22] At conference mealtimes, students vied to be near him, to hear his anecdotes.[23] At Sunday night suppers in Sumner, Orange sometimes told joke after joke, leaving his audience paralysed with laughter.[24] That social dimension – the hilarity and the camaraderie – was a significant element in Orange's appeal, and helps explain the strength of the group that grew up around him: group solidarity was based on more than just doctrine.

Some of Orange's listeners felt his teaching did not always adequately address their scientific, theological or biblical-critical questions.[25] His allegorising sometimes irritated evangelicals beyond his circle, including those of a more Reformed approach such as Les Gosling – who was upset by Orange's attempt to give an allegorical meaning to the 'four anchors' let out from the ship's stern in Acts 27:29 – and those of a scholarly background such as E.M. Blaiklock.[26] At an IVF conference the speaker, T.C. Hammond, quipped, 'We'll leave the significance of the third fig leaf to Canon Orange.'[27] Orange's admirers did not generally adopt his allegorical method in their own ministries.[28]

The earliest Orange Pips included the Revs Harry Thomson (later the head of the New Zealand CMS), Maxwell Wiggins (later a bishop in Africa), Roger Thompson (a leading postwar evangelical minister), Basil Williams, Bob Nicholson, Dick Carson, David Aiken (later vice-principal of the Bible College of New Zealand), Harvey Teulon and Peter Tovey. Later Orange Pips included the Revs Maurice Betteridge (later principal of Ridley College in Melbourne), Maurice Goodall (later bishop of Christchurch), Lester Pfankuch, Graham Lamont, Robert Glen, John Meadowcroft and Wallace Marriott. Most of these served as vicars in New Zealand parishes, mainly in the Christchurch and Nelson dioceses, but many also spent at least part of their ministry as overseas missionaries – most often with the CMS in either South Asia or East Africa. Orange inspired at least forty to enter ordained ministry.[29] Martin Sullivan described the Orange Pips as a 'vast company'.[30] Orange himself commented that in his protégés he saw 'the seeds of thousands'.[31]

Others in Orange's circle went on to become prominent lay people – for example, Edwin Judge, who later became professor of ancient history at Macquarie University. Women, too, were often influenced by Orange, including Hope and Shirley Greenwood and Vera Mott. Orange also made an impact on numerous non-Anglicans who heard him at his evening service, at his

Wednesday night BC and at EU and IVF. In particular, Orange had an effect on Open Brethren, and he sometimes spoke at their Rutland Street Chapel.[32] Through Orange, an intermingling developed of Christchurch's Open Brethren community and its newer evangelical Anglican community: 'our natural relationship was often with Brethren people, rather than anyone else. There weren't too many evangelical Presbyterians around [in Christchurch], and the Baptists tended to stand apart.'[33] Russell Fountain and Hedley Thomas were two Brethren leaders who were strongly influenced by Orange. In the EU, at Crusader Camps and at CSSM missions, evangelical Anglicans and Brethren worked together as as leaders, and marriages between Anglicans and Brethren were a further consequence.

Orange's Evangelical Faith

The son of a doting mother and an alcoholic father, and the second of eleven children, Orange was always serious-minded.[34] At the age of ten he made a faith commitment during a parish mission in Kaikoura, and he became close to his vicar. At twelve, he felt a call to ministry. From 1904, he was involved with St John's Latimer Square in Christchurch, under the ministry of two Low Church, evangelically minded vicars.[35] Orange's diary entries in 1909–12 reveal an intensely devout and lonely young man who oscillated between spiritual despair and elation. He was drearily employed in two department stores. His consuming passion was the church, where he attended three services each Sunday, sang in the choir and taught Sunday School. He had extensive daily devotions, often spent his lunchtime praying in the Cathedral and attended the vicar's Bible Study.[36] He lamented the 'utter godlessness' of his peers, was repelled by 'vulgar' talk and bored by conversations about boxing, racing and girls.[37] He was inspired in 1910 by a parish mission, and on his knees made a 'full surrender'.[38] A few days later he felt his soul 'stirring' and 'knew intuitively' that he was 'born to do great things ... I imagined myself a Missioner swaying a multitude of people.'[39]

There were many indications that Orange was already essentially evangelical. He was earnestly praying for his Sunday School boys' salvation.[40] He understood salvation as by grace, not by works.[41] He wrote that he was 'looking unto Jesus day by day' in the hope of 'being so filled with Him that sin finds no place'.[42] He was influenced by two other members of St John's as well, Harry Funnell and George Stening, who were 'missionary-minded' and 'full of evangelistic zeal'.[43] He was also becoming more aware of differing emphases within Anglicanism. He felt many ministers were not 'truly converted', and 'never preach the Gospel'.[44] Whereas in 1909 Orange had been impressed by a purple chasuble, by mid 1911 he found 'high church' practices 'dreadful'. This view was reinforced when in 1912 he read *Romanism and Ritualism*, a new book critiquing ritualistic trends.[45] In this period Orange appeared to understand the word 'evangelical' primarily as the opposite of 'High Church'.[46] There was less evidence in his diary that Orange was particularly aware of 'modernism', but he was shocked by a newspaper report of some vicars who denied Jesus' divinity and the inspiration of scripture.[47]

In 1911–12, Orange experienced an emotional and spiritual crisis. His time of introspection and melancholy drove him to new spiritual depths: he became more sure of justification by faith, more focused on the Cross, more intent on close study of scripture.[48] 'My great ambition,' he wrote, 'is that love for Jesus may become the one absorbing passion of my life.'[49]

Orange was also influenced by some Open Brethren he knew, who impressed him with their prodigious Bible knowledge.[50] He began reading Brethren literature. At an all-day Brethren meeting at Springston, he was astounded at 'plain but spiritually-minded men talking in an animated and cordial way of the sweetest truths'.[51] He felt that Brethren 'have grasped Scripture truths that Churchmen are hungering for' and that their gatherings were like those of the early church.[52] From a 'brother' Orange heard the fascinating idea that beneath the 'surface' meaning of scripture there lay another, 'under a veil'; he was 'in raptures' as he heard the brother unravel obscurities in scripture.[53] Orange was inspired to adopt a similar approach. He concluded that 'oceans of truth lie before me as yet unexplored and I have a key that will unlock all I need to know'.[54]

Orange was being badgered by some Brethren to escape the 'apostasy' of Anglicanism. Warned by Brethren that he was 'still bound hand and foot by the graveclothes of the System', and informed that the Lord would spew the Anglican Church out of his mouth, Orange was troubled.[55] He fretted that one could attend an Anglican church and gain 'no knowledge of God … no assurance of salvation, nor anything else'.[56] He came close to leaving the Anglicans. However, his vicar persuaded him there was a biblical basis to Church of England doctrine, and Orange resolved to press on towards ordination and preaching the scriptures from an Anglican pulpit.[57]

During the First World War, while staying at College House, Orange studied for a Licentiate of Theology and a BA. He studied Greek and Hebrew (and was tutored in the latter by the local rabbi). He narrowly missed qualifying for his MA when he failed a paper in Syriac.[58] He clashed with the principal of the college, J.R. Wilford, who was a determined Anglo-Catholic:[59] when Orange told Wilford that the ministry of the word was much more important than the ministry of the sacrament, Wilford told Orange he was 'very sad' to hear such views.[60] The night before Orange's ordination in 1919, Wilford told Orange that his theology made him 'not fit to be ordained'.[61] The underlying issue, as one fellow student saw it, was 'opposition between the religious authority of the Bible and that of "Mother Church"'.[62] But Wilford may also have been concerned about Orange's crusading attitude and his sway over young students.[63]

After ordination Orange became a curate in Sydenham. Then, from 1921 to 1923 he went on an extensive world trip, as tutor–companion to a wealthy heir. Back in Canterbury, he served as a locum at Fendalton and then as vicar at Waikari (1924–30). There, Orange devoted himself to concentrated biblical study:[64] 'It really is most absorbing and I am quite thrilled by it … Never before have I been so profoundly impressed with the truth of the Word and its undoubted plenary inspiration.'[65]

Orange developed a consuming passion for teaching scripture. Early Brethren commentaries were a strong influence in shaping his biblical interpretation.[66] His preaching at Waikari was exclusively textual and expositional, with no trace of thematic or topical preaching. Week by week, his diary simply recorded the passage or verse he was expounding.[67] In the morning services, he preached on the passages prescribed in the lectionary. In the evening services, he appears to have chosen favourite texts to preach from that reflected common evangelical themes, such as the new birth and Christian consecration.[68] Orange's approach – whether using the lectionary or not – reflected the traditional Protestant and evangelical emphasis on directly preaching the 'word of God', and the purist notion (held by prominent nineteenth-century evangelical British preachers such as Charles Spurgeon and by Orange's contemporaries such as Scroggie) that biblical exposition was preaching par excellence. Less direct forms of biblical teaching were considered less effective in arousing and nurturing faith.

Orange's spirituality was grounded not only in scripture but in intense prayer.[69] He was convinced that only through prayer could the hard hearts of the people be turned to God: a spiritual awakening 'shall be accomplished by unceasing prayer and by nothing else'.[70] When there was a dramatic increase in the number of people attending church at Waikari, a new spiritual eagerness and a first conversion, he understood those developments as God's response to faithful prayer.[71] His practice of prayer was inextricably linked with his evangelical hunger to see conversions. In that context of prayer, his diary records his constant yearning: 'I must have souls.'[72] Like many Evangelicals,

Orange was anxious about his supposed neglect of prayer: having read E.M. Bounds' *Purpose in Prayer*, he felt convicted of his 'criminal negligence'.[73] In Orange's intense introspection and his deep ache for spiritual breakthrough, there were echoes of celebrated evangelical heroes of faith and prayer such as Robert Murray McCheyne (the saintly Scottish minister) and Hudson Taylor (the founder of the China Inland Mission). Orange would often spend all Saturday evening praying for the services the next day.

Orange was strongly independent, and firmly resisted anyone's attempts to organise him or to tell him what he should think or do. 'I will not,' he wrote, 'be dragooned into anything.'[74] But Orange did not form his ideas alone. He was an avid reader with a huge personal library that reputedly contained 15,000 volumes (30,000 by one account);[75] his books were stored in every room and along both sides of the hallway.[76] Dean Martin Sullivan later claimed that there were few in the Anglican world who read as 'widely or deeply' as Orange.[77] Orange also read extensively from the English evangelical tradition, including such figures as Charles Simeon (celebrated preacher and mentor in the University of Cambridge), William Wilberforce (evangelical humanitarian MP and anti-slavery campaigner), and J.C. Ryle (Bishop of Liverpool).

Orange was certainly familiar with Ryle's *Knots Untied* (1871), a book that provided a strong template for an Anglican evangelicalism and that was much prized by Orange Pips.[78] In *Knots Untied*, Ryle laid out what he saw as the five principles of 'Evangelical Religion', including the 'absolute primacy' of Holy Scripture and doctrines of human sinfulness, the work of Christ, and the role of the Holy Spirit in producing repentance, faith and a fruitful life.[79] Ryle saw High Church views as subverting the Reformation and substituting 'another gospel'.[80] He insisted on the need for personal regeneration; he believed that 'the greater part of those who are called Christian' remained spiritually dead.[81] As for sacraments, he believed it was possible to receive them and be 'none the better for it'.[82] Ryle claimed that, to be true to itself, Anglicanism should always be evangelical: 'I believe firmly that impartial inquiry will always show that Evangelical Religion is the religion of Scripture and of the Church of England.'[83] He lauded the Book of Common Prayer as 'a matchless form of public worship', and the Thirty-Nine Articles as 'eminently Protestant and eminently Evangelical'.[84] In all those areas, Orange held similar views. However, in the tone of his Protestantism, Orange was less tub-thumping than Ryle.

Orange was influenced to some extent by Anglicanism in Sydney. He made several visits there and had close contact with many leading Anglican evangelicals, including Archbishop Howard Mowll, who tried to recruit Orange to work with the Australian Evangelical Unions and, later, as vice-principal at Moore College.[85] Orange also spent time with Marcus Loane (lecturer at Moore and later Archbishop of Sydney), R.B.S. Hammond (a missioner among the poor) and T.C. Hammond (principal of Moore College);[86] he would later share IVF conference platforms with them all in New Zealand. Despite such warm links, and despite believing that the Diocese of Sydney 'is the greatest Evangelical Diocese in the world', Orange had some reservations about Sydney Anglicanism.[87] He was troubled by the controversies, by the driving pace of work expected of the clergy and by the low emphasis placed on the Second Coming.[88] Above all, he perceived a deficiency in Sydney's spiritual tone:

> *I realised that there were very many fine evangelical and godly men in Sydney yet I was conscious of a lack on every hand ... They are able to present doctrine also in a masterly manner but what I miss is the fragrance and sweet savour of Christ. The Scriptures are not presented in such a way as to bring out of them what is Christ in them, so that the house is filled with the ointment.*[89]

It would seem that his devotional approach was not quite in tune with the somewhat more rationalistic, doctrinal and polemical approach of many Sydney evangelicals. For Orange, evangelical belief was never enough in itself, but must also be associated with a depth of spiritual experience.

Orange got to know T.C. Hammond, the emphatically evangelical theologian who had come out from Ireland in 1936 to become principal of Moore College. Hammond was the author of the key IVF theological handbook, *In Understanding Be Men* (1936), another book that was highly valued by Orange Pips. He was impressed by Hammond's 'immense erudition' and his ability to debate.[90] Hammond, who was both solidly intellectual and very entertaining, was a frequent speaker in New Zealand at IVF conferences. Although Hammond was more outspoken and controversial than Orange, and intellectualist rather than devotional in focus,[91] his bold Anglican evangelicalism must have helped reinforce Orange's own position.

There was no chance Orange would ever be a clone of the Sydney evangelicals. He was too much of an individualist to fit into any rigid theological system or identity. He did not quite fit the classic evangelical mould in England, either. He was, for instance, better read in the early church period than in the Reformation – a pattern that was characteristic of those who were more 'Catholic' in tendency.[92] Orange was no classic revivalist: he yearned and prayed for conversions, and saw many, but never gave evangelistic appeals (the practice of urging listeners to come to the front to pray for salvation).[93] He was broadly Reformed in theology, but did not subscribe closely to Calvinism.[94]

He was strongly influenced by the Brethren and often quoted J.N. Darby, but did not accept the details of Brethren dispensational and end-times teaching: one of the Orange Pips recalled him saying about the Second Coming, 'No one will turn to his companion, and say "I told you it would be like this when it happens."'[95]

Orange rejected theological liberalism but refused to accept the label 'fundamentalist'. He deplored the fact that he was regarded as such by the bishop and clergy of his diocese.[96] The 'label', he noted, had become a 'libel'.[97] In theology and identity, Orange was content to be simply 'evangelical'. He openly embraced that label, and used and explained it in his Bible Class.[98] In his diary he used the term repeatedly.[99] Orange, who strongly disliked controversy, was not militant about the label 'evangelical'. For him, to be 'evangelical' was a positive thing. It meant to be 'biblical' and 'spiritual', to teach the scriptures and to emphasise prayer and conversion. He was evangelical in doctrine, but his evangelicalism was primarily experiential, rather than an intellectual system.

Orange's evangelicalism was not narrowly denominational in spirit. He enthusiastically embraced such interdenominational movements as IVF/EU, CSSM, CIM and Keswick,[100] and felt more at home in such settings than in many Anglican contexts. He valued his evangelicalism above his Anglicanism. In that regard he was not typically Anglican; nevertheless he remained a loyal Anglican. Like other Anglican evangelicals he was very appreciative of the Book of Common Prayer and the Thirty-Nine Articles, and claimed the Reformation heritage as his own.[101] One observer saw Orange as 'a classical example of Evangelical Churchmanship of the Charles Simeon mould – loyal to the Church and faithful to the Gospel of Grace unfolded throughout the New Testament'.[102] There were clearly some similarities between Simeon's ministry in Cambridge and Orange's in New Zealand: both were passionately committed to biblical exposition and evangelical work among students, and both were bachelors who fathered a movement among young people.

Unlike his fellow evangelical Anglicans in Sydney or Nelson, Orange was not strictly Low Church. It may be that he continued to reflect the mediating position arrived at by Christchurch Anglicanism at about the time he entered ministry, a compromise between traditional Prayer Book Anglicanism and the newer Anglo-Catholic tendencies being promoted by some.[103] Orange did not adopt the Low Church (and Prayer Book) practice of presiding over communion from the 'north end' of the table.[104] Like most other New Zealand Anglicans of his time, he stood with his back to the congregation.[105] Unlike some of his vehemently 'Protestant' (and often Irish) colleagues in Christchurch, and unlike Sydney and Nelson evangelicals, Orange happily wore a stole.[106] He did not wear 'vestments' (such as the alb, chasuble, or maniple), which he associated with eucharistic sacrifice, and he rejected other Anglo-Catholic and ritualist practices.[107] But he was sufficiently 'High' in his views for an Australian minister to write to Moore College warning them that Orange was 'an Anglo-Catholic posing as Evangelical'.[108] Some Orange Pips – especially those with Nelson links – felt that Orange was too 'High' in his churchmanship, and adopted a more Low Church style.[109] The majority, however, simply followed Orange's approach, and those who took a more staunchly 'Protestant' line in the Christchurch context could be counselled against it.[110]

Privately, Orange felt that much of New Zealand's Anglican Church was 'apostate', unfaithful to the Gospel.[111] As much as possible, he kept aloof from diocesan life, and instead concentrated on his own parish.[112] He went to Synod, duty-bound, but sat in the back and almost never spoke.[113] 'No one,' he declared, 'ever got converted at Synod.'[114] He felt Synod was a waste of time, and 'very dull'.[115] He was very cautious in his dealings with bishops. Orange had been hauled over the coals by Bishop Julius after complaints from Waikari about his insisting on direct giving (rather than fundraising through 'worldly' bazaars, concerts and dances), and at Sumner he was again reprimanded when his curate removed and accidentally broke a memorial crucifix.[116] Orange was conscious that Campbell West-Watson (bishop from 1926 to 1951) had been in CICCU as a young man but had since become liberal, and that the bishop disapproved of his role in launching the Evangelical Union as a rival to the SCM.[117] West-Watson told Orange that conservative evangelicals had 'closed their minds', and his protégés would be of little use in modern parish ministry. Orange respectfully replied that, on the contrary, he had been 'opening' their minds, to 'a line of truth which I certainly never received while at College House'.[118] The intensity and self-righteousness of some of Orange's young charges could raise hackles, and did little to reassure the bishop.[119] In time, as various Pips proved themselves in ministry, Orange's standing with the bishop improved. He had a more positive relationship with the next bishop, Alwyn Warren.[120] But in his Sumner period, Orange seemed to fear that evangelicals would always face 'persecution', and that he should maintain a low profile, keeping his spiritual ministry a 'secret work'.[121]

Although he nursed many private fears and suspicions, Orange tried hard to be peaceable about those he disagreed with. He wrote to a young evangelical who was beginning ministry under a High Church vicar: 'it will do you no harm to have to rub up against something you do not much care for. It tests patience, and charity, and enables you to see Christ in the face of someone with whom you may not agree.'[122] Orange's principal strategy, however, was simply to keep his head down. Among his diocesan colleagues he was socially and theologically isolated.[123] To many, he was an oddball, out of step with the times. It was only in Orange's venerable latter years when his impact was beyond question, and when he was serving in the eminently respectable context of the Cathedral, that he was regarded with more general respect. Dean Martin Sullivan, a liberal, wrote glowingly of Orange: 'Everybody loved him for his worth and goodness', and 'I knew that every time I met him I was in the presence of a man of God.'[124]

In matters such as dancing, smoking, drinking and films, Orange's converts observed much the same code as other conservative Christians in the 1930s and 40s.[125] The tone of the BC, commented one of its members, was fairly 'monastic', and friendships with girls were not considered a priority.[126] To those who requested church dances, Orange retorted that his role was 'feeding the sheep rather than entertaining the goats'.[127] Captured by spiritual ideals, the young people did not generally find the moral code restrictive. They felt they had their minds on higher things. Conservative values were largely assumed. Later, one of the Orange Pips felt Orange's doctrine of 'separation' from the values of the world was 'pharisaical', and it created a 'ghetto mentality'.[128] But such an assessment did not give sufficient weight to the deep personal disgust felt by Orange and his evangelical contemporaries at what seemed to them a serious moral decline in society. Orange was appalled, for instance, at the behaviour of women passengers on a ship who were swearing, drinking, smoking, and 'canoodling' with officers in dark corners.[129]

Orange's Impact

Church services and Bible Classes in Orange's time at Sumner were frequently 'overflowing',[130] with many non-residents attending, but parish statistics reflect only moderate growth.[131] The greatest impact of Orange's ministry was in the Anglican evangelical movement he inspired. His many converts and admirers became a distinctive new strand within Christchurch Anglicanism, a tight-knit and confident group of protégés who were self-consciously 'evangelical' – and 'proud of it'.[132] It was a group that owed its identity jointly (and inseparably) to Orange, Crusaders and the Evangelical Union. For many in that group, it was Orange who most profoundly and indelibly shaped them; one stated that Orange was '*the* influence' of his life.[133] More than one asserted that Orange taught them 'two things': to pray and to preach.[134] Another said Orange's greatest gift was the 'firm conviction that God speaks in his Word'.[135]

Orange's ability to inspire others to enter the ordained ministry was unparalleled in any other New Zealand churchman.[136] It worried many: Principal Parr of College House complained to the bishop in 1934 that four of the six new ordinands were theological conservatives put up by Orange.[137] The following year the Clerical Society called a special meeting to discuss the threat of the diocese being swamped by 'Orangemen'.[138] Some of Orange's BC members later became his curates: Harry Thomson (1936–38), Roger Thompson (1937–41), Basil Williams (1940–42) and David Aiken (1943–47). These men extended the ministry of Orange. Through their ministries many others (such as Maurice Betteridge and Graham Lamont) were converted, especially in the context of Crusaders, and then nurtured by Orange's BC.[139] Aiken, for instance, led the Crusader Union at Christchurch Boys High School, and about half of that group also travelled out to Sumner for Orange's BC.

As the Orange Pips moved into parish ministries of their own, they emulated Orange's ministry. They embraced his evangelical identity. They shared his emphasis on conversion and spiritual growth. They copied his strategies of BC and mentoring young people. Above all they imitated his expository preaching, seeing that as an essential aspect of being evangelical:

> *To be evangelical was to be an expository preacher. This was very clear. The only sort of preaching was expounding the Scripture. This was what Pekoe did, week after week. We simply worked our way through certain books, whether it be in the sermon or the Bible Study.*[140]

The impact of the new Anglican evangelicalism that had arisen was not limited to Christchurch. From the beginning, it would have a revivifying effect on evangelicalism within the Nelson Diocese, New Zealand's only 'evangelical' diocese. Nelson students would come to Christchurch for study, fall under the spell of Orange and then (joined by some Christchurch 'Pips') take up ministries in the Nelson Diocese. Orange's movement also greatly encouraged a nascent Anglican evangelical work in Wellington, and established outposts in other dioceses such as Auckland and Dunedin.

More broadly, Orange's example of 'spiritual' evangelicalism and of devotional biblical exposition left its mark on people of many denominations. His widest influence was through the EUs and IVF. He spoke regularly at the Canterbury EU, at least once a year in each of the other three university EUs, and frequently at EU house parties and national IVF conferences. In those settings, Orange's preaching was often received with awe, and his model of devotional biblical exposition helped shape the future ministries of Evangelicals in many denominations. Graham Miller, for instance, who later became a noted Convention speaker, was greatly impressed as a young man by Orange;[141] like Orange, he spoke quietly, with polished language, rich imagery and great spiritual intensity. Orange's public support for the EUs and IVF made an important contribution to that movement's growth. When overseas, Orange spent time in discussion with IVF leaders such as Douglas Johnson (UK) and Stacey Woods (North America), and helped build the New Zealand IVF's international links.[124]

Evangelical Anglicanism in Nelson

From the mid 1930s, the story of Orange and his Pips began to intersect with the story of the Nelson Diocese, the only New Zealand diocese with a predominantly Low Church style and a moderate evangelical tradition, supported in varying degrees by its previous bishops.[143] Bishop W.C. Sadlier (1912–34), an Irish-born Australian, had recruited many Low Church clergy from England and evangelical clergy from Sydney. In the 1930s two of the latter, O.J. Kimberley and Donald Haultain, were vicars of the diocese's largest two parishes – both essentially evangelical – in Nelson and Blenheim.[144] Bishop W.G. Hilliard, arriving from Sydney in 1934, was a 'staunch Evangelical';[145] he told one of his clergy: 'I am a strong Evangelical, with an emphasis on the strong.'[146] Learned and oratorical, he was a brilliant preacher.[147] Archbishop Mowll preached at Hilliard's consecration, calling for closer ties with Sydney.[148] Hilliard continued to recruit clergy from New South Wales in Australia, most of them Moore-trained and definite evangelicals.[149] They included Paul Kirkham (1935), a vigorous supporter of the evangelical Sydney connection, and Eric Champion (1937). At least one Sydney recruit, however, was not evangelical but more high church, and provoked a furore among other clergy when he introduced candles into the church in Greymouth.[150]

When Hilliard returned to Sydney in 1940, he was replaced by his friend P.W. Stephenson (1940–54), another evangelical Sydney Anglican.[151] Stephenson, regarded by his clergy as as both saintly and scholarly, had previously been a professor of theology in Canada, a CMS missionary in Peshawar and the head of CMS in Australia.[152] He publicly declared to the diocesan synod that he was 'evangelical', giving the three essential emphases of evangelical faith as evangelism, conversion and the Scriptures.[153] Stephenson quickly became the principal leader of the New Zealand CMS[154] and a prominent supporter of the EUs. In churchmanship, Stephenson was emphatically Low Church. In General Synod, he strongly resisted a 1943 proposal to constitute St John's College (which he considered Anglo-Catholic) as a national college for ministry training. He told Synod that 'any province within our Communion that leaves out the need for training men of evangelical conviction in an atmosphere that is in keeping with that conviction – or is at least not opposed to it or scornful of it – is doing a disservice towards the Church as a whole'.[155]

In the wartime conditions of his first few years, Stephenson had been unable to bring in many new ministers. But he did ordain a second minister who had been in Orange's circle, Bernard Machell (1944). The first Orange Pip to be ordained in Nelson had been Bob Nicholson (1938). Meanwhile older evangelical Australian ministers continued to work in key parishes. Probably the most influential of all these was Archdeacon Kimberley at All Saints' in Nelson (1939–49). Kimberley was Low Church and his manner was stern. His theology was conservative with a strong emphasis on Scripture. His parish had a large and active Bible Class, the largest in the Nelson area, and was the seedbed for a number of future ministers.[156]

Notwithstanding its self-consciously evangelical bishops and numerous evangelically minded clergy and laity, the Nelson Diocese in the 1930s and 40s was neither emphatically nor uniformly evangelical. It was more a matter of broad ethos, usually tacit rather than explicit. In a context that was more or less theologically homogeneous, it was felt there was little need to define or declare one's theological position, or to articulate it in relation to other theologies. The diocese, stretched thinly over a vast area of mountains and isolated valleys, and with no university within its bounds, was something of an ecclesiastical backwater. For all that most Nelson Anglicans knew, they were 'just normal Anglican'.[157] The people of Nelson grew up and attended church in an atmosphere of unquestioning faith, in which scripture was 'used and respected' and accepted as simply 'part of the works', and in which the popular diocesan BC camps were always strongly evangelistic.[158] Anglicans growing up in Nelson parishes, including those who were more obviously evangelical in practice, rarely or never heard the term 'evangelical' itself: 'that sort of language wasn't used in [Nelson] – that was all there was in Nelson, except for the Cathedral … in fact I did not know [what an] Evangelical [was] until I came down to Christchurch'.[159] The only descriptor likely to be used was 'Low Church';[160] and Nelson's evangelicalism, in the prewar and wartime period, was rarely a stance that was examined or overt. What would change that, and would gradually lead to a more self-aware evangelicalism in the Diocese of Nelson, was the growing evangelical Anglican movement in Christchurch (where most Nelson ordinands trained), and the critical role of the Evangelical Union in sharpening theological awareness.

By the 1940s it was becoming apparent that, inspired by William Orange's unique mix of spiritual devotion, evocative Bible teaching and gentle conversionism, a new evangelical Anglican stream was being established in New Zealand – in Christchurch, Nelson and beyond.

CHAPTER FOUR

The IVF and a New Evangelical Generation

The Inter-Varsity Fellowship (NZ)

Since they began, the four Evangelical Unions in New Zealand had been a little unsure of how to relate either to each other or to the wider IVF movement.[1] It became clear that they needed to build a national IVF movement, with similar structures to the IVF in Britain, Australia and Canada. So in 1936 the New Zealand IVF was created, on the initiative of the Auckland EU and the Auckland-based Crusader Council.[2] Stacey Woods, an Australian who was leading IVF in Canada, had visited New Zealand the year before and was a catalyst,[3] along with Laird. At Easter 1936 thirty-nine representatives met at Roseneath School in Wellington. The speakers included Laird, Funnell, Pettit and Edwin Orr.[4] In Depression conditions, travel to such an event was not easy, and the five Dunedin delegates competed in national university athletic competitions being held on part of the same weekend, in an effort to get their fares paid to Wellington: Gordon Smith won the three-mile event and Graham Miller came second in the mile.[5] The four EU presidents were all present: Archie Morton (Auckland),[6] Rob Miller (Victoria, a law student, and another son of Thomas Miller), Basil Williams (Canterbury)[7] and Graham Miller (Otago).[8] Jointly, they moved that the doctrinal basis of the new Inter-Varsity Fellowship of Evangelical Unions (New Zealand) (IVF(NZ)) be that of the British IVF.

Understandably, the New Zealand SCM was very disappointed. It had still hoped the 'disastrous' breach might heal, especially as SCM was 'gradually strengthening its own testimony to the central things in Christian faith'.[9] It also admitted there was 'some justice' in the complaints of those who had broken away. But IVF's insistence on biblical infallibility as an essential doctrine was unacceptable to SCM.

The pioneer IVF(NZ) saw itself as an extension of the British IVF movement, on which it consciously modelled itself.[10] Copying British IVF's structures, IVF(NZ) established its various subsections: the Graduates' Fellowship, the Teachers' Prayer Fellowship, the Inter-Varsity Missionary Fellowship and the Theological Students' Prayer Union. The New Zealand student leaders were regular readers of British IVF magazines, as well as the CICCU magazine.[11] British IVF publications (*Effective Witness, Decently and In Order, Problems of Faith and Conduct* and *Evangelical Belief*) laid out the template on which EUs should be organised, and the New Zealand IVF handbook frequently referred to them[12] – in particular the IVF book *Principles of Co-operation*, which firmly discouraged EUs from working with any other movement (i.e. SCM) that did not share a similar doctrinal basis to that of the IVF.[13]

Evangelical Belief (1935) was another core document for IVF(NZ). Subtitled *The Official Interpretation of the Doctrinal Basis of the IVF*, it clarified and explained IVF's teachings.[14] IVF's doctrinal basis, it argued, was consistent with 'the general belief of Christendom', with the two principal doctrinal affirmations of Britain (the Thirty-Nine Articles and the Westminster Confession), and with 'universal Evangelical belief'.[15] The booklet's careful explanations seem to be intended to protect the EUs from both hyperconservative understandings inside the movement and misunderstandings beyond. *Evangelical Belief* insisted that the scriptures are 'the Word of God', through the unique inspiration and revelation of God. It noted that not all parts of scripture are equally important, and that inspiration was not 'mechanical'. Inspiration involved 'the whole personality' of the writers, whose words were nevertheless subject to 'Divine supervision'.[16] *Evangelical Belief* avoided the word 'inerrancy', often favoured in the United States. Biblical 'infallibility' meant that the scriptures, rightly understood, 'will never lead astray', and are 'a true and complete guide'.[17] In relation to the study of the Bible, 'true scholarship' (as opposed to faithless scholarship) had always been legitimate.[18] *Evangelical Belief* likewise insisted on the divinity of Christ, substitutionary atonement and Christ's bodily resurrection. It emphasised the need for regeneration and the work of the Holy Spirit. It asserted both the certainty of the return of Christ, and uncertainty over the details of that event.[19] It ended with reassurances that the IVF was fully committed to 'the Evangelical Protestant position as represented by the chief English and Scottish Reformers', and that it was neither a church nor a sect.[20] Bibliographies followed.[21] Curiously, despite the title, *Evangelical Belief* never commented on the word 'evangelical': the implication of the whole book was simply that the beliefs it expounded were 'evangelical'. *Evangelical Belief* was extremely important in New Zealand IVF for at least a generation. Its main contribution was to define the doctrinal distinctives of the IVF, against the implied backdrop of the SCM.

T.C. Hammond's book *In Understanding Be Men* (1936) was familiar to almost everyone in EU/IVF in New Zealand. An IVF handbook of biblical doctrine, it was written as a resource for weekly EU study groups. As with *Evangelical Belief* and the IVF Doctrinal Basis, *In Understanding Be Men* began with what were essential issues for evangelicals: authority, revelation and scripture. It implied that the foundation of an 'Evangelical' position was to see scripture as the primary authority – in contrast to the 'Catholic' and 'Modernist' positions, which respectively saw the Church and 'Human Reason' as the ultimate authority.[22]

Members of IVF(NZ) and the EUs were likewise familiar with the 1933 IVF booklet *The Quiet Time* (reinforcing the devotional disciplines expected of all serious evangelicals)[23] and the 1934 IVF Bible Study manual *Search the Scriptures*.[24] Another early IVF publication was H.E. Guillebaud's *Why the Cross?* – a defence of substitutionary atonement.[25] EU members also read other British writers with IVF links, such as Daniel Lamont and Rendle Short.[26] The latter wrote *The Bible and Modern Research*, on reconciling new scientific discoveries with biblical teaching.[27] Such IVF and IVF-associated publishing was beginning to redress the scarcity of contemporary evangelical writings at an adequate intellectual level. Howard Guinness's *Sacrifice* (1936) was a strong call to costly service to Christ in such personal areas as money, love and marriage, prayer and vocation. Inside the front cover there was a pledge for readers to sign and date.[28] The book was very influential.[29] It reflected the great spiritual and moral earnestness of the early IVF, and helped define the spirituality of a generation of young evangelicals. It was an age when calls to serious self-discipline may have been more readily received than in the more individualistic post-1960s era.

The New Zealand IVF also adopted as its own the story of the British IVF, especially CICCU's 1910 disentanglement from SCM. That story was told in various published accounts.[30] Although they were restrained in tone, such IVF writings painted SCM in negative terms and laid down an all-important challenge for evangelical students: either they insist on a separate and biblically faithful witness, or they too would lose the Gospel through succumbing to doctrinal inclusiveness. That understanding, and the recounting of the CICCU and British IVF story, were hugely important in shaping the identity of New Zealand student evangelicals.

The same story was at the heart of IVF(NZ)'s own work of history and self-justification, published in 1941.[31] Much more stridently, Basil Atkinson's idiosyncratic *Valiant in Fight* surveyed the whole of church history, with the experiences of the IVF a constant implied backdrop.[32] Atkinson pressed the theme that genuine Christian faithfulness had always involved a heroic struggle for biblical truth and the Gospel: the IVF, a godly remnant standing firm against a floodtide of apostasy, was in the glorious tradition of the martyrs and the Reformers, so misunderstanding, persecution and suffering were inevitable. Atkinson epitomised the isolationist mindset of some 1930s theological conservatives, and was heeded by at least some in the New Zealand IVF.[33]

In all of this – the story, the identity, the theology, the nuances, the subculture – the outlook of the New Zealand IVF was that of classic British evangelicalism, as mediated through the British IVF. The IVF members, asserted the first New Zealand general secretary, were 'residuary legatees' of the Reformation, the Puritans, Wesleyans, CICCU and the early British SCM.[34] In the history that IVF(NZ) claimed for itself, there was trace of American 'fundamentalism'.

IVF and Evangelical Unity

The fledgling New Zealand IVF became a crucial factor in developing a more confident and cohesive evangelicalism, a movement that was both nationwide and transdenominational. A major element in that was the annual IVF conference.[35] For individuals, such conferences were often life-shaping. Francis Foulkes, for instance, considered his first IVF conference (in 1942) the pivotal spiritual event of his early years. He was 'very greatly moved' by Orange's exposition of core Christian doctrine, and inspired by Laird to begin his own lifelong study of the scriptures.[36]

The IVF conferences had a much wider effect than just on individuals, however: they played a critical role in bringing together young evangelicals (and thus future evangelical leaders) from across the whole country and from across the denominations. A photo from the second IVF conference (Easter 1937, Sumner) showed Anglicans, Brethren, Presbyterians and Baptists. The following conference also included some Methodists and members of the Church of Christ (Life and Advent). The IVF conferences brought together the Dunedin (largely Presbyterian) evangelical movement, centred on Thomas Miller, with the Christchurch (Anglican–Brethren) evangelical movement, centred on Orange. They forged links between the South Island evangelical networks of Otago and Canterbury (respectively Presbyterian and Anglican–Brethren), and the more Baptistic–Brethren evangelical community of Auckland. They also encouraged the weaker evangelical movement in Wellington. The IVF and its conferences intensified – and placed on a national level – the interdenominational and intradenominational evangelical mixing that had already typified the Crusaders, CSSM missions and local EUs. Such intermingling led to many interdenominational marriages, too: at the 1940 conference, one Dunedin Presbyterian first noticed his future wife (a Christchurch Anglican) as she peeled potatoes and discussed Calvin.[37]

Importantly, the IVF conferences brought together evangelicals of the same denomination but from different parts of the country, thus strengthening the foundations of future denominational evangelical movements. Northern evangelical Presbyterians mixed with their southern counterparts: a photo taken at the 1940 IVF Conference, for instance, shows three Miller brothers (South Island) and three Kirkby brothers (North Island). Five of the six later became Presbyterian ministers and leaders in the Westminster Fellowship. Christchurch evangelical Anglicans mixed with those in Nelson, Wellington and Auckland. At the 1941 Conference a young evangelical Anglican from Auckland was astonished and heartened by the impressive line-up of Anglican clergy from Sydney and Christchurch, many of them speakers.[38] A photo of that conference includes the Revs Marcus Loane, William Orange, Basil Williams, Walter Wisdom[39] and Harry Thomson – and at least six students who would later become Anglican ministers.

IVF staff also developed strong transdenominational friendships and helped foster a growing evangelical unity. The first IVF travelling secretary, Graham Miller, was appointed in 1938 and was commended to IVF supporters for his 'outstanding gifts', 'sane well-balanced judgement, and true spirituality'.[40] Through his role in the IVF the ardent young Miller (a Presbyterian, and later a leader of the Westminster Fellowship) formed friendships with Anglicans such as Maurice Goodall and Roger Thompson (who later became leaders in the Anglican Evangelical Fellowship).[41] Miller frequently stayed with Brethren stalwarts such as Howell Fountain (Christchurch) and William Pettit (Auckland). Pettit would take Miller out on his medical rounds and talk to him between visits, sometimes lapsing into a Brethren proselytism that contravened the scrupulously interdenominational ethos of IVF. Pettit would ask Miller, 'Why don't you obey the Scriptures in your churchmanship?' (i.e. 'Why don't you join the Brethren?'), and plied him with literature.[42] In Auckland, Miller stayed with the secretary of the Baptist Tabernacle, and with a Church of Christ Life and Advent family.[43] In Wellington, he stayed with Cliff Cocker, the IVF general secretary.[44] Cocker was an evangelical Methodist, and Miller regarded him as someone who 'carried in his soul the deepest strains of evangelical godliness'. Other IVF staff in the 1930s and 40s, such as travelling secretary Basil Williams (1941), similarly moved among evangelicals of many denominations.

Through the IVF conferences, local EU missions and national tours by IVF-sponsored speakers, the evangelical movement was exposed to a number of leading evangelical figures. Orange was one of those – a frequent speaker in all the EUs (visiting all of them at least annually), and also at IVF conferences.[45] It was the EUs and IVFs that gave Orange a national profile among New Zealand evangelicals. Emerging leaders such as Blaiklock likewise gained a national following. IVF-sponsored international visitors were important, too, such as the Irish theologian T.C. Hammond, who was learned, incisive and blunt. His several visits as conference speaker and EU missioner reinforced the use of *In Understanding Be Men*, and helped refute any accusation that the IVF was unscholarly.

IVF–SCM Relationship

The relationship of IVF and SCM was tense. Early in 1938, four representatives of OUEU met with the local SCM at the request of the latter, who wished to explore 'cooperation'.[46] This was a notable meeting, apparently the first since the 1930 breach, and memories of old hurts were still raw. The EU prepared by spending thirty minutes in prayer. Graham Miller spoke on behalf of the current OUEU chairman. He was determined to review the events of 1930, and came prepared with documentary evidence of SCM's exclusion of EU and its subsequent attitude to EU. With the relentlessness of a zealous young lawyer, Miller invited the SCM to read out some of their previous decisions and comments about EU. He chided the SCM for its 'uncharitableness', citing anti-EU material in the SCM magazine. He pointed out that if in fact some SCM members believed the same things as did the EU, the only 'logical' course was for them to join the EU. Combat over, the EU asked that the meeting close with ten minutes' prayer together.

Graham Miller had also met with SCM General Secretary Jim Linton for a frank discussion of their different perspectives.[47] He reported to the IVF that the SCM tacitly conceded responsibility for the 1930 schism, and had now adopted a Barthian theology and become decidedly more 'conservative'. Nevertheless, the 'strict adherence' of the IVF to scripture and the lack of a fixed SCM doctrinal basis were insoluble points of difference, and there was no way the IVF was going to abandon its raison d'être and become reabsorbed into a movement without firm doctrinal safeguards: recurring theological drift was 'inevitable in a movement possessing no precise Doctrinal statement'.

If the SCM had thought that meeting with IVF would resolve the schism, it was being overly hopeful. The same issues and tensions in the relationship of the two movements were evident for many more decades to come. The SCM was still the stronger movement numerically (and would be so until the later 1950s). It was widely respected and continued to stimulate and inspire students, many of whom were often convinced that the SCM was at the cutting edge of church, society and global thinking. But the IVF was there to stay. Through the 1940s its university groups showed a pattern of 'steady though unspectacular growth'.[48] More importantly, the IVF was now producing a steady stream of young evangelical leaders.

IVF Evangelicals Training for Ministry, 1930s–40s

Within a few years of the Evangelical Unions being formed, evangelicals who had been shaped by EU were beginning to train for ministry at the Presbyterian Theological Hall (which was based at Knox College in Dunedin North, and thus often informally referred to as 'Knox'), and at College House (the ministry training centre for the Anglican Diocese of Christchurch, which was similarly based in a university hall of residence). This development was in line with IVF's strategy of bringing into ministry those who would work for 'spiritual life' in the churches and begin 'reviving the school of Evangelical Theology'.[49] It was a phenomenon that would have a considerable effect on the postwar Presbyterian and Anglican churches.

Presbyterian evangelicals at the Theological Hall

In Dunedin, the first of the new generation of EU-influenced Presbyterian ministry trainees was Mervyn Milmine, who had been converted at a meeting addressed by Bissett. Milmine completed an MA at Otago and then began at the Theologicall Hall in 1933. The standard course lasted three years, and while at the Hall Milmine was closely involved in EU. He had earlier been part of Cree Brown's evangelical student group and was one of the founders of OUEU. Over the next few years, there was a steady influx of evangelicals beginning at the Theological Hall, most of them graduates who had been through EU: these included Morrison Yule and Graham Miller (from 1939), Les Gosling (1940) and Rymall Roxburgh (1941).[50]

EU-type evangelicals were still a minority at the Theological Hall. Most of the Hall students were theologically middle-of-the road, shaped by the Bible Class movement and still loyal to the SCM. The EU-associated evangelicals recognised many in that middle group as evangelical 'at heart'.[51] Another minority – most of whom were definitely linked with the SCM – were more overtly liberal. The EU members met frequently for prayer, sometimes under the umbrella of the IVF's Theological Students' Prayer Union. They were keenly aware of their minority status in what was an SCM stronghold, and that they were regarded as creating a division.[52] When they emerged from praying together, they saw the 'sour' looks of their peers, and were aware of the intense pressure on other students not to join them.[53] In general they felt stronger disdain from fellow students than they did from the teaching staff.[54]

In the conservative wider Christian community, the reputation of 'Knox' (the Theolological Hall) was not high. When one Presbyterian was accepted for theological training, his family dissuaded him: 'No, you can't go down there. Professor Dickie is not a believer.' T.C. Hammond also advised him that the Hall was 'a bed of modernism'.[55] In reality the Theological Hall was not, in this period, extremely liberal, but rather 'liberal evangelical'. All the teaching staff had a critical view of scripture, but remained broadly orthodox. Principal Dickie, considered suspect by evangelicals in his theology of the cross, nevertheless believed not only in the divinity and resurrection of Jesus but also in the Virgin Birth.[56] Evangelicals noted, with surprise and much satisfaction, Dickie's more conservative-sounding utterances such as on the occasions when he provocatively expressed preference for fundamentalism over modernism, or for the EU over the SCM. When asked in class if he was a modernist, Dickie answered, 'If I had to choose between being a thorough-going modernist and a fundamentalist, I'd sooner be a fundamentalist. They have convictions.'[57] Dickie was deeply upset by a pacifist chapel sermon in 1941 by SCM member Lloyd Geering; Dickie told his class:

> *I don't suppose the EU would care to have me as its President, but I would far rather be the President of the EU than be President of the SCM of which Mr Geering is a member, for the EU has got a Gospel – even if it's got more than a gospel – and its attitude to the Old Testament in particular makes it more robust in its attitude to war, and the SCM has no Gospel.*[58]

But evangelicals remained unhappy with Dickie's basis of religious authority: his magnum opus dismissed the idea of an 'inerrant book', and elevated 'experience' over Scripture.[59] New Testament Professor John Allan, who was sometimes suspected of an anti-supernaturalist scepticism about scriptural miracles, was nevertheless appreciated by evangelicals for his emphasis on the Reformation doctrine of justification by faith.[60] Professor S.F. Hunter, although very 'critical' in his approach to the Old Testament, appeared still to believe in evangelism and conversion.[61] As for other students, evangelicals were heartened in 1943 when the entire class of thirteen students wrote a complaint after lecturer Helmut Rex appeared to deny the Virgin Birth.[62]

Students associated with EU arrived at the Theological Hall with firm convictions. They had read the IVF books, and often also works by writers such as Ryle, Denney and Machen.[63] They felt they knew what was right in their own system, and what was wrong in a liberal one. They knew what, for them, would be the main points of tension: a critical approach to the Bible, a downplaying of its divine inspiration, authority and reliability, and a liberal theology that questioned miracles and denied substitutionary atonement. They came expecting a 'spiritual battle'.[64] Most EU evangelicals arrived eager to learn new knowledge and skills, but unwilling to have their perspective substantially altered. Some were more defensive than others. A small minority of evangelicals – usually those without a university or EU background – came to Knox expecting to resist most things. Most of them sometimes suffered in silence, though some EU graduates would occasionally challenge the staff, politely cornering a teacher with an awkward question. Graham Miller once asked Professor Hunter, who was teaching on the Old Testament prophets: 'I notice you are using the word "revelation" in the sense of human insight and discernment. Would that be the historic position of the church?' Hunter retorted: 'I would have expected that from the son of your father.'[65]

As Thomas Miller's son, Graham Miller was already a marked man. Trained as a lawyer, he had a sharp mind, an eye for detail and a retentive memory. He was articulate and gracious in manner. He had come first in the Theological Hall's entrance exam, and was being coached in Hebrew and Greek by classics lecturer H.R. Minn. He was a studious reader, and for almost a decade he had been poring over serious works, painstakingly indexing them and taking detailed notes.[66] He had been influenced by Dante, Milton and Cowper,[67] and had devoured theologians such as Edwards, Hodge, Warfield and Machen. He read all the IVF writers.[68] He was reading numerous periodicals, including the *Evangelical Quarterly*.[69] In his first year in Knox, Miller became absorbed by the works of Loraine Boettner, and *The Reformed Doctrine of Predestination* became an integrating book for him: 'If anything was needed to suddenly bring my bits of conservative thinking into a beautiful mosaic, that was the book.'[70] That led on to the works of Kuyper and Shedd, Calvin, Augustine and the Puritans.[71] Unlike many other evangelicals, Miller was not drawn to Christian apologetics.[72] In theology, he was definitely conservative; but nobody could accuse Miller of being ignorant or anti-intellectual, and Dickie considered him the ablest student in his year.[73] Like Geering, who was one year behind Miller at the Hall, Miller went on to make his mark on the postwar New Zealand church.[74] In 1941 he and his wife Flora departed for the New Hebrides (now Vanuatu) for a missionary career characterised by a strong biblicism and by an advanced emphasis on indigenous rather than missionary control of the church.[75]

Rymall Roxburgh was likewise something of a heavyweight. He arrived at the Theological Hall with three degrees already behind him. He was thoughtful, well read and had a prodigious memory. Conscious that 'conservatives' were sometimes assumed to be intellectually weak, Miller and Roxburgh and most EU-associated students worked hard at being good students, and often excelled.[76] As university graduates, several of them studied for the Melbourne Bachelor of Divinity (BD) degree, whereas most Hall students studied at Diploma level only. None, however, were granted scholarships to join other Hall graduates pursuing higher degrees in Europe or Britain. If such an opportunity had been offered, they would probably have turned it down for missionary or parish work: the pursuit of advanced scholarship by New Zealand evangelicals was at least one generation further into the future.

Theological students sometimes shifted in their theological position. Those who had come from a Presbyterian Bible Class background but had not been through university or EU sometimes retained a broad evangelical piety but accommodated their views on scripture to a more liberal approach.[77] Students who had been through EU, however, were less likely to undergo any major theological change. The crucial difference was that EU members had already received their basic theological formation and had already wrestled with issues related to evangelical/liberal distinctives. If they had read and absorbed books like *In Understanding Be Men* and *Evangelical Belief*, they knew where they stood; throughout their years at the Hall, IVF books like those were their constant guides.[78]

Because of their enthusiasm for a closer understanding of the text of scripture, EU-associated theological students often relished learning Hebrew and Greek.[79] They appreciated that historical criticism of scripture made them more aware of conservative 'pitfalls';[80] but they contested some of its presuppositions and conclusions.[81] While they did not necessarily hold to a full doctrine of 'inerrancy' – they all preferred the EU-favoured term 'infallibility'[82] – it was still important to them to defend the essential veracity of scripture, and to find academically convincing responses to sceptical criticism.[83] If they had studied the IVF's explanation of biblical inspiration, they allowed for human factors in biblical authorship.[84] EU-shaped Hall students usually distanced themselves from 'obscurantism' and 'literalism', and became more nuanced in their thinking;[85] but almost all of them retained their evangelical convictions, and became stronger in them.[86] 'The one great consequence of my time in the Theological Hall', asserted one, 'was it confirmed me in the evangelical faith' – primarily because he felt he saw 'the shallowness of the alternatives'.[87]

Evangelical Anglicans and theological training

For Anglicans in the prewar period, ministry training was considerably less academically exacting than the Presbyterian training, in part because it was dispersed among the various dioceses. Even the largest centres of training, St John's in Auckland and College House in Christchurch, lacked much scholarly weight. In College House, the only full-time theological teacher was the principal, Stephen Parr, who taught most subjects and was liberally inclined in theology.[88]

Through the 1930s and 40s, Orange Pips were beginning to enter theological training, mainly at College House. The first of these was Richard (Dick) Carson. With an MA in Classics, Carson was gifted in Hebrew and Greek, and an independent thinker.[89] In 1936 and 1937, Bob Nicholson, Basil Williams and Roger Thompson completed their courses at College House. They were followed by Max Wiggins, David Aiken and Harvey Teulon. Harry Thomson, meanwhile, trained for ministry at Selwyn College in Dunedin.

Unlike most of the Orange Pips, Roger Thompson had not done a prior university degree. He simply 'endured' his theological training.[90] He felt that Parr had 'no influence whatsoever' on his own theology: 'I was so … [influenced] by Canon Orange's biblical truths … that I … rejected these liberals.'[91] Thompson felt that the most common theological change taking place in his time at College House was not evangelicals being subdued by liberalism, but Low Church ordinands being drawn in by the new Christchurch evangelicalism, which was 'vital' and 'exciting'.[92] Max Wiggins, likewise, appeared to keep his theological studies at arm's length:

> It was a real element that I might get knocked back if I expressed evangelical opinions … Stephen Parr … brought textbooks in, and said 'you ought to take note of this, it's important', and it was not much more than annotating textbooks. It was very poor. I topped Old Testament stuff quite easily, because I got a lot of tags to the German critics and put it all in – they thought I knew it all. I didn't really know their stuff, I knew their names … I was getting indications that some of the people examining on the Prayer Book were Anglo-Catholics, so I was very careful how I answered from that point of view.[93]

Wiggins related well to Parr personally, but took almost nothing from him. Wiggins' real teacher was still the vicar of Sumner: 'sitting under Willie Orange, he made Scripture come alive, and you couldn't rubbish it [Scripture] like that, and he [Orange] didn't really do much of the controversial bit, he just made it live'.[94]

The first wave of IVF-associated evangelicals emerging in the 1930s and early 40s from the Presbyterian Theological Hall and from College House was not large,[95] but it was an important development, for all that. It considerably swelled the number of ministers who clearly identified themselves as 'evangelical'.[96] It heralded the coming postwar resurgence, in New Zealand's largest two Protestant denominations, of a new, self-assured evangelicalism. As the war came to an end, many hundreds of other ex-EU members would also be spread across New Zealand, in various professions, and involved in churches and youth work.[97]

Slowly, and just perceptibly, the tide was beginning to creep back in.

PART TWO

A RISING TIDE
1945-65

CHAPTER FIVE

Anglican Evangelicals 1945–55

Postwar Moods

The spiritual mood in New Zealand in the decade or so after the Second World War was similar to that in many other countries: the horrors of war had tempered liberal optimism about human nature, and made some people more receptive to the idea that hope for humanity ultimately depended on God. J.M. Bates, for instance, wrote to the *Outlook* that 'the events of our time have given such a blow to any facile belief in the power of man to save himself'.[1] The advent of atomic weapons and Cold War fears of communism deepened people's sense of human vulnerability and insecurity.[2] At the same time, there was a widespread desire to work for reconstruction and a more secure future. Returning servicemen were often serious about working for a better world. In such an environment of anxiety and activism, and in the height of the postwar 'baby boom', there was a new opportunity for Christianity generally, and in the period from 1945 to 1960 many churches experienced renewed growth and vitality. For many, evangelicalism's confident biblical faith particularly addressed the anxieties of the era. For those who wanted to build a better future, evangelicalism offered strong emphases on outreach, church expansion, children's work and youth work.

The rebuilding of church and faith in the 1950s was against the background of other major changes in New Zealand society: the burgeoning of many new suburbs, the expansion of the welfare state, increased rates of car ownership, new household technologies (including washing machines, electric stoves and refrigerators), full employment, growing affluence (based on unlimited access to the British market for New Zealand meat, wool and dairy products), and the development of secondary education.[3] In the early postwar decades there was a pervasive 'desire for normalcy' focused on family, job, home and section.[4]

That may have reflected a reaction to the deprivations of the Depression, the traumas of war and the anxieties of the Cold War. Through to the late 1960s, New Zealand society was conservative in outlook, retaining a respect for Christianity, church and traditional morality, and emphasising home and family. As in Britain, society retained a pervasive and conventional Christian 'discourse' in its beliefs and values, even if this was often neglected or flouted.[5] The erosive effects of television, the sexual revolution, youth cultural change and a deepening secularism were still at least a decade and a half into the future. New Zealand's Protestant evangelicalism, made stronger and more confident by the EUs and Crusaders and with a new generation of young leaders emerging, was well placed to experience considerable expansion. As the 1950s proceeded, evangelicals were also inspired by reports of a strengthening mainstream evangelical Christianity in Britain and America.

When Orange left the Sumner parish late in 1945, Christchurch evangelical Anglicanism moved with him. His successor at Sumner, Walter Wisdom, a moderate evangelical, was unable to retain Orange's personal following. Orange's relocated Sunday afternoon Bible Class at Tyndale House, a retreat centre in the Cashmere Hills, attracted up to a hundred men and women.[6] Orange retained a very strong sway over the EU and his orbit of influence continued to widen.

Orange's departure from Sumner created the need for a new evangelical parish base. For a few years, the favoured parish for young Anglican evangelicals became St James', Lower Riccarton. The minister at Lower Riccarton was Carl Tanner, a moderate evangelical who warmly welcomed students.[7] Another leading figure at St James' was Andy Pinwill, the leader of the Christchurch Boys High Crusader Union and a contagious enthusiast, who recruited other young evangelicals.[8] Several evangelical ordinands were attending St James', as well as another six who later became ordinands, and numerous other evangelical youth.[9] Many of these were living at College House, which was both a university hall of residence and a theological college, and many continued to sit under the teaching of Orange in his Bible Class at Tyndale House.[10]

Tanner found himself caught between pressures from opposite sides: from the zealous evangelical youth and from more conventional Anglican parishioners.[11] Some of the former felt the latter were not Christian enough. In 1948 there was controversy over a proposed fundraising revue and a scheme to decorate the church ceiling with medieval symbols. Some judged these plans 'worldly' and believed Tanner should resist them.[12] Against that background there was a sudden and puzzling case of church discipline; Tanner lost the trust of many of the young evangelicals and there was a major exodus.[13] Thereafter – if not before – Tanner was suspected by some Orange Pips of being a 'liberal evangelical'.[14]

Roger Thompson at St Martin's Spreydon, 1946-61

Following the troubles at St James', the new regional evangelical hotspot became St Martin's, Spreydon. The vicar was Roger Thompson – the first of the Orange Pips to be appointed as a vicar within Christchurch. From 1946, Thompson had presided over a struggling new parish in a suburb that was less than prosperous (and with much new housing in the Hoon Hay district). St Martin's had no previous evangelical tradition, but had been placidly 'middle of the road'.[15] Thompson was passionately evangelical and an activist. His directness and his uncompromising insistence on people having to be 'saved' had provoked culture shock among some parishioners.[16] His ban on young people's dances put him offside with some parents, and his prohibition on fundraising alienated those who had previously worked hard on fairs and sales ('We liked people to give to God, not ... to give a cabbage').[17] Thompson was also seriously short of Sunday School teachers and BC leaders.[18] Close to resigning, he had gone to see Orange, who told him 'the darkest hours are just before the dawn'.[19] Thompson was thus greatly encouraged one Sunday in 1948, when a group of about eight evangelical young people turned up at Spreydon, followed soon after by another dozen.[20] Joining with a few local youth, they became core members of a new Sunday afternoon BC, and took up roles such as teaching Sunday School.[21]

Thompson modelled his ministry on that of his mentor, Orange, with biblical exposition as its core. Like many evangelical preachers of his time, Thompson aimed to appeal to reason rather than emotion: his hearers were encouraged to have a 'logical and reasoned faith', based on careful study of the Bible.[22] His expositions covered a wide range of subjects. To thwart those he called 'sermon-dodgers', Thompson also preached at the 8 am Holy Communion service.[23] In morning services he followed the lectionary and in the evenings he preached series on biblical books or themes.[24] In his preaching style, he was more 'fiery' than Orange.[25] To some who heard him, his dark beady eyes seemed to bore straight into their souls – but in reality Thompson was shortsighted, and could not see clearly past the front two pews.[26]

Another primary strategy for Thompson was his Sunday afternoon BC, which comprised some 50-60 minutes of uninterrupted Bible teaching, with practical application.[27] Thompson's approach was less typological than Orange's.[28] As at Sumner, the BC was followed by tea, a prayer meeting and evening service. In contrast to Sumner, though, the BC included young women: males sat on one side of the church and females on the other.[29] In church and in BC, Thompson emulated Orange's approach of verse-by-verse exposition, and it made a deep impression on many.[30] Someone who spent two years in the BC recalled:

> For me it was the first time I had ever heard anyone literally open up the Word of God ... The time would fly by – sometimes an hour over one or two verses of Scripture. He made life make sense as the Word was opened up. Principles of Scripture were shown and the Bible became to us the Living Word. We were encouraged to expect fresh truth each time we studied it. The teaching was authoritative and well researched and no one spoke during the hour.[31]

John Meadowcroft was inspired to emulate Thompson:

> Straight biblical exposition ... That was what appealed to me. He and Pekoe made the Bible come alive to me, this explanation of Scripture with Scripture. I never heard that in Nelson, that I was aware of. That would be the mark of his ministry. Roger was also a good evangelist – and a very good pastor as well. But his love was for the word. He gave me the model I have tried to follow.[32]

Other notable features of Thompson's youth ministry were an annual camp on a farm in North Canterbury, and the hospitality of his home. His vocation to ministry was strongly shared by his wife Reena, and even though the family had six children, the vicarage was an open home.[33] After the evening service a crowd of young people would gather there for singing from the Keswick hymnbook (the favourite of many evangelicals in this period) and supper.[34] Several decades later, tributes written for a BC reunion mentioned these gatherings as often as they mentioned Thompson's biblical teaching.[35]

In the St Martin's BC, and to a lesser extent in the parish at large, considerable numbers of people were converted.[36] The BC eventually grew to number about ninety.[37] Some arrived for social reasons, but then were converted.[38] Thompson would give evangelistic challenges from the pulpit. He would not press hard, or ask people to come forward, but would often finish preaching with words such as, 'You know you have to decide for Christ. I will give you two minutes after the sermon, two minutes just to sit and be quiet, or kneel, [to] think over what you have heard.' He would then encourage respondents to tell him later.[39] He would also challenge people personally: on a walk over the hills from Sumner to Lyttelton with forty young people, Thompson asked a young man if he had ever accepted Christ; he drew a line in the dirt with his shoe and said there comes a time when it is necessary to step over the line and make a commitment.

The youth prayed a prayer of response. He had previously been confirmed in another parish, but it had meant little.[40]

In theological position and identity, Thompson was unabashedly and unshakeably 'evangelical'. He had learnt the term from Orange.[41] He had also associated – although he was not a university student – with the Evangelical Union.[42] He and other Orange converts 'were conservative evangelicals and … proud of it'.[43] Thompson did not call himself 'fundamentalist', but felt positive about that term because of his belief in 'the fundamentals of the faith'.[44] He took a conservative position on a number of issues: he personally believed in a literal six-day creation (while respecting those who understood the days as long periods of time); he ruled out theistic evolution. He claimed not to be an extreme literalist, but in contentious matters he 'would line up with the literalists'; for Thompson, liberal academics who sowed doubts were a greater danger than literalists. Like most evangelicals, he believed the Bible contained no errors; but like most evangelicals in the British IVF tradition, he avoided the word 'inerrancy'.[45]

Thompson carried lightly his status as a vicar, and was very approachable. 'Some like to be … called the Vicar or whatever the title was. He [Thompson] was just "Roger" … he didn't carry any airs.'[46] He was straightforward and decisive. He spoke in a cheerful and compelling manner, peppering his talks with humour: evangelicalism was 'a cheerful affair, and that is the way Roger projected himself'.[47] In private, though, Thompson had tendencies towards melancholy and self-doubt.[48]

Like some other evangelicals, Thompson saw the world – and the church – in terms of battle. From his own experience (both at Spreydon and before that at Woodend) he had concluded that within the church there would always be a struggle between spiritual and more worldly emphases – and out in the world there would always be deep spiritual opposition and moral degeneracy.[49] He often signed off letters beneath the words, 'Yours in the fight'.[50] In his memoirs he described himself as a 'soldier' in the 'Church Militant', fighting against the forces of evil and darkness.[51] Thompson wanted the church to be not 'an institution primarily for elderly women and little children', but 'an army on the march', where there was no place for leadership that was 'milk-and-water' or 'lovey-dovey'.[52] Such language was not uncommon among evangelicals, and echoed some of the blunter tones found in scripture. Thompson's polemical style did not, however, indicate any difficulties in relating to people pastorally.

In teaching youth, Thompson assumed the same sort of moral attitudes as had applied in the prewar generation with regard to activities such as drinking, smoking, dancing and going to the pictures.[53] Thompson was vehemently anti-alcohol, and from the pulpit publicly denounced the Black Horse Inn across the road[54] (this was a period when beer and shandies were drunk by working-class people, but other types of alcohol were not widely available, and middle-class people often did not drink alcohol).[55] Most BC members readily accepted such taboos of the evangelical subculture, at least at the time.[56] As with Orange, Thompson's approach to social and moral issues reflected an attitude of 'separation': the Christian who is 'godly' had a duty to keep separate from 'wordly' people and activities. The lifestyle strictures also reflected a positive preoccupation: young evangelicals were often too excited and busy with spiritual activities to be bothered with what they saw as trivial and distracting entertainments. While some overseas neo-evangelical thinkers were beginning to question the evangelical fixation on relatively trivial lifestyle matters and to call for a renewed humanitarian engagement with much wider social evils,[57] in the 1950s such thinking was not yet part of postwar New Zealand evangelicalism.

Thompson had quickly dispensed with church raffles and sales of produce as a means of fundraising. He replaced the annual fair with an annual 'Day of Prayer and Giving'. Influenced by the principles of Hudson Taylor, Thompson saw the 'faith' approach to giving as demonstrating the practicality of trusting God in all matters.[58] Although Spreydon was a working-class district, the stress on consecration and direct giving produced comparatively healthy church finances. At a time when many other Anglican parishes were using financial canvassers, or working with the fundraising Wells Organisation,[59] Thompson scorned such approaches as 'worldly'. He instead instituted 'Our Move Forward', a programme concentrating on evangelism and spiritual growth.[60]

Like Orange, Thompson never adopted a strictly Low Church approach. He wore a stole, and was not a 'north-ender'.[61] He saw himself as simply 'traditional'.[62] He would not, however, have consciously made any concessions to anything High Church. Like Orange, he also kept his distance from the diocese. His awareness that he was part of a small minority reinforced in him a defensive, almost ghetto-like attitude toward the wider church. Of all the Orange Pips, it was arguably Thompson who was the most obviously suspicious of non-evangelicals.[63] He would have nothing to do with the Anglican BC movement or its camps, which he presumably considered weak in theology and evangelism, and social in emphasis. He would have nothing to do with the Melanesian Mission, which he believed was full of 'Anglo-Catholics'.[64] He was extremely wary of the bishop.[65] One of his colleagues felt that Thompson 'saw the bishop with a devil's tail and horn'.[66] Thompson dutifully attended diocesan synod, but rarely spoke there. Since he considered most of those who attended as either liberal or High Church, he felt it 'futile' for Evangelicals to speak.[67] As for diocesan committees, he avoided them as much as possible.[68] One reason for this was that he was too busy: he was 'preoccupied with soul-winning, and going out to find [people] ... and help them spiritually ... and when you have a thriving church you have lots of things on your plate'.[69] It was the next generation of evangelicals, considerably more numerous, better educated and more confident, who would start to emerge from such self-imposed evangelical isolationism.

As with other denominational evangelicals, Thompson's work was not done in isolation. His young people in particular were very much participants within a wider evangelical network, both evangelical Anglican and interdenominational. Many were heavily involved with Crusaders, EU/IVF and CSSM.[70] The activities of these other organisations (such as daily prayer meetings at Crusaders, or the EU executive) could put pressure on young people who were also busy with study and sport. To some extent the evangelical youth existed in a 'hothouse' – spiritually and socially satisfying in itself but somewhat cocooned from the outside world. Through the EU and associated literature, some would find answers to intellectual issues that were sometimes not adequately addressed at church.[71] They were often leaders at CSSM beach missions and at Crusader camps, mixing there with evangelical people from many other churches; or they were office-holders at EU, and many also attended IVF conferences. The evangelical network was small enough at that time to be closely interconnected, each part reinforcing much the same message and values: 'it all said the same thing, [it was] very clear'.[72] In other places and other denominational settings, the precise mix of evangelical organisations differed: Anglican evangelicals had nothing to do with Christian Endeavour, for instance, and usually little or nothing to do with Keswick conventions.[73] But in all contexts the principle was the same: local evangelical churches worked in concert with interdenominational evangelical organisations, each bolstering the work of the other.

For much of Thompson's time at St Martin's, church life was 'booming'.[74] When he arrived, average weekly attendance ranged between fifty and sixty (a total of all congregations). The year he left (1961), the average was 300.[75] In 1960, average Sunday school attendance was over 400.[76] The growth is attributable in part to new housing growth at Hoon Hay, but it largely reflected the vigour of Thompson's distinctively evangelical ministry. There was also the effect of the

1959 Billy Graham Crusade, from which Thompson estimated there were fifty or sixty converts[77] (including some who would already have been in the parish). A new church building, financed by direct giving, was opened at Spreydon in 1959, with an opening-day congregation of 1000.[78] A second parish church, St Andrew's, was begun at Hoon Hay, with ministry there provided from 1959 by retired China Inland Mission Home Director Harry Funnell. As a consequence of the solid growth, the Spreydon–Hoon Hay 'Parochial District' graduated to the status of a 'Parish', gaining the right to be directly involved in the selection of a new minister. When Thompson left, the four local (lay) nominators were thus able to ensure an evangelical succession.[79]

Of all the Orange Pips' local parish ministries in New Zealand, Thompson's at Spreydon appears to be the one that had the greatest effect. Its impact was greatly magnified through it being a ministry that attracted many university students and ordinands. At least thirty persons who spent time in Thompson's BC later became Anglican ministers; by one reckoning, there were thirty-eight.[80] Three of those became bishops, and many became missionaries. They included Bruce Beattie, Maurice Betteridge, Ian Bourne, Brian Carrell (later a bishop), Colin Clark, Gerald Clark (later with CMS, East Africa), Bernard Cox, Peter Edridge, Bill Gaudin, Robert Glen (later with CMS, East Africa), John Greenslade (later with CMS, Pakistan), Fred Greig, Graham Lamont, Gordon Langrell (later with CMS, Singapore), Wallace Marriott (later with OMF, South East Asia), John Meadowcroft (later with CMS, Pakistan), Ian McLellan, Keith Mitchell (later with CMS, Pakistan), Ian Nelson, Henry Paltridge (later with CMS, East Africa, and a bishop), Lester Pfankuch, David Pickering, George Spargo, Ron Taylor (later with CMS, East Africa), Colin Tonks, Dick Tripp, Laurie Wards, Cushla McMillan and Patricia Allan.[81] In some cases, their involvement with Thompson was substantial; in other cases, they still had associations with a home parish, or were only involved at St Martin's while studying in Christchurch, or other formative influences were more crucial. In a few cases, they were also Orange Pips. Some, influenced by later changes in society and church, would consciously develop a style of ministry that was a little less defensive. But by any measure, Thompson had a strong influence on a remarkable number of future Anglican ministers, and thus very considerably reinforced the Anglican evangelical movement begun by Orange.

Apart from ministers already mentioned, many others in Thompson's BC became missionaries[82] – about thirty-five in total.[83] Other BC members became leading lay people in various Anglican parishes, or active in other denominations. Many became teachers and nurses, and some became academics or doctors.[84]

Another long-term consequence of Thompson's ministry at Spreydon was the number of marriages that occurred between evangelical young people associated with St Martin's, including many marriages with future Anglican ministers.

Harry Thomson at St John's Woolston, 1950–61

Another evangelical Orange Pip ministry was that of Harry Thomson at St John's Woolston. Warm and engaging in personality, Thomson was a radiant enthusiast with an appealing sense of fun.[85] He was secured for Woolston through the strenuous efforts of local nominator Les Burgess, a former member of Orange's Sumner Bible Class.[86] Like Thompson, Harry Thomson had earlier been one of Orange's curates at Sumner and had gained further experience as a rural vicar before taking up a parish in a working-class suburb. Thomson was similarly an evangelical activist, and highly energetic. He was an ardent biblical expositor, and passionate about prayer and evangelism. On arrival in the parish he swiftly closed down the dances and Sunday afternoon tennis club and instead began prayer meetings and a Bible Class modelled on that of Orange.[87] Previously a staff worker for CSSM and Scripture Union, Thomson had exceptional gifts in children's work. He taught several classes of Bible in Schools, held children's missions, and personally led the Sunday school (which in 1960 had 300 children). Through the children, Thomson drew many parents to church.[88] In all this he was supported by leading laymen such as Burgess. While Thomson's evangelistic zeal and spiritual intensity made some feel uncomfortable, his parish – previously a conventional parish under a middle-of-the-road ministry – changed markedly in character.[89] Along with Spreydon–Hoon Hay, it became one of the most vigorous parishes in the diocese.[90] However, despite its strong local impact, Thomson's ministry never developed a comparable ministry among university and theological students to that of St Martin's, which remained the favoured gathering place for students.[91]

The Church Missionary Society and Anglican Evangelical Expansion

Thomson had a dual focus: as well as the parish, he had a consuming zeal for overseas missionary work through the New Zealand Church Missionary Society. He worked hard to reinvigorate NZCMS. In 1948 he organised his first Spring School for CMS, featuring both Bible Studies by Orange and missionary speakers, and eight people offered for missionary service.[92] In 1954 he became CMS general secretary, and in 1961 he went full-time. Thomson re-established a clearly conservative evangelical ethos in NZCMS.[93] The movement flourished, and at the peak of his leadership he was responsible for eighty-three New Zealand missionaries.[94] A high proportion of the new generation of NZCMS missionaries initially came from the Bible Classes of Orange, Thompson and Thomson.

Thomson was well aware of CMS's potential to foster homeside Anglican evangelicalism. At the biennial Spring Schools he was careful to have biblical exposition modelled, for those Anglicans who were willing to come to a CMS gathering but would have avoided an explicitly 'evangelical' context. The Spring Schools were a factor in Orange-style evangelicalism steadily gaining greater influence in Nelson, Wellington and beyond. The converse also held: in a diocese such as Auckland, where Bishop Simkin would not allow the CMS to operate officially, Anglican postwar evangelicalism was a relatively late starter.

An important, related strategy of Thomson's was the CMS League of Youth, begun in 1948.[95] With his background in CSSM, Crusaders and EU, it was not surprising that he began a youth movement. The League of Youth became instrumental in promoting evangelicalism among the next generation of Anglicans. Aimed at those from mid teens through to about thirty, and led by young adults, the League was unequivocally evangelical. It promoted not only missionary support, prayer and recruitment, but also conversion, discipleship and local evangelism. The main activity at meetings was Bible study.[96] The League of Youth ran weekend house parties, and sent 'flying squads' out to parishes to run special events. For some young Anglicans – especially those who were not in EU – the League of Youth was the single greatest factor in forming their evangelical identity.[97] That identity transcended parish boundaries. As more Anglican parishes around Christchurch became more evangelical – sometimes as a result of their youth going to League of Youth meetings – the movement steadily extended its reach. Beyond Christchurch, the League of Youth also became active in the Nelson Diocese, with branches in both Nelson and Blenheim.[98] From Nelson, the League spread in 1956 to the Wellington Diocese; Wal Marriott visited Wellington to help get the movement started there.[99] In the same year it began in Dunedin, too.[100] The burgeoning of the League of Youth was indicative of an Anglican evangelical movement that was now incorporating a third generation. The League's growth was not just an isolated development within Anglicanism, however, but was part of a wider evangelical groundswell that was being generated primarily by the new transdenominational youth organisations. The official NZCMS history confirmed that evangelical interconnectedness, when, in relation to this period, it noted that 'NZCMS has drawn its recruits mainly from those active in the SU, Crusaders, IVF and NCF, and ... the League of Youth.'[101]

Evangelical Anglicanism in Nelson, 1945-55

In the postwar era, the evangelical identity and vitality of Nelson Anglicanism strengthened. There were several new clergy from Sydney, all trained at Moore College.[102] Bishop Stephenson also brought committed evangelicals out from England. One of these was Ken Gregory, an ex-British Army officer with a robust evangelistic style. From 1948 Gregory became the diocesan evangelist, conducting parish missions, and running youth camps with a somewhat military style.[103] Other English evangelicals who came to Nelson included James Dyer and George Hull (both in 1950). Stephenson also appointed as his dean Eric Gowing, an English-trained Australian with definite evangelical sympathies.[104]

Between 1948 and 1954, several more Orange Pips became ministers in Nelson. These included Hugh Thomson, Bruce Beattie, Bob Hughes, Maurice Betteridge and Wallace Marriott.[105] The influx reflected the evangelical perception that there was a limit to the number of Orange Pips that the Bishop of Christchurch would be willing to accept. Also, a number of men from the Nelson Diocese entered the ministry. Most of them did university or theological training in Christchurch, where they were strongly influenced by the Evangelical Union, Orange and Thompson. These included Bill Wilkens (1948), John Ford (1949) and John Meadowcroft (1951). Stephenson was also willing to ordain directly evangelical university graduates like Betteridge and Meadowcroft, without their attending a theological college; instead they did some extramural study while working in Nelson.[106]

Analysis of the 1950 clergy list for the Diocese of Nelson suggests at least ten of the thirty-two registered ministers had trained at Moore College.[107] Six of the ministers were Orange Pips. Seven were from England, two of them clearcut evangelicals. Two of the ministers on the list could be described as local evangelicals (but influenced by the Christchurch movement). The rest were New Zealanders who were not overtly evangelical. Several of the younger evangelical ministers were at the forefront of introducing new evangelical emphases and initiatives, such as the very evangelistic diocesan youth camps, the Evangelical Churchmen's Fellowship and the League of Youth. They were strongly supported by the many lay evangelicals in the Nelson Diocese, including such figures as W. Girling (mayor of Blenheim), his son Russell, and Frank Bythell.[108]

A striking new trend after the war was for Nelson ordinands and other Nelson people to be influenced towards a definite evangelical identity through the example of Orange Pips who had gone to Nelson, or through the Orange Pips' influence when Nelson people were studying in Christchurch. There are numerous examples of this process. Bill Wilkens, like most of the Nelson students and ordinands who went to Christchurch, became involved with the EU, with associates of Orange, and with Thompson's parish.[109] John Meadowcroft, who went down to university in 1946, was told by the Orange Pip curate at All Saints' Nelson that there were two student Christian groups, and that he should go to EU.[110] He went to EU (where he first became aware of the term 'evangelical'), often heard Orange speak and teach, resided at College House with several Orange Pips, and adopted a clear evangelical identity.[111] John Ford, from the same parish, went to study theology at College House. Although not in EU, he was drawn into the evangelical network by EU-associated Orange Pips such as Lester Pfankuch and Bob Hughes, who took him to meet Orange and introduced him to evangelical writers such as Bishop Ryle and Griffith Thomas.[112] When Rose Prendergast came over to university from Reefton on the West Coast, her evangelical vicar arranged for her to stay with Roger and Reena Thompson; she joined both St Martin's and the EU, and later married an evangelical minister. John Greenslade, arriving in Christchurch in 1953 from Greymouth, from a non-church family, had had a conversion experience at a camp under the ministry of Ken Gregory.[113] In Christchurch he was drawn into the EU, where he also gained many friends.[114] He became part of St Martin's Spreydon. In both contexts, he commonly heard the word 'evangelical' and took that identity as his own.[115]

Nelson and Christchurch evangelical Anglicans compared

There were subtle differences between the evangelical Anglicanism of Nelson and that of Christchurch. The Nelson style was Low Church; the Christchurch movement was less so. Nelson evangelical Anglicanism had manifold links with the Diocese of Sydney; the Christchurch group had few direct links. Nelson evangelicalism was isolated, uncontested and often not very self-aware; the Christchurch evangelicals were a self-conscious minority: 'The Evangelicals here [in Christchurch] had to know what they stood for, and were perhaps a bit more vocal ... because they had to stand alone against all the liberals and High Church [elements].'[116] The evangelicals in Nelson enjoyed the patronage of unequivocally evangelical bishops; those in Christchurch always trod circumspectly, anxious about how their bishops might regard them. Many of the Nelson evangelical ministers did not have degrees; the Christchurch evangelical ministers were typically university graduates, largely shaped by EU. The Nelson movement reflected the tempo and family atmosphere of a small provincial centre and predominantly rural hinterland, where good relationships were paramount; the Christchurch movement was based in one of New Zealand's largest cities, where more debate and choice were possible. However, as more Orange Pips came to Nelson, and as more younger Nelson ministers became influenced by the Christchurch movement, a degree of convergence was beginning to take place.

Evangelical Anglicanism in Wellington, 1945–55

Rev. W.F. (Bill) Bretton was an important figure in the growth of Anglicanism in Wellington. Bretton was an experienced vicar who emigrated to New Zealand in 1946. A former Cambridge rowing blue and athlete, he was a dynamic and personable church leader.[117] His most influential ministry was at St James' Lower Hutt (1950–56), where his active parishioners included Walter Nash (shortly to become prime minister).[118] A biblical expositor, Bretton applied scripture to life with warmth and directness, and his preaching appealed to a wide audience.[119] He led the liturgy in an unusually compelling manner.[120] He had a gift of putting people at ease, and was a tireless visitor.[121] He worked his curates hard: under Bretton's direction, one of his curates visited over 1000 homes in one year.[122] Bretton reinvigorated St James': services were packed, with congregations of 200 in the morning and 300 at night.[123] There were numerous confirmations: on one Sunday 108 people were confirmed, including twenty-five adults.[124] Bretton's evangelical influence extended beyond Lower Hutt – people came from across Wellington to hear him. His booklet *The A.B.C. of Our Religion*, a commonsense appeal for Christian commitment, was widely used in parish missions.[125] He was often a speaker at Crusaders and EU. He spoke at the College House theological students' retreat and at least two National Council of Churches theological students' conferences.[126] Bretton developed warm links with the Christchurch evangelicals, including Orange. He became a regular speaker at evangelical Anglican conferences in the South Island.

For the first time, there were now three senior evangelical Anglican figures spread across three New Zealand centres: Orange in Christchurch, Stephenson (and then Hulme-Moir) in Nelson, and Bretton in Wellington.

Bretton's protégés

It was not directly through Bretton that evangelicalism established a stronger presence in Wellington, but primarily through some of the younger ministers he had mentored as his curates. Bretton had written to several Wellington colleagues, urging them to identify with an evangelical approach,[127] but he was more successful through recruiting and training up a number of young protégés.[128]

Ian Bourne first met his mentor at a Wellington BC camp; but it was primarily the Christchurch movement that recruited Bourne, when he went to College House for university and theological studies. Rev. Les Morris, a family friend, took the young Bourne along to St Martin's and 'talked like a Dutchman about being evangelical'.[129] Bourne joined St Martin's and EU, was strongly influenced by evangelical peers and became a convinced evangelical.[130] He was confirmed in that at successive IVF and ECF conferences, and at CMS Spring School. In 1956 he became Bretton's curate, back at St James' Lower Hutt.

When Bretton left for Nelson later that year, he was replaced by a vicar who was actively opposed to an evangelical approach, and the congregation halved.[131] Many of the changes instituted by the new vicar related to evangelical subculture: he banned ex tempore prayer at youth meetings, burned the Sunday school's *Golden Bells* hymnbooks (he insisted on 'Anglican' hymns), and forbade his curates (and their wives) from attending the CMS League of Youth.[132]

Bourne was loyally Anglican; however, as with most of his evangelical colleagues, his evangelical theology and practice was more important to him than his Anglicanism. He felt it 'more important to be a biblical Christian than an unbiblical Anglican'.[133] He unequivocally considered himself 'evangelical', and later became an evangelical Anglican leader in the Wellington region. In the parish context, though, where he wanted to extend ministry to everybody, Bourne rarely used the term.[134]

Another curate of Bretton, Doug Edmiston, had experienced a spiritual awakening while walking down Featherston Street in Palmerston North, and felt called to ministry even before he began attending church.[135] At College House (1950–51) he thought his evangelical fellow students too 'pious' and resisted their attempts to recruit him.[136] But in 1951 he became curate to Bretton, who greatly impressed Edmiston and took him to evangelical conferences.[137]

Bretton influenced other curates to become evangelical, too. Ray Somerville was one,[138] and David Pickering was another – a former Lower Hutt parishioner who appreciated Bretton's 'scholarly' approach to issues such as the relationship of faith and science, and was also shaped by Crusaders and EU.[139] While studying at Canterbury and boarding at College House, Pickering gained many evangelical friends.[140] Attending St Martin's, he found Thompson's ministry 'unbelievably powerful'.[141] When Pickering felt a call to ministry, Thompson took him to talk with Orange. Pickering trained at Ridley College (Melbourne), and then became Bretton's curate in Nelson.[142]

Two other evangelical Bretton curates in Nelson were Malcolm Oatway (also from Lower Hutt) and Bernard Cox. Both trained at Moore. Numerous others were influenced by Bretton, including St James' parishioners such as Don Mathieson (later a lawyer and senior TSCF leader), his wife Sally and David Penman (later a CMS missionary, vicar, and Archbishop of Melbourne).[143]

The Evangelical Churchmen's Fellowship

As the postwar era began, it was clear that Orange's ministry had given birth to a significant new evangelical Anglican movement. But that movement's future was not yet assured. With Orange moving away from Sumner and with Orange Pips beginning to disperse to country parishes and overseas, there was some concern about how the movement might be sustained. The strategy that emerged was the Evangelical Churchmen's Fellowship, formed in 1945.[144] The ECF began as a fellowship of like-minded clergy, all of them inspired by Orange. The original organiser – working in collaboration with Orange – was David Aiken, an Orange Pip who was curate at Sumner.[145] Laymen were included in the ECF from the outset but, for a year or two, the ECF was a male-only organisation. Evangelical women such as Vera Mott had to make earnest overtures to Orange before they were allowed to join.[146] The ECF was the vehicle that would shift the Christchurch evangelical Anglican movement from revolving around one individual to being constituted on the basis of a shared evangelical theology and practice. It gave the prospect of preserving the movement beyond the lifetime of its founder and far wider than his personal influence. As the years went by, and as the ECF extended its reach to other dioceses, the number of Anglican evangelicals with personal links with Orange gradually diminished; when Orange died in 1966, the ECF magazine was so concerned with the evangelical issues of the day that it devoted only two of its forty-two pages to a eulogy of its founder.[147]

The ECF's overwhelming preoccupation was to help people be both Anglican and 'evangelical'. Its stated purpose was unity among all those 'who are loyal to the Reformation settlement, and who desire to maintain the position of Holy Scripture in the Church as the supreme rule of faith and practice'.[148] It thus identified itself as a movement whose main concern was to uphold the authority of scripture against what it saw as unscriptural, i.e. High Church practices and liberal theology. The ECF's early material also prominently cited the Thirty-Nine Articles, including the one that stated that 'it is not lawful for the Church to ordain anything that is contrary to God's Word written'. In appealing to the Thirty-Nine Articles, the historic legal basis of Anglicanism, the ECF presumably felt it was on safe ground. It may have hoped to garner support from Low Church and traditional Anglicans, and to reassure other streams of its impeccably Anglican credentials. A few years later, the evangelical arm of the Presbyterian Church would similarly anchor its new movement in adherence to the Westminster Confession. In both cases, the crucial and pervasive concern was not denominational loyalty (important as that was) but to safeguard and promote a biblical basis. At heart the ECF was a society of evangelicals who happened to be Anglican, rather than a society where Anglicanism was paramount and evangelicalism was secondary. Despite its emphasis on the historic Anglican basis, and despite its later attempts to engage with the wider church, the Evangelical Churchmen's Fellowship's name, personalities and preoccupations meant it was always going to be perceived by non-evangelical Anglicans as a fellowship of 'Evangelicals' rather than of 'Churchmen'. There would be no rush by non-evangelical Anglicans to join the ECF on account of its loyal Anglicanism.

Earlier ECF discussions had raised the issue of whether it might be less divisive to strengthen the CMS rather than start a separate evangelical organisation.[149] Similar fears of evangelicals appearing divisive would be raised when a comparable Presbyterian movement was established a few years later. Evangelical movements often included some who were very anxious not to be perceived as separatists. However, in a situation where Anglican evangelicals saw themselves as a tiny minority, it was perhaps inevitable that they would start their own organisation where they could enjoy evangelical fellowship and teaching.

In the United Kingdom and elsewhere in the world there were longstanding precedents for such groups as the ECF, which were a form of church within a church. The medieval church had its monastic orders and reformist movements, and Protestantism had spawned its own intra-church groups. The essential purpose of such groups was to promote sectional interests that could never be adequately served by denominations as a whole. Liberal and High Church traditions had their own organisations, such as the Modern Churchmen's Union. No Protestant theological tradition, however, had been more prolific in forming societies, leagues and fellowships than the Evangelicals. In Britain there were the Evangelical Alliance, the Protestant Reformation Society, the Bible Leagues and countless evangelical missionary societies. In New Zealand, those who had come up through the EUs and IVF – and were now beginning ordained ministry – hankered for a fellowship of similar ethos within their own denominational setting. Over time, similar fellowships to the ECF were established in many other countries, and linked through the Evangelical Fellowship of the Anglican Communion (EFAC), led by John Stott.

The ECF made Orange its 'president'. Its choice of the Bishop of Nelson as its official 'patron' illustrated the characteristic evangelical pattern of listing eminent persons on their organisations' letterhead to lend a respectability they sometimes feared was lacking. When the ECF began to publish the *Latimer Magazine*, for instance, it regularly stated on the back cover that 'The Fellowship … received episcopal sanction and recognition from the late Primate of New Zealand, Archbishop Campbell-Watson.'[150]

In 1947 Aiken left for the Chatham Islands, and Roger Thompson became ECF chairman and its primary leader: 'To a fair extent … [ECF] *was* Roger, [and] Roger *was* ECF.'[151] The organisation began to reflect Thompson's clearcut, quite conservative approach.[152] By March 1947 the ECF had a modest paid-up subscription of seventy-nine,[153] and over the years its membership gradually increased.[154] There was a quarterly newsletter.[155] In 1949 the ECF held four meetings in Christchurch: speakers included Orange, Hammond, Colin Becroft (Scripture Union) and various younger evangelical ministers. The ECF held its first conference in Christchurch at Easter 1946. Bishop Stephenson spoke. A second conference was held at Easter 1947, when the central feature was the Bible Study series by Orange.[156] Stephenson gave addresses on episcopacy (which he saw as consistent with the New Testament but not mandated by it), and on vocation to Christian ministry.[157] At the third conference, in 1950, the Bible Studies were given by Funnell (CIM), and the three main addresses were by Orange. In general, the ECF conferences would be held on alternate years with the CMS Spring Schools. They were never as popular as the Spring Schools, and usually only about half the size. A major aim of the conferences was to model expository preaching. The speakers at ECF conferences included a mix of New Zealand speakers (senior evangelicals such as Orange, Bretton, Stephenson and some of the Orange Pips) and various Australian speakers (mainly from Moore and Ridley colleges).

The ECF conferences became very important in reinforcing evangelical theology and identity. Evangelical books were strongly promoted. A perennial recommendation was Bishop Ryle's *Knots Untied*.[158] Other older works were also recommended, including those by Tomlinson on the reformation settlement and Barnes-Lawrence on communion and the church.[159] The ECF helped to make the Nelson Diocese more consciously evangelical, to bring together evangelicals from there with those in Christchurch, and to nurture evangelicalism in the Wellington Diocese.[160] A sign of the expanding influence of ECF was when its conference was held in Nelson, in 1953. Within the Anglican denomination, the ECF continued the same identity-defining role that the EUs had performed for ministers when they were undergraduates and theological students; because of the ECF, evangelical ministers had less chance of gradually settling into an undifferentiated theological blandness. However, with evangelical ministers widely dispersed and often living in isolated places, the ECF with its newsletters and biennial conferences could not achieve anything like the intensity of a weekly EU. Outside of Christchurch, it only rarely had local events – and even in Christchurch, meetings were held only a few times a year.

The ECF always had a narrower appeal than the CMS, and the CMS offered an easier entry point into evangelicalism. Although the CMS was regarded with suspicion by some high churchmen, it nevertheless attracted the goodwill of some Anglicans who were sympathetic to missionary work but felt the ECF was too partisan. The influence of Harry Thomson and the Christchurch movement, however, meant that the core support of CMS in postwar New Zealand was increasingly conservative–evangelical and theologically aligned with the ECF. The work of each movement complemented the work of the other.

The formation of the ECF helped raise awareness within the denomination at large that a conservative evangelical stream was now a recognisable element in New Zealand Anglicanism, both in Christchurch and more widely. Some may have assumed that an overt and conservative evangelicalism had died out among Anglicans in New Zealand, but the creation and gradual growth of the ECF clearly signalled otherwise.

Evangelical Anglican Ministers in Training, 1945–55

In the 1940s, there had been an early wave of evangelical Anglicans entering ministry, almost all of them Orange Pips. In the early 1950s, many more followed. Some were younger Orange Pips, members of Roger Thompson's congregation, or were from Nelson or Wellington, or were protégés of Bretton. Those categories overlapped. The new evangelical theologues all had strong links with the EU. In all of this, friendships and a sense of belonging reinforced evangelical beliefs and identity.[161] Graham Lamont was one such evangelical in training for Anglican ministry. He was from Christchurch, and lived in College House from 1949 to 1954 while doing his university and theological studies. He attended St Martin's under the ministry of Thompson, and was heavily involved in EU. That was a typical pattern among his evangelical Anglican peers.

The main lecturer at College House in the 1950s was Rev. Monroe Peaston. Although evangelicals respected him as an effective teacher,[162] they regarded him as a 'liberal evangelical'.[163] The other lecturer, Rev. David Taylor, was thoroughly pro-SCM, and was seen as 'liberal' in theology and 'Anglo-Catholic' in churchmanship.[164] The principal – who taught pastoral ministry and not much else – was the Dean of Christchurch, Martin Sullivan.[165] In the liberal tradition, Sullivan was good-natured and practical.[166] In the second half of the 1950s, evangelical students were pleased to welcome Maurice Betteridge – an Orange Pip – as a new part-time lecturer in Hebrew and Church history.[167]

As the 1950s began, about a third of the theological students at College House were evangelicals.[168] There is some evidence that this group, in concert with the EU and with Roger Thompson's ministry at Spreydon, had a more formative effect on some students than did the College House staff. Ian Bourne, for instance, arrived at College House believing that the Bible contained legendary material, but evangelical students persuaded him to embrace an approach that took the Bible as historically true.[169] John Ford arrived at College House without clear theological convictions, but was influenced towards an evangelical approach by Lester Pfankuch, with whom he shared a study.[170]

In the earlier postwar years, evangelical students at College House had felt intimidated, and had tended to 'cocoon' themselves rather than debate or engage.[171] One recalled that 'I saw my job as to pass exams ... you couldn't get into debate with the lecturers that we had.'[172] A few years later, however, some evangelical theologues were trying to be less defensive in their theological studies, and to engage intellectually with liberal approaches. Graham Lamont, for instance, was willing to consider less literal ways of understanding the early chapters of Genesis.[173] His attitude was indicative of a generational shift in evangelical thinking: whereas the Orange Pips had felt themselves part of a small, thoroughly marginalised minority, the next generation of evangelicals had greater numbers, greater theological resources (because of mushrooming evangelical scholarship in the northern hemisphere), and greater assurance:

> *They were much more secure in themselves. They had academic standing and credibility, and that gave them a base from which they could be irenic. They were strong in themselves, so they could be generous to others ... They would debate with anyone, and would do so from a position of strength.*[174]

Less intimidated, the evangelicals were also prepared to question their lecturers and their theological presuppositions. When Martin Sullivan asked Pfankuch about the Crusader Movement, 'Are you fair? Do you present both sides?' Pfankuch replied, 'We are as fair as you are here.'[175]

The younger evangelicals came through their theological studies with their evangelical faith sharpened and 'informed', but intact.[176] They fully retained their belief in the authority of the scriptures.[177] They were still highly critical of liberal theology and methodology, which Brian Carrell depicted as 'contemptible and corrosive'.[178] 'More time,' he asserted, 'was spent on trying to dismantle the Scriptures than to understand what the message really was'. Carrell described the liberal treatment of the scriptures as about as lifegiving as a post-mortem dissection.

While at College House, Carrell did an MA and took extramural BD papers from Otago University. Lamont went on to postgraduate study in the UK. Such students felt frustrated that the postwar renaissance of evangelical biblical scholarship was being ignored by the liberal theological establishment.[179] Through the Theological Students' Fellowship (TSF), the students heard speakers such as Bruce Harris (Classics lecturer in Auckland) and Presbyterian heavyweights Graham Miller and Rob Miller,[180] and they were encouraged to meet evangelical theologues from Knox College and elsewhere. However the primary local support group for evangelical ordinands at College House was not the TSF but the EU.[181]

Lamont, Goodall and Carrell all served as EU presidents. Lamont (ordained in 1954) later became a leading thinker in the Anglican Evangelical Fellowship, and a voice for evangelicals within General Synod. Goodall (ordained in 1951) and Carrell (1956) likewise became evangelical leaders, and both eventually became bishops.

CHAPTER SIX

Presbyterian Evangelicals 1945–55

The 1950s and early 60s were periods of strong growth and optimism in the Presbyterian Church generally. Between 1949 and 1961, 138 new parishes were formed, communicant membership increased by 27 per cent and Sunday school numbers by 43 per cent.¹ The growth reflected both the baby boom and postwar society's interest in moral and spiritual reconstruction. It was in such a context that numerous young EU-associated evangelicals became Presbyterian ministers. Most such evangelicals began their ministries in rural settings; evangelicals believed that liberal members of presbyteries made sure that evangelicals did not receive calls from influential urban churches, by quietly easing their names off parishes' lists of potential ministers.²

One notable new evangelical minister was R.S. (Rob) Miller, another son of Thomas Miller.³ Before the war, as a law student, he had been a stalwart of OUEU and VUCEU, and a president of both. During wartime naval service he had built links with the British IVF leadership.⁴ He began ministry in Central Otago and then became minister of St Stephen's in Dunedin (1950–58). Like his father, Rob Miller concentrated on preaching, Bible Class and Christian Endeavour. He was emphatically 'evangelical' in identity, with a Reformed leaning. He was scholarly and a prodigious reader – especially in Calvinist theology, Scottish church history and the history of missions. Miller spent much time in private prayer, and was a fervent expositional preacher. He later became a regular writer for the Westminster Fellowship, and the second editor of the *Evangelical Presbyterian*. Over the years he published several books and countless articles.⁵

J.D.S. (Jim) Moore, who had previously been a scientist with the Department of Scientific and Industrial Research, was also a product of St Stephen's. Moore was firmly evangelical, but something of an independent thinker in relation to the views of the Millers and the Westminster Fellowship. Ordained in 1950, his ministry was mainly in Otago and Southland. In his first ministry at Owaka in the Catlins, Moore's sense of fun led one young parishioner to conclude that 'being religious and being human was a possible combination'.[6] R.H (Roy) McKenzie was also ordained in 1950, as was Cliff Webster. Moore, McKenzie and Webster all had a background in EU and IVF. Alex Munro, on the other hand, also ordained in 1950, had previously been a home missionary in the isolated West Coast coal-mining settlement of Denniston. Unlike most other leading evangelical Presbyterians, Munro was not a university graduate, so had not been in EU. He had a marked emphasis on prayer and evangelism. His theology was pietistic and revivalist rather than Reformed. Munro was an effective preacher, with a clearcut, authoritative style, and was a frequent speaker at parish missions and Keswick-style conventions.

An interesting new evangelical trio in the postwar Presbyterian ministry were the three Kirkby brothers, all products of the evangelical Hawera parish, and all further moulded by EU. After overseas war service, they all entered the Hall. The oldest and quietest brother, E.L. (Ted) Kirkby,[7] was ordained in 1948, and served in Tapanui, Katikati and Helensville. The third brother, R.W. (Rob) Kirkby,[8] ordained in 1951, was studious in his interests. He became a missionary in the New Hebrides, where he took over from Graham Miller as principal of Tangoa Training Institute. From 1958 he was the minister at Warkworth, and he then became lecturer in Old Testament at BTI.[9] The middle brother, D.A. (Donald) Kirkby,[10] previously president of VUCEU, was ordained in 1950 to the Northland parish of Dargaville. Donald was the most flamboyant of the Kirkbys, and related easily to most people. As a new minister he had appeared to some of his EU friends to be moving into the ecclesiastical middle ground, away from a conservative position, but he was drawn back into the narrower evangelical fold through a Keswick convention.[11] He was an exceptionally gifted preacher and evangelist, and a talented organiser. He was increasingly in demand in many other New Zealand parishes as a missioner. At one such mission, at Gisborne in 1955, there were nightly attendances of up to 500, and nearly 100 responses to appeals on the last two nights.[12] Kirkby also took university missions for EU, in New Zealand and overseas.[13] By 1956 Kirkby was claiming 'a measure of revival' in the Dargaville parish, with 'many ... finding Christ and winning others'.[14] Parish statistics at Dargaville recorded a weekly attendance of 300, the highest in Northland Presbytery.[15] Kirkby moved south soon after this, to be at the heart of the Presbyterian evangelical heyday in South Auckland in the late 1950s and early 1960s.

The Westminster Fellowship

In the late 1940s, the number of Presbyterian ministers who were conservative evangelicals was growing, but still relatively small. They were encouraged in 1950, however, by the founding of a formal evangelical Presbyterian association, the Westminster Fellowship.[16] One of the main reasons for the WF's formation was the sense of alienation and isolation that conservative evangelicals in the Presbyterian ministry felt. They were thoroughly dissatisfied with the liberal theology favoured by denominational leaders. In the PCNZ such theology was being promoted in 1950 in a much-trumpeted book by J.M. Bates, which emphatically distinguished between the Bible and the Word of God, declared that evidence for the Virgin Birth was 'inconclusive', avoided the topic of substitutionary atonement, did not mention the empty tomb, asserted that 'only faith can apprehend' the resurrection, and appeared to endorse universal salvation.[17]

The WF introductory pamphlet identified and expounded its 'primary emphasis' as biblical authority, and gave adherence to the Westminster standards as its 'secondary emphasis'. The critical issue, it asserted, was whether (with the Reformers) the church would locate authority in the 'Word of God written', or whether – in 'reversal' of the Reformation – it would locate authority in the Church itself.[18] As with the IVF, the paramount challenge being addressed by the WF was thus theological liberalism. The establishment of the WF in many ways reflected the suspicious stand-off between those who had aligned with SCM or with EU. There was a strong sense of 'them and us'. Naturally enough, many evangelicals warmed to the idea of associating with like-minded colleagues in a congenial evangelical fellowship.

Both the name and the concept of the WF were borrowed from overseas. The WF stated that it was named after the Westminster Assembly (1643–49), which had 'bequeathed to us our matchless and unsurpassed doctrinal standards'.[19] In the United States, Machen had founded the Westminster Theological Seminary. In the United Kingdom, Dr Martin Lloyd-Jones had since 1941 convened a 300-strong Westminster Fellowship for evangelical and Reformed pastors.[20] The name and concept may have inspired Rob Miller, who had associated with Lloyd-Jones during the war and had attended Lloyd-Jones' (Congregationalist) Westminster Chapel in Central London. In New South Wales, T.P. McEvoy had founded a Westminster Society (1948),[21] and at the New Zealand WF's inaugural meeting a letter of encouragement was read out from 'similar interests and convictions' in Australia.[22] The WF also later received greetings from what it saw as a 'similar' body: the National Church Association in the Church of Scotland.[23]

Church union was another catalyst for the formation of the WF. Evangelicals felt the polarisation between liberals and conservatives was intensified whenever the issue of church union was being debated – as in 1947–48.[24] In New Zealand, the Presbyterian evangelical party line on church union had been clearly laid down by Thomas Miller, who was implacably opposed to church union. In 1946, in conjunction with Wyvern Warin, Miller had formed the anti-union Presbyterian Church League to fight a proposed merger with the Methodist Church.[25] The League was a conscious imitation of a similar organisation in Canada in 1925, and Miller was in correspondence with its leader, Dr John McNab.[26] At the 1947 General Assembly, Miller moved a motion instructing presbyteries and sessions to present the case for staying Presbyterian.[27] The debate was torrid, but Miller's resolution was carried. Early in 1948 Miller composed the League's anti-union 'Open Letter', which was distributed throughout the denomination.[28] The League's campaign helped produce a 41.1 per cent 'No' vote in the 1948 referendum of church members – enough to stall progress toward union. Thomas Miller had died shortly before the results of the vote were known,[29] but his family took pride in the suggestion that their father had been largely responsible for blocking church union.[30] They admired the stance he had adopted and were determined to uphold it. In the 1950s and 60s PCNZ, church union became the cause célèbre of those who were theologically more liberal, while opposition to it became a key identifying mark of conservative evangelicals.[31] In large measure the evangelical opposition to church union was doctrinal, a fear of beliefs being diluted. For at least half a century, conservative evangelicals had been anxious about theological liberalism's erosion of orthodoxy. They saw church union as a Trojan horse by which liberalism would complete its conquest of the church.

Evangelicals, in particular, still felt a deep-seated Protestant apprehension about Roman Catholicism. Evangelical Presbyterians – like many Low Church Anglicans – were horrified at the prospect of anything that might weaken or undermine the emphases and achievements of the Reformation. They strongly identified with the Protestant heritage and claimed its sufferings, heroes and principles as their own. They feared the loss of the Reformation faith in a new, medieval-like ecumenical church that would impose uniformity, ritualism and an authority independent of scripture. It was not just the 'Catholic' ideas of authority, episcopacy, priesthood and the centrality of the eucharist that evangelicals rejected, but a non-Reformed soteriology: above all, evangelicals perceived in both Catholicism and in ecumenism a 'gospel' that they felt required neither repentance nor faith.[32]

There were other reasons, too, for the evangelical Presbyterian reaction against proposals for church union. For one thing, they reacted against the ecumenical rhetoric about the sin of disunity when their own effortless, positive experience had been an evangelical interdenominationalism. They felt that 'ecumenicals' only talked about unity, whereas they had lived it. They insisted that the unity that mattered was spiritual, not formal. Group dynamics were also involved: the stand-off among New Zealand Presbyterians between two rival ecclesiastical tribes.

> [There was] a clear cleavage – EU or SCM, Crusader or non-Crusader, SU or non-SU, which side they would go on. We were against it [Church Union]: 'because these guys are in it, we don't want to be with them' ... It made it pretty easy to know where you were going.[33]

While there were many in the denomination who belonged to neither party but sat somewhere in the middle, it was the polarisation that shaped perceptions.

Resistance to ecumenical proposals also reflected the deep general conservatism of Thomas Miller and clan, whose opposition to church union was instinctive. The Miller family was well aware of historic church re-unions in Scotland, particularly the 1900 merger of the Free Church with the United Presbyterian Church. They identified with the dissident minority which had refused to enter the union and instead formed the continuing Free Church of Scotland (and successfully argued in the courts for the right to Free Church property). The Millers were also very mindful of the Canadian experience of union (and schism) in 1925.

The success of the Presbyterian Church League had encouraged conservative evangelicals. A number of younger evangelical ministers, such as Gosling, Rob Miller and Morrison Yule, began thinking about reconstituting the movement on a 'more positive' basis.[34] In place of a single-issue, ad hoc political machine, they envisioned an organisation that could promote the Reformed faith and also prayer, evangelism and missions.[35] The 1948 AGM of the League asked the executive to bring back proposals for founding such a movement. At the League's executive meeting in March 1949, Rob Miller moved that the 'Westminster Fellowship of the Presbyterian Church of New Zealand' be established, with the primary aim the promotion and defence of the Presbyterian doctrinal heritage as set forth in the Westminster Confession.[36] A circular promoting the Westminster Fellowship was sent out under the name of the League's chairman, Les Gosling. The WF was thus cast as a pro-Presbyterian movement, rather than as an anti-union movement.[37] The concern about church union continued as an underlying motivation.[38] There needed to be 'an on-going plan of re-education for the Church if we were to have a constituency which could intelligently vote for such issues'.[39] A new organisation could maintain a watching brief on church union and could resume the anti-union campaign as required.

It was not just any sort of Presbyterianism that the WF would promote: it exclusively favoured and promoted a self-consciously 'evangelical' Presbyterianism. A principal reason for the WF would be to encourage the growth of evangelicalism within the PCNZ. The WF brand of evangelicalism was both a reaction against the theological liberalism that had developed within the PCNZ, and a natural outgrowth of the more confident evangelicalism inspired in New Zealand by the EUs and IVF. The WF was also a conscious attempt to promote and perpetuate the type of evangelicalism that Thomas Miller had stood for, in much the same way as the ECF was intended to sustain the impact of William Orange's ministry. The WF was in effect 'a *blue-print* for evangelical Presbyterian witness and testimony'.[40]

One of the WF leaders also saw the WF as 'very distinctly' a reaction to the aims of another voluntary Presbyterian group, the Church Worship Society.[41] The evangelical distaste for the modern 'liturgical reform' movement arose out of anxieties that the Presbyterian Church was drifting away from its Reformation roots – including a plain style of worship – in the direction of what an earlier generation had called 'Romanism and Ritualism'. Evangelical Presbyterians were uneasy about written prayers. They believed ministers should pray ex tempore, led by the Holy Spirit and drawing on the language of scripture.[42] Evangelicals felt the liturgies that were being developed were 'ritualistic' and 'hidebound', rendering congregational worship 'ever so tidy but ever so cold'.[43] An early WF figure wrote against 'popish' innovations in worship, calling for worship to be 'simple, spiritual, reverent'.[44] The WF stated that its aim was, among other things, to 'defend our Confessional heritage of ... worship'. The WF's counterpart in New South Wales, the Westminster Society, similarly saw itself as a challenge to 'high church liturgical practices'; its official title was 'The Westminster Society for the Study and Encouragement of Reformed Worship'.[45]

WF beginnings

Les Gosling, minister at St Stephen's, appears to have been the main initial player in the discussions leading to the formation of the WF.[46] Under Gosling's chairmanship the Church League resolved to wind up, and sent out a circular to publicise the new proposal.[47] When evangelicals met together at the 1949 Assembly, some of them were apprehensive that a WF might be seen as dividing the church, and the outcome of the meeting was inconclusive.[48] Graham Miller, away on missionary service in the New Hebrides, did not hear of the initiative until he returned on furlough at the end of 1949 and saw the circular.[49] However, he was at once supportive and pushed for the proposal to be followed through.[50] At the summer Pounawea Convention he called an informal meeting of Presbyterians, who agreed to advertise a meeting in Dunedin to follow the Otago–Southland Synod.[51]

The inaugural WF meeting was held on 28 March 1950 in Burns Hall at First Church, Dunedin.[52] Thirty-four ministers, elders and divinity students – all men – were present.[53] The youthfulness of most who came was promising for the future of the WF. The choices of hymn and reading signalled that a reformist movement was in view.[54] Gosling chaired. Graham Miller gave a weighty address on 'Doctrine'. Quoting scripture, the Scots and Westminster Confessions, Calvin and Kuyper, Miller insisted on scripture as the true source of doctrine, lauded creeds and confessions as the true safeguards of sound doctrine, and explicitly distanced the new movement from American fundamentalism.[55] Gosling outlined the background to the new movement. Rob Miller – a key strategist – moved that the WF be constituted, and moved several motions defining the WF's basis and aims.[56] Gosling was appointed chairman, Yule as secretary and Graham Miller as president.[57] The crucial leadership positions were thus all held by those who had come up through the EU and IVF. In retrospect, Graham Miller saw the WF as raised up by the sovereign purpose of God, the culmination of 'invisible and pulsating influences' at work in the Presbyterian Church of New Zealand.[58] The aim of the WF, as he saw it, was 'warm, positive, and scholarly participation' in the 'reform' of the PCNZ, as a branch of the Reformed Church.[59]

It was suggested that the IVF Doctrinal Basis be adopted. Some objected that it was not a specifically 'Presbyterian' formulation.[60] The meeting then agreed to a basis for the WF:

> ... a full persuasion of the infallible truth and divine authority of the Holy Scriptures, as given by inspiration of God, to be the rule of faith and life; a cordial acceptance of the subordinate standards of our Church, viz., the Westminster Confession of Faith and the Larger and Shorter Catechisms.

Some 'Objects' were also adopted:

> Doctrinal: to explain, expound, and defend the confessional heritage of doctrine, polity, and worship; Practical: to stimulate prayer, to strengthen fellowship, to promote a deeper spiritual life, and to encourage evangelism.

Membership of the WF was to be open to any member of the PCNZ who was in sympathy with the WF's basis and objects. With an emphasis characteristic of evangelicals, the WF basis had thus begun by asserting the authority of scripture: not only was the primacy of scripture a key Reformation principle (and thus often mentioned at the outset of any doctrinal statement), it was also the veracity and authority of scripture that evangelicals felt was most under threat in the liberalised twentieth-century church. The IVF Doctrinal Basis began the same way.

The title of the WF's journal, the *Evangelical Presbyterian*, made it clear that the WF's aim was to promote an 'evangelical' Presbyterianism, and the movement's byline was 'A fellowship of evangelical Presbyterians in New Zealand'.[61] In viewing the PCNZ, the WF claimed the high ground for 'evangelical' faith. The PCNZ, Gosling asserted, 'is *obliged* to be evangelical': it existed to make profession of 'the evangelical faith which is common to all Churches of the Reformation', and it owed its existence to the Free Church, which arose through the fire of evangelical revival in the eighteenth century.[62] In using the word 'evangelical', Gosling made no distinction between the use of the term in Reformation times and its later use from the eighteenth century onwards.[63] To be an 'evangelical' Presbyterian, he explained, involved sharing the common commitments of evangelicals of any denomination: an insistence on the overarching authority of scripture and a preoccupation with individual salvation and evangelism. It meant personal devotion to Christ as Saviour and Lord, spiritual nourishment by scripture, a life of prayer, accepting scripture as God's revelation (rather than just a record of revelation), belief in substitutionary atonement, evangelism, support for missions (especially for evangelical missionary societies), denominational loyalty, and fellowship with other evangelicals regardless of denomination.[64] By contrast, Gosling described anti-evangelical elements within the PCNZ as the 'grievous wolves' of Acts 20:29 who had come among the sheep, who were 'disloyal' to true Presbyterianism, and who were treating evangelicals with 'totally undeserved' opposition and hostility.

Evangelical or reformed?

From the beginning, it was not completely clear whether the WF's theological stance was as much 'Reformed' as it was 'evangelical'.[65] The WF simply assumed that the two emphases were consistent, and that 'the Presbyterian Church stands for the Evangelical Reformed Faith'.[66] In the New Zealand evangelical Presbyterian context of the time, and in a way that was unique to Presbyterians, 'evangelical' and 'Reformed' emphases were inextricably linked. To be an 'evangelical' Presbyterian, in the tradition of Thomas Miller and in the emergent

WF mould, clearly meant embodying both identities. Each identity was held by leading WF people, with varying degrees of explicitness and vehemence, but neither was held to the extent that the other was compromised. In the WF being 'Reformed' meant a commitment to Reformation principles and heritage, and respect for the Westminster confessional documents. It could mean a quiet disdain for an 'Arminian' overemphasis on the role of human free will in salvation (as opposed to the Calvinist emphasis on divine sovereignty). It also usually meant a wariness of evangelistic coercion, separatism, immoderation or doctrinal eccentricities. But it did not mean any unwillingness to cooperate with evangelicals of other denominations; the real enemy perceived by evangelical Presbyterians was not Arminianism, but liberalism.

In many WF supporters, the relationship of the 'evangelical' and 'Reformed' elements in their doctrine appears to have been largely unexamined. Others, such as Graham and Rob Miller, were acutely aware of the issues, and veered toward the 'Reformed' emphasis, as did Gosling.[67] To the Millers, 'Reformed' meant much more than simply Reformation principles in general: it specifically denoted Calvinism, including the particular teachings of the Westminster Confession. Nevertheless, WF leaders as a whole were not pronounced in their Calvinistic beliefs. Don Kirkby and Lewis Wilson, prominent WF leaders, admitted they would be unwilling to 'die in a ditch' for the Westminster Confession.[68] It may be that the majority of WF evangelicals were quite light in specifically Calvinistic doctrine. By the interwar period the Confession and catechisms were rarely taught in the parish, and were largely ignored at the Theological Hall. However the suggestion that the WF represented a Reformed confessionalist strand within the PCNZ, and that the Crusaders, IVF, and the Billy Graham Crusades represented an 'evangelical' stream, cannot be sustained.[69] In the Westminster Fellowship in this period, confessional and evangelical emphases were closely interwoven and were generally held by the same people.

Some WF leaders may possibly have held to a 'Reformed' identity primarily because that was more politically acceptable in the PCNZ than an overtly 'evangelical' one. For many WF evangelicals, the insistence on historic Westminster confessionalism may have owed little or nothing to a hankering after seventeenth-century Reformed doctrine per se. Primarily, the Westminster Confession and catechisms were a strategically useful bulwark in defending conservative Christianity against theological liberalism.[70] Evangelicals were acutely aware of the Westminster Confession's first chapter, which articulated a strong doctrine of the inspiration, infallibility and authority of scripture.[71]

There was a strong sense among some of the WF's founders that the modern church had culpably neglected the church's confessional heritage.[72] Graham Miller was scandalised that the official Presbyterian bookshops did not stock the Westminster Confession or Calvin's *Institutes*, and that bookshop staff appeared not to have heard of Calvin's biblical commentaries.[73] The WF was a conscious attempt to 're-educate' the Presbyterian Church, so that the denomination might once again value its doctrinal foundations and heritage.[74] But it was always going to be an uphill task for the WF to promote the Westminster Confession, which had long been neglected within the PCNZ. If there was any context in which a strong support base for a narrowly Reformed theology could have survived or developed in New Zealand, it might have been among Presbyterians. The denomination as a whole had long since turned away from any tendencies towards a strict Calvinism, and its historic 'Reformed' stance had been much diluted by such factors as the moderating liberalism of the late nineteenth century, the messy outcome of various heresy trials, the marginalisation of P.B. Fraser, several decades of movement towards church union, and the widespread discontinuation of catechetical and confessional instruction. In the John Dickie era at the Theological Hall, Calvin was scarcely in sight.[75] There were also – in a small country – the effects of interchurch mixing, intermarrying, and interdenominational student movements. There may also have been a tendency among New Zealanders to favour a broadly pragmatic style of Christianity rather than doctrinal precision. So while WF evangelicals reasserted the value of historical Presbyterian confessionalism, their embrace of Reformed doctrine was less than complete. Most WF leaders and members were, in essence, evangelicals who had been nurtured by the BC movement and then gained most of their theology from the IVF.

The Westminster Fellowship and the PCNZ

Not everyone welcomed the advent of the WF. Any group setting itself up to reform the church was bound to be met with suspicion. In an era that generally respected authority, church members of a conventional frame of mind were usually content simply to be 'Presbyterian', and disliked the idea of ecclesiastical 'parties'.[76] Those who were less attuned to matters of doctrine saw no need for the WF. Some, with their own conceptions of what it now meant to be 'Presbyterian', may have progressed no further than the word 'evangelical' before immediately rejecting the WF as 'un-Presbyterian'. There were others who saw the WF as 'divisive', even potentially schismatic, and its leaders as presumptuous and disloyal troublemakers.[77] Those of a more liberal theology saw the WF's confessionalism as diehard conservatism, untenable in the modern age. Those inspired by the SCM's ecumenical vision, perceived the WF as obdurate in its opposition to church union. Many Presbyterian leaders recalled with regret or disdain the EU's schism from the SCM – and would have noticed that all the WF leaders had also been EU leaders. J.L. Gray, for example, an older evangelical who had come up through SCM, was uncomfortable with the WF.[78]

In reality, the denominational loyalty of the WF Presbyterians was not in doubt. Even though the WF movement was deeply leery of the PCNZ's liberalising trends, it was loyal to 'Presbyterianism' itself. WF members felt it was they alone who were defending true Presbyterianism against its dissolution into church union, and it was they who were honouring the Westminster Confession while others dismissed it as passé. While the WF was, in part, an expression of theological disaffection, it was also unlikely to be an expression of revolution: it was, after all, a monument to Thomas Miller, and thus emphatically committed to the Presbyterian tradition. What the WF was disloyal to was not Presbyterianism, as they understood it, but to a modern New Zealand expression of Presbyterianism which they judged as no longer faithful to its own roots.

The founding WF leaders were firmly opposed to secession. They had 'not the slightest intention' of leaving the Presbyterian Church;[79] in fact they insisted they would never leave, unless forced out. They considered schism contrary to the biblical doctrine of the church, such as the teachings on unity, and on the wheat and tares (Mark 4:26–29). They were aware of historical examples of evangelicals staying loyal to their denominations despite very hostile contexts.[80] In the face of accusations that it would split the PCNZ, the WF insisted, 'we are not out to divide the Church, but to revive it'.[81] Gosling, at least, also resisted the idea that the WF was 'a church within a church'.[82] Accepting such a sectional identity would have undercut the WF's claim that evangelical Presbyterians, faithful and confessional, were the truest Presbyterians of all.

The Westminster Fellowship and fundamentalism

An issue swirling round the edges of the WF at the time it was formed was whether or not it would be 'fundamentalist' in identity and tone (as opposed to simply 'evangelical' and 'Reformed'). Like the IVF, however, the WF invariably described itself as 'evangelical', and never as 'fundamentalist'. The WF was prepared to accept the latter term only if defined in its original sense: i.e. faithful to the 'fundamentals' of orthodox Christianity.[83]

As with other evangelical bodies in the same period, the WF needed to position itself not only in relation to Christian movements towards broadness, as in ecumenism and liberalism, but also in relation to movements towards narrowness. In the United States, the two polarities were represented by ecumenism, which in 1948 had established the World Council of Churches, and the fiery separatist fundamentalism of Rev. Dr Carl McIntire.[84] Having separated from both the Presbyterian Church in the US and the more conservative Presbyterian Church of America, McIntire was associated with the Bible Presbyterian Church. He was convinced that most of the worldwide church was apostate and deceived by Satan. In 1941 McIntire established the American Council of Christian Churches. In 1948, a few days before the Amsterdam Conference had inaugurated the World Council of Churches (WCC), McIntire had set up the rival International Council of Christian Churches (ICCC).

The ICCC was conservative in all its emphases, rejecting the WCC's modernism, inclusivism and minimalist credal basis.[85] It was in continuity with the early twentieth-century American movement, which had listed fundamentals of the faith and then – in the 1920s – gone into battle against modernists. At one level, the ICCC's basic doctrinal position was similar to that of the British IVF: both held a list of essential doctrines and both insisted on the Bible as the Word of God. But where the ICCC strongly differed from the IVF, and from the emerging American neo-evangelical movement, was in its virulent public denunciation of 'mainstream' Christianity. It was not so much McIntire's beliefs that were extreme, as his militancy. His aggressive polemical tone made many evangelicals uneasy. Evangelical moderate Carl Henry, for instance, described McIntire's magazine the *Christian Beacon* as 'a religious smear sheet in the worst traditions of yellow journalism'.[86] The more moderate conservative evangelical movements were always careful to assert what they believed. But their focus was positive, not negative. They were reluctant to denounce and were anxious to avoid unnecessary controversy. The ICCC recognised no such constraints. It felt a responsibility 'to expose, to offset, and to undo as much as possible the destructive work of the World Council'.[87] There was also an apocalyptic element in the utterances of the ICCC: McIntire feared that the ecumenical movement and the WCC would ultimately establish the apostate 'Babylon the Great'.

The ICCC's explicit commitment to separatism pushed it to the margins of the evangelical church. When, in 1953, a New Zealand branch of the ICCC was formed, with veteran separatist D.B. Forde Carlisle providing leadership, support was meagre, especially among those in the main denominations.[88] McIntire first visited New Zealand in 1950, along with the veteran Canadian Baptist fundamentalist leader T.T. Shields. Graham Miller, on furlough from the New Hebrides, was invited by the Otago Evangelical Bible League to chair the public meeting in Dunedin.[89] Miller, like McIntire, was suspicious of ecumenism.[90] He was probably unaware of the full extent of McIntire's extremism. But at that time Miller himself was under great pressure, and perhaps more open than usual to a militant approach.[91] Although he had been elected first moderator of the newly constituted Presbyterian Church of the New Hebrides, Miller was in dispute with the executive of the PCNZ Missions Committee. The dispute was about the crucial first clause of the constitution of the New Hebrides church, which Miller had drafted. He had been adamant that the clause should avoid the ambiguous words – as in the PCNZ constitution – that the scriptures 'contain' the Word of God. Miller wanted a straightforward statement that the scriptures *are* the Word of God, with no room for ambiguity or confusion.[92] He considered such a formula to be consistent with both the intention of the Westminster divines[93] and the convictions of the New Hebrideans: 'the people were wedded to the Word of God, and this was the thin edge of the radical wedge'.[94] Miller believed that the word 'contained' was interpreted by liberals in New Zealand as 'their classic way of evading the authority of Scripture', their 'trump card' that 'the PCNZ did not regard the Bible as the Word of God'.[95] It was a case, he later reflected, of 'SCM versus EU'.[96]

In insisting on making the change, Miller had attracted vigorous resistance from the NZ Missions Committee. In 1948 he had reluctantly deferred to their wishes, but he gave notice that in 1949, at the first independent Assembly, he would move an amendment to the constitution to achieve the wording he wanted. The day before the 1949 Assembly, Miller received a cable from the Missions Committee instructing him not to proceed with the amendment.[97] But Miller went ahead, arguing that the New Zealand church had no right to dictate the convictions or constitution of a sovereign church: he saw it as 'intolerable, inconceivable insolence' for a missionary-sending church to tell a self-governing church what to do. However, the primary underlying issue for Miller was not the 'divine imperative'[98] of indigenisation and national independence, but the all-important doctrinal question of whether the New Hebridean church would be founded on an unequivocal understanding of the scriptures as the Word of God.[99] To make his point in the Assembly in the New Hebrides, Miller had dramatically ripped out parts of the Bible.[100] Although his amendment was opposed by New Zealand missionaries, it was strongly supported by the New Hebrideans.

Back in New Zealand, and about to be summoned up to Auckland in May to give an account to the Missions Committee, Miller's attitude toward the New Zealand church authorities was one of indignation and defiance. It was in such a mood that he helped promote the formation of the WF, and also agreed to chair the McIntire meeting. Miller sensed his actions sent a 'shudder' through the upper echelons of the PCNZ structure, raising fears that Miller was a fundamentalist schismatic determined to deliver both the New Hebridean church and as much as possible of the PCNZ into the camp of McIntire and the ICCC.[101]

The significance of these incidents involving Miller should not be overemphasised, but they do illustrate an important decision facing evangelicals at that time, both in New Zealand and elsewhere. The issue was whether evangelicals should oppose ecumenism (as represented by the WCC, the National Council of Churches and church union proposals) to the extent that they would become aligned with stridently separatist American fundamentalism, or whether they should remain associated with the softer, more constructive approach of both British evangelicalism and an emerging American neo-evangelicalism. The decision did not in fact prove difficult. At heart Graham Miller and the WF were neither schismatic nor extremist. They were very uncomfortable with the militant tone and the separatist agenda of the fundamentalist ICCC. Anxious about the possibility of the WF somehow being associated in people's minds with the ICCC, Mervyn Milmine had favoured delaying the WF's formation.[102] After his drubbing at the Missions Committee meeting,[103] Miller had no further contact with McIntire or the ICCC.

Instead of being enlisted by the ICCC for separationism, Graham Miller and the WF saw schism as unbiblical, an 'evil thing' which would provoke the withdrawal of divine blessing: it was appealing to immature converts but displeasing to God.[104] When WF member Alex Scarrow left the Presbyterian Church in 1953 to plant an independent church, which later became associated with the Reformed Church and the ICCC, Miller lectured him on the wheat and the tares.[105] Miller was equally dismissive of other New Zealand secessions, such as the United Evangelical Church founded in the 1920s by D.B. Forde Carlisle and A.A. Murray[106] and, later, those who left the PCANZ at the time of the Geering controversy.[107] Another senior WF leader, Morrison Yule, was equally opposed to schism.[108] In this the WF reflected the attitude of Thomas Miller, who, although he considered the PCNZ 'unfaithful' and 'felt the raw end of contempt', 'never for a moment' considered leaving it.[109]

Like their evangelical Anglican counterparts, and like the New Zealand IVF, the WF leaders were thoroughly committed to their denomination. It could be argued that, in their denominational loyalty and in their steady, moderate conservatism, the characteristic evangelical outlook was a middle way between militant separatist fundamentalism and liberal ecumenism. Unlike the liberals, who perceived denominations as symbols of a divided body of Christ soon to be reunited by ecumenism, evangelicals stayed committed to their denominations, their doctrinal standards and their historic distinctives. Unlike the fundamentalists, who could perceive denominations as hopelessly apostate, the evangelicals were still generally hopeful about their denominations, believing them sometimes to be unfaithful in practice but essentially sound in basis.[110]

Westminster Fellowship evangelicals were instinctively wary of the ICCC's extremist style. Yule, for instance, found the ICCC's *Contender* magazine (someone sent him copies) rigid and 'unlovely'.[111] The WF was much more comfortable with the theology and tone of America's National Association of Evangelicals (NAE), formed in 1942. For some years, the WF leaders were hardly aware of the NAE.[112] Similarly, they were only vaguely aware, at the time, of postwar American neo-evangelicals deliberately distancing themselves from the fundamentalists.[113] Such a differentiation would not come into sharper focus until Billy Graham became known in New Zealand, from the mid 1950s.

The WF deliberately avoided association with the ICCC. In 1955, the *Contender* strongly criticised the WF, but the WF executive resolved to ignore the 'outburst'.[114] The next year, the ICCC's Auckland committee mounted what WF saw as 'an attack on the WF', and Ivan Moses took up the WF's cause in an exchange of several letters.[115] The following year, the executive declined an approach from the ICCC and voted to adopt a policy that 'the W.F. would do best if it were not associated with the I.C.C.C.'[116]

While separatism was no part of the agenda of Miller or the WF, a concern for biblical authority certainly was. In that regard, Miller and the WF (as with the IVF) shared a broad affinity with fundamentalism. A few days after being put on the mat by the Missions Committee, Miller was the main speaker at the May 1950 IVF Conference, and had chosen as his theme for all four addresses the authority of the Word of God. But even so, Miller's evangelical theology of scripture was much more subtle than that of a 'fundamentalist' approach: his addresses discussed the relationship of the Written and Living Word, the testimony of the Spirit, and issues of biblical interpretation.[117]

In contrast to the fiery polemicism of some fundamentalists, the WF maintained a restrained and scholarly tone. It did not want to provoke controversy.[118] It had deliberately chosen to style itself as a 'fellowship' – not as a 'league' or even as an 'association'. It aimed to influence the denomination gently and gradually, not to confront or ruffle it. It wished to be 'deliberate, discerning and constructive'.[119] For most of its life, the WF was impeccably polite; after ten years, Graham Miller could fairly claim that in the WF 'the ideal of a warm, positive, and scholarly participation in the reform of this branch of the Reformed Church has been maintained'.[120]

The Westminster Fellowship's early years

After an initial flurry, the early years of the WF were fairly quiet. Executive members were spread across Otago and Southland, and it was seven months before the committee even met.[121] While on furlough and travelling the country in 1950, Graham Miller was active in recruiting members.[122] In 1951 Frazer Barton became president – a respected older evangelical minister, who was elected later that year as moderator of the PCNZ (and who was seen by evangelicals as the only evangelical moderator in the 1950s and 60s).[123] As the 1950s proceeded, the WF experienced steady but unspectacular growth: in 1951 there were 187 members; by 1956 there were 272.[124] The lists of those attending AGMs suggest that the WF had successfully enlisted the support of most known Presbyterian evangelicals who were ministers or divinity students.[125] Almost all who had previously been in EU and IVF had been willing to join. By 1955 the number of ministerial members of the WF stood at forty,[126] at a time when there were about 340 ministers in the PCNZ overall.[127]

Events run by the WF included tea meetings at General Assembly. These meetings gathered together evangelical Presbyterians from across New Zealand – something that would otherwise be impracticable for a small and scattered movement, and which gave a visible national presence to the movement. There was prayer, encouragement, and some planning of strategy for forthcoming Assembly debates. In the North Island, it was 1959 before the WF organised any events.[128] In the South Island, one-day rallies were scheduled by the WF to precede the annual Otago–Southland Synod meetings. Rallies were subsequently held in several South Island centres. The first WF rally (1953) heard papers on the Presbyterian heritage of doctrine, polity and worship, and later rallies were on similar subjects; the outlook of the WF was neither rebellious nor radical, but a serious, historically minded conservatism, calling the Presbyterian Church back to its roots.

The Westminster Fellowship's journal

The main means of spreading news of the WF's existence and promoting its objects was its magazine, the *Evangelical Presbyterian*. Under the editorship of Les Gosling, a former journalist, the *EP* began as a quarterly newsprint tabloid. Its initial editorial stated that the *EP* would be 'the voice of the evangelical Presbyterians', and 'positive'. Avoiding 'heresy-hunting' and 'polemics', it would 'teach and expound the reformed faith in its distinct Presbyterian form'.[129] The first few issues included articles on being evangelical and Presbyterian, the Scottish Reformation, the Westminster Assembly, the doctrine of Scripture in the Westminster Confession, evangelism and missions – and opposing church union, liturgical worship and theological liberalism. Rob Miller took over as editor in 1955 and maintained a similar approach. There was a preponderance of articles culled from overseas journals, most from Scotland, but also from Reformed sources in the United States. In 1955 Miller ran articles on Calvin, the Scottish Reformation, the Westminster standards and the Sabbath.

The *EP* was a solemn magazine, neither racy nor populist. It was produced by earnest, historically-minded confessionalists who were unimpressed by the prevailing trends of the mid twentieth-century Presbyterian Church of New Zealand. A 1955 issue, however, carried two pieces that were unusually enthusiastic in tone – both were reports of the recent Billy Graham Crusade in Glasgow.[130] By 1954, the *EP* had close to 500 subscribers.[131] Copies of magazines were exchanged with the publishers of similar magazines overseas. The WF was always gratified when international readers, such as Douglas Johnson of the IVF, wrote and expressed appreciation of the *EP*.[132] The executive hoped that the *EP*'s influence was 'far from negligible', and that even those who did not agree with the WF 'can't quite ignore us'.[133]

The establishment of the WF had introduced an important new voice into the Presbyterian context in New Zealand. Instead of just a handful of embattled and isolated individuals, as in the prewar period, there was now a national evangelical Presbyterian organisation with support from a growing number of relatively youthful ministers, almost all of them considerably influenced by the IVF. In the early 1950s, the WF was still a small movement, numerically: its heyday was yet to come. But simply by being formed, by publishing its journal and articulating its viewpoint, the WF made an impact disproportionate to its numbers and gave new heart and focus to conservative evangelical Presbyterians.

Among PCNZ ministers, those of IVF and WF stamp remained in the minority. In the pews, however, the biblically and theologically conservative approach of the WF resonated with many. The 'grassroots' of the Presbyterian Church tended to be still quite conservative: 'evangelical and evangelistic without knowing it'.[134] Evangelicals, with their lively style and a focus on young people, were often invited to speak at BC camps or parish missions.

Evangelicals and General Assembly

In presbyteries, evangelicals were usually able to work with other ministerial colleagues. But at General Assemblies they felt 'very much on the outer'.[135] They were always outnumbered, and so usually outgunned by ministers of 'moderate' and 'liberal' persuasion. To the ecclesiastical movers and shakers of the early postwar period, conservative evangelical views were an obstacle to progress and were to be disregarded:[136] 'They would *not* listen. They disdained our contribution, and swept it aside.'[137] The crucial issue – and recurring flashpoint – was often church union. Lacking critical mass, evangelicals were easily quietened: 'The other side amassed a big scrum down in the front pews … so they could get up and be on their feet at the microphone in no time.'[138] Sometimes evangelical speakers were harassed by repeated points of order. Sometimes there was brow-beating:

> *Time after time somebody would pop up from those liberals down at the front to blast the last evangelical who had spoken, to demolish him … not his argument, [but] to castigate the man and call him out of date and all the rest of it.*[139]

Evangelicals also believed the business of Assembly was 'managed', with some on the floor allowed 'inside knowledge'.[140] Given all those perceptions, many evangelicals found Assembly 'chilling'.[141]

Evangelicals and the New Life Movement

Despite their sense of embattlement at General Assembly, evangelical Presbyterians in the 1950s still found a positive point of contact with their denomination: the New Life Movement, launched in 1949.[142] Essentially a lay movement, and influenced by similar campaigns in Scotland and elsewhere, the NLM was not overtly 'evangelical' but was nevertheless tacitly so in its core emphases on spiritual renewal and church-based evangelism. These reflected the broadly evangelistic piety of many of the PCNZ's lay leaders, most of them products of the Bible Class movement. Aiming to draw in the support of as many as possible, the NLM leadership was careful to avoid any hint of partisan theology. But the NLM's aims meshed well with those of evangelical ministers, many of whom became enthusiastic supporters, interpreting and adapting its programmes to their own ends.[143] Leading evangelical ministers such as Graham Miller, Arthur Gunn, Don Elley and Don Kirkby were frequent speakers at New Life missions in other parishes.[144] Of all the New Life missioners, Don Kirkby stood out as the most effective, and was much in demand.[145]

One of the founders of the New Life Movement was Norman Perry of Opotiki, a layman.[146] Perry came from a conservative background and had studied at BTI. In the 1930s he had served as a missionary with BTI's Māori mission in the Eastern Bay of Plenty. Through reading Roland Allen, involvement with Māori (including members of the Ringatū movement), war service with YMCA and wider denominational involvement, Perry had broadened in his outook, but was still at heart evangelical, especially in his vigorous interest in evangelism.[147] He placed a high value on unity, and was uncomfortable with evangelical sectionalism. He did not normally use the term 'evangelical' of himself: he felt it compromised unity, and 'took too long to explain'.[148] Perry sometimes read the *Evangelical Presbyterian*, but he questioned the need for the WF, and never joined it. He related well to the leading evangelicals, who all respected him.

The other main leader of the NLM was Tom Steele, a farmer (also from Opotiki), who had been much influenced by the BC movement.[149] His evangelical piety showed through when he spoke at Assembly.[150] Other NLM leaders included the Revs A.D. (Arthur) Horwell, the dynamic (and theologically non-aligned) Director of Ministry, W.P. (Bill) Temple (who was broadly evangelical), and Don Kirkby.

In evangelical parishes, NLM programmes took on a strongly evangelistic flavour, and included strenuous campaigns of evangelistic home visitation.[151] In parishes of a more liberal or traditional ethos, theological reservations could mean that little or no place was given to evangelism in implementing NLM programmes.[152] Another component of the NLM was the 'Stewardship Campaigns'.[153] Evangelicals related the holistic emphasis on the 'stewardship' of time and abilities to their existing stress on Christian consecration, and related its financial aspects to biblical concepts of tithing.[154] In all this, the New Life Movement strengthened conservative evangelicals' confidence.

The New Life Movement of the 1950s was not directly related to the Presbyterian evangelical movement inspired by Thomas Miller and the IVF, but in its own way it reflected the more evangelical mood in the postwar church.

Chapter Seven

EU/IVF and the Postwar Evangelical Resurgence

We stand for sane conservatism.[1]

As the 1950s began, there were EUs in the four university colleges,[2] five teacher training colleges, and in Massey Agricultural College.[3] At Ardmore Teachers' College, evangelical students had taken over the leadership in a Christian Union, which then affiliated with IVF.[4] At Massey, too, EU had replaced SCM.[5] By 1960 the number of EUs had grown to fifteen, and by 1964 to eighteen, including the University of Waikato EU, Lincoln College EU, North Shore Teachers' College EU, Dental Nurses' EUs in Wellington and Christchurch, Overseas Christian Fellowships in Wellington and Christchurch, and Ilam School of Engineering.[6] There were also numerous Nurses' Christian Fellowships, and IVF-related Theological Students' Fellowships in four theological colleges.[7] In 1950 the combined number of students in IVF student groups was 400 at the most, about 3 per cent of New Zealand's total of 15,000 students.[8] By 1960 the combined membership of EU groups was 1000 and growing.[9]

As student groups lost at least a third of their members at the end of each academic year, they were vulnerable to fluctuating numbers and the regular loss of experienced leadership. After the exodus of students at the end of 1955, for instance, only two previous members of the Massey EU stayed through to the beginning of the new year in 1956.[10] But the corresponding growth of the Crusader Movement in secondary schools (200 unions by 1964, with a combined attendance of 4000) ensured that university EUs had a constant stream of new recruits. Guinness's strategy appeared to be working.

The growth of the EUs reflected the postwar major expansion of education at all levels. In the mid 1960s the babyboom contributed to a further swell in

EU numbers. But demographic factors alone do not account for the growth of the EUs: in the same context in which the EU/IVF movement was steadily expanding, the SCM was shrinking. The growth of the EUs and the decline of the SCM were occurring in New Zealand's highly secular university environment, which suggests that evangelicalism (with its more definite doctrines) was better able to hold its own in such an environment than was liberalism (with its more open approach). A pioneer SCM chaplain acknowledged the appeal of the 'authoritative' beliefs of the EUs, and reflected that the 'woolliness' of the SCM had taken its toll.[11]

The Canterbury EU

The EU at Canterbury was still dominated by Anglicans, almost all of them associated with Orange or his protégés, and also often with College House. Anglican members of the EU executive were meeting at College House when fellow theologue Bob Lowe (not an evangelical, and later a prominent Christchurch vicar) burst through the door and exclaimed, 'Ah, the Fundies with their mean little thoughts and mean little ways!'[12] From 1949 there was a long succession of Anglican EU presidents, mostly from Christchurch but some from Nelson;[13] it was not until the late 1960s that there were a number of presidents from other denominations.[14] Russell Fountain was a prominent Brethren supporter of the Canterbury group. Presbyterian members included Lewis and Challis Wilson, who both later became ministers. There were very few Baptists, reflecting the predominance of Anglicanism in the province of Canterbury. EU meetings and house parties at Canterbury were often addressed by William Orange, Roger Thompson and Harry Thomson. There was also teaching from Brethren (e.g. Howell Fountain, and Jim Cross, a local science teacher), from R.J. Thompson (minister of Opawa Baptist) and from visiting IVF staff workers like Ivan Moses.[15]

Many of the Canterbury EU members served as leaders at CSSM beach missions, and in Crusader unions, camps and conferences. In such settings they developed their skills, mixed with Canterbury's wider evangelical Anglican and Brethren community, and worked alongside SU staff workers such as Colin Becroft and Lewis Wilson. The records – both at Canterbury and in all other EUs – constantly point to such an interdenominational mixing and cohesion within the evangelical network, especially among those active in the evangelical children's and youth movements.

A highlight of the early 1950s for the Canterbury EU was the 1952 mission by Howard Guinness, who attracted an attendance of 1900 students and argued persuasively for Christian faith.[16] Other notable visitors to EU included Edwin Orr (1956), John Stott (1958) and Alan Cole (1958). By the early 1950s the Friday night Canterbury EU meetings often had an attendance of 150.[17] By 1960 the EU had a signed-up membership of 128. The weekly routine included the morning daily prayer meeting, in the tradition of CICCU. The EU was one of the largest student clubs, but its focus – apart from missions and evangelism – was essentially inward. In that respect it was no different from most churches. Individual members were often involved in wider student life, including sports clubs and student leadership, but the overwhelming preoccupation of the EU was with the formation of its members rather than with the life of the university.

In the postwar era the EU clearly dominated the Christian student scene in Canterbury. As elsewhere, the eclipse of SCM by EU among young future leaders was indicative of wider shifts in New Zealand Protestantism.

The EU at Otago and Victoria

With medical students from all over New Zealand, and a large number of Presbyterian divinity students, Otago University was a strategic setting for the EU. Both elements helped give OUEU a unique character. The EU/SCM rivalry was perhaps at its most acute in Otago. Many ordinands at the Theological Hall held leadership roles in either EU or SCM. When new university students arrived the two movements vied hard to recruit them.[18] Samuel McCay went to both, was 'very comfortable' in EU, but found SCM '*very* abstruse'. By the mid 1950s OUEU was larger than the local SCM group.[19] By the mid 1960s OUEU had attendances of 175 and was the second largest EU in the country.[20]

The EU at Victoria continued to struggle against the background of Wellington's more secular atmosphere and the weaker base of evangelical churches in that city.[21] The particularly anti-religious culture of Wellington's university college was also observed by SCM. Their first chaplain (Martin Sullivan, from 1946) described Victoria as 'the most secular of the secular', and noted the influence of the principal, Sir Thomas Hunter, a 'freethinker' who held 'all religious views in contempt'.[22] In 1945 the EU at Victoria had only thirty-five active members.[23] By 1956 it had still no more than sixty-five, even after an influx of new members following a mission in 1955.[24] It continued to nurture future evangelical leaders: the 1956 executive, for example, included Guy Jansen (later a leader in the field of Christian music), Don Mathieson (later a law lecturer and prominent evangelical Anglican layman), Peter Warner (later a Presbyterian minister and a missionary) and Wilf Malcolm (later general

Rev. Thomas Miller (c.1940).

Photo: Presbyterian Research Centre

St Stephen's Young Men's Bible Class, 1940. The photo shows about eight future evangelical ministers, including Rob Miller (3rd row, 5th from L) and Rymall Roxburgh and Morrison Yule (4th Row, 5th and 7th from L).

Photo: Presbyterian Research Centre

St Stephen's Christian Endeavour (1942). Photo: Presbyterian Research Centre

Left: Assembly Evangelist Rev. John Bissett (L), and Rev. E.R. Harries (R), 1927. Photo: Presbyterian Research Centre
Above: Rev. Joseph Kemp, founder of the New Zealand Bible Training Institute. Photo: Baptist Research Centre

The Ngaruawahia Christian Convention (c.1932) was held beside the Waipa River. Photo: Les Rushbrook Archives, Laidlaw College

'Blind Evangelist' Andrew Johnston, with his wife and soloist, Nellie.

Photo: *Reaper*, 30 November 1933

W.P. Nicholson, an Irish evangelist who toured New Zealand in 1933–34.
Photo: *Reaper*, April 1933

Dr Howard Guinness.
Photo: TSCF

Dr John Laird.
Photo: TSCF

This New Zealand Bible Training Institute 'caravan' was used in the mid-1930s for evangelism and literature distribution.
Photo: *Reaper*, April 1933

Crusader Camp at Ponui Island (Hauraki Gulf), where they have been held since 1932. Photo: Chamberlin family

Crusader Camp devotions. Photo: Chamberlin family

William Orange (c.1919).

Photo: Latimer Fellowship

Rev. William Orange in the 1930s, during his time in Sumner parish.

Photo: Latimer Fellowship

Sumner Bible Class Retreat, Scarborough, 1943. From L: John Judge, Rex Hollis, Ray Blakely, Crellin Dingwall, Maurice Betteridge, Edwin Close, Lester Pfankuch, Edwin Judge, Bruce Thomson. Photo: M. Betteridge

Inaugural conference of the New Zealand IVF, 1936, Roseneath School, Wellington. Photo: TSCF

The four EU presidents at the 1936 Roseneath conference, with John Laird. From L: Basil Williams (CUCEU), Archie Morton (AUCEU), Laird, Rob Miller (VUCEU), Graham Miller (OUEU). Photo: TSCF

J. Graham Miller, first Travelling Secretary of the New Zealand IVF. Photo: Presbyterian Research Centre

IVF conference, Easter 1937, Sumner. Front row: Rymall Roxburgh and Max Wiggins (2nd and 3rd from L). The clergy are (from L) Dick Carson, Harry Thomson and W. Orange. Photo: TSCF

IVF conference, Christchurch, 1941. The Latin motto means 'In Christ we live, we conquer'. The clergy are (from L) Marcus Loane, Orange, Thomson, Basil Williams, Walter Wisdom. Photo: TSCF

The first Evangelical Churchmen's Fellowship conference, 1946. Front row, from L: David Aiken, Paul Kirkham, – , Bishop Stephenson, W. Orange, L. McNee, H. Thomson, R. Thompson, – . 2nd row, from L: Bob Nicholson, Vic Maddock, Bernard Machell, Carl Tanner, Vernon Leaning. 3rd row: 1st on L: M. Betteridge. Photo: M. Betteridge

IVF conference, John McGlashan College, Dunedin, 1947. Photo: TSCF

Leaders at a Crusader Camp, Charteris Bay, 1949. Front row, 3rd and 4th from L, are John Meadowcroft and Lewis Wilson. Photo: J. Meadowcroft

A group from St Martin's Bible Class (Spreydon), 1949, with Rev. Roger Thompson. Photo: B. Carrell

St Martin's Bible Class (Spreydon), 1950. Photo: J. Meadowcroft

CMS League of Youth Easter House Party, 1958.
Photo: B. Carrell

Rev. Graham Miller, 1950.
Photo: Presbyterian Research Centre

Rev. Donald Kirkby.
Photo: Presbyterian Research Centre

Professor E.M. Blaiklock.
Photo: Baptist Research Centre

Rev. Arthur Gunn, c.1966.
Photo: Presbyterian Research Centre

IVF conference, Paekakariki, 1952. Photo: TSCF

IVF conference, Auckland, 1958.
Photo: TSCF

IVF conference, at the new Bible Training Institute site in Henderson, Auckland, 1962. Photo: TSCF

IVF conference, Woodend, Christchurch, 1965. Photo: W.J. Roxborogh

secretary of NZIVF, a university teacher and vice-chancellor of Waikato University). By the early 1960s the EU in Victoria had seventy members, whereas SCM had forty.[25] By 1965 it had 100 members.[26]

The Auckland EU

As with other EUs, the EU in Auckland received a flood of new students in the immediate postwar era, including many returned servicemen. Thomas Miller, who had visited all the EUs in 1945, felt that AUCEU was the strongest at that time.[27] The 1946 president was Ian Kemp (grandson of BTI founder Joseph Kemp, and later a Baptist minister, missionary and Bible College lecturer). Professor Blaiklock was a frequent speaker, and the Auckland EU's mentor and luminary. A visitor in 1955 reported that Professor Blaiklock was:

a tower of strength ... His weekly Bible Expositions gather about 80, which exceeds in size any other meeting held in the College. His witness in the town, his 'leaders' to the papers, his Sunday preaching, and his influence on the Staff are outstanding.[28]

Other frequent speakers at AUCEU in this period included John Deane (BTI principal and a Baptist minister from Australia), R.A. Laidlaw (Brethren businessman) and Roland Hart (a Baptist minister).[29] Deane was a notable new arrival in New Zealand evangelicalism, and a voice of theological moderation.

By contrast, the influence in Auckland of EU pioneer William Pettit had faded. As he aged, Pettit had become more sectarian in outlook. In 1958 – against the counsel of Laidlaw, Deane and almost the entire evangelical establishment – Pettit had held public rallies to denounce the forthcoming Billy Graham Crusade, on the grounds that it was sponsored by 'modernists and unbelievers'.[30] Such an outlook could not be accommodated within the canons of moderation and interdenominationalism that underlay the IVF and Crusader evangelical consensus. In a *Reaper* editorial, Blaiklock publicly rejected Pettit's view;[31] Blaiklock wrote against those (unnamed) persons of 'rigid and brittle theology' who are 'survivors ... wounded by a crude liberalism of a generation ago, who have been unable to cease firing after the battle is done'.

The Auckland EU's membership continued to increase. In the 1950s it overtook SCM,[32] and by 1959 it had 125 members.[33] By 1960 the average attendance was 150, a 25 per cent increase at a time when the overall university roll had increased only 7 per cent.[34] Such growth, which was also experienced by many other evangelical organisations and churches in this time, represented the general evangelical groundswell of the late 1950s; but it also reflected the encouragements of the 1959 Billy Graham Crusade. By the early 1960s, AUEU had 200 active members and was the largest student club in the university.[35] By 1964 its membership was said to be 260, making it the biggest EU in the country.[36]

As elsewhere, the Auckland EU was regularly replenished by ex-Crusaders. Strong Crusader groups feeding into AUEU included that at Westlake Boys, where there were several evangelical teachers, including the contagiously enthusiastic Alex Black.[37] Another trend in AUEU was the increase in members from mainline churches. Whereas the EU in Auckland had previously had a strong Baptist and Brethren base, by late 1959 half its executive were either Anglicans or Presbyterians: this was interpreted as indicating 'a growing evangelical trend in the larger N.Z. denominations'.[38] That trend prompted the IVF general secretary to reflect that 'evangelicalism is certainly far more respectable in the Church life of the country as a whole than it was even ten years ago'.[39]

Emphases on Reason and Evidence

In a university setting where faith was often questioned, Evangelical Unions were constantly looking to demonstrate the evidences for Christian faith. The Massey EU, for instance, had a series of addresses in 1951 entitled 'Why Believe?'[40] A few years later the same EU declared that its aims were 'to provide an intelligently thought-out Christian witness, to show that the Christian Faith is grounded on evidence strong enough to satisfy the tests of higher learning and to help the members by fellowship and service' (prayer and evangelism were not mentioned, but were probably assumed).[41]

At a popular level, the apologetic thrust in many EUs was complemented by the use of the Moody Bible Institute's 'Fact and Faith' films. One EU screened four of these in 1951 alone.[42] The films were intended to counter the assumption that the scientific study of nature undermined Christian faith. They did not explicitly attack the theory of evolution, but instead confidently focused on the marvels and intricacies of nature as evidence of God's design. *Dust or Destiny*, for instance, revealed not only 'the wonders of the human heart and eye', but 'the remarkable homing-pigeon and the flight of the bat', and 'the incredible spawning habits of the grunion'.[43] Evangelical Unions were particularly keen for science students to see such films. In the late 1960s the majority of AUEU meetings had an apologetic focus,[44] and the stated aim of VUEU main meetings was 'showing that Christian faith is reasonable'.[45]

Emphases on reason and evidence (historical, archeological, scientific and philosophical) were also marked in many of the books being promoted and read in EUs in the 1950s and 60s,[46] most of which were published by the British IVF. They included works such as Rendle Short's *Why Believe?* and his *Modern Discovery and the Bible*,[47] F.F. Bruce's *Are the New Testament Documents Reliable?*,[48] Hallesby's *Why I Am a Christian*,[49] Tasker's *The Narrow Way*,[50] Johnson's *The Christian and his Bible*,[51] Pollock's *The Cambridge Seven*,[52] and *The New Bible Commentary*.[53] Many of these, such as those by Bruce and Short, went to many editions. Some non-IVF books were also influential, including Morison's *Who Moved the Stone?* and Pollock's *A Cambridge Movement*.[54] C.S. Lewis's apologetic works were also extremely popular.[55] Along with IVF classics such as *Search the Scriptures* and *In Understanding Be Men*, the new evangelical works shaped the outlook of at least another generation of EU people, and they were also popular in the wider evangelical scene.

Together, the IVF publications provided a moderate and intellectually coherent apologetic for conservative evangelical faith. Confidently addressing various intellectual challenges to faith, the IVF library was highly strategic in the buttressing and recovery of postwar Protestant evangelicalism. While many ordinary Protestants were scarcely aware of the IVF, they would nevertheless be affected by it, through the diffused influence of IVF literature on many ministers and lay leaders.

In 1958, three leading figures in British IVF all produced books. Martyn Lloyd-Jones' *Authority* defended scripture as the true source of unchanging truth.[56] John Stott published *Basic Christianity*.[57] With his clarity, instinctive balance and careful biblical explanations, Stott was emerging as the principal voice of moderate British-style evangelicalism. His 1958 mission to American universities raised his international profile and provided the basis for his book.[58] J.I. Packer wrote *'Fundamentalism' and the Word of God: Some Evangelical Principles*.[59] The title was definitely not intended as an endorsement of 'fundamentalists', but was rather an indignant response to evangelicals being publicly pilloried by British liberals (especially Ramsay and Hebert)[60] as 'Fundamentalists' – with Billy Graham one target, and IVF another.[61] Packer used the word 'fundamentalist' only in quotation marks, and noted that the term was one that most British evangelicals had always rejected.[62] He described the designation 'fundamentalist' as 'objectionable' and 'contemptuous', combining 'the vaguest conceptual meaning with the strongest emotional flavour'.[63] Packer's book was a spirited restatement of mainstream evangelical Christianity in relation to authority, scripture, faith and reason. He refuted 'demonstrably false' caricatures, such as the claim that evangelicals believed in the mechanical 'dictation' of scripture. Evangelicals at their best, he argued, had never been either anti-intellectual or sectarian. He insisted that evangelicalism was in continuity with historical Christianity, and that it was 'Liberal Protestantism that is obscurantist and heretical and a deviation'. Liberalism's main flaw, he argued, was its unscriptural submission to human opinion: 'authentic Christianity is a religion of biblical authority' and anything less is 'impertinence'.[64] Packer's work became 'the standard evangelical apologia'.[65] Within the New Zealand IVF it was strongly promoted – more than any other book – for at least a decade.[66]

Emerging IVF writers – soon to become prolific – included Michael Griffiths,[67] Michael Green[68] and Francis Schaeffer.[69] Their works persuasively defended Christianity against the backdrop of new moods in contemporary thought and culture, such as the emphasis on personal freedom. Meanwhile, there was an increasing flow of academically credible evangelical commentaries and theological books, reflecting the postwar recovery of evangelical scholarship, especially in the United Kingdom. Works included the IVF's *New Bible Dictionary* (1962),[70] Packer's *Evangelism and the Sovereignty of God* (1961)[71] and the exegetical work of scholars such as R.V.G. Tasker, Leon Morris and F.F. Bruce.

The aim of the literature being promoted in EU and IVF circles was not to reframe Christian faith in the light of modern science and scholarship, but to bolster it. The SCM diet of reading was intellectually broader and more open, and reflected a passion for keeping up with the latest writers, theologians and fashions of thought: those in SCM 'read a lot of books that we [in EU] never bothered to read'.[72] The literature being read in EUs could be intellectually rigorous, but it was invariably committed to a classical (and evangelical) Christian position: one way or another, the IVF type of books 'all reinforced what you believed'.[73] Nevertheless, from the 1960s they increasingly represented a serious critical engagement with modern secular thought.

Inter-Varsity Fellowship teaching and reading often had a profound effect on EU members, and was the single greatest influence in their Christian formation. Not only was their faith retained, but there could be what amounted to a Christian intellectual awakening. 'For the first time', recalled a member of the Victoria EU in 1952, 'I realised the gospel could be understood by the mind.'[74]

The IVF movement was about Christian robustness and clarity. It was never about theological sophistication or freewheeling speculation. The constant exhortation was to faithfulness, not exploration. Exploration was good, but only within the bounds of faithfulness, and insofar as it deepened faithfulness.

The IVF could never forget its origin as a movement of reaction against what it considered doctrinal deviancy. Adherence to the doctrinal basis continued as the non-negotiable foundation of the movement, and was required of student leaders and of all speakers at EU and IVF gatherings. Anxiety about 'unsoundness' was never far away, and evangelical orthodoxy was very carefully guarded. Even though each EU was theoretically 'autonomous', local office-bearers were usually fastidious in toeing the IVF line, and would frequently seek the advice of IVF staff, including of the general secretaries.

As it grew in numbers and confidence, IVF in New Zealand gradually became a little more relaxed. General Secretary Warner Hutchinson was especially noted for his stress on exploring and thinking through the faith. There were always those in EUs who thought a bit differently or with more doctrinal latitude.[75] Despite the constant promotion of IVF publications, EU members read material from other perspectives as well, and were not necessarily convinced by every word that issued from the IVF press: a future IVF(NZ) general secretary admitted that in the 1950s he sometimes 'began to recognise limitations of [IVF] viewpoints, or began to exercise differing judgement on the material in hand'.[76]

The most eloquent and learned exponent of evangelical Christian 'rationalism' in New Zealand was Professor Blaiklock. In his 1952 IVF presidential address, he spoke of his concern for rationality in Christian faith, especially among Christian university students.[77] 'A Christian', he claimed, 'is the truest rationalist' – because Christian faith alone 'makes sense', and because Christian conviction is 'the most truly integrating of all ideas'. Faith always involves rationality. 'Our faith is a reasonable one,' he declared, and we 'are not asked to believe without the assent of our minds'. Blaiklock insisted that reason is not contrary to faith, but a solid foundation for faith: 'we must accept the reason of man as a legitimate road to God, and must be prepared to submit the tenets and attitudes of religion to its test'. Reason is foundational to human nature, he argued, and to deny its validity is 'to scorn the image of God within us'. Blaiklock therefore decried the 'widespread revolt against reason' that was becoming evident in modern art and literature, which reflected 'the insane theory that the intellect is of no consequence'. By contrast, the rational Christian should be 'a fountain of sanity in a mad world'.

Blaiklock was troubled by any hint of irrationality of thought or behaviour among evangelical students: it caused him 'pain'. It included 'crudity of … language' and shallowness in public prayer, 'stupidity in exposition', and 'boisterous' song-leading. Perhaps it was unavoidable that such an erudite figure as Blaiklock would be irritated by anything that compromised gravitas or clarity of thinking. Two decades on, he would be moved to paroxysms of rage and despair at the irrationality he perceived in the neo-Pentecostal movement: 'The sound of hammering on the nails that close the coffin of the IVF is insistent in my ears. Lose the intelligent and we lose the lot – and I *do* know universities in four continents.'[78]

Instead of irrationality, Blaiklock exhorted, IVF students should model 'sanity, confidence and scholarship'. They should always be mindful of how they may be seen by others. Evangelical students must exhibit 'grace', 'clarity', 'culture, charm and polish'. They must integrate their faith, life and studies. They must aim for excellent academic results. They must read widely. As students and graduates, they must form

> ... an intellectual Christian élite of laymen informed in matters of faith and thought, aware of the scholarship that lies in and around their convictions, and trained in the exposition of what their minds have stored, in such language and form as befits the scholar.

Blaiklock had no time, however, for the sort of rationalism that led to religious scepticism and theological liberalism. He attributed part of the blame for the rise of the latter to those who 'held the faith and neglected scholarship'. But he was greatly heartened by the more recent recovery of (conservative) 'Christian scholarship'.[79]

Blaiklock was decidedly nervous about university missioners. He had an aversion to triumphalism: 'missioners descend on the place and gain the impression that they have done marvels, and know nothing of the subtle damage left behind.'[80] When it was first mooted that EU pioneer Howard Guinness be brought back to New Zealand for another round of university missions, Blaiklock wrote, 'I view the whole project without enthusiasm', and, 'I like Guinness immensely but should be horrified to let him loose in a public meeting of students'. Blaiklock brushed away an assurance that Guinness had now matured: 'Basil Williams' opinion, or that of any other outside opinion, weighs nothing with me.' Blaiklock was moved primarily by an intense protectiveness of his own more scholarly style of Christian witness – which could be undermined by emotional mass meetings – and by a concern for his own academic reputation: 'I don't want my work hindered by well-meaning efforts from outside ... I wish I could make plain to you how difficult some matters look from the point of view of staff, and how ultimately important that view is.'[81]

The concern for academic respectability was not unique to Blaiklock. The IVF leadership always craved that, along with ecclesiastical respectability. It never passed by an opportunity to list eminent supporters: the letterhead of every EU listed the names and academic qualifications of all fifteen men on the IVF Board of Reference, which included university teachers, senior churchmen and people in various professions.[82]

EU Missions

Despite Blaiklock's nervousness, the IVF in the 1950s continued to arrange evangelistic missions in universities and training colleges. Dr Howard Guinness (by then rector of St Barnabas in Sydney) conducted university missions in Otago and Canterbury in 1952, in Auckland and Victoria in 1955, and again in Auckland in 1959. In Otago, the names of thirty-two respondents at Guinness's meetings were recorded as 'helped and desiring further contact'.[83] Sixteen of these were already EU members (including some on the mission's organising committee), one was an SCM member, and only five were recorded as 'converted'. Respondents were listed by denomination, as this was still an era when almost everyone had at least a nominal church affiliation. In Canterbury, the results were loosely reported as 'at least a dozen converted';[84] nevertheless, members of the Canterbury group felt that the mission had made a 'tremendous impact' on the university.[85]

When Guinness returned in 1955, the publicity material was framed as an appeal to reason. The pamphlet was titled 'Can a Thinking Man be a Christian?', and asserted that Christianity 'demands from all honest-thinking men and women a thorough and open-minded consideration'.[86] Guinness – a medical doctor, author of *The Sanity of Faith*, and someone who had spoken in 'every university in the British Empire' – would present the faith 'in a reasoned, logical way'. His topics indicated a marked apologetic emphasis, with such titles as 'Where Science and Faith Meet', 'Five Good Reasons for Believing that Jesus Christ is the Son of God', and 'Christian Sex Morality is Psychologically Sound and Medically Up to Date'. The pamphlet recognised that Christian faith 'does present intellectual difficulties to some thinking men'. However, once one comes to accept the divinity of Christ, difficulties with miracles and the resurrection are resolved. In a later newspaper account, it was noted that Guinness believed that 'the truth of Christianity is essentially reasonable'.[87]

Guinness's meetings in Auckland were chaired by the professors of modern languages, classics, obstetrics, law and botany. In Wellington, a special service at St Paul's Cathedral was attended by 700. At Victoria University College over 200 students came to hear Guinness's talk on sex, and were crammed into a room 'packed to suffocation'.[88] The topic was a sign of changing times. In

Auckland, where twice-daily meetings attracted similar numbers, someone turned up dressed as the devil. It turned out to be a member of the SCM. Guinness reported that 'on the whole' the devil 'behaved very well'.

A newcomer to the New Zealand Christian student scene in 1952 was missioner David Stewart, an Australian Baptist minister and former CIM missionary. John Deane had previously been Stewart's minister and had presumably arranged the visit. Stewart had a strong academic background in mathematics and theology, and was a persuasive Christian apologist and biblical expositor. In 1952 he did missions in AUC, VUC, Massey, and at Ardmore and Wellington teachers' colleges.[89] In Victoria, he captivated Wilf Malcolm with a more intellectual conception of Christian faith.[90] In 1965 Stewart would commence a more permanent role in evangelicalism in New Zealand with his appointment as principal of the BTI, where he strengthened the Institute's cross-denominational character and its academic standards.[91]

In addition to the overseas missioners, who usually went the rounds of several of the larger university EUs, smaller EUs would also often call on New Zealanders to conduct local missions. The Massey EU, for instance, had Don Elley lead a mission in 1960 and Wynford Davies in 1961.[92]

The EU missions to university students were constrained by several factors: the prevailing outlook in the university setting was religious scepticism; EU groups in New Zealand were generally better at building up Christian students in faith than at converting non-Christian students;[93] EU was regarded with suspicion by many students, staff and church leaders; and it was difficult to attract the attention of the university with just one week of special meetings, especially when most New Zealand university students were non-residential. Nevertheless, the 1950s to the 1970s was a period of relative openness to Christianity, and an EU mission could still generate significant student interest. The number of converts was not huge, but the missions had more impact than university missions did a few decades later, when society was more pluralistic and secular.

In the early 1960s the IVF coordinated an annual round of 'teaching missions' by overseas academics, including Dr Hermann Sasse (1962), W.A. Andersen (1963), Dr Bernard Ramm (1964) and Dr Klaas Runia (1965).[94] These were intended to offer a scholarly defence of Christianity in the university setting, in dialogue with modern intellectual movements. The missions were not seen as evangelistic, but as an adjunct to evangelism.[95] Both the strength and the weakness of the teaching missions was their sheer intellectualism, in isolation from the more experiential dimensions of evangelicalism; it was not the sort of approach that would have appealed to EU pioneer William Orange, who last addressed an EU in 1965 and died the following year.

A Network of People Shaping People

The work of the IVF was very much embodied in actual people. Through conferences, correspondence and personal contacts, younger leaders in the movement were constantly being influenced by IVF staff and older leaders. There was an unending process of evangelical beliefs, values and behaviours being modelled and transmitted to emerging generations of evangelicals. It was a web of influence that operated across the whole country: from his base in the Canterbury EU, for instance, Graham Lamont came to know people like Kevin O'Sullivan, Ivan Moses, Bruce Nicholls, Ian Kemp and Colin Becroft, all of them based in the North Island. He was impressed by their 'intellectual sharpness' – their willingness to think and debate.[96] Others in the same EU had appreciated the trio of stalwarts sometimes known as the 'BBC' of IVF – Becroft, Buist and Cocker – who were meticulous custodians of the IVF vision. Warner Hutchinson and Wilf Malcolm would inherit the mantle and have considerable personal influence. So, too, did various travelling secretaries: those mentioned above (Moses, Nicholls, Kemp) and also Ken Roundhill, Frank Stephens, Ruth Moses and Ken Ralph.

Warner Hutchinson and Wilf Malcolm

The general secretary of the IVF, with much potential influence over future Christian leaders, had one of the most strategic evangelical roles in New Zealand. The IVF was very conscious that the role involved theological leadership.[97] Late in 1958, Warner Hutchinson became the first full-time general secretary. A Congregationalist minister from the United States and a former IVCF staff worker, Hutchinson strongly affirmed core evangelical commitments, and rejected both fundamentalist and neo-orthodox conceptions of scripture.[98] He held the line against cooperation with a doctrinally inclusive SCM, but his manner was not defensive.[99] Hutchinson critiqued evangelicalism for sometimes reducing faith to doctrinal formulas, and for its neglect – at that time – of humanitarianism.[100] He encouraged students to explore their faith intellectually and to engage with other viewpoints.[101] He plied them, especially the theologues, with books and articles to extend their thinking.

Hutchinson had a marked influence on many IVF students.[102] Some others were uneasy about his emphasis on love, rather than truth, as the essence of

Christianity.[103] His relatively open attitudes were questionable in the eyes of some earlier IVF leaders: this was the time, Graham Miller suspected, when the IVF in New Zealand 'was beginning to swither'.[104]

Late in 1962, Hutchinson moved on. IVF resolved to find a new general secretary who was unaffected by either a defensive 'fundamentalism' or an anti-intellectual 'activism'.[105] They settled on Wilf Malcolm, who served for five years before resuming his university teaching career. Brethren in affiliation, Malcolm had been much influenced by IVF, and was resolutely interdenominationalist in outlook.[106] He aimed for a 'catholicity' of Christian conviction: to hold to 'irreducible' evangelical beliefs while avoiding what was 'sectarian'.[107] As an academic, he stressed the 'intellectual character' of IVF, offering a Christian understanding within the validity of the university's pursuit of knowledge and truth.[108] He noted that 'within the university world of learning and scholarship' it had not been easy for the movement 'to maintain its distinctive witness to the authority and functions of the scriptures and yet properly resist some of the stricter formulations ... pressed upon it by those of fundamentalist convictions, especially of the American variety'.[109]

The Vexed Relationship of IVF and SCM

In postwar New Zealand, relations between IVF and SCM remained very uneasy. The two organisations constantly fretted about each other, generating huge amounts of correspondence and written material – for the IVF at least, much more than on any other matter.[110] The SCM, which was committed to Christian unity, continued to deplore the schism with the EU as sinful and tragic. From the mid 1930s, influenced by the neo-orthodoxy of Barth and Brunner, SCM had moved away from a more radical and sociopolitical focus, to one that emphasised church, sacraments, ministry, theology, biblical and doctrinal study, evangelism and prayer.[111] Aware of that shift, the SCM argued that a permanent breach in student Christian work was more unjustified than ever: that the two movements were now practically the same.[112] However, internally – and sometimes externally – the SCM continued to criticise the IVF as divisive and narrow-minded.

The IVF recognised signs that the SCM had shifted, but did not feel that it had come far enough. The SCM, they felt, regarded the Gospel as 'a matter of speculative discussion', whereas the IVF saw it as 'the essence of revealed truth'.[113] The SCM, they suggested, acknowledged the divinity of Jesus, but in practice seemed to regard him 'more as Leader and Teacher than as Saviour'.[114] The IVF believed in revelation, but the SCM, they noted, 'welcomes all points of view'.

The IVF represented 'Christian Faith', but the SCM represented 'religion'.[115] The IVF was 'conservative', but the SCM fluctuated 'from pseudo-conservatism to extreme liberalism'. The IVF was custodian and heir to authentic Christian faith, whereas the SCM wished to whittle away at that orthodoxy. The IVF, they claimed, 'definitely supports the historic creeds', whereas the SCM 'frequently opposes' them.

At the heart of the matter were the questions of authority and salvation. The SCM, according to the IVF, had a different epistemological basis: the SCM held not to the Scriptures themselves but merely to their 'echo', in a subjectively discerned and nebulous 'Word of God'.[116] The SCM, IVF alleged, had a different soteriology: they neither believed in universal human alienation from God nor in the necessity of individual spiritual regeneration.[117] The IVF believed that the SCM had become so shaped by its 'overriding principle' of 'inclusivism' that it had replaced 'specific saving faith' in Christ with a 'general' faith in God.[118] Consequently, in these two areas – scriptural authority and soteriology – 'the battle of the Reformation' was being 're-fought with every SCM approach to the EU'.[119] A former EU student recalled:

> There were two things that we fought for as students. I can remember having great debates with [the] SCM crowd, in university days. There were two things only, really. One was the defence of Scripture – the inspiration and authority of Scripture, and ... the other thing was ... Substitutionary Atonement, and we weren't going to give an inch. It was all very simple, ... two issues that distinguished an evangelical from other people.[120]

The SCM, the IVF reasoned, did not truly respect IVF's position: if the SCM *did* accept it, then 'why [did it] not adopt the IVF Doctrinal Statement and join us?'[121] The SCM, the IVF kept hearing, continued to whisper that the EUs were schismatic spoilers: but the true history, the IVF insisted, was that the EUs had been forced into existence 'because the SCM leaders would not allow the Evangelical witness within the framework of the existing organization'.[122]

The perceived theological thought patterns of SCM people were often dissected and critiqued by IVF people. One such critic – thoughtful, ardent, unswervingly orthodox and penetratingly logical – was lawyer Malcolm Buist. A lifelong friend of Graham Miller, and a fellow Presbyterian, Buist had been an early member of VUCEU. He had resigned from SCM in the mid 1930s, after his misgivings about SCM theology had become overwhelming. He had especially reacted against SCM's willingness to entertain any view. In the early postwar decades, Buist was probably IVF(NZ)'s most stern and unbudging defender of IVF doctrinal purity and identity. Although his critique of SCM could at times be overstated, he was always keen to analyse and expose the 'theoretical presuppositions' of the SCM movement.[123]

Like many of the IVF people, Buist insisted on consistency of thought, an attribute he felt was lacking in what he saw as an amorphous and rootless SCM. Buist could not abide the implication, for instance, that there was more than one road to salvation; or that substitutionary atonement was an optional doctrine. He also could not abide the SCM's willingness to give a platform to both evangelical and anti-evangelical viewpoints. In his own way, Buist and his IVF colleagues were expressing a yearning for Christian faith to have solid and dependable intellectual foundations. SCM thinkers shared that desire, but sought such foundations in what they saw as necessary accommodations to modern knowledge and thought, rather than in rigorous adherence to historic doctrines. In spirit, Buist was modernist in his relentless concern for logicality and philosophical coherence. But he was also in deep reaction against modernism in his thoroughgoing determination to be credally and biblically faithful. In those patterns of thought, he was not unlike many other evangelicals around the world: they shared modernity's rationalistic cast of mind, but rejected modernity's more critical and sceptical conclusions.

In keeping with its own principles, the SCM expressed hopes that the SCM/IVF breach might be healed. Meanwhile, to 'lessen the scandal of disunity', SCM members were urged to keep seeking to 'cooperate' with EU in such areas as joint prayer, discussions and missions (and when the SCM found 'the other group's attitudes hard to understand', to maintain an outlook of 'charity').[124] Given that the IVF's preconditions for cooperation with SCM could never be met, the SCM was setting itself up for perpetual frustration. Pressure to cooperate was always felt most acutely at the local level, where EU members often felt some tension between personal friendships and the IVF policy of declining cooperation.[125] The IVF head office theoretically acknowledged the autonomy of each EU, but in practice ensured each EU's compliance with the IVF policy.[126] In 1965, for instance, the general secretary wrote firmly to CUEU to remind them that, constitutionally, 'no joint activities are to be undertaken with any bodies that do not share a statement of doctrinal belief in sympathy with that of the IVF doctrinal basis'.[127] Similarly, he declined an invitation to attend the SCM conference as a 'fraternal delegate' because 'the presence of official IVF delegates ... would be by implication a toleration of the teaching content of the conference'.[128]

Related issues of cooperation arose with the promotion of university chaplains by the SCM and then the National Council of Churches (NCC). As a student-led group, the EUs felt no need for chaplains. The IVF suspected NCC appointees would be de facto SCM chaplains but 'on the NCC payroll',[129] that EUs would be expected to support the chaplains, and that chaplains would agitate to reunite EU and SCM. The first NCC chaplain, in Canterbury, was seen as hostile towards the EU.[130] The IVF adopted the policy that university chaplains should serve everyone, but that the EUs would not use any who did not subscribe to the IVF Doctrinal Basis.[131]

IVF and the Methodist Church

It was perhaps frustration among SCM leaders that inspired the *Methodist Times* in New Zealand to print a vitriolic anti-IVF article in 1955, from the pen of Britain's leading liberal Methodist, Donald Soper.[132] The article castigated the IVF as a 'short cut to authority' which appealed to the 'unsophisticated adolescent'; the IVF suppressed doubt, and could not withstand the scrutiny of 'intellectual honesty'. In its 'disastrous intolerance', Soper asserted, the IVF is fostering a 'religious fascism' and 'totalitarianism' based on 'the violence of fear'.

The IVF president thought it 'mean and despicable' of the Methodist Church in New Zealand to print such an article, especially at the beginning of the university year, and that its inclusion in its official paper showed 'that there is within the hierarchy of the Methodist Church a deep hatred towards IVF'.[133] But in keeping with its style of avoiding controversy, IVF in New Zealand appears to have let the matter die away rather than protest and fuel a controversy.

Some Internal IVF Conflict

In general, among those involved in IVF, the movement fostered a high level of evangelical unity, with a common sense of purpose that transcended denominational and provincial barriers. In the late 1940s, however, the closeknit evangelical leadership circle in New Zealand also had to work through some passing internal tensions, relating to Orange and Tyndale House – the new evangelical conference and study centre on the hills near Christchurch.[134] Tyndale House was bankrolled by L.B. Miller, a prominent Christchurch businessman and member of the Open Brethren. Through his Cashmere Evangelical Trust (CET), Miller was a generous supporter of Christian work, especially the IVF. The 1945 IVF Conference was held at Tyndale House, and a special service was held to dedicate the venue for the use of IVF, SU and the Crusader Movement. Orange accepted Miller's invitation to leave Sumner and become resident warden. Orange hoped to devote himself to Bible study and exposition, devotional retreats and IVF. He relocated his Bible Class to Tyndale

House, which also became the favoured venue for IVF, EU, the Crusader Movement, ECF and CMS, and a symbol of evangelical unity. In practice, however, the Miller–Orange and CET–IVF partnerships both proved difficult. The IVF, always anxious for its reputation, was nervous about being formally associated with another organisation. It was sensitive about the CET as a 'rich uncle' which might influence IVF policy, and about its own powerlessness within the CET.

In 1947, Orange resigned as warden. He freely acknowledged Miller's generosity and zeal, but clearly his and Miller's approaches were at odds. Orange, a studious loner, had wanted to run intimate devotional retreats, trusting God for invisible spiritual outcomes. Miller, the self-made entrepreneur and man of action, wanted large events, publicity and quantifiable 'results'. Long accustomed to working in his own way and very sensitive about pressure, Orange chafed at working under direction. He resented questions being raised 'as to how the work was progressing, or whether there was even any work being done at all'.[135] Miller lost confidence in Orange.

Auckland members of the CET, including BTI Principal John Deane, took the side of Miller.[136] Miller's relationship with IVF soured. IVF decided to withdraw from the CET.[137] Matters were further complicated when Blaiklock weighed in. Blaiklock already had a negative opinion of Orange: he strongly rejected Orange's typological approach, did not respect his scholarship, and felt his reputation in IVF circles was undeserved. Blaiklock rebuked IVF for its 'grave and hasty error of judgement'.[138] The IVF general secretary feared Blaiklock might conceivably force a schism in the IVF, perhaps by inducing AUEU to withdraw.[139] There was some strain felt, too, in the Crusader movement, which also involved many IVF leaders.[140]

The dispute was kept very much behind the scenes, however, and was successfully resolved. Many people were involved in trying to heal the breaches, among them Lewis Wilson, Colin Becroft, Ken Roundhill, H.R. Minn and William Pettit.[141] IVF's return to Tyndale House for its 1949 Conference, with Orange giving the presidential address, marked a positive step forward. The IVF General Committee gave much attention to restoring a good relationship with the CET.[142] Letters expressing warm Christian concord were mutually exchanged, and there was relief all round.[143] By early 1950, L.B. Miller was once again an enthusiastic supporter of IVF.[144] Blaiklock's relationship with the IVF leadership continued to be somewhat taut, but in 1949 he was duly re-elected as an IVF vice-president, and president in 1952.

The CET/IVF dispute did not reveal any major or enduring rifts in New

Zealand evangelicalism. It was a passing (and discreetly handled) family blow-up, mainly precipitated by personal clashes. If anything, the dispute illustrated just how interwoven, at a personal level, the New Zealand evangelical network was, made up as it was of Christchurch Anglicans and Brethren, the IVF and Crusader movements, Auckland Baptists and the BTI; several key figures had been involved, including Orange, Miller, Cocker, Deane and Blaiklock. The dispute tested the strength of New Zealand's evangelical leaders' commitment to unity, but showed that in fact they were anxious to see unity maintained.

The IVF and Evangelicals in the United States

After the Second World War, the IVF was often seen as a leader of New Zealand evangelicalism. This leadership role was illustrated in 1950, when America's National Association of Evangelicals (NAE) was wanting to make contact with New Zealand evangelicals. The NAE was unsure how to do so, but wrote to a Youth for Christ member in Wellington, who passed the letters on to the YFC leadership, who consulted the Crusader Council, who suggested that IVF was the appropriate body to write to.[145] The NAE, under the chairmanship of neo-evangelical H.J. Ockenga, introduced itself as representing 1.5 million 'responsible evangelicals'.[146] The adjective 'responsible' implicitly differentiated the NAE membership from the more militant, separatist, 'fundamentalist' type of evangelicals associated with McIntire's ICCC. The IVF general secretary at the time, Cliff Cocker, had not heard of the NAE before, but was immediately sympathetic to what it seemed to represent.[147] He was at least vaguely aware of the ICCC (McIntire also visited New Zealand that year). Cocker wrote to his US counterpart, Stacey Woods, asking him to give IVF the 'low-down' on the different configurations of American evangelicals.[148]

Woods wrote back at length, explaining that there were three 'actual or potential' worldwide Christian organisations: the WCC, NAE and ICCC.[149] The ICCC, he explained, was headed up by 'a rather notorious man', McIntire, who held to an excessively rigid doctrine of separation, and whose 'methods and manners' in attacking the WCC – and all those associated with it – seemed less than Christian. The NAE, Woods wrote, had little time for the WCC, but wanted to be positive and to avoid condemning those it disagreed with. Woods enclosed an NAE flier, including a statement of faith, which avoided narrow doctrinal definitions, focused on positives and emphasised the new birth.[150] The NAE appeared to position itself as a moderate, evangelical alternative to both liberal ecumenism (as in the WCC) and militant separatist fundamentalism (as represented by the ICCC). Woods thought that IVF people would feel at home with the NAE point of view and 'manner', and also noted that the NAE was seeking links with the World Evangelical Alliance based in Britain.

This correspondence confirmed again that the natural affinities of the IVF (in New Zealand and elsewhere) were not with militant separatist American fundamentalism, but with the more moderate evangelicalism embodied by both the American neo-evangelical movement and much of British evangelicalism.

Because New Zealand's cultural, theological and ecclesiastical orientation in the early 1950s was still essentially towards what was British rather than American, there was limited knowledge of, or interest in the NAE in New Zealand. However, the Second World War (and the influx of American troops and the victory in the Pacific) had heightened New Zealand's awareness of America – as did the Cold War and the Korean War. A sign of increasing American influence on the evangelical churches of New Zealand was the postwar importation of Youth for Christ, an evangelistic youth organisation.[151] Later in the 1950s, the Billy Graham Crusade would increase the American influence on New Zealand evangelicalism.

The Evangelical Ministers' Fellowship

From the early 1940s the IVF had dreamed of sustaining its influence with EU graduates through the Graduates' Fellowship (GF).[152] Part of the plan was the Evangelical Ministers' Fellowship (EMF), a subsection of the GF intended to bind together those EU graduates who were in the ministry of New Zealand churches.[153] The vision was for a growing body of IVF-style evangelical ministers continuing to encourage one another, and faithful to the IVF Doctrinal Basis. The EMF was also intended as a common witness, an expression of evangelical ecumenism. To keep ministers reading, there would be a postal exchange library of theological books. Along with other IVF graduates, it was hoped that EMF members would subscribe to the *NZ IVF Magazine,* the GF *Bulletin* (with an EMF section), and the British IVF magazine.[154] Ministers would write articles and book reviews for the newsletters, would gather in their regions for prayer and fellowship, and would have occasional conferences (usually in association with an IVF conference). The EMF's first secretary, Mervyn Milmine, and chairman, Les Gosling, were both Presbyterians.[155]

In practice, the EMF struggled. As an IVF organisation it held no appeal for graduates without an EU background. J.L. Gray, an older evangelical with an SCM background, responded to an invitation to join EMF with a curt comment that 'signing of such statements is *divisive*'.[156] But the main problem that EMF faced was enlisting the active support of EU graduates themselves.

They were prepared to be listed as members, but usually could offer little more. New evangelical ministers were inevitably preoccupied with the present rather than wanting to focus on something linked with their university past. Where evangelical ministers had any energy for activities outside the parish, they tended to devote it to activities such as extra speaking engagements (at BC camps, Crusaders, EU, or parish missions), local inter-church evangelistic campaigns, supporting overseas mission societies, responsibilities in synod or presbytery, or involvement in ECF or WF, Keswick and CE. With ex-EU ministers dispersed over the whole country, many of them in remote rural parishes, EMF lacked critical mass in almost every region: it could only function as a movement based on correspondence and occasional newsletters, and thus failed to generate much momentum. EMF members, it appears, may have shared in the general lack of commitment among GF members to systematic scholarly reading, writing articles – or paying subscriptions.[157] It was a matter of both genuine busyness and the characteristically pragmatic orientation of many New Zealanders. EMF office-bearers were themselves too busy to do much.[158] They were often at a loss to know what should or could be done.[159]

Because of the relatively small number of EU graduates in the ministry, the EMF membership was broadened to include non-graduate ordained ministers.[160] In 1946, the EMF had only forty-five members.[161] A third of these were Presbyterian, the Anglicans and Baptists had about ten members each and there was a smattering of Congregationalists and Methodists. In 1950 a strategic IVF document discussed the EMF, which still had only seventy members.[162] It acknowledged that the EMF existed 'largely in form and name only'. Apart from 'practical difficulties' there were basic issues of identity and purpose:

> [I]t may be that an artificial fellowship is being forced and that the natural line of development would be an Evangelical Fellowship in each denomination where active work is accomplished and each denominational fellowship linked together in the EMF.

The report went on to note the formation of the ECF and the WF:[163] the implication was that the EMF should give way to such denominational bodies. From the outset, some Presbyterian ministers had voiced a lack of enthusiasm for the EMF.[164] In his 1946 report, the EMF president had indicated 'there is the real conviction amongst many Evangelical ministers that their real contribution to the Evangelical cause lies within their own denomination', and he agreed that 'an interdenominational movement must take second place'.[165]

By 1956 there were around ninety on the EMF mailing list,[166] but the increase reflected the growth in evangelicalism rather than the vitality of the EMF itself. The majority were Presbyterians, followed by Anglicans then Baptists. The Presbyterian and Anglican members listed largely coincided with those in WF and ECF.

The EMF lingered for some years yet. The newsletter continued to carry brief reports of new books by evangelical scholars, and in 1957 about twenty-five members attended a conference.[167] In the same year Betteridge, the outgoing secretary, felt 'more strongly than ever' that an interdenominational evangelical fellowship of ministers could make a crucial contribution to the New Zealand church, as a 'spearhead of biblical theology'.[168] But the incoming secretary, Maurice Goodall, soon concluded that for most of its members the EMF was 'a good thing', but 'on paper only'.[169] In 1960 a Christian Graduates Fellowship (CGF) committee noted 'the practical cessation of all EMF activity', and recommended that provision for it be deleted from the IVF constitution.[170] The motion amending the constitution explained that closing down EMF was 'largely in favour of more effective avenues of activity by members within their denominational movements'.[171]

The lasting impact of the EMF was obviously limited – some who had had association with it later completely forgot it had ever existed. The EMF was a failure: its specific goal of a widespread interdenominational fellowship of studious evangelical ministers was not realised. But its aim of encouraging evangelical ministers was assumed by the ECF and the WF. Despite the EMF's demise, in the next decade there was a steady increase in the number of conservative evangelicals in the ministry of the main denominations.

IVF Graduates

Overall, the Graduates' Fellowship did not thrive. Most graduates refocused on their work, families and church. Some subscribed to *Inter-Varsity* (NZ) and the *Christian Graduate* (Britain), but in 1950 there were GF study groups only in Auckland and Christchurch.[172] IVF graduate movements had similar struggles in Australia and the United States. Bruce Harris, a university lecturer who was familiar with IVF graduate work in Britain, put considerable energy into strengthening the New Zealand movement.[173] In 1957 the CGF had 734 members, and groups functioning regularly or occasionally in up to seven cities.[174] Nevertheless a British graduate in New Zealand for several years never encountered any CGF members.[175] In the early 1960s, the groups in the four main centres – often largely supported by university staff – met several times a year for study sessions, overseas speakers and conferences.[176] The focus was on fellowship and teaching. Auckland also had a subgroup for medical doctors. By far the strongest CGF subsection in New Zealand was the Teachers' Christian Fellowship, which had enough critical mass to run viable conferences.[177]

In 1965 Harris launched the Tyndale Fellowship – based on the IVF's British and Australian counterparts – with the aim of fostering evangelical scholarship.[178] A draft IVF inventory of likely Tyndale supporters offers a tentative profile of the evangelical theological establishment in New Zealand in 1965, including four members of the Auckland Classics Department, lecturers at BTI and Baptist College, some theological students, twenty-seven Presbyterian ministers (all associated with the WF), fifteen Anglican clergy, four Brethren, and one woman (W.B. Lewis).[179] The first few TF speakers included E.M. Blaiklock and F.F. Bruce.[180]

IVF graduates and theological shifts

Not all those involved in EU as students continued 'evangelical'; many of them later embraced a different theological position and identity. Some moved away from any Christian belief; others adopted a more radical Christian theology. Ex-EU people who made such transitions included Ian Cairns, who had chaired the OUEU committee organising the Guinness mission in 1952 and was later an Old Testament lecturer in Indonesia and a moderator of the PCNZ. One of those listed as 'converted' in the 1952 OUEU mission was George W. Armstrong, later a controversial 'frontier theologian' at St John's Theological College.[181] Laurie Barber, later a Methodist minister and lecturer in religious studies at Waikato University, had been an executive member of Massey Agricultural College EU in 1951–52.[182] James Veitch – who later taught religious studies at Victoria University, was a protégé of Lloyd Geering, and was active in such bodies as the Jesus Seminar and the Sea of Faith – had previously been part of Crusaders, OUEU and TSF. Irvine Roxburgh, who later endorsed a 'secular' Christianity, had been involved in OUEU and in Thomas Miller's parish of St Stephen's.[183] Donald Shaw, who shared the same background of OUEU and St Stephen's, wrote an article vehemently denouncing evangelical attitudes.[184] John Greenslade, who in the 1950s was involved in CUEU and in the 1970s was a leader in the Latimer Society, later repudiated an evangelical outlook.[185]

Some others who had been in EU developed a more complex or nuanced theological identity, within a broader churchmanship, but retained strong evangelical sympathies that owed much to their background in IVF. Examples include Ian Breward (professor of Church history at the Theological Hall, 1965–82),[186] who commented, 'I would not have been in the ministry if it were not for the Evangelical Union in Auckland. I drew my theological and spiritual sustenance from that kind of tradition, and have continued to do so.'[187] He also noted the strong influence of Blaiklock, Harris and Minn, of mentors in the Massey College EU, and of IVF General Secretary Warner Hutchinson.[188] Samuel McCay, a Presbyterian parish minister with a strongly denominational focus, stayed evangelical in doctrine and practice but resisted what he saw as evangelical factionalism and 'negativity'.[189] Simon Rae (Presbyterian minister, missionary, theological educator) retained some evangelical emphases, but also widened his views.[190]

Changes in theological conviction and identity reflected a variety of factors, both personal and contextual. Sometimes it was a reaction to the more rigid or combative aspects of evangelicalism;[191] or those concerned were looking to reposition themselves into a less isolated ecclesiastical identity within their denomination. Pressure from peers could help provoke shifts in theological stance. Those who changed most were influenced in varying degrees by the liberal theology and methodologies that prevailed in theological colleges. Some were influenced by new mentors, or through wider reading. Some became less certain about the distinctives of an evangelical theology and moved into the theological middle ground. Some, on the rebound, swung from a defensively held conservative stance to a defensively held radical one.

IVF and the Ferment of the 1960s

At the start of the 1960s, New Zealand society was still relatively conservative. But the social and intellectual ferments that were affecting youth in the rest of the Western world were beginning to be felt in New Zealand too. Such upheavals, well canvassed elsewhere, included the elevation of individual choice and experience, widespread questioning of authority, nonconformity, the rejection of Christian beliefs and values, the contraceptive pill, television, less censorship, a music culture celebrating free love and the use of drugs, existentialism, and – among liberal churchmen – the advocacy of 'secular theology' and the 'new morality'. It was against that background that IVF and the EUs sought both to maintain the evangelical faith and to make some accommodations to the way it was expressed. New themes began to appear in IVF books and in the topics at EU meetings: freedom, sex and social concern. These trends intensified in the decade after 1965. One expression of the new climate of experientialism was the advent of 'neo-Pentecostalism', the 'tongues-healings-prophecy' movement that began to be discussed in IVF documents from the early 1960s.[192]

'Sane Conservatism'

In the postwar period, the New Zealand EU/IVF movement had come of age. By the late 1950s, it had overtaken the SCM.[193] In the words of Professor Blaiklock, its most eminent sponsor, the movement stood for a 'sane conservatism'.[194] By deliberately 'securing and shaping the faith' of large numbers of future church leaders,[195] the EUs and IVF had also begun to reshape New Zealand Protestantism.

CHAPTER EIGHT

Anglican Evangelicalism Expands, 1956–65

Evangelicalism is Anglicanism, and Anglicanism is Evangelicalism.[1]

Growth in Christchurch

In the late 1950s, the flagship of evangelical Anglican ministry in the Christchurch Diocese was still that of Roger Thompson at St Martin's, with energetic expository preaching and lots of young people attending. Harry Thomson, likewise, had a vigorous but more localised evangelical ministry at St John's Woolston. But both of these notable ministries came to an end in 1961. Somewhat surprisingly, Thompson moved to a country parish in the Nelson Diocese. Less surprisingly, Harry Thomson resigned from parish ministry so as to concentrate on his principal passion, the CMS.[2] Nevertheless, in the late 1950s there was a marked expansion in the number of other evangelical Anglican ministries in Christchurch.

One of the new evangelical ministers, in the new suburb of Bryndwr, was Les Morris at St Aidan's (1957–61). Morris, from a Brethren and Methodist background, had been strongly influenced by Orange and Thompson.[3] He was an uncomplicated conservative and a passionate and gifted evangelistic speaker.[4] Some of his evangelical colleagues wondered 'how much he was really an Anglican'.[5] He energetically built up the new parish, and later succeeded Thomson at Woolston.

Maurice Goodall at Shirley

In the late 1950s, St Stephen's in Shirley joined those Christchurch Anglican parishes that were becoming definitely evangelical in identity and ethos. The main catalyst was the vicar, Maurice Goodall (1959–67). Goodall, an

Orange Pip, had been a president of CUCEU and was openly evangelical. The parish had already been heading in an evangelical direction under Goodall's predecessor, Geoffrey Schurr (1953–59), who was assisted by a Church Army officer, J.T. Withers. The parish had an evangelical group of about forty young people with links to the CMS League of Youth, some of whom (including Bob Barrett and Phil Thomas) later became ministers.[6] Under Goodall, a younger man with a definite evangelical identity, there was an intensified emphasis on prayer and a new weekly 'Bible Study and Prayer Meeting'.[7] The preaching became verse-by-verse exposition.[8] The focus of the evening service was on youth, and it became a 'magnet' for many.[9] The parish magazine became more evangelistic, demonstrating a preoccupation with topics such as the Cross, scripture, personal faith and missionary visitors; there was considerably less material about buildings and social events.[10] Schurr had promoted the annual fundraising Dolls' Show,[11] but there was no sign of such schemes in the Goodall era. Whereas Schurr had worked with the Wells Organisation to raise parish income,[12] Goodall instituted a Stewardship Programme that emphasised direct giving and Christian commitment in general.

Goodall was an outstanding organiser and developed busy programmes for every age group.[13] As always, a ministry like this depended on lay people, such as BC leader Ross Elliott. Goodall's ministry was also strengthened by evangelical influences beyond the parish: his young people were very active in the League of Youth, in Crusaders and EU, and in summer camps led by Thompson and the Spreydon parish. Goodall maintained strong friendships with other evangelical clergy, including Pfankuch, Marriott, Morris, Lamont and Thompson.[14] The Christchurch evangelical clergy were a tight network, leading a growing cluster of like-minded parishes: in 1965, for instance, visiting speakers to the Shirley parish included Harry Thomson, Roger Thompson, Lester Pfankuch, Robert Glen, Elizabeth Purchas, Max Wiggins and John Hewlett.

In the mid 1960s Goodall arranged a parish mission at Shirley, with nightly meetings and many submeetings. The missioner was Lance Sheldon, rector of Holy Trinity (Adelaide). Goodall recalled having a 'huge' argument with Bishop Alwyn Warren, who objected to the parish bringing in an evangelical from overseas rather than using a local man such as Martin Sullivan: 'You just want someone of your own outlook, don't you?'[15] The bishop was no doubt right about that: the fact was, evangelicals rarely trusted non-evangelicals to do evangelism, especially in their own territory; only card-carrying evangelicals could be trusted to present the whole Gospel, with sufficient 'soundness', conviction and urgency. The mission went ahead and there were numerous conversions.

Under Goodall's leadership it seemed, to those who were part of it, that the Shirley parish 'grew dramatically'.[16] The statistical returns are more nuanced. Between 1960 and 1965, the average Sunday school attendance in the Shirley parish increased from 370 to 539. In 1960 the BC roll increased from 100 to 141, and then remained much the same. In 1960 there were fifty-eight confirmations.[17] The parish was already large when Goodall came. The impression of spectacular growth may also reflect the very strong sense of spiritual commitment and evangelical activism among the young people. Another encouragement was that the parish was beginning to export young adults to other ministries:[18] from Goodall onwards, an overt evangelical succession was established in the Shirley parish, in a similar way to what had become established in Spreydon, Woolston and Bryndwr.[19]

Graham Lamont at Spreydon

The Spreydon–Hoon Hay ministry vacated by Roger Thompson was taken up in 1962 by Graham Lamont, one of those who had moved there from St James' (Lower Riccarton) in the late 1940s. Lamont had been heavily involved in Crusaders and EU. Ordained in 1954, he had served in four other parishes. Lamont openly identified himself as evangelical, and was very conscious of continuing the evangelical tradition begun by Thompson.[20] For Lamont, being an evangelical minister meant preaching from the Bible and seeing people converted.[21] In presenting the intellectual bases of Christian belief, Lamont reflected the evangelical rationalism and evidentialism that was common in this period, especially among those of IVF background:

> *We were concerned to stress the fact that the Christian faith is based on objective historical events (e.g. the resurrection) ... Personal subjective experiences (e.g. testimonies) are important but at most they can be confirmations of objective truths about Christ and salvation ... we were concerned to try and ensure that appeals for commitment were made on the basis of a presentation of the gospel that was intellectually 'honest' and not simply emotional.*[22]

Lamont did not have quite the same popular appeal as his predecessor, but the parish continued to grow. In 1965 the average Sunday school attendance was 520.[23] Lamont maintained the Sunday afternoon Bible Class, with 80–100 young people coming from many parts of the city. As with Thompson, Lamont was conscious of his dependence on lay people and assistants.[24] There were also some differences between Lamont and his predecessor. Lamont was willing to be called a 'conservative evangelical', but 'disliked intensely' being labelled 'fundamentalist'[25] – whereas Thompson would not have cared.[26] Thompson believed in a literal six-day creation[27] – whereas Lamont interpreted the days in Genesis 1 as long periods of time.[28] As a firm evangelical, Lamont saw many doctrines as 'non-negotiable'; but he tried to be less dogmatic on secondary issues, such as church union,[29] and, like some others in his generation, he was less convinced about some of the evangelical subcultural moral taboos such as dances and films.[30]

Lamont did expositional series but also preached according to the lectionary, and sometimes gave topical series on themes such as 'Love and Marriage' or 'Sickness and Death'. He ran an informal Saturday night outreach to young people which was pre-evangelistic rather than directly proselytising.[31] At one such event he led a discussion about sexual morality after screening a slightly risqué secular film. Such innovations in content and method reflected growing evangelical concern about the social ferment unsettling the Western world in the 1960s, a climate of questioning and radicalism which was also beginning to affect New Zealand.[32] In an era of rock 'n' roll, the Beatles, student protests, increasing promiscuity, the 'death of God' theology and 'the new morality',[33] some issues were being discussed much more directly and urgently by evangelicals than twenty years earlier.

Intellectually, Lamont had been shaped primarily not by Thompson but by the EU and his own university and theological studies. Lamont reflected a new attitude among some Anglican evangelicals, who were consciously trying to help develop an Anglican evangelicalism that was ecclesiastically more open, and more intellectually engaged with non-evangelicals. Well read and confident, he was willing to become actively involved in debates in the diocesan and General Synods.[34]

Other Christchurch evangelical ministers

In this period a number of evangelical ministers were serving elsewhere in the diocese, often outside the Christchurch urban area. From 1955, Maurice Betteridge was at Lincoln and lecturing at College House, and R.E. (Ted) Coulthard became vicar at Otaio–Bluecliffs and later at Lincoln. Unlike most of the newer Christchurch evangelical ministers Coulthard was from Auckland, a product of Crusaders and the EU, and a protégé not of Orange but of Blaiklock.[35] From 1956, Brian Carrell did two curacies then became vicar of Hororata. In 1957, Harvey Teulon became the vicar of Highfield (Timaru). The same year, Dick Tripp became a curate and was later vicar of Bryndwr and Methven. In 1960, Colin Tonks was ordained. A 1959 register of ECF members in the Christchurch Diocese listed a total of fourteen clergy: Orange, Thompson,

Thomson, Teulon, Coulthard, Goodall, Betteridge, Lamont, Morris, Funnell, Wisdom, J.J. Flewellen (Avonside), A.E. Rolleston (Hororata) and B.W. Don (Methven).[36] The list did not include all known evangelicals (it did not, for instance, include Carrell or Tripp), but it indicated something of the growing strength of evangelical Anglicanism in the Diocese. Relative to the total number of clergy in the Christchurch Diocese, this was still a small minority. But it was an expanding minority.

In addition, the diocese had several more evangelical clergy serving overseas as missionaries, including John Meadowcroft, Peter Tovey, Max Wiggins, Wallace Marriott, R.A. Carson, Gerald Clark, John Greenslade, Lester Pfankuch and Hugh Thomson. Some of these would soon return to parish ministry in the Christchurch Diocese, including Pfankuch,[37] Thomson,[38] Carson[39] and Greenslade.[40] Returning missionaries like these increased the number of Orange Pips – and protégés of Orange Pips – who were now fanning out across the Christchurch parishes. Although they were all part of the same movement, they were not a completely homogeneous group: Carson, for instance, was more scholarly and less polemical than some more populist evangelicals.[41]

An Anglican 'Bible Belt'

By the mid 1960s, there were a considerable number of Christchurch parishes of a definite evangelical stamp – notably St Martin's (Spreydon), St John's (Woolston), St Stephen's (Shirley) and St Aidan's (Bryndwr). That group of parishes constituted what was sometimes referred to among evangelical ministers themselves as an Anglican evangelical 'Bible Belt'.[42] They would soon be joined by St Timothy's (Burnside) and St John's (Latimer Square). Several more parishes were less consistently or less emphatically evangelical but nevertheless had a number of evangelical ministers: these included Belfast–Styx, Avonhead and Cashmere.[43] Together, all these parishes represented about a third of the urban or suburban Christchurch parishes. Several rural or non-Christchurch parishes were also developing a tradition – not always continuous – of having vicars or curates of an evangelical stamp: these included Waikari, Lincoln, Hororata, Methven and Highfield. In 1961 Morris replaced Thomson as the vicar at Woolston, thus consolidating the evangelical character of that parish. In Bryndwr, Morris was replaced by Carson; and in Woolston, by Pfankuch. It was clear that evangelical parishes were now insisting on an evangelical minister to replace those who moved on, and that the expanding muster of evangelical clergy within the diocese was being moved around within a growing circuit of evangelical parishes.

A pattern of evangelical succession like this depended on the parishes having become strong enough to have full 'parish' status (with the right to elect nominators), rather than just 'parochial district' status (where the appointment rested with the bishop). The growth of a cluster of consciously 'evangelical' parishes in the Christchurch Diocese, and the proliferation of evangelical ministries in many other parishes besides, had been gradual rather than sudden; but it was nevertheless a momentous development. It represented a situation very different from that prevailing in 1930 when Orange had begun his rather lonely evangelical ministry at Sumner.

Evangelical parishes and the Billy Graham Crusade

There can be no question that the 1959 Billy Graham Crusade made an important contribution to Anglican evangelical growth in Christchurch, especially in those parishes with evangelical ministers. The Spreydon–Hoon Hay parish, for instance, estimated that it gained fifty new members from the Crusade.[44] A follow-up mid-week 'Christian Training Course' led by Funnell attracted up to 100 people.[45] The Shirley parish, which received seventy cards giving the details of those who had made 'decisions', welcomed many respondents into church and especially into the Bible Class.[46] In another parish where the vicar 'totally opposed' the Crusade, many Anglican enquirers were nevertheless referred. An evangelical curate gathered them into an adult confirmation class – which was an unusual thing in itself – of thirty to forty people. These included his own father, who was of Irish Catholic background.[47] The Crusade also had an effect in some country parishes, at least those with evangelical ministers. In Waikari there were some who made a decision at the Crusade but they tended to be people already associated with the parish. There was no great infusion of new people but rather a spiritual 'quickening' of the congregation.[48] In Kumara on the West Coast, the minister encouraged people to attend. Some did, and some leading lay people were 'brought to conscious commitment'.[49]

The Billy Graham Crusade was clearly a decisive event for many individuals. A survey of parish statistics held by the Christchurch Diocese, however, does not reveal any pronounced upswing in congregational numbers, Bible Class membership or confirmation figures in evangelically-minded parishes in 1959–60. It appears that the Crusade made a conspicuous contribution to the growth of evangelical parishes, but that it was only one of several factors encouraging growth. The Crusade coincided with a period when evangelical parishes (and many other Anglican parishes) were already experiencing definite growth. That growth was reinforced by the Crusade, but was also explicable quite apart from the Crusade: the sustained work of the evangelical ministers, Bible Classes and League of Youth was probably more important.

Nevertheless, the Billy Graham Crusade (and reports of similar crusades in Britain and the US) appears to have had a definite effect on evangelical morale: the 1959 Crusade very publicly displayed and authenticated a conservative evangelical approach to matters of faith. It demonstrated – at least to evangelicals – that old-fashioned biblicism and straight-talking appeals for decision still had currency in the public domain, that evangelicals were innovative and energetic, and that evangelical initiatives could give a lead even to an ecumenical body such as the National Council of Churches.

CMS League of Youth in Christchurch, 1956–65

In this period, the CMS League of Youth was in its heyday in the Diocese of Christchurch. Its monthly Saturday night meetings, with frequent challenges to deep commitment, attracted up to 150 young people. The speakers were missionaries on furlough, or local evangelical clergy.[50] Apart from its primary overseas mission focus, the League of Youth also had a vigorous emphasis on local and city-wide evangelism. One of those converted through an evangelistic barbecue held by the League was Bob Robinson, a young 'agnostic' who had gained a scholarship to attend Christ's College and was therefore required to attend church.[51] The speaker was Les Morris. To Robinson it seemed as if it was the first time he had ever heard the gospel, and he was greatly stirred. The next morning, sitting in church, he had a conversion experience. He later became a CMS missionary and NZCMS general secretary, and an evangelical theologian and lecturer.[52]

The League of Youth drew youth from the principal evangelical parishes of Shirley, Spreydon, Woolston and Bryndwr, who then came to know one other. The League therefore played a role in unifying the youth of the Christchurch Anglican evangelical movement and in giving them a common sense of evangelical identity.[53] The League also had a wider influence: it drew in some young people from parishes where the minister himself did not identify with the evangelical networks, but where the young people did. As with other evangelical youth organisations such as Crusaders, and especially the EUs, the League of Youth was led by youth themselves, and was an important training ground for emerging leaders. League of Youth leaders in this period included David Powell, Derek Eaton,[54] Phil Thomas,[55] Tony Andrews[56] and Dale Oldham.[57] The League of Youth also encouraged its members to attend the CMS Spring Schools, where evangelical youth were drawn into the general community of Anglican evangelicals.[58]

Anglican Evangelical Growth in Nelson, 1956–65

In this period, evangelicalism became more vigorous and overt within the Nelson Diocese – and more homegrown. The influence of Sydney evangelical Anglicanism was maintained, but the influence of the Christchurch evangelical Anglican movement grew, and the proportion of definitely evangelical clergy in Nelson increased.

The new bishop, Frank Hulme-Moir (1954–65), continued the episcopal succession in Nelson of Sydney evangelicals who had trained at Moore College. His election had been strongly promoted by fellow Australian Paul Kirkham, vicar of Blenheim.[59] Hulme-Moir, a large, cheerful man with a powerful voice and charismatic personality, was a popular bishop. With his experience as an army chaplain, his 'manly faith' and his large fund of stories, he related very well to 'the common man' and was the sort of speaker who could establish rapport with a crowd of workers in a meat-processing plant.[60] He was a very effective missioner. His strengths were pastoral and practical rather than theological.[61] He had definite evangelical convictions, and in his correspondence he was explicit about his evangelical stance and agenda.[62] On arrival in New Zealand, he immediately assumed the chairmanship of the New Zealand CMS. He also warmly supported the China Inland Mission, and endorsed two of his younger clergy who joined the CIM for missionary service in Southeast Asia.[63] He quickly established links with the EUs and IVF(NZ), and became a frequent speaker at their events.[64] Every year he hosted an interdenominational spiritual life convention.[65]

Hulme-Moir's wife Dorothy was a very effective Bible teacher.[66] She ran a weekly lunchtime Bible Class at Bishopdale that was sometimes compared to that of Orange in Christchurch, and had a powerful influence on many laity and young people in Nelson city and environs (whereas her husband's work, and his impact, was diffused over the whole diocese).[67] She often wrote Bible Studies for *The Witness*, the diocesan newpaper,[68] and was a prominent supporter of evangelical missionary work, EU and IVF. Mrs Hulme-Moir was not universally popular, however, and some struggled with her personal directness and her adamant views on such matters as teetotalism and dancing.

Hulme-Moir actively recruited evangelical clergy for his diocese. In 1956, he succeeded in enticing his friend W.F. Bretton across Cook Strait. Bretton had been the dynamic evangelical vicar of Lower Hutt. He became Dean of

Nelson, thus strengthening the senior evangelical leadership in Nelson. Bretton was a frequent parish missioner, and closely mentored a tight coterie of curates, including David Pickering and Malcolm Oatway. Hulme-Moir also brought into the diocese a number of clergy from the Diocese of Sydney, including Kelvin Tutt, a fervent evangelical.[69] He also recruited John Hewlett, a Moore-trained Aucklander who served as curate at Nelson's All Saints' (1955-58), and who showed great energy with young people and evangelism. Hewlett received strong personal encouragement from Hulme-Moir.[70] As a zealous young evangelical, Hewlett felt that the Nelson Diocese was not quite as evangelical as reputed – that it was more just Low Church and traditional Anglican.[71] The All Saints' youth became very involved in the League of Youth, and in evangelism at camps and in other parishes. Hewlett sensed 'a minor revival'.[72]

Meanwhile strong youth work was being done in other parishes, such as in Stoke (under Tutt), Richmond (under Machell) and Blenheim (under Kirkham). Together with All Saints', these parishes represented a fresh wave of energy in the Nelson Diocese.[73] At the heart of that was a group of evangelical ministers who were determined to preach the Gospel and to develop strong youth work. Such fervour and activism were characteristic of the evangelical movement. As elsewhere, the leaders of the evangelical Nelson youth refused to countenance the popular demand for dances, but instead ran Saturday night Bible Studies.[74]

The flourishing of evangelical youth work in this era partly reflected the vigour and conviction of its leadership, but it also reflected the height of the postwar babyboom and the consequent effects on church life across New Zealand. This was a period when church pews were often full and Sunday schools were overflowing; when many people in New Zealand communities acknowledged at least nominal Christian faith and were still willing to support the church financially – and sometimes attend.

A survey of the clergy roll for Nelson Diocese in 1963 indicates that of the thirty-four clergy listed, ten were graduates of Moore College; nine of those were evangelical.[75] A smaller proportion (four) were from England, all of them evangelical.[76] The remainder (twenty-three) were New Zealanders. Of those, sixteen were definite evangelicals, and the other five tended towards a midde-of-the-road or 'liberal evangelical' outlook – though some of them nevertheless attended ECF conferences.[77]

Overall, the proportion of evangelical clergy in the diocese had risen (twenty-eight of the thirty-four), because by 1963 a higher proportion of the diocese's clergy from New Zealand were evangelical. Some of the evangelical

New Zealanders came from evangelical parishes within the Nelson Diocese (such as Noel Bythell and George Spargo from Blenheim, and Barry Loveridge from All Saints' Nelson). Six of them were Orange Pips: Donald Williams, Bernard Machell, Bob Nicholson, Bruce Beattie, Bob Hughes and Roger Thompson. At least three – David Pickering, Dennis Barrett and Malcolm Oatway – came from Wellington, through Bretton. Several others, such as Ian Nelson and Bernard Cox, had come through Thompson's Bible Class at St Martin's Spreydon; some others had done so while studying in Christchurch.

When the make-up of Nelson clergy from 1963 is compared with that in 1950, it becomes apparent that Nelson Diocese was gradually becoming less of an outpost of the Diocese of Sydney, and more obviously a gathering place for New Zealand evangelical Anglican clergy. The reason was not a weakening of the Sydney connection, but rather the steady growth of evangelical Anglicanism within New Zealand. That homegrown Anglican evangelicalism had developed primarily in Christchurch, but had also grown stronger in the Nelson Diocese itself. Nelson evangelicalism had been nurtured by the conferences, publications and personal networking of ECF and CMS. In the 1960s, Nelson evangelicals were less isolated and felt increasingly part of a buoyant, expansionist evangelical movement that now spanned two dioceses.

With its Low Church style of worship and its majority of evangelical or evangelical-leaning clergy, Nelson was unique among New Zealand dioceses. The evangelical ethos of the diocese was reflected in the diocesan newspaper, *The Witness*: its pages gave the impression that, with no contrary opinion in the diocese against which an evangelical approach needed defending, Nelson's evangelicalism was generally assumed rather than advocated, and implicit rather than explicit. *The Witness* promoted an everyday style of Christianity that was practical, moralistic and mildly biblicist. While the word 'evangelical' rarely appeared in *The Witness*, there were innumerable signs of evangelical piety and outlook, such as the regular features on prayer, the frequent apologetic and devotional articles, the tone of the monthly Bishop's Letter, and numerous enthusiastic reports of great responses to the evangelistic appeals given at Easter Camps.[78] *The Witness* contained no trace of anything High Church or theologically liberal, and in this period there was just one report on an NCC conference.[79] There were warm commendations of IVF, and of the interdenominational Keswick-style convention at Renwick which featured talks on revival and missionary speakers from 'faith' mission societies.[80] There were extensive, glowing reports on the Billy Graham Crusade (which was relayed to Nelson and other provincial areas by 'landline').[81]

A succession crisis

Given the increasing vitality of evangelicalism in the Nelson Diocese, evangelicals were confident another evangelical would be elected as bishop after Hulme-Moir returned to Sydney in 1965. The electoral synod met twice, late in 1964. Bretton had hopes, but limited support.[82] An Orange Pip who had been in Australia for over twenty years was nominated by Kirkham, an Australian. Evangelical clergy were dismayed when there was firm and coordinated lay resistance to the prospect of another bishop from Sydney. The opposition, articulate and persuasive, was centred on the Cathedral, which was characteristically less Low Church and evangelical than the diocese as a whole. It included some people who had come from other parts of New Zealand, and argued that it was time for Nelson to drop its unique Sydney connection and to become more like all the other New Zealand dioceses.[83] Evangelical laity did not agree, but were less prominent in the electoral synod than some of other sympathies. The opposition to the 'Australian' nominee was not explicitly theological, but was perhaps implicitly so. There may have been an underlying reaction to the conservatism of the Sydney clergy, and the outspoken views of at least one bishop's wife on such matters as alcohol and dancing.[84] More than one evangelical minister felt that the opposition was 'anti-evangelical'.[85]

At a second meeting of the electoral synod, the anti-Australian bloc backed another nominee, but evangelical clergy as a whole did not support him.[86] Unable to reach a decision, the synod ceded its power to nominate the next bishop to its 'Commissary' (Bishop A.H. Johnston of Dunedin), who nominated his own dean, P.E. Sutton. Evangelical clergy in Nelson were 'dejected' that their new bishop was a High Churchman.[87] However, Sutton was doctrinally conservative, and fair-minded. While the Low Church and evangelical character of the diocese was diluted during the time of Sutton's episcopate, mainly through his choices of new clergy, it would endure.

Anglican Evangelical Growth in Wellington, 1956–65

When Bretton left the Wellington Diocese in 1956, the new senior evangelical in the diocese was Charles Haskell, a former CMS missionary in Karachi.[88] Originally from All Saints' in Nelson, Haskell was staunchly evangelical.[89] He came to Wellington to serve as general secretary of the Anglican Board of Missions, and from 1964 as vicar of Naenae. The number of evangelical ministers in the Wellington Diocese was growing. An ECF membership list for 1958 lists eight such clergy, widely scattered. While R.J. Taylor and I.G. Bourne were serving in rural parishes across the Rimutaka Ranges,[90] two younger evangelical clergy had become ministers in expanding new suburbs, giving them an opportunity to grow sizable churches of an evangelical flavour: Edmiston at Tawa–Linden (1958–67) and Somerville at Naenae (1959–63).

At Tawa, Edmiston's parish had a Sunday school of 500 (and forty teachers) and a BC of over 100.[91] Edmiston preached expositionally, and often invited people to pray prayers of commitment.[92] Like many of his evangelical colleagues, he was heavily involved with youth, and frequently went on camps with them. Within the parish, he did not explicitly parade his evangelical identity: 'I got on with the job ... I was a biblical Christian, I was an evangelical, but I never wrote it all over the wall.'[93] Such a reserve about theological labels was common, and pragmatic. It saved complicating the message or creating unnecessary barriers. Evangelicals were often happy to let congregations assume that a biblicist and evangelistic Christianity was simply normative Christianity. In the late 1950s and early 60s, evangelical ministry was being conspicuously modelled in the preaching and films of Billy Graham, and seemed to be vindicated by the apparent flourishing of evangelical-style parishes.

Edmiston and the other Wellington evangelicals appeared to avoid some of the moral and ecclesiastical taboos held by their older counterparts in the Christchurch and Nelson contexts: Edmiston happily used the fundraising Wells Organisation and enjoyed coordinating an annual fair.[94] Beyond the parish, he generally avoided diocesan roles: he wanted to concentrate on the parish. At synod meetings, he often slipped out for a walk.[95] But he was prepared to be a member of the diocese's Youth and Missionary committees, two areas characteristically of great interest to evangelicals. He was also willing to become chair of the Wellington branch of CMS,[96] and to join the executive of the 1959 Billy Graham Crusade (on which he was in charge of 'follow-up' for the Wellington meetings).[97] The Crusade had a 'huge influence' on Tawa parish: twenty-four parishioners trained as counsellors, there were fifty referrals, and Edmiston felt he took courage in both pulpit and personal evangelism.[98]

For Anglican evangelicals in the Wellington Diocese, fellowship with other evangelicals was extremely important. These included lay Anglicans such as Kevin O'Sullivan in Palmerston North, and Kaye Johnston and Ken McKay in Wellington.[99] The first ECF meeting in Wellington was initiated by Roger Thompson asking Edmiston to host a small gathering of evangelicals in the Tawa vicarage.[100] The meeting was not to be public. Even so, Edmiston felt it necessary to seek the permission of the bishop, who lectured him on the 'middle-of-the-road' approach of the diocese – and then gave permission. Thompson and Edmiston's caution illustrates the extent to which many evangelical Anglicans in New Zealand still felt themselves irregular and illicit, and obliged to creep around the margins of most dioceses. It was not uncommon among evangelicals to feel that their ministry emphasis was well received by many lay people, but regarded with suspicion by ecclesiastical colleagues and authorities.[101]

Edmiston and Somerville helped establish a CMS Spring School in the North Island.[102] The first school, in Wellington in 1960, attracted up to 250 people at evening sessions.[103] The CMS was widely respected, and was an unthreatening path into evangelical Anglicanism. At the Spring Schools and ECF Conferences the isolated evangelicals of the Wellington Diocese met others, heard the teaching of the likes of Harry Thomson and Roger Thompson, and were consolidated in an evangelical identity.

An Evangelical Anglican Toehold in Dunedin

For at least half a century, the Diocese of Dunedin had been known for its High Church tendencies. St Matthew's, on the south side of the city centre, had been markedly Anglo-Catholic under the ministry of Archdeacon W. Curson-Siggers (1896–1922).[104] Archdeacon W.A. Hamblett (1922–52) followed, with a ministry which was Low Church, and supportive of missionary work, the Bible Society, the EU and later the ECF. Urban depopulation, however, had led to serious decline, and in the 1950s closure of the parish was being considered. After Hamblett's retirement attendance dwindled to about ten.[105] Meanwhile parish nominators 'fought for three and a half years' with Bishop Johnston to get an evangelical vicar.[106] The eventual result was the appointment of Rev. Kenneth Gregory (1955–59). A former British army officer, Gregory was an evangelical firebrand. In Nelson, he had been diocesan evangelist. His peremptory, no-nonsense approach began to turn St Matthew's around.

When Gregory left for Karachi, he was succeeded by an Orange Pip, Maurice Betteridge (1959–65). Betteridge had a strong preaching and teaching ministry. When he arrived at St Matthew's, the Sunday morning attendance was about forty. By the time he left, it was 200–300.[107] A young student arriving at St Matthew's from a small country church found the 'zeal and passion' of the congregation almost 'overwhelming'.[108] Like many other Orange Pips, Betteridge consciously emulated his mentor:

> *I preached four times a Sunday, two morning services, afternoon Bible study, and an evening sermon. You see, I replicated Pekoe. The strength of it was simply an expository preaching ministry.[109]*

At 5 pm every Sunday there was the Bible Class, a solid Bible exposition for one hour.¹¹⁰ Then there would be tea, followed by a prayer meeting and the evening service. The evening service would be mainly of university students, but also often included people invited from off the streets. After church, some sixty or so would go to the vicarage for supper and a 'sing-song'. All this was a familiar pattern, derived from Orange and implemented by numerous Orange Pips. The details varied, but the underlying aims and strategies were always the same.

As the sole evangelical Anglican church in Dunedin, St Matthew's drew people from all over the city. Vicars of the parishes that such people came from were often less than impressed.¹¹¹ The Bible Class and evening service also drew many non-Anglicans, such as Graham Stanton, a Presbyterian who was later professor of New Testament at King's College, London.¹¹²

In 1965 Betteridge left for Australia, where he eventually became principal of Ridley College. But the evangelical succession in St Matthew's was firmly established, and his next three successors would be Brian Carrell, Wallace Marriott and John Meadowcroft.¹¹³ St Matthew's transformation into an evangelical stronghold was a strategic development. As a church with a strong ministry among students, in an important university city, St Matthew's had a disproportionate influence on New Zealand Anglicanism. Over the years it preserved and bolstered the evangelical identity and fervour of a large number of young Anglicans who were studying in Dunedin.¹¹⁴

Anglican Evangelicals in Auckland, 1956–65

An overt Anglican evangelicalism was slow to get established in Auckland parishes, in part because of the staunchly High Church tendency of Bishop Simkin (1940–60), who resolutely opposed anything he considered un-Anglican, including the CMS and evangelicalism. The effect of his episcopate was to discourage evangelical clergy from entering the diocese. As a result, there was no minister in Auckland who might have developed a strong evangelical parish, and Anglican evangelicalism in Auckland remained a self-consciously clandestine movement with a barely visible presence. Evangelicals often felt isolated, cold-shouldered by their vicars or by the bishop.¹¹⁵

From the 1940s through to the 1960s, a group of about ten evangelical Anglicans in Auckland had often gathered in an informal Bible Study and prayer fellowship at the home of retired vicar Llewellyn Foulkes, and later at Stan Rosser's, a school teacher and former Church Army officer.¹¹⁶ Most members were lay people, drawn from parishes across Auckland.¹¹⁷ Many of the younger attenders had made Christian commitments through the influence of Crusaders or EU.[118] In imitation of secret wartime resistance movements, they nicknamed their group 'The Underground'. From time to time they received visitors from Christchurch, or CMS missionaries, or Sydney people such as Loane or Hammond in town for an IVF conference. The Auckland 'Underground' saw itself as an informal branch of the ECF.[119]

In 1955, Rev. R.T. Everill, a former TCF worker, became vicar of Papakura, south of Auckland, and was there until 1963. In 1958 he was the sole clerical member of the ECF in the Auckland Diocese. In 1961 Rev. Leo King, who was broadly evangelical, became vicar of St Andrew's Epsom and served there until 1965. More significantly, in 1963 Rev. Guy Nicholson became vicar of Ellerslie–Mt Wellington.

Nicholson's conversion in 1946 had been spiritually intense. Before his conversion, he had attended Orange's Bible Class while studying in Christchurch. In Wellington, he had been mentored by Colin Becroft and ran the Crusaders at Wellington College. From that time on, Nicholson had called himself 'evangelical' – by which he meant an emphasis on the new birth and the Cross. A respondent at one Crusader meeting was Edgar Hornblow (later a leading Methodist evangelical); but another boy, Paul Reeves (later archbishop and governor-general), attended once only. Although Nicholson was deeply moved when he saw believer's baptism within the Baptist church, he had stayed Anglican, influenced by Orange's reported assertion that the Anglican Church was 'a very good fishing ground'. After a year in the Nelson Diocese as a stipendiary lay reader in Greymouth, Nicholson went to England for theological training at Oak Hill (London), became a curate under an evangelical vicar, attended Keswick, and had been very impressed by Billy Graham's preaching when he heard him in London at the 1954 Harringay Crusade.[120]

When Bishop Simkin retired in 1960, he was succeeded by E.A. Gowing, who was more open to evangelicals.[121] The way opened for Nicholson to fufil his hope of serving in an Auckland parish. Through members of the 'Underground', a nominator for Ellerslie parish became aware of Nicholson. The parish had been High Church. It may have helped that the nominator had gone forward in the 1959 Billy Graham Crusade. In Ellerslie, Nicholson was cautious, but concentrated on preaching the Gospel, and a number of people were converted.[122] His preaching was 'crisp' but 'stirring'.[123] Nicholson's parish became known among Anglican evangelicals as a safe haven. Some evangelical students at St John's College started attending, as did evangelical young people from elsewhere.[124] Nicholson worked with Open Air Campaigners and Lay Institute for Evangelism, and spoke at AUEU, Crusaders, BTI and the Rotorua

Keswick Convention. But he would never speak at the diocesan synod, which he intensely disliked, and believed himself the only ordained evangelical Anglican in the diocese.[125] He was only 'dimly aware' of the ECF.

Nicholson's ministry in Auckland represented a quiet but noteworthy extension of New Zealand evangelical Anglicanism. He would be followed in Ellerslie by other definite evangelicals;[126] but evangelicalism had not yet taken hold in any larger parish in the Auckland Diocese, or in any parish with a strong ministry among university students. In the upper North Island, evangelical Anglicanism remained a weak presence for some time to come.[127] That situation would only change when charismatic renewal became a catalyst for a different type of evangelical growth.

The Evangelical Churchmen's Fellowship, 1956–65

Lacking staff, funds or facilities, the Evangelical Churchmen's Fellowship was for some years little more than just a fellowship of like-minded people. By 1959, however, it was buoyed by increased membership (331), by the Billy Graham Crusade, and by plans to start an ECF periodical.[128] The conference theme of the 1959 Dominion Conference, held at Tyndale House, was 'Our Glorious Heritage': the ECF was not wishing to promote something new, but to reinforce and revive something old. Almost all the addresses were on some aspect of scriptural authority, demonstrating the characteristic evangelical conviction that the scriptures gave a foundation and template for every aspect of the church's life. Hulme-Moir, Orange and Bretton all gave talks on scriptural authority, and Betteridge spoke on 'Reform through the Word'.[129] Other speakers related scripture to worship (Somerville), to ministry (Edmiston), to sacraments (Glen), to 'sound doctrine' (Lamont), and to revival (Gregory). Haskell spoke on ministry recruitment. The array of speakers from four dioceses (Christchurch, Nelson, Wellington and Dunedin) perhaps reflected an aim to draw in scattered evangelicals and to emphasise the nationwide potential of Anglican evangelicalism. The line-up included no laymen or women. The format of the printed programme card was almost identical to that of IVF conference brochures, and would have seemed familiar to many of those attending.

The ECF did not institute a formal monthly committee meeting until 1961,[130] when Graham Lamont was elected to the new office of clerical secretary, to address enquiries in the areas of doctrine, practice and liturgy, and to relate to theological students and libraries. The meeting was not particularly confident about the ECF's effectiveness; two members of the committee bemoaned widespread ignorance in the church about both the ECF and 'evangelical principles'. Two meetings later, a member of the committee questioned why the ECF even existed.[131] One of its leaders wrote a letter noting how many Anglican authorities frowned on any group perceived as fostering an ecclesiastical 'party'.[132] The ECF, he wrote, must maintain its freedom to associate (for study and fellowship), but must also be careful not to be seen competing with official Anglican programmes and events. In addition, members of ECF must take the fullest possible part in the affairs and councils of the wider church. In these few sentences, he had captured the tension faced by any evangelical subgroup: to guard its life, it must be distinct; but to have influence, its members must also engage with the wider church. The ECF's younger leaders would be increasingly concerned to do the latter.

The E.C.F. Review

In the spring of 1959, the ECF began publishing a quarterly journal, the *E.C.F. Review*.[133] The editor was Roger Thompson, whose editorials and articles outlined the evangelical position with clarity and firmness. People often seek a definition of the word 'evangelical', he wrote, and he was happy to give one: 'An evangelical is one who holds devotedly and loyally to the great basic doctrines of orthodox Christianity, together with that particular emphasis which is accorded those doctrines in the pages of the New Testament.'[134] His two principal categories of evangelicalism were thus doctrinal orthodoxy and the New Testament Gospel. Thompson also endorsed Simeon's insistence that evangelicals give primary focus to 'Christ, and Him crucified'. He listed doctrines held and emphasised by evangelicals: the authority of scripture (taking precedence over tradition and reason), substitutionary atonement, justification by faith, assurance of salvation, the priesthood of all believers,[135] and the 'right of private judgement'.[136]

One of the main aims of the *Review* was to educate and assure evangelical Anglicans that – as both evangelicals and Anglicans – they were not 'strangers in a strange land', but could hold their heads high. They were loyal and true Anglicans, rather than troublemakers, sectarians or eccentrics. The ECF existed, Thompson claimed, 'for the preservation and extension of the traditional orthodoxy of our beloved Church of England, to which we as Evangelicals most happily subscribe'.[137] Thompson quoted Hammond's claim that 'an Evangelical is a true son of the Church of England, and abides loyally by Scripture, the Articles and the Book of Common Prayer' – thus implying that evangelicals were the most authentic, faithful Anglicans of all, and Tractarians and liberals were the aberrant ones.[138] Thompson followed Packer in arguing that evangelicals must not be content to be merely a tolerated minority. Instead, they must insist that 'theologically ... we *are* the church of England'.[139] The *Review* thus encouraged its readers to claim the high ground as Anglicans. Such a stance was based not just on history: it reflected growing evangelical confidence, based on church growth, the success of the Billy Graham Crusade, and the new wave of articulate, scholarly writings coming out of Anglican evangelicalism in Britain.

Articles in the *Review* were chosen to reinforce and defend the evangelical position: pieces on scripture and its authority, justification, the history of the evangelical tradition in England, Holy Communion as sacrament not sacrifice, preaching, revival, repentance, the biblical warrant for infant baptism, parish evangelism, the dangers of sacerdotalism, apostolic succession, and prayers for the dead. There was only one article on moral matters – a reprint of an Australian item rejecting raffles and ballroom dancing.[140] There was a curious snippet (from an Australian source) suggesting that the European Common Market was part of a Roman Catholic strategy to reverse the Reformation.[141] Towards the end of his editorship, Thompson was beginning to perceive growing threats, and to publish articles against them: ecumenism,[142] church union,[143] the undermining of the Thirty-Nine Articles[144] and Prayer Book revision.

Thompson eulogised both the 1662 Book of Common Prayer and the Thirty Nine Articles. The Prayer Book, he wrote, was a thing of 'beauty, genius and abiding strength': it was 'unparalleled in the field of Christian literature, and unsurpassed in its power to awaken the conscience, touch the heart and stir the will of the worshipper'. Also, being 'undeviating in its fidelity to N.T. truth', the Prayer Book was a 'bulwark of scriptural and spiritual truths', and central to Anglicans' 'priceless and glorious heritage'.[145] The Thirty-Nine Articles, he claimed, expressed truths that are 'eternal and unchanging'. But to avoid according them the respect due only to scripture, he added that they also 'invariably defer to the eternal and abiding Word of God'.[146]

The *E.C.F. Review* frequently reviewed new evangelical titles from overseas: this was a major function of the publication. In the vast number of cases, the books it recommended came from evangelical scholars in Britain, most of them Anglican. In addition, the *Review* regularly publicised the evangelical *Church of England Newspaper* and *The Churchman*.[147] On occasion, it made appreciative comments about the new evangelical American magazine, *Christianity Today*, established as an evangelical alternative to *The Christian Century*.[148] At first, Thompson himself was the main contributor to the *E.C.F. Review*. From time to time, there were articles by other New Zealanders, including Bishop Hulme-Moir, Betteridge, Haskell, Goodall, Machell, Aiken, Lamont, Funnell and – the sole non-Anglican – J. Oswald Sanders. Surprisingly, the *Review* never included any article by the ECF president, William Orange.[149] Overseas contributors (usually by way of reprint) included evangelical luminaries from the past, mostly Simeon and Ryle, and contemporaries such as Leon Morris, John Stott and – above all – James Packer. Thompson no doubt respected Packer for his incisive scholarship and unflinching orthodoxy. Thompson was always likely to appreciate someone who could make such assertions as 'the extent that you deviate from the evangelical position, you deviate from Christianity itself' – and even 'Evangelicalism is Anglicanism, and Anglicanism is Evangelicalism'.[150]

Soon after he retired as editor, Thompson wrote an article in which he deplored the inroads into the church of both 'apostasy' (i.e. liberalism) and 'unreformed doctrines and practices' (i.e. High Church tendencies).[151] In both cases, the problem was 'a failure to recognise the Holy Scriptures as the divinely-given norm in all the life of the Church'. Thompson declared himself unimpressed by 'complacent ... institutional Christianity with its harmless, toothless, soporific routine-ism'. The need today, he wrote, was for 'another Reformation', recalling the church to the scriptures. In what might possibly have been a subtle warning to his younger evangelical colleagues, Thompson declared that the church needed men of courage, not compromise:

> *This Space-age Church needs men who are not afraid, not ashamed, to own their theological convictions ... Every spiritual revival, every reformation, every evangelical awakening in the Church has been at the cost of ecclesiastical promotion and popularity, and has been purchased by blood, sweat and tears.*

Such metaphors were characteristic of Thompson, but some of his evangelical Anglican successors would soon adopt a different tone.

The ECF as a lay movement

The ECF was not just a movement of ministers. In Christchurch in particular, it attracted into leadership a notable group of laity. These included builders Ron Mauger and Alf Wright. Don Laugeson, the managing director of a large bus company and 'discipled' by Joe Simmons (the pioneer of the New Zealand work of the Navigators),[152] became a passionate evangelist.[153] Hedley Thomas, a businessman from Sumner parish, had been a close associate of Orange. So had foundry owner Les Burgess, who was very active in the Woolston parish, and prominent in the diocesan synod. Stockbroker Archie Scott was an ECF leader and a lay canon in the Cathedral.[154] He was a major financial backer of the ECF, especially after it purchased Latimer House. He was strongly traditional, and sometimes clashed with the younger evangelical clergy. He objected to the first warden of Latimer House having a beard – which in the 1960s may have seemed to him a symbol of social radicalism.[155] As a whole, the lay leaders of ECF tended to be conservative in their evangelical convictions and practice. They considerably augmented the ECF's resources of energy, practical expertise and finance, and increased its credibility and appeal among non-clergy. On occasion, some of them would visit parishes as a lay mission team, as laymen speaking to laymen.[156]

The ECF and the wider evangelical nexus

The ECF was part of a wider evangelical Anglican network. Evangelical Anglicans were usually active in both ECF and CMS: Don Laugeson, for instance, was also vice-chairman of NZCMS. There was collaboration with regard to speakers: when the CMS sponsored conference speakers such as John Stott in 1961, the ECF movement was strengthened as much as the CMS. There was also partnership with regard to literature, through the CMS Bookshop.

The ECF was also part of a wider transdenominational evangelical network. Its members had strong links not just with with CSSM, Crusaders and IVF, but also often with newer ministries such as YFC and the Navigators. In contrast to earlier times, evangelical Anglicans had a much stronger presence in the Bible Training Institute: by 1963, BTI had twenty-one Anglican students.[157] The ECF became a party to many interdenominational evangelical discussions – for instance, when there was discussion about possibly issuing a combined evangelical invitation to Billy Graham to return to New Zealand, the ECF was naturally part of that conversation.[158] When the Presbyterian evangelicals in the Westminster Fellowship were seeking a partner in an evangelistic broadcasting venture to the New Zealand public, they approached the ECF[159] (but ECF's concern about Anglican denominational sensitivities outweighed its interest in such a transdenominational partnership).[160] When a New Zealand Evangelical Alliance was mooted, ECF leaders were part of the conversation, but some Anglican evangelicals were apprehensive about being swamped by evangelicals with a less traditional ecclesiology.[161] When ECF leaders felt the need to discuss 'the growth of evangelical witness' in the Dominion, they wrote to the groups with which evangelical Anglicans had some broad affinity: WF, the Methodist Revival Fellowship, IVF, SU, the CSSM and Crusader Movement, BTI, the Keswick Convention movement, and the Canterbury and Dunedin Evangelical Alliances.[162] When the issue of church union became increasingly insistent, leaders of the ECF gathered with WF and the Methodist Revival Fellowship leaders to explore various possible scenarios.

Evangelical Fellowship in the Anglican Communion

The ECF's life was stimulated, from 1961, by the formation of the international Evangelical Fellowship in the Anglican Communion (EFAC). This new grouping, committed to 'Biblical truth and Reformation principle',[163] reflected the postwar renaissance of evangelicalism within the Church of England. In Britain, the Church of England Evangelical Council had been formed to relate to EFAC. The primary thinker and emissary of EFAC was its secretary, John Stott. EFAC recognised that Anglican evangelical fellowships around the world were often 'isolated and fainthearted', and it sought to encourage such groups. It was at pains to emphasise that its purpose was 'not partisan in any narrow or negative sense, but positive and eirenical'. It hoped to strengthen biblical and reformation principles within the worldwide Anglican communion, and to re-establish the 'comprehensiveness' of the Anglican Church in those parts where evangelicalism was weak or absent. The significance of EFAC for New Zealand was that it strengthened the confidence of the ECF in its Anglican identity, and gave more direct access to the resources and leaders of Anglican evangelicalism in the United Kingdom.

Latimer House

In Orange's later years, the ECF developed the vision of an evangelical study centre based on Orange's library, initially with Orange as residential warden. The vision was in some ways a re-emergence of that which had created Tyndale House, but now safely within the bounds of Anglicanism. The Latimer Foundation (NZ) Inc, with the subtitle 'Biblical Research Foundation', was founded to own and manage the centre, and a property was purchased in Creyke Road.[164] The name chosen for the new centre – 'Latimer House' – was in imitation of the evangelical prototype in Oxford (UK), where Dr Packer was warden.[165] The Foundation appears to have been undersubscribed, and dependent on the generosity of Scott.[166] After Orange's death in 1966, Latimer House was re-established in Waimairi Road, close to the new sites of the university and College House.[167] The library holdings were culled of older titles, and progressively expanded to reflect new evangelical scholarship.

A Generational Windshift

Within the New Zealand evangelical Anglican movement, some generational differences began to emerge. The ECF included traditional evangelical elements, especially among laity and the older clergy. The older Anglican evangelicals such as Roger Thompson knew what had worked for them, and saw little need to distinguish between non-negotiable evangelical principles and those things that reflected an earlier societal context. They were aware they were considered the 'tight and narrow' generation and that the next generation had a different outlook.[168] The younger Anglican evangelical leaders tended to be less partisan and adversarial in their evangelicalism and more friendly towards other ecclesiastical streams.[169] As a result, they could sometimes be suspected of being a little 'unsound'.[170]

The older Anglican evangelicals had been moulded primarily (and directly) by Orange, whereas many of the younger evangelicals had been influenced by the IVF's Warner Hutchinson, by a more open fare of theological reading, and by a changing society. The older Anglican generation had grown up as part of a tiny minority, whereas the younger leaders had the confidence of knowing they belonged to a movement that was increasing in numbers, clout and intellectual firepower. Emerging ECF leaders such as Lamont, Goodall and Carrell wanted to steer the movement away from any pious 'other-worldliness' or 'gloomy reactionism' towards a confident, outward-looking stance.[171] They wanted to interact constructively with issues being debated in the wider church and society, such as church union, intercommunion, liturgical reform, and the social implications of the Gospel. Unlike their older colleagues, the younger evangelicals did not regard involvement in the diocese as unspiritual and fruitless. They wanted to debate, to be part of the decision-making and to exert influence.[172] Before synod meetings they met together to go through the agenda and to work out stances and strategies.[173]

Latimer Magazine

The shift from a less reactive attitude was reflected in the ECF journal. Early in 1961, Goodall spoke to the ECF in Christchurch about the need to emulate the tone of the *Church of England Newspaper* and to avoid a 'negative or protesting' attitude.[174] Change was inevitable: there were several energetic younger evangelicals on the ECF executive in Christchurch – and Thompson, now isolated in Nelson Diocese, was not well positioned to counsel otherwise. In June 1963 there was a discernible modification of tone and content in the ECF journal.[175] Goodall became associate editor. The journal's title was changed to the *Latimer Magazine* – presumably to emphasise the movement's historic Anglican credentials. There was a reassuring statement about continuing support for a 'reformed and protestant position', but a broader outlook was also signalled. The *Latimer Magazine* would 'encourage constructive thought and understanding of the truths of the Gospel' rather than promote 'narrow party loyalties'. A new column was begun: 'News and Views' by 'Eutychus'. It became clear that Eutychus was the sort of evangelical who was open to new developments. 'By all means let us work and think hard on the Doctrinal truths we must teach and defend,' Eutychus wrote, but 'in our anxiety to defend the truth of the Articles we must be careful to recognise them as documents of the 16th Century'. In the next issue, Eutychus reported on younger evangelical theologians in the UK, and welcomed Michael Green's rejection of evangelical isolationism and his call for evangelicals to enter into scholarly evangelical engagement with the whole church.[176]

The next month, Thompson's retirement as editor was announced. He was replaced by an editorial board made up of Pfankuch, Goodall, Lamont and Carrell.[177] A new editorial outlook became apparent. Successive issues carried positive (or at least constructively critical) articles on church union and prayer book revision; there were articles discussing the 'new morality'[178] and the emerging pentecostal movement,[179] and there were endorsements of the evangelical call to social action.[180] Thompson continued to have a voice, however, writing articles under the pseudonym of 'Veritas', and describing himself as 'a plodding Evangelical of the Old School'.[181] Whereas Thompson had extolled the 1662 Prayer Book[182] and struggled to countenance any thought of revision, the new generation of Anglican evangelical leaders were cautiously in favour of a more accessible, modernised liturgy. Evangelicals like Goodall, Lamont and Carrell argued that the crucial issue for evangelicals was not the perpetual preservation of the 1662 form of the Prayer Book, but the application of Cranmer's evangelical principle that there should be nothing in the liturgy inconsistent with scripture.[183] To help shape new liturgies, evangelicals must be constructively involved. To that end, they closely critiqued emerging liturgies.[184] Some of them later became members of the official drafting groups. But ECF was still prepared to contemplate legal action to block changes (such as prayers for the dead) that were inconsistent with the Protestant principles enshrined in the 1662 religious settlement which followed the turmoil of the English Civil War.[185]

Intercommunion

There was unanimity among Anglican evangelicals that communicants of other denominations should be allowed to participate in Anglican services of communion.[186] They passionately believed it was 'the Lord's table', not an Anglican one.[187] They felt a restrictive approach was biblically, theologically and historically untenable.[188] Such an outlook also reflected the very positive evangelical experiences of interdenominational fellowship in contexts such as Crusaders, CSSM, the EUs and IVF. Evangelicals like Lamont – versed in Anglican history and theology – argued robustly that a closed communion was at odds with the spirit and practice of the Anglican reformers, and that an exclusive approach was an expression of much more recent Tractarian understandings of ordination and the eucharist. The issue of intercommunion had been sharply raised in 1960, when Bishop Warren wrote to Anglican delegates about to attend an NCC Youth Conference advising them that 'no loyal Anglican' should take communion at a non-Anglican service or encourage a communicant of another denomination to communicate at an Anglican service.[189] Anglican evangelicals were highly indignant. Lamont helped to shape a new approach in the Christchurch Diocese, and was asked by Bishop Pyatt to outline it to the archbishop. At the 1970 General Synod, evangelicals successfully promoted a legislative proposal to accept intercommunion.

Church Union

With regard to church union, Anglican evangelicals were not constrained by any strong evangelical 'party line', as were their Presbyterian counterparts in the WF. Thompson wrote in 1963 that the ECF was not happy with church union, giving six reasons.[190] But younger Anglican evangelicals were often more positive about church union than their seniors, and more prepared to look beyond Anglican traditions and denominationalist assumptions. They thought there might be a positive biblical mandate for church union.[191] Others accepted the practical arguments about denominationalism's wasteful duplication of resources.[192] They felt church union was 'likely', given its apparently strong support among the 'vast majority' of the members of the five negotiating denominations, and that to believe otherwise was 'ostrich-like'.[193] They decided the wisest evangelical strategy was to work for the best possible basis for union, one 'in accordance with God's will'. By that they seemed to mean a union with an orthodox basis of faith within which evangelical doctrines were 'recognised'. Such doctrines included the inspiration and authority of scripture and justification by grace through faith alone.[194] They also meant that there would be freedom for evangelical practices such as prayer meetings, evangelistic missions and expository preaching. Consequently, the younger evangelical leaders, although still offering 'constructive criticism',[195] were willing to participate in explorations towards an acceptable basis of union. They were aware that their evangelical contemporaries in England were engaged in similar explorations.[196]

When the ECF leadership had talks about church union in 1965 with their evangelical counterparts in the WF and with the Methodist Revival Fellowship,[197] some of the younger ECF leaders felt uncomfortable with the implacably anti-church union stance of the WF leaders.[198] Carrell had already decided that Arthur Gunn's arguments against church union were 'very thin', and that they 'magnify minor issues'.[199] He felt Anglican evangelicals could do more by staying within the union movement than by withdrawing from it. Following the meeting with the WF, the ECF leaders rejected the WF's intention to stay out of union and to form a continuing Presbyterian Church. They argued that the New Testament emphasises fellowship rather than separation, and that, even in an apostate church, faithful witness is possible. They passed resolutions that church unity in the New Testament is of a 'visible organic nature', and that the ECF is 'therefore committed to the pursuit of organic unity'.[200] They feared that the WF secession would weaken evangelical attempts to establish a biblically sound basis for a united church, and would undermine the position of those evangelicals who entered the united church.[201] They asked the WF to reconsider its approach. Carrell, unhappy with Gunn's 'militant' outlook, quipped that the issue might be resolved by nominating him as one of the new bishops. Within a few years, however, the deepening controversy in the Presbyterian Church over the radical views of Professor Geering induced some Anglican evangelical leaders to be more cautious about church union. The controversy may have pressed home to the Anglican evangelicals that theological liberalism was stronger in the Presbyterian context than in their own, and may have helped them to understand some of the intensity of WF fears about doctrinal indifferentism in the proposed united church.

Continuing British influence

In this period, younger ECF leaders in New Zealand were strongly influenced by the strengthening Anglican evangelical movement in England, which in 1967 ran the pivotal National Evangelical Anglican Congress at Keele. As in Britain, the younger Anglican evangelicals in New Zealand believed they were on the ascendancy, and were uncomfortable with the ghetto outlook they discerned in a previous evangelical generation. Lamont, Goodall, Bourne and Carrell actively engaged with the wider denomination. Bourne, for instance, intentionally sought to be on various decision-making bodies, including General Synod, the Standing Committee of the Diocese, and the Prayer Book commission.[202] While New Zealand's younger evangelical Anglican leaders all appreciated the new American neo-evangelical magazine *Christianity Today*

(1956–),²⁰³ their reading diet was still primarily British. Lamont, for instance, was sometimes reading American writers such as Henry, Lindsell and Carnell (along with earlier authors such as Warfield and Machen, and Reformed writers such as Van Til and Ridderbos); but his reading was still principally from the IVP and from Church of England evangelicals. His favourite writers included Bruce, Stibbs, Guthrie, Buchanan, Tasker, Morris and – above all – Packer and Stott.²⁰⁴

A new movement secured

Orange's death in 1966 quietly marked the passing of an earlier era. The Anglican evangelical movement begun by him had blossomed in Christchurch, had spread to Nelson and Wellington, and had established toeholds in Dunedin and Auckland.

The intergenerational changes of mood discernible in the Evangelical Churchman's Fellowship by the early 1960s were evidence that the evangelical Anglican movement in New Zealand was no mere fading afterglow of the William Orange phenomenon, but was a movement that had successfully reproduced itself in at least two more generations. Instead of ossifying, the Anglican evangelical movement was accepting new leadership and grappling with new intellectual, ecclesiastical and societal challenges. Increased confidence led evangelicals to be more assertive on some issues, and more relaxed on others. Nevertheless, emerging Anglican evangelical leaders continued resolutely 'evangelical' in identity and conviction. When the 'God is Dead' debate made its impact in New Zealand, through J.A.T. Robinson's *Honest to God* and the Geering controversy, Anglican evangelicals of all ages were of one mind in speaking and writing against such views.²⁰⁵

CHAPTER NINE

Presbyterian Evangelicalism Expands, 1956–65

Inextinguishable witness, inextinguishable opposition.[1]

The South Auckland Evangelical Phenomenon

Notwithstanding the postwar recovery in New Zealand of evangelical Presbyterianism, there had been no clear geographical centre to that growth; there was no Presbyterian equivalent to the evangelical Anglican movement based on the diocese of Christchurch. Presbyterian evangelicalism had natural affinities with many parishes in rural Otago–Southland, but apart from there, Presbyterian evangelical ministers were spread fairly thinly across most of the country. In part that difference reflected the stronger national focus of Presbyterianism, where ministers all attended the General Assembly, all read a national Presbyterian publication, and commonly moved from one region to another. From the 1950s, however, South Auckland became a notable evangelical Presbyterian stronghold. At that time south of the Auckland metropolis rather than part of it, South Auckland had previously been predominantly rural, and remained quite conservative in outlook. It is arguable that at least a broad evangelicalism was the prevailing ethos of Presbyterianism in South Auckland, and that the more overt evangelicalism of the 1950s and 1960s developed in fertile soil.

J.G. Miller at Papakura, 1953–65

In 1952, Graham Miller returned from the New Hebrides and accepted a call to First Church, Papakura. The parish was 30 kilometres south of Auckland, in a town that was becoming an outer suburb. First Church was already more or less evangelical in outlook, and had previously been under the ministry of Geordie

Yule, a biblical conservative and passionate conversionist.[1] There had been an unsuccessful attempt to block the call to Miller by Rev. Dr Ian Fraser, a liberal member of South Auckland Presbytery.[3] Fraser would have known that Miller was conservative, capable and determined.

Graham Miller was subdued and gracious in manner, and effortlessly eloquent. He had a piercing intellect. He could show a dry humour, with a strong sense of irony and a droll turn of phrase, but he was essentially a serious man. He was instinctively conservative in doctrine, habits and manners, and was relatively impervious to modern fashions of thought or behaviour; he much preferred what he felt had stood the test of time. He valued propriety, duty and order. He retained most of the convictions and views of his father, whose memory he revered.

But Miller was not inflexible or merely conventional: as a missionary in the New Hebrides, he had brought a fresh perspective to many issues and had been a vigorous champion of indigenisation. He was also capable of sudden and emphatic changes of mind, such as his (later) endorsing of women's ordination.[4] He was not given to self-doubt. He was certain he was adhering to what was true, and right, and blessed by God. He was completely unabashed at being in a minority, either in society or among ministry colleagues. Reversals neither surprised nor discouraged Miller. He was deeply grounded in the writings of Calvin, and saw problems and setbacks as part of the mysterious outworking of divine providence. He was intensely loyal to Presbyterian doctrine and order, but scornfully dismissive of modern Presbyterian theological liberalism, and distrustful of its devotees. He struggled to understand why – to his eyes – liberals knew so little of their biblical or confessional heritage. He saw them as superficial and faddish, and he resented their presumption that they were the intellectuals and that 'conservatives' were the obscurantists.

Miller's ministry at Papakura was distinguished primarily by his exceptional gifts as a preacher. He saw the faithful, regular exposition of the scriptures as the crucial element in generating spiritual life and commitment, and as the heart of his ministry. He impressed on his congregation that their 'central duty' – twice on Sundays, and carrying Bible and notebook – was 'to come and listen to the Word of God'.[5] Advance notice of his expositions constituted the primary content of his monthly, one-page parish newsletters, which were distributed by a team of fifty to the letterbox of every known Presbyterian household.[6] 'I did not fill the sheet up with news, or funnies … I just let them keep this centrality of what the preaching would be about, and I am sure that gradually mastered the thoughts of the congregation.'[7]

Miller's exposition was based on intensive study of the biblical text. Eager to convey the force of the original as it had first struck him, he avoided using commentaries. His preaching was doctrinal, expressing a deep and unshakeable faith, and with a marked spiritual tone. His language was poetic and evocative, rich with allusions and quotes (he read widely, systematically recording quotable material). His application was clear and forthright: behind his quiet voice and mild manner, Miller was very insistent. His preaching was directed at teaching and inspiration, rather than evangelism. He did not give evangelistic 'appeals', believing that the Holy Spirit 'had his own way of evoking response' that was 'diverse and profound'.[8] Miller's unusual abilities as a preacher were widely acknowledged by his evangelical colleagues, one of whom, later familiar with the preaching of John Stott and Jack Hayford, rated Miller as the finest expositor he had ever heard.[9] Miller acknowledged the influence on his preaching of Rev. George B. Duncan, a frequent speaker at the English Keswick Convention,[10] but there were likely to have been other influences too, especially Thomas Miller and William Orange.

Miller's ministry helped generate pronounced congregational growth: 'it was only a few months and they didn't have seating room – and this of course cheered them up immensely, because they had never [previously] been able to pay their budget'.[11] In the first six months, the giving increased 80 per cent.[12] The number of communicant members went from 174 in 1953 to 463 in 1957.[13] The congregations were also swelled by trainee teachers and engineering students from Ardmore, many of whom came to hear Miller.[14]

One of Miller's strategies for evangelism was the use of the Communicants' Class, which prepared youth and adults for public profession of faith and church membership. By the time he left Papakura in 1965 he had received 279 people into church membership by profession of faith.[15] In the 1950s and 1960s, many people in society still commonly approached the church when they wanted to be married, or their children to be baptised. Miller made the most of interviews with such couples, often inviting them into his Communicants' Class. Like most of his WF colleagues, he combined a Reformed theology of infant baptism with a keen eye for evangelistic opportunity. Another evangelistic strategy, effective in a societal context where many people still had some known affiliation with a church denomination, was the use of trained visitors to make calls on 'Presbyterian' households. This strategy was recommended by the New Life Movement, and was widely implemented by evangelical parishes.

For nurturing Christian maturity, First Church had half a dozen adult Bible Study groups (with a focus on instruction rather than fellowship). Miller began a weekly Adult Bible School, in lecture style, with every communicant member encouraged to attend. There were separate men's and women's prayer meetings; the men's meetings were held at the demanding time of 7 am on Sundays. Notwithstanding his strongly Reformed theology of divine sovereignty, Miller also appeared to endorse the more revivalistic idea that the amount of spiritual 'blessing' was related to the amount of prayer that had been occurring.[16] Miller taught the Senior Bible Class at Papakura, attended CE, was chaplain to the Boys' and Girls' Brigades, and spoke at BC camps, Crusaders and EU. His ministry was sharply focused on spiritual ends, and traditional social groups such as the Women's Guild and Women's Fellowship were very rarely mentioned in the newsletters.

First Church often received visits from overseas missionaries on furlough.[17] Ideologically committed to 'indigenous' principles, and with extensive crosscultural experience in the New Hebrides, Miller became quite involved with Māori – in Papakura, and also in such contexts as the Ngaruawahia Convention, the United Maori Mission, and annual BC return visits with Māori youth in Murupara.[18] Some Māori joined First Church and its daughter churches, but Miller sensed they often seemed ill at ease in predominantly Pakeha settings, and he decided it was more fruitful to provide strong support to the Maori Evangelical Fellowship and its new Papakura work led by Tia Matiu. In his time, several members of First Church moved to the Bay of Plenty to take up full-time work with the Presbyterian Maori Synod.[19]

Miller's ministry at Papakura coincided with what appears to have been an unusual public receptivity to Christianity in New Zealand in the late 1950s, in the years leading up to the 1959 Billy Graham Crusade. Such a spiritual atmosphere is not readily explained, but it was widely felt by many evangelicals, and was reflected in enlarged congregations, packed Sunday schools and overall church growth. When the Billy Graham Crusade occurred, its effect on the churches came as a 'crowning encouragement' rather than something entirely new.[20] Miller's parish hired a fleet of buses to take people into Auckland to the Crusade. The parish received sixty-nine decision cards, and Miller visited all the individuals concerned. About half of the respondents were known to him, and were seeking assurance of faith or were making recommitments. The other half represented conversions, mostly of people he did not know. There was only one respondent who 'did not advance'.[21] Many were received as new members into First Church.[22]

The effect of the Crusade was also felt on the nearby Ardmore Teachers' College: about half the student body attended the Crusade, many responded, and the weekly meeting of the Christian Fellowship grew from 50–60 to about 140.[23] The effects of the Crusade were experienced – in Papakura and elsewhere – as an incomparable 'outpouring' of spiritual 'blessing' that continued for months: many people in both church and community responded readily to calls to conversion or recommitment, congregations had a new fervour (often reflected in the singing), and there was 'revival in the heart of ministers'.[24]

The congregation at Papakura continued to grow. Morning services in 1960 were attended by up to 250 adults; evening services by up to 180.[25] The church was often overflowing in the morning, even after cutting the congregation twice to help establish new churches in neighbouring new suburbs: eighty communicants were sent to Papakura East in 1959 and thirty-eight to Takanini in 1961. Miller claimed that 'whenever we'd give them away, by the end of the year we'd nearly always got the same number back again', and official statistics corroborate that claim.[26] Influenced by historical accounts of past awakenings, Miller was preaching – in hope and expectation – a series about revival. The high tide was sustained for about eighteen months, and then Miller began to notice a drop in numbers at the evening service. He and his evangelical colleagues talked among themselves about a coming spiritual regression, which they termed a 'Counter Reformation', when the 'times of refreshing' would come to an end.[27] The content of a 1964 newsletter suggests the parish's spiritual fervour remained high: from 1963 to 1964 weekly giving doubled, and it was planned to give half of the income away to missions and to have a monthly day of prayer.[28] But Miller was also acutely aware of a group of young men in the church who had previously professed faith and then became 'impervious' to 'spiritual truth'.[29]

A distinctive feature of Miller's ministry at Papakura – and one that his evangelical colleagues in this period did not generally emulate – was his introduction of Christian Endeavour, which had been so important in his own formative years and which he had also used in the New Hebrides. Miller channelled younger converts into CE, which was additional to the BC and pitched for those eager for deeper spiritual growth. Miller also saw the CE as a wholesome alternative to Saturday night dances. While Miller had sat silent and disapproving, his session had given permission for a square dance. In reaction, Miller had started up CE.[30] Miller felt a persistent pressure to allow dances among the youth. Churches in this period commonly allowed dances, and many of the Ardmore students at First Church came from such churches. A member of the BC stood at the manse door and remonstrated: 'Why *can't* we have dancing? Don't you know that Papatoetoe [St John's] have ninety people every Saturday night?' But Miller asked how many of those also attended church on Sunday night.[31]

Within New Zealand, Miller regularly spoke at Keswick-type conventions including those at Pounawea, Rotorua (where he was chairman) and Ngaruawahia, and was an outstanding speaker in such contexts.[32] He also frequently spoke at parish teaching missions.[33] At one parish mission in a small town he spoke for ten consecutive evenings from Romans, with the crowds increasing from 200 to a peak of 530.[34] He spoke at numerous Presbyterian BC Easter Camps. At one of those, in the Bay of Plenty, he reluctantly gave an 'appeal', to which over 100 responded.[35] He was often invited to speak in EU and IVF contexts. In 1955 and 1959 he gave the presidential address at the IVF Conference. In evangelical contexts, whether Presbyterian or interdenominational, Miller's speaking was well received, but he felt that, in official Presbyterian contexts, his contribution was often barely tolerated. When he spoke at the 1964 Theological Hall students' retreat, the atmosphere was 'frosty' and the questions antagonistic, and he realised that as chairman of the Westminster Fellowship he was regarded with considerable suspicion.[36]

Internationally, Miller's expositional gifts were reflected in invitations to speak at numerous overseas conferences, including IVF conferences. In 1963 he was invited to speak at Keswick (UK), where 5000 heard his expositions of Hosea.[37] Miller also spoke at similar evangelical conventions in Australia (Belgrave Heights and Katoomba), North London, Ireland (Portstewart) and India.[38] In Keswick-type settings, Miller consciously avoided preaching according to a classic Keswick holiness or 'second blessing' formula, which sat uneasily with his Calvinist understanding. He kept such emphases in mind, but assumed the freedom simply to expound scripture with a spiritual emphasis on consecration.[39]

From the mid 1950s, Miller was writing up to half of each year's *Daily Notes* for Scripture Union in the UK. With a worldwide readership in some 120 languages, such notes increased Miller's international profile.[40] He also wrote some daily Bible notes for the *Outlook*. His pamphlet 'Baptism in the Presbyterian Church' reflected a widespread concern in the church that many parents in the 1950s society felt a need to do the right thing by their children and have them 'done' (as if baptism were some sort of innoculation) but then, after the ceremony, were rarely or never seen again.[41] Miller provided an explanation of infant baptism and emphasised the need for parents themselves to profess faith and become involved in the life of the church.

In the Presbytery of South Auckland, Miller became the obvious leader and spokesman of the growing group of evangelical ministers. He became very active in the WF. Within the national church, he was a member of the Overseas Missions Committee, and from 1954 he was also a (dissident minority) member of the Church Union Committee. While at Papakura, Miller had up to twenty younger protégés who later went into ministry, missionary service or theological teaching, or did some training for such work. These included Alistair McKenzie, Garth McInnes, Kenneth Ralph, Bruce Ralph, Graham Adams, Graham Hughes, Ed Norton, Thomas Strahan, Dennis Fitzpatrick, Roy Masters, Ian Keals, Marcus Willitts, Pierce Hobbs and Don Murray.[42] Some of those later reacted against the perceived narrowness of the WF,[43] and others ceased to identify themselves as evangelical.

Towards the end of his time in Papakura, Miller received several approaches to serve elsewhere. A number of BTI staff and board members who knew Miller well through the Ngaruawahia conventions wanted him to succeed John Deane as BTI principal; but Miller believed that Blaiklock (who was BTI president) was unwilling to have a Calvinist in such a position.[44] In 1965, Miller accepted an invitation to become principal of Melbourne Bible Institute. His public farewell at the Auckland Town Hall, arranged by the Evangelical Alliance, highlighted his interdenominational evangelical leadership. Tributes or prayers were given by Donald Kirkby (WF), John Pritchard (Auckland Evangelical Alliance), Muri Thompson (Māori Christians), A.E. Williams (Keswick) and R.A. Laidlaw (BTI). The *Challenge* ran a large, two-page feature on Miller, expressing the view that New Zealand was losing 'one of its most gracious, able, and spiritual leaders'.[45] By contrast, the Presbyterian *Outlook*'s tribute was both belated and restrained. The piece's (evangelical) author praised Miller's loyalty and graciousness, but avoided referring to his theology – or the Westminster Fellowship.[46]

Donald Kirkby at Pukekohe, 1957–69

In 1957, Donald Kirkby moved from Dargaville to the bustling country town of Pukekohe. As interim moderator overseeing the selection process, Graham Miller had strongly encouraged the call. St James' had a long evangelical tradition.[47] Kirkby was an evangelical preacher of exceptional confidence and flair;[48] his preaching was intelligent, well prepared, eloquent and dynamic. A young bank officer in the town, encountering expository preaching for the first time, was 'totally gripped': he 'could not get to church fast enough' and often could not sleep afterwards.[49] There were full congregations morning and night.

By 1962 average weekly church attendance peaked at 620, including over 300 children.[50] St James' became the largest congregation in the presbytery and the second largest in the upper North Island.[51]

Kirkby was a hands-on, charismatic leader. He was able to establish rapport – especially with men, with whom he shared a strong interest in sport.[52] He had a gift in personal evangelism. He had strong organisational ability, and worked to mobilise his whole parish along evangelical lines, not least in the area of systematic outreach visitation by teams of lay people. He established a Saturday night pre-communion service, attended by up to 200. He taught a large midweek meeting (Bible study and prayer), and also the Senior BC. He laid great emphasis on prayer and prayer meetings, and published a Prayer Diary for daily use. He actively fed people into his communicant classes, which ran in three-month series, and there were numerous professions of faith;[53] the Billy Graham Crusade led to thirty-six professions of faith at the next communion service.[54] A new church building was opened in 1961. There were some limited attempts to reach out to Pukekohe's Māori, Chinese and Indian communities.[55] To at least one observer, the state of St James' Pukekohe seemed akin to 'revival'.[56] Such an exceptional flourishing of the church cannot be directly attributed either to the work of Kirkby or to the effects of the Graham Crusade; rather, the late 1950s in New Zealand was a period of 'unusual spiritual receptivity and fruitfulness'.[57] Evangelical ministries did not produce that spiritual upswell, but were very effective at tapping in to it.

In Kirkby's time, twenty-three people entered full-time Christian work.[58] There were many who went into Presbyterian ministry, including Tom Woods, John McKinlay, Neville Harris, Pat Connell, Graeme Murray, Ken Campbell, Brian Weston, David Jack, Bert Schoneveld and Rod Harris.[59] Elinor Papesch went to Deaconess College. Several church members went to BTI,[60] and several became missionaries.[61] In support of missionaries, Kirkby established the St James' World Missionary Fellowship, which produced extensive mission prayer notes and ran missionary conventions.[62] Kirkby argued that a church's support for missions is a measure of its spiritual state, and that 'a Church which has an aggressive and sacrificial missionary policy is bound to be a live, thriving Church with evidence all about it of the blessing of God'.[63] His strong missionary interest was also associated with a pronounced emphasis on Christian giving, much of which went to overseas missions.[64] Like other evangelical parishes, St James' had no hesitations about supporting nondenominational missionary societies, and felt that Presbyterian missionaries in such societies were ignored by denominational authorities.[65]

Kirkby was theologically astute, and clearly evangelical by conviction. But he was less rigorously or systematically Reformed than Graham Miller. Whereas Miller had 'much more the legal mind', Kirkby was more 'the dynamic warm evangelist'.[66] Privately, at least, Kirkby was less committed to the Westminster Confession than some of his WF peers.[67] He was friendly in his attitude to non-evangelicals.

More than any of his evangelical colleagues, Kirkby was in wide demand outside the parish. In 1955 he had been absent from his previous parish for a total of four months, speaking at camps and New Life missions.[68] More than Miller, whose primary gift was in teaching, Kirkby was an evangelist. He would not hesitate to give an 'appeal'. As a missioner, he made much of his experiences as a pilot in the Fleet Air Arm, and he was a lively raconteur. Of all the New Life missioners of every theological stripe, he was probably the most effective.[69] He carried a heavy load of speaking engagements, both in New Zealand and overseas. In the early 1960s, for instance, these included missions (in Melville, Manurewa, Greymouth, Taupo and Dunedin), four BC camps, a School of Evangelism, a Ministers' Refresher Course, lectures at the Theological Hall, an OUEU house party, and the Belgrave Heights Convention (Melbourne).[70]

Like most of his evangelical colleagues, Kirkby was on the leadership councils of several evangelical organisations.[71] But unlike most of his evangelical peers, he was also on several national PCNZ committees (and convener of one). With his warm personality and his focus on church growth and evangelism, rather than on controversial issues of doctrine or church union, he was more acceptable to the wider church than were some other evangelicals.[72] He was an appealing and enthusiastic advocate for the evangelical cause. Some colleagues wondered if he exaggerated his successes.[73]

Kirkby's ministry at Pukekohe ended with his sudden resignation in 1968, but he later had an international ministry with Youth with a Mission.

Arthur Gunn at Manurewa, from 1961

When Rev. A.G. Gunn arrived from Scotland in 1961 at St Andrew's Manurewa, it was clear that a powerful new evangelical constellation had formed in the Presbytery of South Auckland: Miller, Kirkby and Gunn. All three openly and unequivocally identified themselves as evangelical, and actively championed evangelical theology and praxis. All three were gifted, articulate, energetic and determined.

Arthur Gunn (1912–1999) was the son of another New Zealand minister, James Gunn, who was a friend of Thomas Miller.[74] With a background in youth and children's work, lay preaching and BTI, Arthur Gunn had excellent organisational abilities and a formidable intellect.[75] He had helped Robert Laidlaw found the Christian Business Men's Association, had been a CIM missionary in China, and did wartime service as an RAF pilot. Accepted for the ministry but unable to find accommodation in Dunedin for his wife and baby, Gunn had switched to New College in Edinburgh, hoping to do a BD and PhD and eventually return to New Zealand.[76] There is no evidence he avoided Knox on theological grounds.[77] Ordained in 1950, he was minister in two Scottish parishes. The second of those, St David's (Glasgow), had 2000 members and the largest Bible Class in Scotland.[78] At one communion service, 126 new members had joined. Gunn had also a mid-week children's programme with an attendance of 400.

At Manurewa, where he followed a gently evangelical predecessor, Sefton Campbell,[79] Gunn was clearly an outstanding parish minister. With considerable personal presence, he preached strongly and was always well prepared.[80] His preaching was instructional rather than evangelistic. Both in preaching and in leadership style, he was fairly authoritarian. He had boundless energy and was prodigiously hardworking – the epitome of an evangelical activist. He had nothing of the quietist streak that was in Graham Miller. Whereas Miller was content to leave some things to the sovereign wisdom of God, Gunn preferred to organise.[81] He was diligent and effective in pastoral visitation, and organised a large team of twenty-eight elders to do likewise.[82] He had another team of volunteers to deliver a newsletter to those who had missed church. Every Sunday night after church a different elder would be organised to bring people in his pastoral district to the manse for supper.

As in Papakura and Pukekohe, congregational numbers grew: average weekly attendance in Manurewa peaked at 470 in 1959.[83] Such growth was not unique to evangelical parishes, however. In the same period St John's Papatoetoe (the only large parish in the presbytery with a non-evangelical ministry) had similar growth to St Andrew's – but less growth than First Church Papakura or St James' Pukekohe.[84] As with Miller and Kirkby – though not to the same extent – Gunn also spoke at various Christian conventions in New Zealand and Australia.[85] When Gunn spoke at a parish mission in Pukekohe, there were attendances every night of 400.[86] But by far Gunn's most prominent activity outside of the parish was his work writing, editing and speaking for the Westminster Fellowship.

Arthur Gunn was less measured than Miller, and more combative than Kirkby. At a personal level, he was friendly, relaxed and affable, with a strong sense of humour. He was also an outspoken advocate of conservative evangelical views, and a fearless polemicist. He could sometimes overstate his case: his dismissiveness towards other theological positions (whether Roman Catholic, liberal or ecumenical) offended some. Gunn showed no deference to those who saw themselves as the leading lights of the PCNZ. Through his comments in General Assembly, in the *Evangelical Presbyterian* and in the media, he became perceived by liberals and moderates within New Zealand Presbyterianism as the bête noire of WF-style evangelicalism. As a New Zealander who had done his ministry training overseas, Gunn may have been resented by some as an outspoken outsider. The denominational authorities were also irritated by Gunn's willingness to make unofficial comments about Assembly to the media, who often sought him out.[87] Gunn was not motivated by anger or hostility, but by cool-headed conviction: he was matter-of-fact, and not intense. He was not trying to be provocative, just standing up for what he believed;[88] as a strong individualist, he was unfazed by hostile reactions.

Other new South Auckland evangelical ministers

The new parish of Papakura East firmly identified itself with the evangelical ethos and practices of its parent church, First Church. Its first minister was Lewis Wilson.[89] Brought up in inland Canterbury, Wilson had been converted through the Open Brethren, had been moulded by the Crusaders (and Laird), and had gone to BTI.[90] In Christchurch, he had been influenced by Orange and other Anglican evangelicals, and had been the president of the Canterbury EU.[91] He had spent three years in Dunedin as a Crusader Movement staff worker.[92] Returning to his Presbyterian roots, Wilson had trained at the Theological Hall, excelling in biblical languages and exegesis.[93] He had actively interacted with critical scholarship, but retained a scholarly evangelical position on scripture. There had been a liberal attempt to block Wilson's call to his first parish (Rangiora), probably because of his Brethren and EU background. His opponents, he asserted, 'put two and two together and made about ten'.[94]

In outlook, Wilson was moderate and thoughtful. As with many other evangelicals in Crusaders or Scripture Union, his evangelicalism centred on evangelical conversion and experience rather than doctrine. He held to evangelical doctrines, but in a positive rather than negative way. He accepted being called a 'conservative evangelical', but strongly rejected a fundamentalist identity and evangelical 'extremes'.[95] Although he was a founding member of the Westminster Fellowship (and on its executive), he was ambivalent about aspects of the Westminster Confession.[96] Wilson represented a different

Westminister Fellowship style to that of Arthur Gunn, with whose narrower views and polemical style Wilson was uncomfortable.⁹⁷ Also, while Wilson voted against all the specific proposals for church union, he was unconvinced that being evangelical required opposition to church union in principle.⁹⁸ A younger evangelical recalled him asking: 'Who do we owe the greatest debt to, the [British] evangelical Anglicans, or the evangelical Presbyterians?'⁹⁹ Wilson was one of the few leading Presbyterian evangelicals who was respected and trusted across the whole denomination, both for his abilities and graciousness.¹⁰⁰ Someone who had moved away from the evangelical stream eulogised him as

> *unquestionably ... one of NZ's outstanding biblical scholars of his generation. His scholarship was driven by his love of the Scriptures but also by his determination that the Evangelical 'position' would be as disciplined, as academic and as robust as the prevailing Liberal 'positions' of the day ... There was a substance in his careful and caring scrutiny of Scripture that was enthralling as well as infectious.*¹⁰¹

Despite Wilson's constructive attitude toward the wider church, he shared the deep sense of ecclesiastical isolation which was the prevailing experience of Presbyterian evangelicals of his day, and felt his gifts were underutilised by the national church.¹⁰² When Wilson left Papakura East to pursue PhD study in London, he was replaced by J.N.A. Smith, a WF stalwart.¹⁰³

Meanwhile, from 1961 to 1967, John Brinsley was the first minister of the new evangelical parish of Manurewa South–Takanini, where the session clerk, Ian Thomson, was also the secretary of WF. When Brinsley arrived, about half the church members were converts of the Graham crusade.¹⁰⁴ Over the next few years the membership doubled, the Sunday school numbered 360, and there were twelve parishioners either in full-time Christian work or training for it.¹⁰⁵ As elsewhere, such growth could be attributed to several factors working together: a population boom, urbanisation, the spiritual receptiveness in the late 1950s and early 1960s, emphases on conversion and consecration, the expansionist vision of the New Life Movement, and the characteristic evangelical activism of the minister and leading lay people. Brinsley, like other evangelicals committed to expository preaching, took two morning services, an evening service, a CE, a BC and a Communicants' Class, and during the week there was much pastoral and evangelistic activity.¹⁰⁶ This was a period, Brinsley later reflected, when 'conversions' came 'readily'.¹⁰⁷ Beyond the parish, Brinsley did numerous missions in other parishes, and spoke frequently at BC and Crusader camps.¹⁰⁸

From a nominally Presbyterian family in Dunedin, Brinsley had been taken to the Open Brethren by neighbours and had a conversion experience in a Lionel Fletcher mission.[109] At Waitaki Boys' High he had been recruited by Lewis Wilson for Crusaders.[110] The main influence forming Brinsley as an evangelical had been EU.[111] In the same period (the 1950s) Brinsley had exhibited the sort of interdenominationalism that was common among evangelicals: on Saturday nights he attended CE at St Stephen's Presbyterian, and on Sundays he attended his local Presbyterian church in the morning, a Brethren BC in the afternoon, and St Matthew's Anglican in the evening.[112]

Brinsley expressed his evangelical faith in a positive way, and had enjoyed his time at the Theological Hall (1958–60). He realised that liberals categorised him as 'conservative', but the theological label he owned was 'evangelical'.[113] He freely used it, but mainly among other ministers rather than in the parish. He did not differentiate himself as a 'conservative evangelical': 'you were either evangelical or liberal' and 'that was the only evangelicalism we knew'.[114] Brinsley knew the 'favourable' sense of 'fundamentalist' (believing in the fundamentals of the faith), but saw the term as American, and did not use it;[115] he was also aware of the pejorative term 'Fundie', meaning ultraconservative. Brinsley respected the Westminster Confession, and thought Chapter One (on scripture) 'absolutely magnificent'.[116] But his interest in the WF as an organisation was not primarily doctrinal. He felt the greatest benefit of the WF was how it encouraged those who were passionate about evangelism and overseas mission.[117] He thought it went much further in such matters than did the national church. While Brinsley accepted the WF party position on church union, he was more open in principle than some of his evangelical colleagues.[118] Like many others, he had enjoyed fellowship across the denominations, and greatly admired evangelical Anglicans such as Maurice Betteridge and those in the UK.[119]

In the rural areas of South Auckland, other evangelicals were also in ministry, and were encouraged by the increasingly evangelical atmosphere of the presbytery. In Te Kauwhata, a dynamic ministry was conducted by Tom Woods (1960–65).[120] In 1960, average church attendances of 382 were recorded – a remarkable figure for a small town.[121] In Tuakau, another rural township, there was Rex Lange, called there on the initiative of Graham Miller.[122] His energetic ministry (1957–62) was characterised by strong preaching, Bible Classes, home prayer and study groups, the Billy Graham Crusade, numerous professions of faith (twenty-eight in 1959), a parish mission with Sam Green, a stewardship campaign and a major building project.[123] With a background in farming and home missionary work, but not in EU, Lange's evangelicalism was conversionist and activist but not heavily doctrinal, and he had some wariness of evangelical narrowness.[124] He was succeeded by A.C. (Cliff) Webster, who became very active in the WF. Other evangelical ministers in the South Auckland Presbytery included A.H. Lowden (Drury), E.E. Dyason (Mauku) and D.R. Allen (Waiuku). By 1965, in contrast to most other presbyteries, a strong majority of ministers in South Auckland were associated with the WF.

Presbyterian Evangelical Ministries Around New Zealand
Auckland

Of the four main cities, Auckland had by far the greatest minority of evangelical ministers. That probably reflected the historical underlying strength in Auckland of interdenominational evangelicalism, and the evangelical sympathies of many laity: Auckland was the city of Kemp, Fletcher, Laidlaw and Blaiklock, and of BTI. In the 1960s evangelical growth among Presbyterians in Auckland mainly occurred at the periphery, in new suburbs, where the mood of confident expansion may have been especially favourable to an evangelical strain of Christianity. The proliferation of evangelical ministries in Auckland was of concern to at least some liberals.[125] By 1960 there were a number of evangelical ministers, most of them quite moderate in their evangelicalism: Ernie Walsh at St Helier's (1951-64), Jim Gunn at Titirangi (1953-66), Ian Grant at Orakei (1955-61), Douglas Watt at Mt Eden (1953-67),[126] Bert Tweedie at Birkenhead (1958-67), Gwilym Jones at Mangere (1958-61) and Stan Nicholls at Avondale (1955-62).

In the early 1960s the number of evangelicals in Auckland swelled further: Morrison Yule came to Ponsonby (1960-75); in 1961 David Sage went to Mangere East, John Graham to Glen Eden and Bill Temple to Kohimarama. Subseqent new arrivals were Robert Blaikie (St Helier's, 1962),[127] Rex Lange (Forrest Hill, 1963),[128] Challis Wilson (Orewa, 1963), Ted Kirkby (Helensville, 1964), Reg Poolman (Owairaka, 1964), Tom Wilson (Kumeu, 1964), Tom Woods (Trinity-Glendowie, 1965), Russell Kenward (St Helier's, 1965) and Arch Davie (Glenfield, 1965). Some of those (such as Temple and Blaikie) came from overseas and stood aloof from the WF, but others (such as Yule, Kirkby and Sage) had EU backgrounds and were leaders in the WF. Many of the parishes would develop an evangelical identity and succession.

Wellington, Christchurch and Dunedin

No similar concentration of evangelical ministers developed in any of the other three main centres. In Wellington, Les Gosling was at Island Bay

(1958–68), where his parishioners included Arnold Nordmeyer, leader of the Opposition.[129] Gosling lacked WF colleagues in other Wellington parishes.[130] Unlike most other WF leaders, Gosling was appointed to numerous PCNZ national committees, partly because he was in Wellington and partly because he was committed to working constructively with the wider denomination. In 1967, he became editor of the *Outlook*.

In Christchurch, the number of WF-associated evangelicals was similarly sparse. Wynford Davies, a protégé of Lloyd-Jones and an appealing evangelical preacher, arrived from Wales to become minister of New Brighton (1960–63).[131] His evangelicalism reflected his background in Welsh Calvinistic revivalism and the British IVF. The fact that he had been in the national rugby team for Wales also commended him to many New Zealanders. J.S. Scarlet joined the Christchurch Presbytery in 1962, A.S. Munro in 1963, and R.H. Wells in 1964. Alex Munro's evangelical ministry at Hornby became particularly influential. His biblically conservative preaching attracted disaffected Presbyterians from other Christchurch parishes, and people from other denominations.[132] For some years, he was chairman of the Evangelical Alliance of New Zealand.[133]

In Dunedin, there was a small group of evangelical ministers: Rod McKenzie at St Stephen's (1958–77),[134] Hessel Troughton (a BTI graduate and former missionary in Japan) at Ravensbourne (1949–67),[135] Jack Smith at Kaikorai (1955–65), Challis Wilson at Wakari (1956–63), and J.A. Mitchell in the rural hinterland at Strath Taieri (1956–62).

Evangelical Presbyterian ministries in provincial New Zealand

In Hamilton's Knox Church, Rowland Harries had a lively Bible preaching ministry (1958–68) with a strong conversionist emphasis.[136] In the year following the Billy Graham Crusade (relayed by landline to the Te Rapa racecourse), his congregation almost doubled: 'There was a sensitivity to things spiritual right through the community at that time.'[137] Stephen Clark was another evangelical minister in Hamilton, at Melville (1959–67). Clark had been shaped by Scripture Union, CSSM and the Crusader Movement, and was greatly influenced by Laird. His emphasis was evangelistic and devotional, and he disliked doctrinal controversy.[138] Both he and Harries had come into the ordained Presbyterian ministry after previous interdenominational evangelistic ministries and had been at BTI, and were less influenced by IVF than some. I.D. (Ian) MacGregor was yet another Hamilton evangelical minister, based at Frankton (1957–67). His ministry had a similar flavour to Harries' and Clark's, with numerous parishioners later going into ministry or mission.

In the Bay of Plenty, there was a smattering of evangelical ministers, including A.C. Webster at Murupara (1957–63), F.A. Hume at Opotiki (1956–65), M.G. Milmine at Rangitaiki (1957–64), W.J. Milligan at Whakatane (1954–66), G.A. McKenzie at Matata (1963–67)[139] and E.L. Kirkby at Katikati (1954–64).[140]

In Wanganui East (1955–60), and later in Wellington, there was Don Elley – who had been firmed up in his evangelicalism through such influences as EU, Graham Miller (who introduced him to the Keswick movement), Edwin Orr (who spent ten days in Whanganui during his 1956 tour of New Zealand) and the Billy Graham Crusade.[141] Elley developed a ministry as an evangelist, frequently speaking at parish missions and BC Easter Camps. He recalled that at one such camp there were eighty-four 'first-time decisions'. He also spoke at the Ngaruawahia and Rotorua conventions, and in university missions.[142] From 1962 to 1964 Whanganui also briefly had an evangelical firebrand in the ministry of I.B. (Ivor) Davies from Wales.[143]

In the Deep South – reflecting factors such as Free Church roots, late nineteenth-century revival, the influence of Andrew Johnston and, perhaps, rural conservatism – the three southernmost presbyteries (Clutha, Mataura and Southland) had a relatively high proportion of evangelical ministers, including Cliff Dunn at Owaka (1957–64),[144] G.A. McKenzie at Lumsden (1957–63), Hugh Reid at Gore (St Andrew's, 1953–67),[145] G.A. McLean at East Gore (1962–75), Bill Wallace at Mataura (1949–69), Jim Moore at Wyndham (1954–63),[146] Bill Moore at Limestone Plains (1951–67), Roy McKenzie at Otautau (1963–69), Dallas Clark at Merrivale–Waiau (1958–66) and Norman Sheat at Tuatapere (1956–65). All of those were supporters of the WF. Many new ministers of other theological persuasions also began their ministries in the rural south. Evangelicals suspected that the national church was attempting to break up the evangelical concentration: one of them asserted, 'It was a deliberate move, you could see it.'[147] But it may simply have been that the number of ministerial vacancies in the rural south exceeded the available supply of new evangelical ministers.

Outside the three southern presbyteries, evangelical ministries in the South Island were less common. A notable exception was the ministry of Rob Miller in Blenheim, in the new Wairau parish (1958–66). Miller was very hardworking, with a robust and scholarly Bible preaching ministry, and there was vigorous development in such areas as youth work, mid-week meetings, missionary support and new buildings. Also, with his strong family background at Pounawea, Rob Miller established the Mid-New Zealand Convention at Renwick.[148] In 1966, he accepted a call to Tasmania.[149]

In general, Presbyterian evangelical ministers were still dispersed across the whole nation, lacking critical mass in most regions. Westminster Fellowship evangelicals tended to be ministers in rural and suburban parishes, and in this period were almost never called to large city churches.[150] Although spread fairly thinly and unevenly, by 1965 evangelical ministers had nevertheless established a noticeable presence across the Presbyterian Church in New Zealand. One indication of such growth is that, in 1965, over one in four Presbyterian parish ministers were paid-up members of the WF.[151]

The Westminster Fellowship in the Late 1950s

From its base in Dunedin, the WF self-consciously maintained an 'evangelical testimony'.[152] It held regional rallies.[153] It published reprints of booklets such as P.B. Fraser's *A Brief Statement of the Reformed Faith* and B.B. Warfield's *Christian Baptism*. It distributed pamphlets on 'What is an Evangelical?',[154] and sold titles by Reformed theologian Loraine Boettner.[155] It purchased mass copies of Packer's *Fundamentalism and The Word of God* to give to divinity students.[156] It responded to Blaiklock's provocative assertion (in the *Reaper*) that Calvinism was a 'virus' which 'paralyses eagerness, zeal, and enterprise' and was thus one of four hindrances to evangelistic effort.[157]

Meanwhile, with Rob Miller as editor (1955–62), the bi-monthly *Evangelical Presbyterian* developed as a solid Presbyterian journal. It had a strong historical and confessional focus, and by 1957 had a print run of 1100 copies.[158] The greatest number of articles were from Miller himself. Many others were from writers long since passed away, especially Warfield.[159] Miller also reprinted pieces from Fraser's *Biblical Recorder*.[160] Only one or two New Zealanders contributed to most issues.[161] The predominance of articles from overseas sources reflected the *EP*'s large number of exchange arrangements with other journals.[162] There were frequent articles on Presbyterian doctrine and distinctives,[163] on the Westminster standards,[164] and some on evangelicalism.[165] There were innumerable articles on historical figures: on Calvin, heroes of the Scottish Reformation (Hamilton, Wishart, Knox), Jonathan Edwards, Scottish evangelical Andrew Thomson, missionary pioneers (e.g. Alexander Duff), the Princeton theologians (Hodge, Warfield, Machen) and Scottish Presbyterians generally. There were pieces on the Great Awakening, the Disruption and the 1859 Revival, and almost an entire issue on the pioneer Free Church in New Zealand. Only one Anglican (Ryle) received attention.[166] Curiously, there were no articles on the Church Fathers (or anyone else pre-Calvin), and none on Puritans or Pietists. There were numerous articles opposing church union, several Sabbatarian pieces and a few pieces – conservative but not extreme – on gambling, temperance and dancing.[167] There was only one brief article on eschatology,[168] and a serialised feature on evolution (sceptical, but open to the earth being very old).[169] There was warm commendation of the Keswick conventions, Billy Graham and IVF – and in a recommended booklist, eleven of the eighteen titles in the theology section were from IVF.[170] The magazine consistently identified with evangelicalism, especially in its historic Scottish Free Church expression, but also in its Princetonian and British IVF forms. The sole mention of 'fundamentalism' was that the term was 'confusing'.[171]

A Reinvigorated Westminster Fellowship

At the end of 1961 a very important change took place in the leadership of the Westminster Fellowship. The executive was reconstituted in South Auckland, where there was a growing pool of younger, highly energetic, evangelical ministers, and staunch support from many elders. Many other evangelicals were close by in Auckland. A very capable new leadership team was formed. The chairman was Graham Miller, an evangelical of obvious stature. The new editor of the *Evangelical Presbyterian* was Arthur Gunn. The other ministers on the executive were Morrison Yule, Donald Kirkby, Rob Kirkby, Lewis Wilson, John Brinsley, David Sage, Mervyn Milmine and John Poon.[172] Significantly, all of them had previously been closely involved in EU and IVF. The executive included no ministers who were not graduates, and no older evangelicals who had come up through the SCM only. The laymen on the executive were H.F. Thompson, G.I. Thomson, Norrie Fitzpatrick, M. Murphy, R. Clarke, R. Freeland, R.J. Wardlaw and S.S. Green. The only woman on the executive, Mrs W.B. (Winfred) Lewis (BA, BD), had a strong background in British IVF.[173]

The WF's level of activity was set to increase to a remarkable new level. Rob Miller had worked very hard, but Arthur Gunn's pace and output were phenomenal. He often astounded his executive colleagues with the amount of copy he could produce, and he seemed to them like 'a prophet from heaven'.[174] Under Gunn's editorship, the *EP* rapidly grew in both size and circulation. In 1963, the bimonthly *EP* was sixty-four pages long.[175] By 1964, the print run was up to 6000 (though that included many free promotional copies, including those distributed to divinity students);[176] by 1965 there were 3500 paid subscriptions.[177] Gunn's editorship meant definite shifts in focus and tone. Book reviews and serialised Bible Studies remained, and there were the customary evangelical articles on the nature of scripture.[178] There were still a few weighty doctrinal pieces, often by the former editor.[179] There was a little on Calvin and Calvinism.[180] There was a brief article on the Second Coming,[181] one on the Sabbath,[182] but nothing on evolution.[183] The flow of historical biographies suddenly ceased, as did all the contributions from those long deceased. Overall, the focus became more contemporary, and more related to praxis. There were new extended series on prayer and missionary work, and articles on expository preaching, evangelism, revival, church music, the IVF, Keswick, BTI and new Bible translations.[184]

The editorial tone also became more indignant and anxious. Gunn compiled a new multi-page feature 'Window on the World', intended to give news of 'church trends throughout the world which are of particular concern to evangelicals'.[185] There was material expressing alarm about 'a moral landslide of extreme danger', the sexualisation of the media, promiscuity among youth, and liberal advocacy of 'New Morality'.[186] Gunn and his sources saw modernity as morally depraved, and theological liberalism as complicit.[187] There was also polemic against universalism, neo-orthodoxy, theological 'double-talk', the theology of the NCC, and J.A.T. Robinson's secular theology.[188]

Gunn's primary preoccupation was ecumenism, which he saw as the doorway to ecclesiastical calamity. He believed Protestantism was perilously close to reversing the Reformation and capitulating to Rome. Gunn saw Roman Catholicism as benighted and oppressive, and as the enemy of the Gospel and spiritual freedom. 'The Westminster Fellowship', he wrote, is 'opposed absolutely to the darkness, superstition, and cruelty of the Roman Catholic system.'[189] What outraged him most of all was that Protestantism – seriously weakened by theological liberalism – might be handed on a plate to Rome by the ecumenical movement. 'All roads,' he wrote, 'are now leading to Rome.'[190] He declared that liberals – who 'don't really believe' in Protestant truth – were happy to sell out to and rejoin Roman Catholicism, for the sake of unity. But the 'one world-wide church' that the ecumenicals desired was the same church that Luther had rejected, and because of that same church 'our forefathers dyed the Scottish heather red with their blood in defence of Presbyterianism'.[191] Gunn's apprehension intensified when, in 1965, the Anglicans joined the church union negotiations in New Zealand. Gunn claimed that, notwithstanding the negligible difference between evangelical Anglicans and Presbyterians, it was the Anglo-Catholics who were laying down the terms of church union,[192] and those terms were calculated to ease re-union with Rome: 'I have not the slightest doubt … that we will … become Anglicans … and that later on we will be asked to commit suicide as Protestants.'[193] One of Gunn's headlines summed up his fears: 'The Liberal Protestant Landslide Towards Rome – Via Anglicanism'.[194]

Gunn's editorials were strongly stated.[195] But his primary technique in the *EP* was to quote rather than comment: he scoured large numbers of liberal, ecumenical and Roman Catholic publications (including *Zealandia*) and extracted quotations documenting the theological, spiritual and moral bankruptcy of the movements he feared. In successive issues Gunn printed snippets revealing wrongs he perceived about Catholics, such as persecution of Protestants, policy about Catholic–Protestant intermarriage, the Catholic Enquiry Centre, Catholic support for lotteries, parishioners reading *Zealandia* during the mass, Mariolatry, transubstantiation, the wealth of the Vatican and high rates of illiteracy in Catholic countries. He similarly documented the failings of ecumenism, such as the decline of the SCM, liberal curricula, radical left-wing political sympathies in the WCC, the problems of the United Church in Canada (and the vigour of Canadian Presbyterianism), the heterodox statements of leading liberals (for example, Lord Soper and Bishop Pike) and the desire of some ecumemists ultimately to fuse all world religions.[196] In every issue there were also longer articles, most of them reasoned and moderate in themselves, that were critical of Roman Catholicism and ecumenism.[197] In varying degrees, Gunn's colleagues on the WF executive shared most of his apprehensions, but none of them articulated Gunn's scenario of impending disaster with quite the same clarity or passion. Whenever they themselves wrote for the *EP*, especially in the occasional editorial, they wrote with what appeared to be a deliberately milder tone.[198] Whenever they compiled 'Window on the World', they featured positive news (for example, items about Billy Graham, IVF, Crusaders, the persistence of Christianity in the USSR and China, and overseas missions).[199]

Alongside his work on the *EP*, Gunn drove an ambitious programme of publications, mostly small booklets written by WF members. In 1964, for instance, ten titles were published.[200] Many of the WF publications were little more than tracts, usually reprints of *EP* articles. Initial print runs of most titles ran to several thousand. Sales were vigorous, and many titles were reprinted;[201] by the mid 1960s, the WF reported sales of 50,000 publications per year.[202] The WF programme of publications was unparalleled among New Zealand evangelical movements. It reflected the extraordinary vision and energies of Gunn. It also expressed the heady reformist zeal and confidence of a movement that saw itself as bringing spiritual and doctrinal renewal to a whole denomination. They were intent on re-educating the PCNZ.[203] They saw their movement as akin to the Scottish evangelicals who worked together with Andrew Thomson in the 1820s to reform the Church of Scotland from moderatism to evangelicalism; by negative analogy, they were also inspired by the effect of the Jesuits and the Tractarians.[204] As reformists, the WF leaders saw the flood of WF publications as a 'brilliant break-through', dramatically increasing the WF's impact.[205]

Some of the WF publications, such as Gunn's *Visitation Evangelism* and *Elders' Roll Book and Handbook*, were related to parish-based evangelism, a forté of the WF evangelicals in South Auckland.[206] Such titles reflected, in part, the influence of similar overseas campaigns of visitation evangelism such as the 'Tell Scotland' programme.[207] Another tool for church growth was the WF communicants' manual *Christ Our Life*; the WF was pleased when the manual was also adopted by the PCNZ – but felt ruffled that the PCNZ suppressed the names of the book's WF authors.[208] Some WF titles were evangelistic, such as *I Want to Know God* (Elley) and *After Death What?* (J.G. Miller).[209] Some were pastoral: *How Can I Overcome Temptation?* (Milmine) and *What Shall Be My Work?* (W.M. Ryburn).[210] Some WF publications were booklets of about fifty pages. These included doctrinal and didactic works such as *Authority of the Bible*,[211] or R.S. Miller's *Our Presbyterian Faith*,[212] and his scholarly appeal for Sabbatarianism, *His Day or Ours?*[213] There were also the popular glossy-covered Bible study booklets for personal or group use, such as *Nehemiah* (R.W. Kirkby), *Jonah* (J.G. Miller), *Romans* (D.A. Kirkby), *Ephesians* (Gunn), *Colossians* (J.G. Miller), and *1 John* (W.B. Lewis).[214] In addition, the WF produced a solid and wide-ranging *Book List*.[215]

The booklet *Evangelicals and the Ecumenical Movement* (J.G. Miller and A. Gunn) addressed the church union issue.[216] So did briefer works such as *Statement on the Draft Basis of Faith* (1962), *Ten Reasons Against the Present Church Union Proposals* (1965), and *Why We Say 'No' to an Act of Commitment* (1965).[217] A 1964 pamphlet, *What Is the Westminster Fellowship?* (J.G. Miller), was mild and reassuring in tone and obviously intended to allay suspicion.[218] A more polemical offering was the WF's attack on universalism, *Is Hell Empty After All?* (Webster and Taylor).[219] Other titles were ethical, such as Gunn's *Sex and the Christian*,[220] or Webster's tract against alcohol, *It's a Trap*.[221] Among the flurry of publications coming from the WF in the early 1960s, there was nothing on evolution or eschatology: neither subject was a preoccupation among WF evangelicals.[222]

Almost all of the WF's writers were New Zealanders, but the WF did publish a small amount of material from overseas sources, e.g. *The Roman Catholic Church* (Lloyd-Jones),[223] *Dancing and the Christian* (Dwight Small),[224] and A.F.

Olsen's anti-ecumenical *It's a Scandal*.²²⁵ Some in the executive felt that the latter two pamphlets, sourced from America and published by Gunn without authorisation from the executive, were 'harmful' to the WF, presumably because they were too narrow and strident, and from a 'fundamentalist' American context.²²⁶

In the early 1960s, the WF was clearly in an expansionist, missionary mood. An office and secretary were arranged to handle dispatch.²²⁷ Eleven area committees were established.²²⁸ Annual 'Rallies', held in various cities and regional centres, featured exposition, prayer and information about WF.²²⁹ In 1965, Gunn made a nationwide whirlwind tour ('Tell the Church'), addressing WF rallies in sixteen different centres over a period of nine days.²³⁰ AGMs, which always included both biblical exposition and an address called 'Blueprint for the Future', attracted up to 300.²³¹ In 1964, the WF held its first national conference, on the theme of 'Renewal of the Church', also with 300 present.²³² This conference, with its unity and confidence, arguably represented the peak of the WF's influence, which seemed to be expanding on every front.²³³ A dramatic development occurred in 1964 when WF stalwart and executive member N.C. (Norrie) Fitzpatrick and his wife decided to gift their home and 40 acres of farmland at Karaka to WF.²³⁴ The WF began to dream of an evangelical conference and study centre, dedicated to the 'renewal and revival' of the PCNZ. Donald Kirkby compared its potential to that of St Ninian's in Crieff, or even Calvin's Academy in Geneva.²³⁵

The WF's international connections

Evangelicalism was characteristically internationalist in spirit, and the WF's focus was always wider than New Zealand alone. The WF continued to have considerable links with overseas evangelicalism. It corresponded with kindred organisations (such as the Protestant Reformation Society, Scottish Reformation Society and Northern Ireland Evangelical Group), and designated overseas agents such as J.D. Douglas in the UK. Some WF leaders also made personal contact with evangelicals overseas.²³⁶ Another international focus of the WF was its involvement in the work of the Far East Broadcasting Company (FEBC), an evangelical radio station broadcasting into Asia and the Pacific from Manila. Several members of the WF executive (including Gunn, Miller, Fitzpatrick and Brinsley) were enthusiastic supporters of the FEBC.²³⁷ The WF became responsible for weekly biblical expositions; the tapes were cut in South Auckland.²³⁸ The broadcasts could also be heard in New Zealand on shortwave radio.

A somewhat unexpected factor was the WF's influence on conservative evangelical Presbyterians in Australia. Graham Miller, Gunn and Kirkby spoke on Keswick platforms in Australia, raising the profile of the WF. Rob Miller and Gosling preached from the pulpit of Robert Swanton, the leader of a resurgent Reformed Presbyterianism in Victoria.[239] The WF had official 'Representatives' in five states, with their names listed on the *EP*'s inside cover.[240] By 1964 there were 603 Australian subscribers to the *EP*, WF publications were selling well in Australia's Presbyterian bookshops, and a sample *EP* was sent to every Presbyterian minister in Queensland.[241] WF rallies were held in numerous Australian centres: in 1964, for instance, Gunn addressed rallies in Brisbane, Toowoomba, Sydney and Melbourne, and reported considerable interest in the establishment of similar fellowships.[242] There was already such a fellowship in Queensland, and others were founded in New South Wales and Tasmania.[243] Before his departure to Australia, Graham Miller told the WF that 'the spiritual destiny of our two countries lies together' and proposed at the AGM that the WF be renamed 'The Westminster Fellowship of Evangelical Presbyterians in Australia and New Zealand'.[244] The proposal was not accepted in New Zealand, but it was indicative of how strong the Australian connection had become.[245]

The WF and the Reformed Churches of New Zealand

The Westminster Fellowship in this period carefully maintained its policy of avoiding any contact with the International Conference of Christian Churches. When the *Contender* implied that the WF had invited the NZICCC to send representatives to the WF conference, the WF chairman immediately wrote a letter refuting that claim, and also wrote to the *Outlook* stating that the WF had no connection with the ICCC.[246] The WF had no desire to be associated – in reality or in perception – with a militant separatist group. By contrast, the WF was happy to host a visiting leader of the National Association of Evangelicals.[247] The *EP* included articles from the NAE, but never any material from the ICCC.[248]

A related issue was the WF's connection with the Synod of the Reformed Churches of New Zealand, a small cluster of churches which reflected the more conservative side of schism in the church in Holland, and which was affiliated with the ICCC.[249] Its adherents looked askance at the confessional latitude of the PCNZ,[250] but took considerable interest in the WF. An *EP* editorial in 1962 expressed WF admiration of the Reformed denomination and 'gladly and joyously' extended 'the hand of friendship'.[251] Some Reformed leaders privately called for WF ministers to leave the PCNZ and join them in a denomination that was anti-modernist, anti-ecumenical and anti-Catholic, and that maintained church discipline.[252] WF leaders, however, buoyed by the groundswell of popular support they were receiving within the PCNZ, insisted that they were witnessing the beginnings of divine 'renewal and revival' in the Presbyterian Church, and that they had no intention of abandoning the thousands of faithful church members who looked to them for leadership.[253]

Despite considerable common ground (in such areas as biblicism, Reformed theology and distrust of theological liberalism and ecumenism), there were still considerable differences between the Reformed and WF groups. There were disparities in how far each group took its doctrinal tendencies, and the tone in which they articulated them: the Reformed Synod people were rigorist on most issues, whereas the WF leaders were still constrained by a concern for balance and moderation. There were dissimilarities in ecclesiology, too: the Reformed group based their sense of legitimacy – and purity – on the fact of being visibly separate, whereas the WF leaders were content to be a reformist element inside a greater whole. The WF hoped not for a pure church but for a revived church, or at least an improved church. The Reformed group felt safely quarantined from those they considered apostate, whereas the WF group still wished to persuade their co-denominationalists and were prepared to coexist with those they disagreed with. These divergent approaches broadly reflected the differences between a more militant and separatist conservatism (with some similarities to American 'fundamentalism') and the milder and non-separatist conservative evangelicalism modelled by the IVF.

The WF and schism

Within the WF there were different shades of feeling about church union. Some Executive members (e.g. Wilson and Brinsley) were open to union, if an acceptable basis could be found, but some (e.g. Gunn and Miller) were inclined to resist union on almost any basis. Miller's objections to ecumenism reflected his thorough theological critique of that movement, and had been fortified by a recent work by Lloyd-Jones: for evangelicals, the basis of unity was common doctrine; for ecumenists, doctrine was 'divisive'.[254] Miller was nevertheless prepared to be a voice within the Church Union Committee, engaging with the issues from an evangelical perspective. Miller saw separation as a last resort, but Gunn became increasingly impatient with the PCNZ, and seemed to see church union as an opportunity for evangelicals to separate into a remnant of the Presbyterian Church that would stay out of union.[255] In 1962, the WF executive hammered out a careful memorandum and sent it to the *Outlook*.

The statement noted that there was no reference to church union in the WF constitution, that the WF was 'not ... inherently opposed' to it, and that 'in an ideal evangelical context [the WF] might conceivably participate in fostering such a union'. But in the 'menacing climate of today's world', and 'in loyalty to the Reformed heritage', the WF could not afford to be neutral. Basing its views on scripture, it would participate in the debate 'with serious purpose'.[256]

Once the Anglican Church joined the church union negotiations, the WF attitude hardened: the WF leaders could not accept the loss of the historic doctrinal standards; they recoiled from what they saw as a requirement for reordination; they were anxious about the authority that bishops might exert over evangelical ministers and congregations; they wanted to retain elders and a simple non-liturgical worship.[257] They believed Anglican demands were being dictated by a High Church outlook (with exclusive views on ordination and communion) rather than by the traditional Reformed Anglican position (which had welcomed intercommunion with other Reformed churches).[258] For Gunn, at least, these objections were compounded by his attitude to Roman Catholicism.[259] Miller shared similar concerns, but they were expressed in a more restrained way, and with strong historical awareness.[260] While he felt the Protestant Church had temporarily slipped its moorings and succumbed to 'collective delusions', he was optimistic that – in the sovereign purpose of God – the 'swelling testimony' of international evangelicalism would soon lead to Protestantism's renewal.[261]

The WF executive agreed that it opposed participation in the 'Act of Commitment'. But Gunn wanted to go further and presented the executive with proposals for a 'Continuing [Presbyterian] Church'. In a prolonged debate, a majority of the executive appeared to regard Gunn's proposal as 'premature and unfortunate'.[262] Two months later, the executive passed a resolution prohibiting him from publishing his paper in the *EP*.[263] In the Annual Report, Graham Miller pointedly wrote, 'We disown any thought of separation. We shall take our full and responsible part in the church union proposals now before the Church.'[264] Miller thus echoed his words of a year earlier:

> Let us be quite clear ... we hold no brief for schism. Rank and untamed spiritual pride can appeal to Scripture in support of its separatist position, it can appear very right, very earnest, and very cogent; but it can prove an antichrist.[265]

Later, in 1966, Miller was present in the London meeting where John Stott publicly opposed Lloyd-Jones' apparent call for evangelical 'separation' – and Miller firmly agreed with Stott.[266]

Opposition to WF

The Westminster Fellowship was regarded with considerable suspicion and hostility, and the WF saw its opposition to church union plans as the main contributing factor to such 'prejudice'.[267] There were many evidences of antipathy. Westland Presbytery railed against any group other than the Presbyterian Bookroom publishing Presbyterian books, and complained to the PCNZ Doctrine Committee about alleged heresy in the WF's *Elders' Roll Book* and *Visitation Evangelism*.[268] A large city church in Whanganui withheld permission from the WF to use its facilities for a rally.[269] The moderator (J.S. Murray) refused to attend the WF Conference and took exception to his name being used on the tentative programme.[270]

A 1962 issue of *Forum*, the church's magazine for ministers, contained two spirited denunciations of the WF. Both articles referred to church union and to Arthur Gunn. One of the pieces charged the WF with self-righteousness, literalism, negativity, factionalism, and trying 'to influence the rest of the Church'.[271] The other article – by a minister who had come up through St Stephen's (Dunedin), BTI, EU and IVF – accused his former evangelical friends of narrowness, intolerance, bias, defensiveness, lack of charity, disloyalty to the church, self-congratulation, presumption and arrogance, and with no right to the name 'evangelical'.[272] Four decades later, a WF insider recalled the article as 'bitter'.[273] In the next issue, a liberal minister castigated the WF 'sect' for 'shameless' and 'blasphemous' vilification of others. The WF lacked 'elementary churchmanship' and was as blinkered as 'an aged draught-horse'.[274] In 1963 a crude bogus letter, written as if it were from the WF, was posted to every presbytery.[275] As the only organised opposition to the prevailing tendencies within the PCNZ, the WF naturally provoked apprehension and antagonism. The WF was seen as a reactionary, backward-looking phenomenon, unjustifiably resisting more enlightened theologies. It was a threat to progress, obstructing ecumenical dreams that seemed close to realisation. The WF also attracted resentment from ecumenical elements beyond the PCNZ. On the opening day of the 1965 Assembly, a Methodist minister was quoted in the *Otago Daily Times* describing the WF as a 'highly organised group' which was 'unscrupulously attacking the [Church Union] Commission's efforts' – prompting Gunn's response that as 'the only group in the negotiating churches exposing in print the weaknesses, fallacies and ambiguities of the present proposals', the WF was bound to face opposition.[276]

Antipathy towards the WF can be taken as evidence that the WF had established itself as an important voice within the PCNZ, an articulate conservative evangelical voice with effective organs of communication and growing popular support. Critics of the WF recognised that its leaders were 'able and devoted' and highly energetic, and that they conveyed an 'air of authority' that appealed to many.[277] The vigour of the WF-associated ministries and parishes within South Auckland, and the confident expansion of the WF itself, made the WF seem all the more dangerous to those who regretted its existence. In large measure, the tensions reflected the continuing rivalry of the two competing strands within the postwar PCNZ: those inspired and nurtured by the SCM, and those inspired and nurtured by the Evangelical Unions and IVF.

There was another element in the mix: the public face and voice of the WF had increasingly become Arthur Gunn, and his frequent inclusion in the *EP* of material against Roman Catholicism and ecumenism left the WF vulnerable to being misconstrued as negative and divisive. In 1964, a carefully worded letter from two Knox students and signed by nineteen others chided the *EP* for 'intolerance' towards both Roman Catholics and liberals, and for failing to fulfil the WF's stated aim of being 'as constructive and helpful as possible to the whole church, especially in the field of communication'.[278]

At Assembly, most evangelicals still felt intimidated by the phalanx of liberals and ex-moderators seated in the front rows.[279] But as the evangelical stream grew in numbers, and as the WF grew in influence, some Presbyterian evangelicals became more willing to speak out at Assembly. The South Auckland group provided leadership, and evangelicals often met together before Assembly to coordinate strategy.[280] But it was still difficult for evangelicals to join a debate: 'if an evangelical point of view was put up it would be countered, and despised, and there were some very vociferous speakers'.[281] The evangelicals believed there was an 'iron-clad' solidarity against them, and that liberals 'mutually supported one another like the shields on the back of a tortoise'.[282] Most often, the rallying point for both WF evangelicals and for opposition to the WF was church union.

Neither Arthur Gunn nor Graham Miller was given to timidity, and both were willing to enter the fray. Gunn was an effective debater, with a capacity for putting things in a memorable way.[283] He could also provoke hostility by being overly trenchant, or too sweeping in his assertions. When he rose to speak, there was 'shuffling of the feet, murmuring, sighing' on the floor of Assembly.[284] The prejudice against Gunn was such that many were unable to listen to what he said: 'Arthur Gunn would get up and say something that was perfectly good, but it went down like a lead balloon.'[285] On occasion Gunn faced open personal antagonism, and was 'very unfairly treated'.[286] An evangelical recalled an incident when a moderator 'got the whole Assembly to jeer at Arthur Gunn' – the moderator 'fired the first shot, and then several liberal speakers took the cue and got up to lambast Arthur'.[287]

Graham Miller was also a marked man,[288] but usually got a better hearing, out of respect for his knowledge, eloquence and 'obvious Christian disposition'.[289] He was a skilled debater who spoke quietly and graciously, but with piercing reason, with a mastery of Assembly procedures and with great tenacity. He was 'steel clothed in velvet'.[290] 'He said things so nicely, but he had terrific punch. Quite devastating, from the point of view of logic … The fellows … didn't have an answer for him.'[291] He was also unperturbed by reversals. An evangelical newcomer to the PCNZ Assembly, Wynford Davies, thought Miller was 'clarity all through', and 'most impressive' (but when he said so to some liberal ministers on the steamer across Cook Strait after Assembly – one of whom was Geering – the temperature of the conversation suddenly plummeted).[292]

Miller's brother Rob, likewise trained in law, was also a careful, scholarly speaker, incisive in his thinking, and very well informed on Presbyterianism's historic and Reformed heritage. Sam Green, an evangelical elder from Dargaville and WF president, was a pleasant, 'rollicking' speaker who was able to sway Assembly.[293] So could Les Gosling, who was an impassioned debater. Feisty, opinionated and individualistic, Gosling was widely liked, and his fiery indignation could change Assembly's mind.[294] Lewis Wilson, known to be moderate and scholarly, was also usually well received.

Sometimes it was the WF itself that was under attack at Assemblies – as in 1965, when church union plans were advancing rapidly and there were several moves at Assembly against the WF. A minister from Auckland objected to the WF publications.[295] The clerk of Dunedin Presbytery supported a motion that Assembly 'direct' the WF to delete from its title the words 'within the Presbyterian Church of New Zealand'.[296] After the vote on church union, evangelicals signed their dissent.[297] Immediately afterwards, they tried to present an overture about protecting the property rights of those parishes not entering church union. It was countered by an unusually haughty amendment that the overture should only be received pro forma, and that Assembly should record a five-point statement of why it 'does not accept the premises of the overture'.[298] At the same Assembly, the South Auckland Presbytery was accused of mishandling a disciplinary issue, and WF members felt that the opportunity was being taken by some to vent a 'malignant dislike' of the WF.[299] The enduring memory of Assembly among Presbyterian evangelicals from this period is that they were vigorously opposed by the prevailing church party, and were sometimes the objects of 'astounding acrimony'.[300] Even those evangelicals who went out of their way to be generous towards those they disagreed with felt pushed to the margins.[301] Nevertheless, evangelicals – believing that they made a disproportionate contribution within the denomination to overseas mission, congregational mission, youth evangelism and church growth – comforted themselves with the thought that in the church at large they were 'too numerous, useful and successful to be overlooked'.[302]

Evangelical critique of the WF

The WF was criticised not only by liberals and ecumenists, but also by some evangelicals who were troubled in particular by the negative style of Arthur Gunn. In 1962, a letter to Gunn and the Editorial Board from Dunedin objected to a judgmental tone in the *EP*. The writer claimed the WF was exhibiting a 'lovelessness' more akin to 'the works of the flesh' than 'the fruit of the Spirit'.[303] A copy was sent to another executive member, with a letter expressing the primary concern that the respect for the evangelical cause that had been built up by the IVF and EU was being destroyed.[304] In 1964, the WF received a 'severely critical' letter from an evangelical minister in Invercargill.[305] A year later, WF supporter Rowland Harries wrote deploring a 'spirit of intolerance dividing WF from the rest of the Church'.[306] In the same year, an *EP* article by Gosling contained at least three thinly veiled repudiations of Gunn's editorial style.[307] Within the executive, Miller was one of several temperate voices. As chairman, he sometimes quietly restrained his colleague.[308] The majority of the executive supported 'a more moderate line' than that adopted by Gunn.[309] In 1965, Donald Kirkby wrote an editorial disavowing 'unbalanced thinking leading to extremes in emphasis, and a striving for the truth divorced from grace'.[310] Gunn's polemical approach was not reined in sufficiently to avoid some damage being done to the image of the WF; but on the other hand his forthrightness appealed to many, and was one reason why the WF attracted much support.

After Miller left New Zealand, and against the background of advanced church union plans and the mounting Geering controversy,[311] Gunn appeared increasingly willing to consider denominational schism, and the unease of some moderate evangelicals intensified.[312] In July 1966, with the support of Gosling, eleven evangelical students at the Theological Hall (all of them associated with EU, IVF and the WF) wrote to the WF expressing distress.[313] They acknowledged the great popularity of the WF among laity, reflecting widespread dissatisfaction with liberal theology, but the unsubtle 'populism' of the *EP* had been at the cost of 'responsible theological leadership', and over the last three years the WF had 'gradually alienated itself from almost all the University-trained students in the Theological Hall'. The WF had failed to represent 'fairly and objectively' those views it did not share; it had failed to show love for the whole church; instead of engaging the Church's attention it had repelled it. The letter indicated that the WF's opposition to church union was a major obstacle.[314] Such heavy insider criticism – from the sons and protégés of WF leaders – did not bode well for the WF, which forfeited the support of some in that generation.[315] It was the EU and IVF that had nurtured the leaders of the WF and given them a theological vision and assurance. However, to the extent that the WF had substituted populism for the moderate tone characteristic of the IVF, and denunciation for positive witness, it had weakened its leadership among some IVF-trained evangelicals. Also, while the IVF had always been respectful of denominations, the more assertive denominationalism of the WF may have sat uneasily with the ethos of Christian interdenominationalism that was characteristic of IVF and related evangelical organisations. By no means all evangelical divinity students were concerned about the tone of the WF, however: another group of them wrote to the executive expressing strong support for the WF.[316]

Such internal disagreements within Presbyterian evangelicalism indicated that, despite an apparently easy unity in the earlier postwar decades, the evangelical movement was no longer so ideologically cohesive. The unease was not about basic doctrine, but about tone and style. The misgivings that had become apparent also add weight to the contention that separatism and militancy were not the prevailing character or mood of the New Zealand evangelical movement. The evangelical outlook and tone fostered in New Zealand by Laird, the Crusaders and the IVF – and embraced by successive generations of evangelical leaders – was essentially moderate and reformist, rather than truculent or separatist.

Both the robust external opposition to the Westminster Fellowship and the differing perspectives within the two generations of IVF-trained Presbyterians were indications that, by the mid 1960s, evangelical Presbyterianism in New Zealand had become an increasingly vigorous and influential movement. Since the early 1930s, when Thomas Miller had been a lonely voice and the Evangelical Unions had scarcely begun, evangelical New Zealand Presbyterianism had come a long way.

Conclusion

New Zealand evangelicalism grew markedly in the first two decades after the Second World War. There was a big increase in the number of evangelical churches, students, ministers and lay leaders. In the 1920s and 30s, evangelical Christians had often been regarded as old-fashioned Bible-thumping reactionaries; but by the late 1950s evangelicals had a new assurance and vibrancy, and were making an impact that could not easily be dismissed. As Warner Hutchinson remarked in 1959, 'evangelicalism is certainly far more respectable in the Church life of the country as a whole than it was even ten years ago'.[1]

The seeds of that New Zealand evangelical recovery were planted in the prewar period, from about 1930. A decisive factor in the evangelical renaissance was the EU/IVF movement, which gave evangelicals a clear name and identity, restored their intellectual confidence, and brought them together across denominations and across the nation. For disaffected conservative Presbyterian minister Thomas Miller, in Dunedin, partnership with the Evangelical Union offered a way of reasserting evangelical faith, and of raising a new generation of future evangelical Presbyterian leaders. In Christchurch, William Orange inspired a large number of young protégés with his unique style of devotional Bible teaching, and modelled a way of being both explicitly 'evangelical' and loyally 'Anglican'. The EU and IVF were decisive in consolidating and extending Orange's influence. From the 1940s onwards, successive waves of those shaped by Miller, Orange and EU/IVF were moving through theological college and entering church ministry, where they would reproduce the evangelical model they had been steeped in, characterised by prayerfulness, conversions, exposition, Bible Classes, 'sound' doctrine and missionary support.

By 1965, the new Anglican evangelical movement had established evangelical ministries in a sizable bloc of Christchurch parishes, had helped reinvigorate the evangelical character of Nelson Diocese, had a growing presence in Wellington, and had gained beachheads in both Dunedin and Auckland. Likewise the evangelical Presbyterian movement had greatly expanded in the postwar era, especially in the dynamic South Auckland context. In both denominations young evangelical leaders – all of them moulded by EU and IVF – had established flagship evangelical organisations. The Evangelical Churchmen's Fellowship and the Westminster Fellowship became significant new voices within New Zealand's Anglican and Presbyterian denominations. In the case of the latter, the WF directly challenged the liberal directions of the denominational leadership. The WF was in part a delayed outcome of the 1930s SCM/EU schism, an event which helped shape theological contours for decades to come. By the late 1950s the EUs had eclipsed the SCM, a development symbolic of the rise of evangelical vis-à-vis liberal Protestantism. For at least two decades into the postwar era, EU/IVF was a crucial defining and unifying element in the resurgent New Zealand evangelicalism.

The new evangelical identity brought to New Zealand by the EU and IVF reflected the conservative British evangelical tradition. The IVF was conservative, but was neither extreme nor militant. It rejected 'modernist' theological reductionism, but was not anti-intellectual. It was opposed to ecclesiastical separatism, and it avoided controversy over secondary issues. Its tone was quintessentially moderate. It stood for 'sobriety and balance', for 'sane conservatism'. The ethos of moderation was in part because the IVF put a premium on gaining and retaining acceptance. But it was also instinctive, in a former colony where the majority of people still considered themselves British. To the extent that evangelical leaders in New Zealand became aware of the competing streams within Christianity in the United States, they felt a ready affinity with the positive, peaceable type of American evangelicalism being promoted in the US by the NAE, Billy Graham and *Christianity Today* – and they firmly rejected the militant fundamentalism of the ICCC.

In the mid-twentieth century, various evangelical organisations – including BTI, Scripture Union, Keswick, and especially EU/IVF and Crusaders – contributed to an increased unity within New Zealand evangelicalism by bringing together evangelicals from within and across various denominations. For a time, at least at leadership level, New Zealand evangelical Protestantism was more cohesive than ever before. But there was not uniformity. Within the New Zealand IVF movement itself, different strands and emphases were discernible, such as the more spiritualising approach of Orange and the more rationalistic outlook of Blaiklock. Within the Presbyterian evangelical movement, some were more Reformed and confessionalist, and some were more experientialist or activist. Within the Anglican evangelical movement, Anglican tradition was important for some, and less important for others. In both the Presbyterian and Anglican movements, there were some intergenerational differentials: leaders who had been part of a small beleaguered evangelical minority were more likely to be defensive and isolationist, and emerging leaders whose experience had mainly been that of an ascendant evangelicalism were more likely to engage confidently with other viewpoints. The relative cohesiveness of evangelicalism in the 1950s and 60s was remarkable, but could scarcely last: as evangelicalism expanded further, and as New Zealand society experienced major changes, the fragmentation of evangelicalism became inevitable.

Was the emerging evangelical movement in New Zealand reactive or positive? Unsurprisingly, it was both. Conservative elements in the SCM and in various denominations had been unhappy with theological modernism, and the arrival of the Evangelical Unions had provided a means of reasserting a more biblicist approach. Likewise, the ECF and WF created safe environments for anti-modernists. But, arguably, the impulse behind the evangelicalism was primarily positive: those of a more conservative faith simply wanted to get on with Christian faith, personal piety, nurture, Bible study and evangelism as they had always understood it. The evangelicalism which emerged mid-century was in some ways a more refined and intellectually robust version of earlier pietism and revivalism.

Another question is the extent to which evangelical Protestantism in mid twentieth-century New Zealand was distinctive. Broadly speaking, it was not distinctive at all. It had much in common with evangelical Protestant Christianity anywhere: the same Bible, similar doctrines and emphases, the same devotional disciplines, a comparable range of spiritual experiences and many equivalent (or shared) organisations. By its very nature, evangelicalism is international, with similar features in most contexts. As elsewhere, evangelical faith and practice were filtered and constrained by various denominational traditions, which were often much more important than any distinctives of New Zealand nationality.

Since, before about 1970, New Zealand highly valued its cultural affinities and links with Britain, it was inevitable that the greatest overseas influence on New Zealand evangelicalism in the period of this study was British evangelicalism. That influence was both direct (through particular denominations, books, organisations, ideas, immigrants, and speakers) and also indirect (through many shared cultural assumptions and values). The influence from the United States was considerably less. Earlier New Zealand evangelicalism had been influenced to some extent by American revivalism, and there had also been various introductions of American hymns and organisations. In the postwar period, the most significant American influence on New Zealand evangelicalism was the preaching and methodology of Billy Graham, especially through the 1959 Crusade.

Because of the broadly similar history of New Zealand and Australia as antipodean British migrant colonies, evangelical Protestantism in both countries experienced many similar cultural, theological and ecclesiastical influences. Along the way, this book has illustrated various commonalities, including the importance in both countries of Keswick-style conventions, Bible institutes, IVF, the Billy Graham Crusade and missionary societies such as CIM. Evangelical speakers visiting from the Northern Hemisphere (e.g. Guinness and Stott) often visited both countries. The New Zealand IVF movement regularly looked to Australia for its conference speakers and university missioners, and New Zealand figures such as Graham Miller and Don Kirkby were frequent convention speakers and missioners in Australia. There were exchanges of evangelical leaders between the countries (e.g. Lionel Fletcher, David Stewart, Graham Miller). There were ongoing links between the Nelson and Sydney dioceses. In both countries, evangelical Protestantism became more vigorous and assured in the 1950s and 60s; both countries experienced heightened spiritual receptivity in the late 1950s. Nevertheless, there were features of evangelicalism in each country that had no parallel in the other – for instance, there was nothing in New Zealand that closely resembled Sydney evangelicalism.

The distinctiveness of New Zealand's evangelical Protestantism derived from the unique mix of New Zealand's geography, demographics, regions, denominations and personalities. New Zealand is long and narrow, and several regions (including three of the four main cities) had their distinctive denominational concentrations, which helped give New Zealand some of its various evangelical flavours. There was the more Presbyterian character of Otago–Southland evangelicalism, the Anglican–Brethren character of the Christchurch movement, the more Low Church style of Anglicanism in Nelson, and the more Baptist–Brethren constituency of Auckland evangelicalism. But such regional differences were not grounded in any strong cultural differences, and in a fairly small country no part of the evangelical community had sufficient critical mass to remain insulated from other parts. There was also much interdenominational mixing and intermarrying. Key contextual factors affecting New Zealand's evangelicalism were thus the country's relatively small population and (at that time) its relative cultural homogeneity.

In the New Zealand evangelical scene, various personalities made their mark. Some figures stand out: the gentle, spiritual biblicism of Orange; the lonely resoluteness of Thomas Miller; the shepherding, movement-building skills of John Laird; the evangelical intensity and energy of Roger Thompson; the warmth and missionary focus of Harry Thomson; the gravitas and erudite oratory of Blaiklock; the gracious but piercing eloquence of Graham Miller; the cool-headed combativeness of Arthur Gunn; the flair of Don Kirkby; and the irenic evangelical Anglicanism of people like Maurice Goodall.

Another way of highlighting the distinctive story of mid twentieth-century New Zealand evangelicalism would be to suggest some defining moments. At the time, some of them would have seemed fairly insignificant events. In 1926, for instance, E.M. Blaiklock was appointed to a university lectureship in Auckland – and thus gained a platform from which he would later become a leading voice in postwar New Zealand evangelicalism. In 1928, Thomas Miller missed out on a parish in Melbourne and instead moved to a Dunedin parish strategic for student work – and thus later became the leader of Dunedin and Presbyterian evangelicalism. A number of events took place in 1930: William Orange transferred from rural seclusion to a parish on the outskirts of Christchurch – and began the work that would later make him the leader of Christchurch and Anglican evangelicalism; Cree Brown wrote to Dr Howard Guinness inviting him to New Zealand – and thus the Evangelical Unions became established; Dr John Laird came ashore when his ship visited Auckland – and thus there arrived someone who would became a unifying figure among New Zealand evangelicals; in the Otago University CU, someone moved a resolution that the EU be declined permission to affiliate with the SCM – and thus there began a critical schism within New Zealand Protestantism. In 1936, representatives of the four EUs met in Wellington to establish a New Zealand IVF. In 1945, the Evangelical Churchmen's Fellowship was founded, and in 1950 the Westminster Fellowship. In 1948, a group of evangelical young people turned up one Sunday at St Martin's Spreydon – energising what was to become a highly influential evangelical Anglican ministry among young people in Christchurch. In 1950, Graham Miller and the WF resolved to have no contact with the ICCC. In 1959, Billy Graham held his first New Zealand crusade. In 1962, the WF executive was relocated in South Auckland – thus beginning a dynamic new phase in the Presbyterian evangelical movement. In 1963, some younger evangelicals took editorial control of the ECF magazine – heralding a less defensive style of evangelical Anglicanism. Together, these events helped a new type of evangelicalism develop in New Zealand in the mid twentieth century.

This book has tracked the recovery of a more conservative Protestantism, at a time when a more liberal Protestantism had peaked and then was beginning to decline. It has been beyond the scope of this study to explore the reasons why, at a more philosophical level, those two processes were occurring. Some comments from overseas, however, are relevant. Stuart Piggin attributed evangelicalism's 'tenacity' to the transcendence of its 'meaning system', its possession of an authority (scripture) that was 'external to social norms', and the powerful socialising influence of its families and institutions.[2] Steve Bruce, comparing IVF and SCM student groups from a sociological perspective, noted the advantages of theological conservatism over liberalism: clear beliefs and boundaries, simplicity, more active promotion and 'product profile', stronger differentiation from secularism, a greater commitment required of participants and an effective network of separate organisations which sustain faith.[3] Such insights could readily apply to the evangelical movement examined in this book.

Many different metaphors could be applied to describe the emergence of a renascent evangelicalism in postwar New Zealand: images of windshift, rebirth, foundations and rebuilding, seeding and growing. But another appropriate metaphor is a tidal one. The image arose from the words of a key informant, who suggested that 'gradually, without any trumpets blaring, God brought this quiet tidal movement up the estuary, and one by one the rocks and snags were covered'.[4]

In 1930 the evangelical tide was at its lowest ebb. Almost imperceptibly, in the 1930s and 40s, the tide had begun to turn. By the late 1950s the tide was visibly coming back in.

Epilogue: A Glimpse of What Came Next

This book covers only the period up to 1965. But some readers might be thinking about what has happened in New Zealand evangelicalism in the period since 1965. The following brief and tentative overview is offered.

All the indications are that the evangelical tendency within New Zealand Protestantism has continued, but in a more diverse and fragmented way – and against the wider backdrop of a decline in active Christian adherence among New Zealanders. From the 1970s onward, as in many other Western nations, new moods of personal freedom and self-realisation (and a new disdain for authority, conformity and duty) increasingly produced major changes in New Zealand society's religious and moral outlook. There was a growth in religious scepticism, and in indifference to organised religion. Opportunities for Sunday sport, leisure and shopping increased. Church-going gradually became less popular, many long-established denominations became smaller, and census figures for church affiliation decreased. Television and other media became less sympathetic to Christian faith. At the same time the number of religious options multiplied, including new age spirituality and Eastern religion. Infusions of people from non-Western nations swelled the number of New Zealanders belonging to various non-Christian religions.

New Zealand's collective memory of a more Christian past gradually diminished. The greatest decline among churches was experienced by the main Protestant denominations, particularly in those congregations which were more traditional or more liberal. Many evangelical churches and denominations also declined, but evangelical Christianity generally fared somewhat better, especially when churches combined an evangelical theology (of one sort or another) with a more contemporary style. Meanwhile new denominations and independent churches proliferated, most of them conservative in theology.

In the 1970s and 80s, the evangelical student movement experienced further growth. In 1973 the IVF renamed itself the Tertiary Students Christian Fellowship. In the same period, the SCM became comparatively small. Later in the century, the number of theologically conservative student organisations multiplied, and the number of students in TSCF groups reduced. By 2012, for instance, there were about twelve different Christian student groups at the University of Auckland – some of them, such as Student Life, had been imports from the United States, some were associated with particular churches, and some represented cultural minorities. Across the country's campuses Christian student work in all its many flavours remained predominantly evangelical in character, even though many groups would not have identified themselves by that label.

The mid twentieth-century liberal directions of the Presbyterian denomination were not sustained. In the late 1960s, the principal of the Theological Hall, Lloyd Geering, repudiated orthodox Christian doctrines and advocated a radical 'secular theology'. Successive General Assemblies reaffirmed much of what he had denied, and his views had relatively little support among those who remained within the Church. The Presbyterian denomination was still theologically fractured, but over the last few decades the proportion of evangelically-minded ministers and laity gradually increased. Reasons for that include the ongoing effects of the postwar evangelical resurgence (including the work of the IVF/TSCF movement), the impetus of charismatic renewal, and the influx of Pacific and Asian streams (whose churches, in all denominational contexts, were usually theologically conservative).

In the Anglican Church, the evangelical movement continued to expand, and established new parish bases across the country. In some places, including Auckland, the charismatic movement was an important catalyst for evangelical expansion. From the 1990s, the Nelson Diocese strengthened its evangelical ethos. Despite evangelical and charismatic growth, other theological streams retained a considerable influence over Anglicanism in New Zealand. Other Protestant denominations continued in similar paths to those they had previously adopted. The evangelical ethos of the Baptist churches was consolidated, and the Open Brethren movement remained biblicist in character. The Methodist Church followed a more liberal course, and at the end of the century experienced an exodus of some of its more theologically conservative elements.

In the last three decades of the twentieth century the charismatic renewal movement, with its emphasis on the work of the Holy Spirit, had a major influence on many New Zealand churches, including many Baptist, Presbyterian and Anglican congregations. The movement reflected new cultural moods in society, including greater emphases on freedom, experience, expressiveness and intimacy. Charismatic renewal often appealed to those who were already evangelical in outlook. For many, the charismatic movement also helped change the nature of what it meant to be evangelical: an emphasis on ongoing spiritual experience replaced an emphasis on conversion, and worship and 'prayer ministry' could gain priority over expositional preaching. In charismatic contexts, evangelical identity often became less clear, or less important, or could be seen as different to being 'Spirit-filled'.

From the 1970s, Pentecostal churches experienced major growth, and became a much more prominent element within Christianity in New Zealand. Pentecostal churches often combined conservative theology with boisterous worship, upbeat music and appeal to youth. Pentecostals could be very active in establishing new churches, and the number of Pentecostal denominations proliferated also. Many Pentecostal leaders and recruits had backgrounds in evangelical and mainline denominations. In some respects Pentecostalism was a type of de facto evangelicalism, which shared with other evangelicals emphases on salvation and biblical authority. In other respects Pentecostals' preoccupation with the baptism and gifts of the Holy Spirit made them a distinct new movement, one that was very confident of being at the vanguard of a new thing which God was now doing. Pentecostals did not identify with the older evangelical movement, which they sometimes saw as passé. Pentecostals often celebrated a different history than the evangelicals, venerated different heroes and looked in different places for new inspirations. In the last few decades the influence of the United States on New Zealand society has grown, and many New Zealand churches reflected that; Pentecostal churches were perhaps among those most influenced, not least with the adoption of mega-church models and sometimes tendencies toward prosperity teaching.

The mid twentieth-century ecumenical dream ended in disappointment. Plans to unite the five Negotiating Churches fell apart in the mid 1970s and were abandoned. The National Council of Churches was disbanded in 1988, and its successor body in 2005. The failure of ecumenism was indicative of how much the church scene in New Zealand had shifted. The dominance of New Zealand Christianity by mainline churches had come to an end, and liberal theological leadership had faded.

The sort of evangelicalism that was ascendant in New Zealand in the mid twentieth century was to some extent eclipsed by new movements, which were broadly evangelical in character but not explicitly so in name or identity. In one form or another, however, the evangelical impulse remained strong.

Perhaps the tide was still rising.

Notes

The symbol ¶ indicates paragraphs in the transcripts of oral history interviews, copies of which are lodged in the New Zealand Evangelical Archive of Christianity, Deane Memorial Library, Laidlaw College, Henderson, Auckland.

Abbreviations

ADMNH	'A Day's March Nearer Home'	JM	John Meadowcroft interview
BR	Bob Robinson interview	JRB	John R. Brinsley interview
BRC	Brian Carrell interview	KO	Kevin O'Sullivan interview
BTD	Barry T. Doig interview	LW	J. Lewis Wilson interview
DE	Doug Edmiston interview	MB	Maurice Betteridge interview
DO	Dale Oldham interview	MF	Marjorie Foulkes interview
DNZB	*Dictionary of New Zealand Biography*	MG	Maurice Goodall interview
		MW	Max Wiggins interview
DP	David Pickering interview	NP	Norman Perry interview
DW	David Wood interview	PK	Paul Kirkham interview
EP	*The Evangelical Presbyterian*	RDE	R. Donald Elley interview
ERH	E. Rowland Harries interview	REC	R.E. Coulthard interview
FM	Frances Milmine interview	RMG	Robert M. Glen interview
GF	Graduates' Fellowship	RR	Rymall Roxburgh interview
GL	Graham Lamont interview	RT	Roger Thompson interview
GMY	G. Morrison Yule interview	SC	Stephen Clark interview
GN	Guy Nicholson interview	SM	Samuel McCay interview
HT	Harvey Teulon interview	SR	Simon Rae interview
IB	Ian Breward interview	TM	*Thomas Miller*
IGB	Ian Bourne interview	VM	Vera Mott interview
JBM	John B. McKinlay interview	WD	Wynford Davies interview
JF	John Ford interview	WM	Wallace Marriott interview
JG	John Greenslade interview	WJR	W. John Roxborogh interview
JGM	J. Graham Miller interview	WW	Bill F. Wilkens interview
JH	John O. Hewlett interview		

1 Introduction

1. Robert Withycombe, TSCF NI/1. This book generally uses lower case for 'evangelical' when it is a noun, except where evangelical people themselves used upper case.
2. Myk Habets and Tim Meadowcroft (eds), *Gospel, Truth and Interpretation: Evangelical Identity in Aotearoa New Zealand* (Auckland: Archer Press, 2011); Peter J. Lineham, *No Ordinary Union: The Story of the Scripture Union, Children's Special Service Mission and Crusader Movement of New Zealand 1880-1980* (Wellington: Scripture Union in New Zealand, 1980); John Roxborogh, 'Mapping the Evangelical Landscape in New Zealand', in Susan and William W. Emilsen (eds), *Mapping the Landscape. Essays in Australian and New Zealand Christianity. Festschrift in Honour of Professor Ian Breward* (New York: Peter Lang, 2000): 318-31; Douglas Pratt (ed.), *'Rescue the Perishing': Comparative Perspectives on Evangelism and Revivalism* (Auckland: College Communications, 1989); Bryan Gilling (ed.), *'Be Ye Separate': Fundamentalism and the New Zealand Experience* (Hamilton: University of Waikato and Colcom Press, 1992).
3. See e.g. Bernard Ramm, *The Evangelical Heritage: A Study in Historical Theology* (Grand Rapids, Michigan: Baker Book House, 1973): 23-40.
4. D.W. Bebbington, *Evangelicalism in Modern Britain: A History from the 1730s to the 1980s* (London: Unwin Hyman, 1989): 1; 'Introduction', Mark A. Noll, David W. Bebbington, George A. Rawlyk (eds), *Evangelicalism: Comparative Studies of Popular Protestantism in North America, the British Isles, and Beyond, 1700-1990* (New York, Oxford: Oxford University Press, 1994): 4-5.
5. Ibid.: 2-4.
6. Mark A. Noll, *American Evangelical Christianity: An Introduction* (Oxford: Blackwell, 2001); Timothy Larsen, 'Defining and Locating Evangelicalism', in Timothy Larsen and Daniel J. Treier (eds), *The Cambridge Companion to Evangelical Theology* (Cambridge: Cambridge University Press, 2007): 1-14.
7. E.g. John Charles Ryle, *Knots Untied, Being Plain Statements on Disputed Points in Religion from an Evangelical Standpoint* (James Clarke and Co: London, 1954. 31st Edition): 10-13, 80-93; T.C. Hammond, *What Is an Evangelical?* (Beecroft: Evangelical Tracts and Publications, n.d.): 5-8, 14, 17; D.M. Lloyd-Jones, *What Is an Evangelical?* (Edinburgh: Banner of Truth, 1992): 37-61, 68-85.
8. J.W.R. Stott, *What Is an Evangelical?* (London: Church Pastoral Aid Society, 1977), cit. Bebbington, *Evangelicalism*: 4.
9. J.I. Packer, *'Fundamentalism' and the Word of God: Some Evangelical Principles* (London: IVF, 1958): 38; similarly J.W.R. Stott, *Christ the Controversialist: A Study in Some Essentials of the Evangelical Religion* (London: Tyndale Press, 1970): 32.
10. Noll, *American Evangelical Christianity*: 14-15.
11. See e.g. Mark A. Noll, *The Rise of Evangelicalism: The Age of Edwards, Whitefield and the Wesleys* (Downers Grove and Leicester: InterVarsity Press, 2004); John Wolffe, *The Expansion of Evangelicalism: The Age of Wilberforce, More, Chalmers and Finney* (Nottingham: IVP, 2006); D.W. Bebbington, *The Dominance of Evangelicalism: The Age of Spurgeon and Moody* (Nottingham: IVP, 2005); Douglas A. Sweeney, *The American Evangelical Story: A History of the Movement* (Grand Rapids: Baker Academic, 2005); George M. Marsden, *Reforming Fundamentalism: Fuller Seminary and the New Evangelicalism* (Grand

Rapids: Eerdmans, 1987); George M. Marsden, *Understanding Fundamentalism and Evangelicalism* (Grand Rapids: Eerdmans, 1991); Joel A. Carpenter, *Revive Us Again: The Reawakening of American Fundamentalism* (New York, Oxford: Oxford University Press); Noll, *American Evangelical Christianity*: 2.

12 Robert Webber, *Common Roots: A Call to Evangelical Maturity* (Grand Rapids: Zondervan, 1978): 31-33.

13 J. Gresham Machen, *Christianity and Liberalism* (New York: MacMillan, 1934): 2-8.

14 The idea of 'anti-intellectualism' is complex. Any popular theology (conservative or liberal) was likely to have many adherents whose views were relatively unexamined. A more telling issue may be whether a movement's *leadership* regarded study as helpful or dangerous, important or less important. 'Fundamentalists' were often suspicious of academia, but some of their leaders were nevertheless quite intellectual in their opposition to modernism.

15 Cf. J.R. Stone, who argues that 'evangelicalism is a fiction': Jon R. Stone, *On the Boundaries of American Evangelicalism* (New York: St Martin's Press, 1997): 2, 12, 15, 73-116, 179. Similarly: D.G. Hart, *Deconstructing Evangelicalism: Conservative Protestantism in the Age of Billy Graham* (Grand Rapids: Baker Academic, 2004): 17-19.

16 A. Donald MacLeod, *C. Stacey Woods and the Evangelical Rediscovery of the University* (Downers Grove: InterVarsity Press, 2007); Keith and Gladys Hunt, *For Christ and the University: The Story of the InterVarsity Christian Fellowship of the U.S.A., 1940-1990* (Downers Grove: IVP, 1991).

17 See e.g. Bebbington, *Evangelicalism*; Randle Manwaring, *From Controversy to Co-existence: Evangelicals in the Church of England, 1914-1980* (Cambridge: Cambridge University Press, 1985); Kenneth Hylson-Smith, *Evangelicals in the Church of England, 1734-1984* (Edinburgh: T & T Clark, 1988); Ian M. Randall, *Educating Evangelicalism: The Origins, Development and Impact of London Bible College* (Carlisle: Paternoster Press, 2000); Harriet A. Harris, *Fundamentalism and Evangelicals* (Oxford: Clarendon Press, 1998); Rob Warner, *Reinventing English Evangelicalism, 1966-2001: A Theological and Sociological Study* (Milton Keynes: Paternoster Press, 2007); Oliver Barclay, *Evangelicalism in Britain, 1935-1990* (Leicester: IVP, 1997).

18 See e.g. David Goodhew, 'The Rise of the Cambridge Inter-Collegiate Christian Union, 1910-1970', *Journal of Ecclesiastical History* 54, 1 (January 2003): 62-88; IVF Booklet No. 1, *A Brief History of the Inter-Varsity Fellowship of Evangelical Christian Unions* (London: CSSM, 1928); D. Johnson, *Contending for Faith: A History of the Evangelical Movement in the Universities and Colleges* (Leicester: IVP, 1979); F.D. Coggan (ed.), *Christ and the Colleges: A History of the Inter-Varsity Fellowship of Evangelical Unions* (London: IVFEU, 1934); J.C. Pollock, *A Cambridge Movement* (London: John Murray, 1953): 159-62, 167-74; cf. Tissington Tatlow, *The Story of the Student Christian Movement of Great Britain and Ireland* (London: SCM, 1933): 380-88; Ruth Rouse, *The World's Student Christian Federation: A History of theFirst Thirty Years* (London: SCM, 1948): 292-93; Robin Boyd, *The Witness of the Student Christian Movement: 'Church Ahead of Church'* (Hindmarsh, SA: ATF Press, 2007); 25-29.

19 Ian M. Randall, *Evangelical Experiences: A Study in the Spirituality of English Evangelicalism, 1918-1939* (Carlisle: Paternoster Press, 1999).

20 Harris, *Fundamentalism and Evangelicals*: 45, 48-49; Bebbington, *Evangelicalism*: 207-09, 227; D.F. Wright, 'Soundings in the Doctrine of Scripture in British Evangelicalism in the First Half of the Twentieth Century', *Tyndale Bulletin* (1980): 87-106; Bebbington, 'Evangelicalism in Modern Scotland', *Scottish Bulletin of Evangelical Theology* (1991): 10-11.
21 Manwaring, *From Controversy*: 17-56.
22 Randall, *Educating*: 51, 95-96, 139.
23 Bebbington, *Evangelicalism*: 259-60.
24 Manwaring, *From Controversy*: x-xi, 44-45, 51; Randall, *Educating*: 18; Harris, *Fundamentalism and Evangelicals*: 51, 54; Derek Tidball, *Who are the Evangelicals? Tracing the Roots of Modern Movements*. (London: Marshall Pickering, 1994): 47, 49, 89; Goodhew, *The Rise*; Johnson.
25 Goodhew, *The Rise*: 64, 86-88.
26 E.g. Clive Calver and Rob Warner, *Together We Stand* (London: Hodder and Stoughton, 1996): 19-20; John Stott, *Fundamentalism and Evangelism* (London: Crusade for the Evangelical Alliance, 1956): 20-24.
27 Bebbington, *Evangelicalism*: 182, 222.
28 Ibid.: 275-76; cf. James Barr, *Fundamentalism* (London: SCM, 1977): 2-6.
29 Harris: 1, 9-10, 12, 14, 19-56, 86: similarly Warner: 28.
30 George M. Marsden, 'Fundamentalism as an American Phenomenon: A Comparison with English Evangelicalism', *Church History* 46 (June 1977): 215-32; David Bebbington, 'Evangelicalism in Modern Britain and America. A Comparison,' in Mark A. Noll, David B. Bebbington & George A. Rawlyk (eds) *Evangelicalism: Comparative Studies of Popular Protestantism in North America, the British Isles and Beyond, 1700-1990* (Oxford: Oxford University Press, 1994): 183-212; Bebbington, 'Evangelicalism in its Settings: The British and American Movements Since 1940', in ibid.: 365-88.
31 John G. Stackhouse, Jnr., 'More Than a Hyphen: Twentieth Century Canadian Evangelicalism in Anglo-American Context', in *Amazing Grace*: 375-400; David Bebbington, 'Canadian Evangelicalism: A View from Britain', in G.A. Rawlyk (ed.), *Aspects of the Canadian Evangelical Experience* (Montreal: McGill-Queens University Press, 1997): 38-54; R.P. Burkinshaw, 'Conservative Evangelicalism in the Twentieth-Century "West": British Columbia and the United States', in *Amazing Grace*: 317-48; Mark A. Noll, 'Learning a Lesson from Canada,' *American Evangelical Christianity: An Introduction* (Oxford: Blackwell, 2001): 237-61; Mark A. Noll, 'Canadian Evangelicalism: A view from the United States', in G.A. Rawlyk (ed.), *Aspects*: 3-20; John G. Stackhouse, Jnr., *Canadian Evangelicalism: An Introduction to Its Character* (Toronto: University of Toronto Press, 1993): 12-17.
32 Stackhouse, 'Hyphen': 385.
33 Stackhouse, *Canadian Evangelicalism*: 89-108; Stackhouse, 'The Emergence of a Fellowship: Canadian Evangelicalism in the Twentieth Century,' *Church History* (June 1991): 247-62 (253-54); Burkinshaw: 338-39.
34 Several works deal with the religious history of Australia and New Zealand in the same volumes: H.R. Jackson, *Churches and People in Australia and New Zealand, 1860-1930* (Wellington: Allen and Unwin, 1987); Ian Breward, *A History of the Churches of Australasia* (Oxford: Oxford University Press, 2001); Emilsen (eds), *Mapping*.
35 Stuart Piggin, *Evangelical Christianity in Australia: Spirit, Word and World* (Melbourne: Oxford University Press, 1996).

36 See e.g. Brian Dickey (ed.), *Australian Evangelical Dictionary of Biography* (NSW: Evangelical History Association, 1994); Brian Dickey, 'Evangelical Anglicans Compared: Australia and Britain', in *Amazing Grace*: 215-40.
37 New Zealand's Diocese of Nelson was not a parallel, as it was neither large nor influential.
38 James Belich, *Paradise Reforged: A History of the New Zealanders from the 1880s to the Year 2000* (Auckland: Penguin Books, 2001): 11, 27-108; cf. Keith Sinclair, *A Destiny Apart: New Zealand Search for National Identity* (Wellington: Unwin Paperbacks, 1986).
39 Belich: 157-88.
40 W.H. Oliver, 'Christianity among the New Zealanders', *Landfall* 20 (1966): 4-20; Oliver was writing about a period a generation later, when eighty per cent of marriages were still conducted in church. Note also: John Stenhouse, 'Secular New Zealand, or God's Own Country?', in Bruce Patrick (ed.), *New Vision New Zealand* III (Auckland: Tabernacle Books, 2008): 79-92.
41 NZ Department of Statistics, *Census of Population and Dwellings* 1896: xlvi-xlviii; 1926, vol. xv.
42 Peter Matheson, 'The Contours of Christian Theology in Aotearoa New Zealand', in Emilsen (eds): 255-72; Jackson; Breward, *Australasia*: e.g. 194, 196, 198, 423-25.
43 Belich: 163.
44 Brian Carrell, 'Evangelical Anglicans and the Canterbury Settlement' (Paper presented to the Latimer Fellowship in Christchurch, 13 October 2000).
45 Peter J. Lineham, 'How Institutionalized Was Protestant Piety in Nineteenth-Century New Zealand?' *Journal of Religious History* 13 (1985): 370-82 (377).
46 Right Rev. Max Wiggins, interview, 2 November 1999 (hereafter MW), ¶26, ¶28, ¶62.

47 See e.g. Marie Peters, *Christchurch – St Michael's: A Study in Anglicanism in New Zealand, 1851-1972* (Christchurch: University of Canterbury, 1986): 37, 40-41, 100-01, 104; John Dickson, *Shall Ritualism and Romanism Capture New Zealand? Their Ramifications in Protestant Churches* (Dunedin: Otago Daily Times, 1912): 1-66.
48 Right Rev. Brian Carrell, interview, 1 October 2001 (hereafter BRC), ¶303-06.
49 David G.S. Rathgen, 'The Church in New Zealand 1890-1920, with Special Reference to W.A. Orange' (Joint Board of Theological Studies Licentiate of Theology thesis, 1969): 68-75; MW, ¶23-25.
50 For insights into the theological character of the Auckland Diocese and its ministry training, see: Allan K. Davidson (ed.), *Living Legacy. A History of the Anglican Diocese of Auckland* (Auckland: Anglican Diocese of Auckland, 2011); Davidson, *Selwyn's Legacy: The College of St John the Evangelist, Te Waimate and Auckland, 1843-1992* (Auckland: College of Saint John the Evangelist, 1993).
51 *The Church News for the Diocese of Christchurch* (January 1930-December 1930).
52 For overviews of Presbyterian theological history in New Zealand, see: Davidson, *Christianity in Aotearoa. A History of Church and Society in New Zealand*, 3rd edn (Wellington: Education for Ministry, 2004); Dennis McEldowney (ed.), *Presbyterians in Aotearoa* (Wellington: Presbyterian Church of New Zealand, 1990); Ian Breward, *Grace and Truth. A History of the Theological Hall, Knox College, Dunedin, 1876-1975* (Dunedin: Theological Education Committee, Presbyterian Church of New Zealand, 1975); Matheson, 'Contours': 255-72; Breward, *Australasia*.

53 Belich: 163. Of those, 28 per cent regularly attended.
54 Jackson: 6, 11.
55 See e.g. R.R. Mclean, 'Scottish Piety: the Free Church Settlement of Otago, 1843-1853', in John Stenhouse and Jane Thomson (eds), *Building God's Own Country: Historical Essays on Religions in New Zealand* (University of Otago Press, Dunedin, 2004): 21-31; Alison Clarke, 'A Godly Rhythm: Keeping the Sabbath in Otago', in ibid.: 46-59; Alison Clarke, '"Tinged with Christian Sentiment": Popular Religion and the Otago Colonists, 1850-1900', in John Stenhouse and G.A. Wood (eds), *Christianity, Modernity and Culture. New Perspectives on New Zealand History* (Adelaide: Australian Theological Forum, 2005): 103-31. Free Church personnel and ethos were also predominant across New Zealand Presbyterianism as a whole: Rollo Arnold, 'The Patterns of Denominationalism in Later Victorian New Zealand', in Christopher Nichol and James Veitch (eds), *Religion in New Zealand* (Wellington: Tertiary Christian Studies Programme, 1983): 96.
56 John Collie, *The Story of the Otago Church Settlement, 1848-1948: A Century's Growth by a Southern Sea* (Christchurch: Presbyterian Bookroom, n.d. [c.1948]): 304.
57 Robert Evans and Roy McKenzie, *Evangelical Revivals in New Zealand: A History of Evangelical Revivals in New Zealand, and an Outline of Some Basic Principles of Revivals* (Paihia: Colcom Press, 1999): 56-62.
58 Bryan Dudley Gilling, 'Retelling the Old, Old Story: A Study of Six Mass Evangelistic Missions in Twentieth Century New Zealand' (D.Phil. thesis, University of Waikato, 1990): 114-72.
59 Mark A. Noll, *The Princeton Theology, 1812-1921: Scripture, Science, and Theological Method from Archibald Alexander to Benjamin Breckinridge Warfield* (Grand Rapids: Baker, 1983); P. Helm, 'Scottish Realism', *Dictionary of Scottish Church History and Theology*: 759-60.
60 Gray was at North East Valley (1906-17) and later Hawera (1917-23). 'The Fire of God' (ms, 1932). A later arrival, in 1912, was Geordie (George Morrison) Yule, who had been converted under evangelist W.P. Nicholson: Rev. G. Morrison Yule, interview, 12-13 August 1999 (hereafter GMY), ¶13-23.
61 The BC movement was begun in 1889 at St John's Wellington by George Troup, a definite evangelical (as was J.C. Jamieson the first travelling secretary, 1903-07). In 1918 the movement appeared still 'fervently and passionately evangelical': G.M. Yule (Sen.), 'The Church Over The years', *Evangelical Presbyterian* (February 1954): 1. Note Maureen Nola Garing, 'Four Square for Christ. The Presbyterian Bible Class Movement, 1902-1972: Its Background, its Rise, its Influence and its Decline' (MA thesis, Victoria University of Wellington, 1985). Similar movements were begun by Methodists, Anglicans and Baptists.
62 Rev. Dr J. Graham Miller, interview, 23-25 November 1999 (hereafter JGM), ¶104.
63 See Geoffrey King, 'Organising Christian Truth: An Investigation of the Life and Work of John Dickie' (Ph.D. thesis, University of Otago, 1998): Dickie, Professor of Systematic Theology from 1910-42 and principal from 1929, was a contrast to his intensely evangelical predecessor, John Dunlop, who was in the classic Free Church evangelical tradition (ibid: 28-29). Dickie had a critical view of the scriptures (71, 116), rejected penal substitution, and reflected the subjectivist theologies of Schleiermacher and Ritschl (55-57, 75).

64 Deeply committed to Westminster confessionalism and the Free Church tradition, Fraser was an ardent and scholarly evangelical, and prolific writer. He was also influenced by the Princeton school, and had personal links with B.B. Warfield. In 1909 he was commended by Assembly for *A Brief Statement of the Reformed Faith. A Help for a Better Understanding of Our Christian Faith. In Agreement with Recognized Standards of Presbyterian Churches Throughout the World. A Living Creed for Today*. Fraser became an increasingly agitated defender of historic Reformed orthodoxy, and from 1914 to 1935 was editor and publisher of the *Biblical Recorder*, a monthly paper. Allan K. Davidson, 'A Protesting Presbyterian: The Reverend P.B. Fraser and New Zealand Presbyterianism, 1892–1940', *Journal of Religious History* (December 1986): 193–217; *EP* (May 1957): 9; *Outlook* (27 November 1940): 7; JGM, ¶814–15.

65 Doctrines which were being rejected included the eternal punishment of the unsaved, and substitutionary atonement – the teaching that Christ achieved salvation by dying in the place of sinners.

66 'Great Bible Demonstration in Auckland', *Reaper* (April 1929): 26–42 (27, 29). Kemp organised the gathering, attended by 3000, as a counter to the visit of H.D.A. Major, the editor of *The Modern Churchman*.

67 *Outlook* (10 February 1930): 26. For revivalist hymnology, note Gilling, 'Retelling': 429–87.

68 *Outlook* (2 June 1930): 5–6, 27; ibid (7 July 1930): 23. JGM, ¶115: 'Jesus was the hero to follow … The Bible Class appeals were not biblical appeals' (JGM, ¶117); cf. *Outlook* (21 February 1940): 4–5, 9, 13, 17, 23, 29. Note discussion of 'manly Jesus' in Geoffrey Troughton, *New Zealand Jesus. Social and Religious Transformations of an Image. 1890-1940* (Bern: Peter Lang, 2011): 191–230.

69 'Waiting for the Troubling of the Pool', *Outlook* (24 November 1930): 3–4.

70 *Outlook* (17 November 1930): 16.

71 Gibson Smith, 'The League of the Burning Bush', *Outlook* (15 September 1930): 29–31 (30).

72 'How to Be Saved', *Outlook* (9 June 1930): 31.

73 E.J. Tipler, 'The Prayer Meeting', *Outlook* (8 September 1930): 6.

74 *Outlook* XXXVII (22 December 1930): 6.

75 W. McLean, 'Has Protestantism Anything to Learn from Roman Catholicism?' *Outlook* (22 September 1930): 7.

76 E.g. D. Sutherland to Editor, *Outlook* (24 March 1930): 7; C. Duff to Editor, *Outlook* (27 October 1930): 21.

77 E.g. T.W. Armour, 'The Nineteenth Centenary of Pentecost,' *Outlook* (2 June 1930): 4–5.

78 But by 1931 J.V.T. Steele was writing about Calvin's affinities with Karl Barth.

79 E.g. J.L. Gray, 'The Sin of Prayerlessness', *Outlook* (22 September 1930): 28.

80 Harries (1872–1953) had been converted in the Welsh Revival. He was minister at St James' (Auckland) from 1924–34, and frequently spoke at Keswick-type conventions. Douglas Ireton, 'O Lord How Long? A Revival Movement in New Zealand, 1920–1933' (MA thesis, Massey University, 1985): 68–69; *Proceedings*, 1954: 7–8; Evan R. Harries, *Receive Ye the Holy Spirit* (London: Marshall Morgan & Scott, [c.1937]).

81 E.g. *Outlook* (2 June 1930): 32; (15 December): 29.

82 *Outlook* (25 August 1930): 19.

83 *Outlook* (16 November 1931): 16; (21 September 1931): 17.

84 E.g. Isaac Jolly, 'Our Lord's Appeal to the Old Testament Regarding his

Death', *Outlook* (18 May 1931): 18.
85 A.M. Richards, 'The Adventure of the SCM', *Outlook* (2 March 1931): 5–7.
86 *Outlook* (18 May 1931): 13; J.V.T. Steele, 'The Theology of Karl Barth', *Outlook* (25 May 1931): 19.
87 E.g. *Outlook* (6 October 1930): 5.
88 E.g. *Outlook* (22 June 1931): 6. The Federal Council of Evangelical Free Churches (UK) included Baptists, Congregationalists, Methodists and Presbyterians – the 'Free Churches'; cf. the call for a union of the 'Evangelical Churches' of New Zealand, *Proceedings*, 1918: 19.
89 E.g. NZBTI advertisement, *Outlook* (1 December 1930): 36.
90 E.g. *Outlook* (23 June 1930): 5.
91 *Outlook* (7 July 1930): 3.
92 *Outlook* (22 December 1930): 6.
93 J.V.T. Steele, 'The Theology of Karl Barth', *Outlook* (25 May, 1931): 20.
94 Shirley – Vestry Minutes, 1951–57; ibid., 11 August 1957; Minute Book, Sumner Parish, 5 May 1927–33 November 1960; Vicar's Report, Minutes of Annual Meeting, 21 April 1937.
95 Data from interviews was correlated with other sources wherever possible, and a few informants proved to have impressively accurate recall. Caution was taken in relation to informants reading back into their memories their more recent attitudes.
96 Keith W. Sewell, 'Christian Historiographical Methodology: Some Foundational Considerations', *Lucas* 15 (June 1993): 1–13 (13).
97 Cf. Marsden, *Reforming Fundamentalism*: xi; Warner: 20–22.
98 G.A. Rawlyk, 'Introduction', in G.A. Rawlyk (ed.), *Aspects*: xix.

Chapter One: Thomas Miller and Friends

1 J.D. Salmond to Miller family, [1948], cit. [J. Graham Miller, Robert Strang Miller and Thomas F. Miller], *Thomas Miller, MA: A Family Tribute by His Sons* (Christchurch: Presbyterian Bookroom, 1949), hereafter *TM*: 56.
2 Davidson briefly noted Miller's significance as 'the foremost evangelical minister', and St Stephen's as an evangelical 'rallying place'. He mentioned Miller's vigorous preaching, his loyal Presbyterianism, his 'evangelical ecumenism', and his opposition to modernism and church union (Allan Davidson, 'Depression, War, New Life', in *Presbyterians in Aotearoa*: 106; Davidson, *Christianity in Aotearoa*: 113). Also: Simon Rae, 'Thomas Miller', *Southern People*: 344–45.
3 Thomas Miller. Miscellaneous undated ms. sermon notes, given to author by J.G. Miller, e.g. 'The Unchanging Word of Christ' (Hebrews 1); 'The Sovereignty of God and Freewill of Man' (John 15: 16); 'No Cross, No Crown' (1 Peter 4: 1–5).
4 GMY, ¶70, 246; J. Graham Miller interview, ¶441; Rev. Rymall Roxburgh interview, 2–3 November 1999 (hereafter RR), ¶336.
5 JGM, ¶75.
6 GMY, ¶70; similarly Mrs Frances Milmine, interview, August 2002 (hereafter FM), ¶18.
7 H.H. Rex to Marion Miller, letter [1948] cited *TM*: 70.
8 In 1927 he had sought a call in Australia, but it did not proceed: JGM, ¶577. His ministry at St Stephen's was preceded by others with evangelical tendencies, including W. Fairlie Evans (1917–24) and J.M. Simpson (1925–28).
9 Newcomers included the Cree Brown family (previously Open Brethren) and H.R. Minn (classics lecturer, and previously Exclusive Brethren).
10 J.G. Miller, 'A Day's March Nearer Home' (unpublished memoirs, typescript, n.d., hereafter ADMNH) 1: 47 (subsequently published in part as *A Day's March Nearer Home: Autobiography of J. Graham Miller*,

Edinburgh: Banner of Truth, 2010).
11 The family had been in the United Presbyterian Church (1847–1900): JGM, ¶69.
12 L. Barber, 'Gibb, James, 1857–1935', *DNZB* II: 165–67.
13 JGM, ¶71.
14 *TM*: 12; JGM, ¶72–73.
15 *TM*: 11.
16 JGM, ¶71.
17 *TM*: 17–18.
18 *TM*: 19–36; unidentified newspaper clipping, June 1916, in J.G. Miller papers.
19 JGM, ¶79–81.
20 *TM*: 32, 34, 63, 65–67; ADMNH 1: 8–9.
21 JGM, ¶83–84.
22 JGM, ¶604. The assailants were later taken to court. For PPA, see e.g. Miles Fairburn, 'The Farmers Take Over (1912–1930)', in Keith Sinclair (ed.), *The Oxford Illustrated History of New Zealand* (Auckland: Oxford University Press, 1990): 211–36.
23 Thomas Miller, 'The Inerrancy of Scripture', *Outlook* (14 November 1916): 17.
24 J.G. Miller to Peter Barnes, 30 April 1987.
25 Miller, 'Inerrancy'.
26 JGM, ¶97–99. Elliott (1845–1929), from Ireland, was minister of Kent Terrace in Wellington (1886–1920).
27 [R. Miller], 'Previous moves for Church Union in New Zealand', *Evangelical Presbyterian* (May 1957): 8–10.
28 Miller, speech notes: ADMNH 13; JGM, ¶98.
29 *TM*: 85.
30 *TM*: 57.
31 'The Inspiration of the Bible', *Reaper* (April 1929): 43–46; 'The Inspiration of the Bible. II: The Bible on the Bible', *Reaper* (May 1929): 65–69; 'The Inspiration of the Bible. III: The Conservative and Modernist Views Compared', *Reaper* (June 1929): 88–92; 'The Inspiration of the Bible. IV: The Conservative and Modernist Views – Their Results Compared', *Reaper* (July 1929): 120–23.
32 *Reaper* (April 1929): 43.
33 Ibid.: 44.
34 *Reaper* (April 1929): 43; *Reaper* (June 1929): 90–91.
35 *Reaper* (July 1929): 120–21.
36 Thomas Miller, *Archaeology and the Bible: A Romance and a Vindication* (Dunedin: Evangelical Bible League of Otago, 1934): 7.
37 Ibid.: 9–12.
38 JGM, ¶507, 517.
39 *TM*: 58.
40 Machen to F.E. Robinson, 25 June 1925, cit. C. Allwyn Russell, *Voices of American Fundamentalism: Seven Biographical Studies* (Philadephia: Westminster, 1976): 43–44.
41 GMY, ¶180.
42 Ibid.: ¶262.
43 JGM, ¶97.
44 Reformed eschatology tended to be amillennial or postmillennial. Machen, whom Miller admired, described premillennialism as heresy. Miller did not obviously adopt any particular position, but regarded the details of the second coming as unimportant: JGM, ¶671.
45 Miller was less explicitly or technically Calvinist than his son Graham was to become: JGM, ¶441, ¶444.
46 Miller was impressed by W. Gray Dixon, *The Romance of the Catholic Presbyterian Church* (Melbourne: Board of Religious Education, Presbyterian Church of Australia, 1930).
47 ADMNH 1: 46.
48 *TM*: 38.
49 JGM, ¶199.
50 ADMNH 1:50.
51 JGM, ¶46–54.
52 JGM, ¶56; J. Oswald Sanders, *The Divine Art of Soul-Winning* (London: Picketing & Inglis, 1937). Miller's desk drawer contained tracts for handing out, including Laidlaw's *The Reason Why*.

53 Miller's views are probably reflected in those of his son: 'The era of .... good responses ... seemed to peter out with World War I ... The cigarette in the mouth became a commonplace ... the contraceptive became a commonplace ... you can trace it to the insidious influences of World War I' (JGM, ¶109).
54 JGM, ¶190.
55 Morrison Yule went to an Auckland district PBCM camp in the 1930s and was 'most disappointed'. The 'main feature appeared to be the Mount Eden BC clothed in red shirts splattered with black arrows all over them' ganging up against the contingent from St David's. 'There was no spiritual emphasis or desire with either group.' Yule believed that the PCBM, was theologically 'middle of the road, scared to go too far'; there were 'restraining hands somewhere ... watching the movement and not allowing it to get too hot'. Nevertheless, the Presbyterian BC movement was 'often a means of distinct Christian commitment'. (GMY, ¶78, 83, 85, 87).
56 JGM, ¶111.
57 Miller opposed shaving on Sundays, but his son Graham 'never quite saw his point of view' (ADMNH 1: 57).
58 'The instinct of it came out of the Scriptures ... [the] old things have passed away ... I never sensed any harsh directives of legalism' (JGM, ¶192–95). However some St Stephen's youth – in retrospect anyway – found the code of behaviour 'a bit narrow' (name withheld, interview, 15 November 1999).
59 See *TM*: 66. In 1930 the group had 360 members: Cree Brown to Guinness, 16 September 1930, TSCF A2c.
60 RR, ¶120, 123.
61 With no upper age limit, CE was not strictly a youth movement.
62 CE was begun in 1881 by an American Congregationalist, F.E. Clark, promoted by F.B. Meyer, and became established in Britain in 1888: Miller, 'The CE Movement', *Outlook* (12 October 1931): 5f.
63 Thomas Miller, 'The CE Movement'.
64 RR, ¶158; JGM, ¶214. Graham Miller found the training 'excellent', and commented: 'I attribute any gift of speaking to the training that came in CE ... you were meant to speak sense' (from a manuscript).
65 JGM, ¶214.
66 RR, ¶162; JGM, ¶227.
67 Street was also representing the National Sunday School Union of Great Britain and the Band of Hope: CE Otago Union, Miss J.M. Street, Papers re Visit of, 1929, 91/44/17.
68 *Evening Star* (12 April 1929); *Otago Daily Times* (13 April 1929).
69 JGM, ¶218. Seventy years later, Miller's son recalled her message from Romans 16 (and her 'huge mouth').
70 CE, Otago Union, Executive Minutes 1929–33, 91/44/11; Minute of appreciation, 7 October 1948, in minutes of 19th Annual Meeting, 9 October 1948.
71 Rowland Harries (Rev. E. Rowland Harries, interview, 16 August 1999, hereafter ERH), ¶27. There were unions in several prominent inner-city churches, including the Baptist Tabernacle, Pitt St Methodist, Beresford St Congregational and St James' Presbyterian. Combined rallies were held.
72 CE was not necessarily so. In the US, CE had 'often gone liberal' (RR, ¶162). LMS-based churches in the Pacific Islands developed CE extensively, but – perhaps reflecting twentieth century Congregationalism generally – that work did not appear conspicuously evangelical (personal observation in New Zealand, 1980s).
73 The word 'evangelical' does not appear in: CE Otago Union, Executive Minutes 1929–33, 91/44/11.

74 Waiwera South (1934), Gore (1935), Pounawea (1936), Mosgiel (1937), Mataura (1938).
75 CE Otago Union Convention Committee, Minutes 1936–40, 91/44/3. Frequent speakers included Miller, Andrew Johnston (BTI evangelist), Hedley Bycroft (Congregational Minister) and Charles Kennedy (Mataura).
76 The Otago CE Union used Keswick hymnbooks.
77 *Outlook* (24 February 1930): 10.
78 The Pounawea Convention was started in 1908, with leadership by H.B. Gray.
79 Ireton: 47; Dr Bruce Harris, letter, 30 May 2001. The Ngaruawhia convention movement was initially founded by A.A. Murray in 1921.
80 GMY, ¶489; JGM, ¶261. J.G. Miller listed those districts as Gore, South Clutha, Waiwera, Warepa, the Catlins and Waikaka.
81 JGM, ¶262; RR, ¶114–16. Originally from Southland, Sanders experienced a spiritual awakening at Pounawea as a young man and after that regularly attended the convention: J. Oswald Sanders, *This I Remember* (Eastbourne: Kingsway, 2002): 137.
82 JGM, ¶265–66, 270–72. Keswick theology emphasised victory over sin through the enabling of the Holy Spirit.
83 GMY, ¶481; JGM, ¶275.
84 JGM, ¶262.
85 ADMNH 1: 60–61. 'This proved a turning point in my life ... All things had become new'. Another person deeply moved by the Convention was future missionary Cliff Mitchell, who was later murdered in Ethiopia.
86 'Pounawea 1929', *Outlook* (29 February 1930): 29.
87 RR, ¶205.
88 J.V.T. Steele, 'Calvinism or Pietism', *Outlook* (30 November 1931): 9–12.
89 George Morrison Yule, 'Calvinism or Pietism', *Outlook* (18 January 1932): 26–27; E.M. Blaiklock, 'The Pounawea Convention', *Outlook* (18 January 1932): 28.
90 ADMNH 1: 49; *Proceedings*, 1930, Appendix XXX, Report of Life and Work Committee: 194.
91 GMY, ¶54. Bissett (1868–1943) accepted a call in 1910 to the Auckland Central Mission. He was Assembly Evangelist from 1918–34 and ordained by Assembly in 1921.
92 J.S. Somerville, *Jack in the Pulpit: An Autobiography* (Dunedin: McIndoe, 1987): 36.
93 In 1932, for instance, his parish missions included Waiuku, Ponsonby, Te Kuiti, Fitzroy, Mayfield and Mauku: 'Life and Work [Committee] Report', Appendix XVII, *Proceedings*, 1933: 131.
94 *Proceedings*, 1918, Appendix I, Report of Life and Work Committee: 57.
95 RR, ¶87–89, 97–98. Roxburgh had earlier been influenced by Methodist home missionary Hedley Bycroft.
96 Milmine 23; *Proceedings*, 1981: 112; *Proceedings*, 1981: 119; GMY, ¶52; Somerville: 36–37.
97 Graham Miller claimed Waikaka Valley parish was affected 'for years' (JGM, ¶175); see also *Outlook* (22 October 1941): 7.
98 Report, Life and Work Committee, *Proceedings*, 1930: 82.
99 Charles W. Malcolm, *Twelve Hours in the Day: The Life and Work of the Rev. Lionel B. Fletcher D.D.* (London and Edinburgh: Marshall, Morgan and Scott, 1956); and Fletcher's own books (see bibliography).
100 Piggin: 86–87.
101 Davidson: 106. In 1932 Fletcher left New Zealand for Britain, to become [CE] 'Empire Evangelist', Otago CE Executive Minutes, 16 February 1932.
102 JGM, ¶170.
103 John Laird to Mervyn Milmine: 24 July 1931.
104 Nicholson first made his impact in New Zealand as a speaker at the 1933 Ngaruawhia Easter Convention: 'Our Evangelistic Page,' *Outlook* (12

June 1933): 24; (1 May 1933): 28. A month in Auckland ensued, with nightly meetings in Scots Hall: ibid. (22 May): 24; (12 June): 28; 'Rev. Wm. P. Nicholson's Mission in Auckland,' *Reaper* (28 September 1933): 62–64. Campaigns followed in main cities and many provincial centres.

105 Informants frequently claimed that Nicholson's converts were more enduring than those of many other evangelistic campaigns e.g. Rev. Stephen Clark, interview, 16 August 1999 (hereafter SC), ¶266; RR, ¶199; JGM, ¶305; GMY, ¶54.

106 GMY, ¶55–57, 61; SC, ¶265.

107 Miller got a call from the clerk of Presbytery, reporting complaints. He explained that the statement originated with Dr Alexander Whyte (minister of Free St George's Church, Edinburgh, and principal of New College, 1909–21), who said it in the pulpit. The next morning his students stamped their feet in disapproval, and Whyte responded [J.G. Miller's paraphrase]: 'Gentleman, I gather there is some disapproval of what I said yesterday in St George's. Permit me to add that not only is the road to hell paved with the skulls of Presbyterian ministers, but there is enough material coming on to keep it in repair for all eternity': JGM, ¶303; SC, ¶265.

108 Dickie had taught at the Hall since 1910, and was appointed principal in 1929.

109 GMY, ¶306.

110 Thomas Miller, 'Rev. W.P. Nicholson in Dunedin,' *Reaper* (30 November 1933): 213–14. The two men became lifelong friends and corresponded thereafter; *TM*: 58.

111 JGM, ¶306. Sixty-five years later, Graham Miller felt the humour sometimes 'regrettable' and ungracious, reflecting a 'barbaric North of Ireland language of strife'.

112 GMY, ¶554; GMY, ¶332.

113 During his 1926 CICCU mission at Cambridge, Nicholson's bluntness surprised some and outraged others, but he had an 'indelible' effect on the CICCU (Pollock: 219–29; Coggan: 71. Archbishop A.M. Ramsay never quite forgave CICCU for inviting Nicholson, and always consequently thought of evangelicals as anti-intellectual and overly emotional (Barclay: 29); 'That one evening created in me a deep and lasting dislike of the extreme evangelical style of evangelism' (cit. Randall, *Educating*: 99).

114 George MacLean, Jack Smith, Jack Johnson, Rod McKenzie, C.A.G. McKenzie, Bob Weir: GMY, ¶62; J.S. Scarlet, *Proceedings*, 1984: 103.

115 Advertisement, *Outlook* (1 December 1930): 36.

116 Ibid.

117 'The Importance of the Bible Training Institute', *Reaper* (July 1927): 104–13. See also: J. Oswald Sanders, *Expanding Horizons: The Jubilee History of the New Zealand Bible Training Institute* (Auckland: Institute Press, 1971); Graham C. Stoop, 'Continuity and Change: Reflections on the Theological History of the Bible College of New Zealand', *Reaper* (1992): 16–18.

118 GMY, ¶59, 100–01, 104; JGM, ¶290, 300.

119 'Sanders, John Oswald: 1902–1999', *DNZB* 4: 449–50. Sanders was on BTI staff from 1926 and Superintendent from 1933. He was CIM Home Director of Australia and New Zealand from 1946, and CIM General Director from 1954. He was a prolific writer.

120 JGM, ¶174.

121 John S. Thomson, *Light in Darkness: The Story of Andrew M. Johnston 'The Blind Evangelist'* (Gore: Gore Publishing Co., 1975): 23, 32.

122 'The Otautau Revival', *Reaper* (28 June 1934): 122; 'United Methodist and Presbyterian Mission at Tuatapere',

Reaper (December 1934): 265; JGM, ¶173.
123 C.J. Tocker, 'A Remarkable Mission', *Reaper* (November 1934): 237–39.
124 GMY, ¶283.
125 Thomas Miller, 'The Inspiration of the Bible. Introductory and Textual', *Outlook* (20 August 1923): 3–5.
126 Thomas Miller, 'Preparation for the Ministry', *Outlook* (8 November 1926): 16, 18.
127 John Dickie, 'Preparation for the Ministry', *Outlook* (20 November 1926): 25.
128 Thomas Miller, 'Preparation for the Ministry', *Outlook* (20 December 1926): 8; 'Preparation for the Ministry and Other Matters. A reply to Dr Dickie', *Outlook* (24 January 1927): 6–7.
129 John Dickie, 'Ministerial Training?' *Outlook* (14 February 1927): 5–6.
130 Thomas Miller, 'Ministerial Training', *Outlook* (4 April 1927): 5–6.
131 John Dickie, *The Organism of Christian Truth: A Modern Positive Dogmatic* (London: James Clarke and Company, n.d. [1931]): 266–78. Dickie asserted, for instance, that the Bible is 'not inerrant' and that he adopted a middle position between fundamentalism and modernism: 7–8.
132 Isaac Jolly, 'Principal Dickie and the Atonement', *Outlook* (4 January 1932): 27–28. King (246) describes Jolly's critique as 'fairly compelling'.
133 *Proceedings*, 1932: 26.
134 The text of the speech is in *The Biblical Recorder* 24 (May–June 1932): 86–90, under extended headlines: 'Modernism in New Zealand. Attack in Presbyterian Assembly. Address by Rev. Thos. Miller, M.A. on Professor's Theology. Excluded from "Official" Organ'.
135 Several ministers of conservative evangelical sympathies were present and could have seconded the motion.
136 JGM, ¶94–96.
137 *Biblical Recorder*, ibid: 86. Much later, and in the same venue (St Paul's Christchurch), similar dynamics were at work in the 1967 debate relating to Principal Geering.
138 *Proceedings*, 1932: 27.
139 A brief item gave the wording of both Miller's item and the motion that was carried, and noted that the vote was 'overwhelming': 'The Organism of Christian Truth', *Outlook* (7 March 1932): 5.
140 Note King's reflection that 'the treatment' which Fraser, Miller and Jolly received at the hands of Dickie and some of his friends and colleagues helped build an enduring conservative fear of liberal conspiracy, censorship and control, 'fears which have been … part of the New Zealand Presbyterian psyche ever since.' (250–51).
141 The Synod, a leftover from the 1901 union, would not have wanted to rule in matters relating to theology.
142 *Proceedings of the Synod of Otago and Southland*, 1932, bound with *Proceedings of the General Assembly of the Presbyterian Church of New Zealand*, 1933: 297, 300–01.
143 *Proceedings*, 1935: 21–22.
144 *Proceedings*, 1940: 38.
145 R.S. Miller, 'In Memoriam: Rev. D.N. McKenzie', *Evangelical Presbyterian* (September 1962): 55–56. McKenzie was minister of West Taieri.
146 E.g. *Outlook* (24 December 1940): 3; (26 November 1941): 3; (1 April 1942): 3.
147 John Dickie, D.N. McKenzie, Thomas Miller, 'The Case against Church Union: Twelve Reasons'. *Outlook* (25 March 1942): 15.
148 *Outlook* (1 July 1942): 9.
149 E.g. D. Sutherland, *Outlook* (3 September 1941): 23; (16 July 1941): 23; T.G. Calder, *Outlook* (22 April 1942): 9.
150 *Outlook* (4 March 1942): 29–30.
151 *Outlook* (10 August 1931): 27; *Proceedings*, 1930: 82.
152 J.V.T. Steele, 'Calvinism or Pietism,' *Outlook* (30 November 1931): 9.

153 E.R. Harries, 'Our Evangelistic Page', *Outlook* (8 June 1931): 28; (3 November 1930): 28; (20 July 1931): 36.
154 *Outlook* (16 November 1931): 20.
155 Ibid.
156 The 1935 Assembly re-established the committee under a new convener and with different sympathies. Life and Work Report, Appendix XXXV, *Proceedings*, 1936: 257–62.
157 Jolly died in 1938, Fraser in 1940.
158 Bissett took a position with BTI, and died in 1943. Harries spent ten years in Syria with the British Syrian Mission, and died in 1953. 'Our Evangelistic Page' was replaced by the 'Life and Work' page.
159 ADMNH 1:14
160 Breward: 257. A similar 'sub-zero rating' was given in mainline Protestant circles in America to one of Miller's heroes, Machen, who was seen as a 'troublemaker and sectarian crank' (Marsden, *Understanding*: 184).
161 St Stephen's average attendance was 210 in 1929, 180 in 1944.
162 *TM*, 38–39 cf. Graham Miller, 'St Stephen's Presbyterian Church, North Dunedin: Record of those who entered full-time Christian service during or soon after the ministry of Rev. Thomas Miller', ADMNH 1, which gave a more cautious figure of twenty-three.
163 Yule was also much influenced by his own father.
164 Irvine Roxburgh later moved away from an evangelical position.
165 Sage married Miller's daughter Margaret.
166 E.g. David Paulin, Stan Lamb, Bill Carr, Betty McDonald, Aileen Wilson, Walter Pullar, Ina Cormack.
167 E.g. Nora Morris (South Seas Evangelical Mission), Ken Roundhill (WEC), May Roy (CIM).
168 Laird to Miller, n.d., cit. *TM*: 47.
169 Salmond to Miller family, cit. *TM*: 56.

Chapter Two: The Evangelical Unions

1 Dozens of interviewees were asked the question: 'When did you first become aware of the term "evangelical"?' Almost invariably they indicated that it was through the Evangelical Union, e.g. Kevin O'Sullivan, interview, November 2001 (hereafter KO), ¶50; MW, ¶35. The exceptions were those few (e.g. Graham Miller, Morrison Yule) who had grown up in families that were theologically very aware and who believed they knew the term earlier, and those who first encountered it in BTI (e.g. Rev. J. Lewis Wilson, interview, 1 November 1999 (hereafter LW), ¶104.
2 The beginnings of the Evangelical Union and Inter-Varsity Fellowship in New Zealand have previously been noted primarily in: *N.Z. Varsity Papers No. 2: The Inter-Varsity Fellowship of Evangelical Unions (N.Z)* (Wellington: IVF, n.d. [1940]); Lineham, *No Ordinary Union*, which drew on some of the same archival sources as this study.
3 Cree Brown to Guinness (19 March 1930, TSCF A2c) and to [G.B.] Nicholson (19 March 1930, TSCF A2c).
4 Barclay: 20.
5 Christine Berry, *The New Zealand Student Christian Movement, 1896–1996. A Centennial History* (Christchurch: Student Christian Movement of Aotearoa, 1998). Ch. 1: 8–13; Ch. 2: 7–8; W.H. Pettit, 'Experiences in Christian Work Among New Zealand Students', in *N.Z. Varsity Papers No. 2*: 22–36; Archie Morton to Merv[yn Milmine], n.d., copy, TSCF N7/76).

6   Pettit (see P.J. Lineham, 'Pettit, William Haddow: 1885-1985', *DNZB* 3: 398-99) had been a foundation member of the Otago CU, and twice its president. He considered SCM once 'definitely evangelical' ('Experiences': 23), and its spiritual high-water mark an Australasian conference in 1909.
7   Coggan: 189.
8   Baptist Tabernacle (Joseph Kemp), St James' Presbyterian (E.R. Harries), Beresford St Congregational (Lionel Fletcher) and Howe St Brethren (where Pettit was a leader).
9   'Auckland'. Typescript history, n.a., n.d., B1/066, TSCF.
10 Coggan: 191.
11 [Cree Brown] to Guinness, 19 March 1930, TSCF A2c; ibid., 29 March 1930, TSCF A2c. Members included Hallam Howie, Trevor Knight, Vine Martin, Marion Thomson, Jack Strang, Mervyn Milmine, Lilian Jefferies, Naomi Grey.
12 Lineham: 38-51.
13 B. Griffiths to A. Stewart, 6 October 1930, SCM file 31 (cit. Lineham: 51).
14 Cree Brown to Guinness, 19 June 1930, TSCF A2c; 'The Universities of New Zealand', *Terminal Magazine of the Inter-Varsity Fellowship of Evangelical Unions* III, 3 (1931), TSCF A2c/20. Guinness's reports on his visit to New Zealand were slapdash. He guessed at numbers, misspelled names and called Auckland the capital.
15 Cree Brown to Will[iam Pettit], 19 August 1930, TSCF A2c.
16 Cree Brown to Guinness, 19 March 1930, TSCF A2c; Cree Brown to Guinness, 29 March 1930, TSCF A2c.
17 M.G. Milmine to Rymall [Roxburgh], 4 October 1948, TSCF N7/75.
18 'Evangelical Bible League, Dr Howard Guinness, Special Appeal for Prayer', [1930], TSCF A2c.
19 Lineham, 'Evangelical Witness'.
20 Robert A. Laidlaw (1885-1971) was a noted Auckland businessman. Converted in Dunedin at the 1902 Torrey mission, he was a leading member of Howe St Brethren, a major supporter of BTI and a frequent speaker and missioner. It was claimed that by the time of his death his pamphlet *The Reason Why* had been printed sixteen million times and translated into thirty languages. Ian Hunter, *Robert Laidlaw: Man for Our Time* (Auckland: Castle Publishing, 1999); Graham C. Stoop, 'Laidlaw, Robert Alexander Crookston: 1885-1971', *DNZB* 3: 271-72; R.A. Laidlaw, *The Reason Why* (Auckland: Institute Printing and Publishing Society, n.d.); R.A. Laidlaw, *The Story of 'The Reason Why'* (Auckland: G.W. Moore, 1969).
21 Guinness, 'The Universities of New Zealand', in the *Terminal Magazine* III, 3 (1931), TSCF A2c/20.
22 Lineham: 46.
23 *Terminal Magazine* III, 2 (1931), TSCF A2c/19. Coggan: 190-91.
24 Cree Brown to Guinness, 19 March 1930, TSCF A2c; to Nicholson, 19 March 1930, TSCF A2c; to Pettit, 19 August 1930, TSCF A2c.
25 'EU-SCM Relations', TSCF N7/62a, 1946, 4.
26 They noted that at its 1926 Conference NZSCM committed itself to a modernist outlook, and there were objections to conservative material in the bookstall: Morton to [Milmine], n.d., TSCF N7/76.
27 Bebbington, *Evangelicalism*: 259.
28 27 October 1930. E.g. Jansen moved 'that affiliation be declined' and the vote was unanimous. 'Extracts'; O. Eaton to the Sec. OUEU, 30 October 1930, TSCF N7/80.
29 Milmine to SCM, 9 April 1931, TSCF N7/81. Also: 'Extracts', 20 April 1931, TSCF.
30 E.g. [IVF] General Secretary to the Editor, *Methodist Times*, Auckland, 24 July 1945, TSCF N7/74; Morton to [Milmine], n.d., copy, TSCF N7/76.
31 Milmine to [Roxburgh], 4 October 1948, TSCF N7/75; to Robert

Withycombe, 27 July 1971, TSCF A1/81.
32. 'Extracts', 29 July 1931, 22 September 1931, 20 September 1934, 26 September 1935.
33. Milmine to [Roxburgh], 4 October 1948, TSCF N7/75. They were Hallam and Tennyson Howie.
34. Cree Brown to A. Stewart, 6 October 1930 (SCM file 30), cit. Lineham 45.
35. E.g. 29 July 1931, 'Extracts'. Otago CU executive resolved to inform EU that 'we resent the introduction of a Christian speaker to the university over the heads of the SCM'.
36. JGM, ¶162.
37. John Deane to T.C. Cocker, 19 March 1947, TSCF A3c.
38. Prior to 1961, when they became universities, the University Colleges of Auckland, Victoria and Canterbury were University Colleges of the University of New Zealand.
39. *Terminal Magazine* III, 3 (1931), TSCF A2c/20.
40. 'Auckland', typescript. The ESF basis used the word 'inerrant'. The IVF basis addressed a wider range of doctrines.
41. VUCEU Annual Report, 31 August 1945, B1/074, TSCF; AUCEU Annual Report, 31 August 1945, TSCF B1/074; ADMNH 1: 72.
42. J.G. Miller, 'Annual Report', 1936, cit. D. Penman, MS. history of IVF, n.d., TSCF A2c.
43. JGM, ¶611; 'Notes of Discussion between O.U.E.U. and S.C.M. (at request of S.C.M.) re Co-operation in the University', 14 March 1938, TSCF N762.
44. JGM, ¶612; similarly GMY, ¶95.
45. Buist to the Secretary, SCM, VUC, 25 July 1935, TSCF N7/70.
46. In morality, the EU considered the SCM 'worldly' and risqué. EU members understood, for instance, that SCM held house parties without camp parents – something 'not done' in those days: FM, ¶14.
47. 7 November 1936, 'Extracts'.
48. GMY, ¶95–96. Yule claimed Owen Baragwanath, once very active in SCM, was heard referring to the SCM as the 'Scarcely Christian Movement'. Buist argued that the SCM's desire to 'allow free expression of all shades of opinion' meant it only paid 'lip service' to biblical revelation. Its doubts meant it lacked 'power from on high', and it experienced 'a generally low level' of spirituality and consecration: Buist to Secretary, SCM, VUC, 25 July 1935, TSCF N7/70. At least one (overseas) SCM insider denied it was truly liberal (Boyd: 149–150).
49. Berry, Ch. 3: 1.
50. J.M. Bates, 'Memorandum on the Relationship of the SCM to the EU', c.1945, n.p., NZSCM papers, MS papers 1617: 632, ATL, cit. Berry Ch. 3: 8.
51. For instance, *Principles of Co-operation* (London: IVFEU, n.d.).
52. Colin [?] Becroft to Jack [McQueen], 13 August 1941, TSCF B4.
53. RR, ¶370.
54. E.g. Dr C.F. Andrews, who came to NZ as an SCM university missioner in 1936. JGM, ¶611; H. Yolland, 'Is Rev. C.F. Andrews a Trustworthy Leader of Christian Thought?' *Reaper* (25 June 1936): 97–100.
55. E.g. B.H. Williams to [Becroft], n.d. [1941], TSCF B4; Williams to Becroft, 2 September 1941, TSCF B4.
56. Williams to Jack [McQueen], 7 September 1941, TSCF B4.
57. A.M. Richards, 'The Adventure of the SCM', *Outlook* (2 March 1931): 5–7.
58. J.A. Linton [SCM General Secretary], 'Student Christian Movement', *Outlook* 23 February 1938: 30.
59. FM, ¶13.
60. E.g. R.A. Carson, who was on the executive of the CUCEU while a vice president in the SCM group.
61. RR, ¶180–81. Stevely (1886–1950), from the United Free Church in Scotland, had studied under James Denney and James Orr, was minister

62 at First Church from 1930 and a popular preacher.
62 ADMNH 1: 83. Minties were a lolly.
63 Thomson, a protégé of Orange, was at Selwyn College preparing for Anglican ministry. Other early OUEU presidents included Cuth Stewart, Gordon Smith, Colin Morrison and Jack McQueen. Other early OUEU members included Jean Hanning, Alister Loan, Marjorie and Ruth Pettit, Eunice McLean and Caleb Tucker: RR, ¶178.
64 MW, ¶35; LW, ¶69.
65 'Tour of the New Zealand Colleges by the Rev. Thomas Miller, M.A.,' n.d. [1945], TSCF C5/2. This room, in the university's old central-city site, was also known as the room where Ernest Rutherford began his research.
66 Peter Lineham, 'Evangelical Witness at Canterbury University: A History of the EU/CU 1930–1974', unpublished paper, TSCF archives, 1974: 26.
67 Monthly teas in 1936, for instance, were attended by about 100: *NZ Inter-Varsity News Bulletin* (July 1936).
68 Dr Bruce Harris, letter, 30 May 2001; KO, ¶19. Local churches contributing students to EU included St James' Presbyterian, Beresford St Congregational and West Street Church of Christ (Life and Advent).
69 KO, ¶19.
70 KO, ¶18–19.
71 Harris letter.
72 'A.U.C. Evangelical Union, 1939'.
73 *The NZ Inter-Varsity News Bulletin* (July 1936); *The New Zealand Inter-Varsity Supplement* (November 1941.
74 Ibid. Blaiklock and John Laird also spoke. In 1939, Orange was invited by all four EUs to speak at their annual house parties: *New Zealand Inter-Varsity Supplement* (July 1939).
75 These three were cited by Francis Foulkes, for instance, as critical influences upon him: 'The Richness of Life. Recalling the Past'

(unpublished memoirs, typescript, n.d.): 11, 13.
76 KO, ¶10, 13–15.
77 'Notes for incoming president'. Raymond Honey, 3 December 1949. B2/12, VUCEU, TSCF.
78 Ibid.
79 VUCEU, Annual Report, 31 August 1945, B1/074, TSCF.
80 JGM, ¶248.
81 MW, ¶40.
82 JGM, ¶497.
83 RR, ¶365; ERH, ¶62.
84 Rev. Maurice Betteridge, interview, 26 November 1999 (hereafter MB), ¶84; RR, ¶327; JGM, ¶495–96, 512.
85 ERH, ¶61, 68, 70. Harries was reflecting on his background at BTI (1934–35), where many were happy to wear the label 'fundamentalist'; similarly LW, ¶126–28. Note also Orr's 1936 comment *en passant*: 'I am an evangelical, a fundamentalist' (Orr: 49). But Orr had spent much time in North America.
86 In Britain, the differentiation of the two terms was less apparent in the 1930s than later, and British evangelicalism was closer to American fundamentalism than it was half a century later (Barclay: 13).
87 IVFEU TSPU circular, April 1939, TSCF I1/035.
88 RR, ¶364.
89 OUEU, [introductory] card, 1944, TSCF.
90 The Doctrinal Basis made no reference to creation or evolution. In relation to eschatology, the DB simply asserted an 'expectation of the Personal return of the Lord Jesus Christ'.
91 Max Wiggins, IVFEU TSPU circular, April 1939, TSCF I1/035.
92 Ibid.
93 Note: IVFEU(NZ). *N.Z. Inter-Varsity Papers No. 1: Organic Evolution: The Theory Critically Examined. The Argument for the Negative in Students' Debate, Otago University on the Subject 'That the Weight of Evidence Supports*

the Theory of Evolution'. Wellington: published for the IVFEU (NZ) by A.H. and A.W. Reed, 1940.
94 T.C. Hammond, *In Understanding Be Men: A Handbook on Christian Doctrine For Non-Theological Students* (London: IVF, 1936).
95 E.g. Dr Bruce Harris, who wrote that it 'opened my eyes to serious theological writing' (letter, 30 May 2001).
96 The 1877 Education Act, bypassing denominational rivalries, stipulated that primary schools be 'secular'. That provision was anti-sectarian rather than anti-religious, but a more rationalistic understanding of the secular clause gradually gained ground. Secondary schools were not required to be secular, and often had hymns or prayers at school assemblies, but were influenced by the secular atmosphere of primary and tertiary education.
97 The English Crusader movement targeted grammar school pupils and met outside the schools on Sunday afternoons. It refused to affiliate the New Zealand movement (Lineham: 62).
98 KO, ¶8, 10.
99 Lineham: 79.
100 Dr John Laird, *No Mere Chance* (London: Hodder and Stoughton, 1987): 52–53. Note Don Biggs and Lawrie Becroft (eds). *The Ponui Story. Celebrating 75 Years of Scripture Union Camping* (Wellington: Scripture Union New Zealand, 2006).
101 David Wood, interview, November 2004 (hereafter DW), ¶7.
102 Biggs and Becroft: 11.
103 Ibid.: 13.
104 Ponui Scripture Union Camps Visitors Book (1967).
105 Lineham: 73.
106 AUCEU Annual Report, 31 August 1941, B1/070, TSCF.
107 E.g. Ponui Scripture Union Camps Visitors Books, 1951–75.
108 KO, ¶12.
109 Laird: 33–34, 37–40, 43–44; Lineham: 52–56. In 1933 Laird began to work with CSSM as well as Crusaders, and in 1934 the two movements were united, in association with the Scripture Union.
110 Laird, 40–42, 46; Lineham, 54–55.
111 JGM, ¶162.
112 JGM, ¶232; ADMNH 1: 92; FM, ¶22.
113 CSSM Council Minute Book, 1930–1933, 699, SU (UK), cit. Lineham: 65.
114 RR, ¶109.
115 Laird counselled the first IVF staff worker not to 'go overboard' on Calvinism: JGM, ¶233.
116 RR, ¶358.
117 RR, ¶338–42.

Chapter Three: William Orange and Orange Pips

1 David G.S. Rathgen, 'The Church in New Zealand 1890–1920, with Special Reference to W.A. Orange' (Joint Board of Theological Studies Licentiate of Theology Thesis, 1969); Lineham, *No Ordinary Union*: e.g. 79; R.A. Carson, 'Some Reflections on the Life of W.A. Orange', *Latimer* 111 (August 1992): 19–22; Jeremy Clark, 'The Evangelical Ministry of William A. Orange, 1930–1945' (Auckland Consortium of Theological Education B.Th. Research Essay in Church History, M.C.D., 1995); ibid.,'Orange, William Alfred, 1869–1966, *DNZB* 4: 391–92; L.E. Pfankuch, 'The Reverend W.A. Orange, Vicar of Sumner 1930–1945', in *All Saints Church, Sumner Centennial. Parish of Sumner/Redcliffs* (no publisher: n.d.); Stuart Lange, 'Orange Pips and the Evangelical Churchmen's Fellowship, 1945–1972', *Churchman* (September 2011); ibid., 'Spirit and Reason: Canon Orange and Professor Blaiklock as Contrasting Exemplars of Evangelical Identity in Mid-Twentieth Century New Zealand', in Habets and Meadowcroft (eds).
2 Carson: 20.

3   E.g. Max Wiggins, Harry Thomson, Maurice Goodall.
4   Rev. Graham Lamont, interview, December 2001 (hereafter GL), ¶2.
5   Rev. R.M. Glen, interview, 27 October 1999 (hereafter RMG), ¶9.
6   Orange showed no interest in women. He wrote, referring to a colleague, that 'like myself, Aubrey is … not in the least sylph-conscious, and wastes no time at all dame-dreaming': Orange to G. Nicholson, 1 February 1950.
7   Vera Mott, interview, 21 April 2006 (hereafter VM), ¶3; *The Messenger* (May 1944; May 1945).
8   RMG, ¶12.
9   Interview with the Ven. R.A. Carson by R.M. Glen, 20 December 1989, ¶4; RR, ¶332. See e.g. 'A Sermon Preached by Canon W.A. Orange at the ECF Quiet Day at St Augustine, Cashmere, 1 June, 1964', *Latimer Magazine* (July 1964).
10 JGM, ¶236.
11 Roger Thompson, *This Is the Victory. The Church – Dormant or Militant. Some memoirs of a Kiwi 'Sin-Buster'* (Christchurch: privately published, 1995: 9).
12 JGM, ¶236.
13 Rev. Roger F.N. Thompson, interview, 1 November 1999 (hereafter RT), ¶370.
14 MB, ¶32.
15 Canon Basil H. Williams, 'Passing of Canon William Alfred "Willie" Orange', *Challenge Weekly* 24, 28 (23 July 1966): 6–7.
16 RMG, ¶12.
17 Glen, in Thompson/Glen interview, ¶10.
18 Hutchinson, 'Interview with Professor Edwin Judge' (37). 'The extraordinary thing is that though I think the methodology was wrong, its effect was profound.'
19 Coulthard/Glen interview, ¶17.
20 JGM, ¶236. Miller compared the effect of Orange's preaching to that of Savonarola in Florence, where the man taking shorthand notes wrote 'at this point I was overcome with weeping and could not go on'. 'Further tributes', *Challenge* (6 August 1966): 12.
21 *The NZ Inter-Varsity News Bulletin* (October 1937): 11.
22 RT, ¶26.
23 JGM, ¶236.
24 RT, ¶370.
25 RR, ¶333; Carson/Glen interview, ¶12.
26 JGM, ¶236; GMY, ¶89; O'Sullivan, ¶18; Minn to Moses, 31 October 1948, TSCF N12/49; Rev. Harvey Teulon, interview, 29 September 1999 (hereafter HT), ¶16: 'I had too much of a scientific background … I could not feel that typology had any empirical basis'.
27 Russell Fountain, interview by P.J. Lineham, n.d.; also R.M. Glen recollection, August 2006.
28 E.g. Carson/Glen interview, ¶4, 11; Coulthard/Glen interview, ¶18; Hutchinson, 'Interview with Professor Edwin Judge' (37).
29 'ECF News', *Latimer Magazine* (April 1964).
30 Rev. Martin Sullivan, 'Like a Father', *Challenge Weekly* (23 July 1966): 6–7.
31 Thomas/Glen interview, ¶46.
32 Fountain, interview by Glen, 30 November 1990, ¶27.
33 MB, ¶128.
34 Rathgen: 123–27.
35 H. Purchas and later P.J. Cocks. Ibid.: 129–32.
36 Diary: 25 May 1910; 31 January; 1, 2 February 1911.
37 18 January, 5 April 1909; 2 November 1911; 18 January 1909.
38 22–29 October 1910.
39 7 November 1910.
40 16 July 1911.
41 Ibid.
42 22 July 1911.
43 'Obituary: The Rev. H.W. Funnell', *E.C.F. Review* (August 1962). Funnell left in 1909 for Moody College and service with CIM.
44 8 September, 6 November 1911.
45 27 May 1912. John Dickson, *Shall*

Ritualism and Romanism Capture New Zealand? Their Ramifications in Protestant Churches (Dunedin: Otago Daily Times, 1912).
46   27 September, 6 November 1911.
47   25 November 1911.
48   E.g. 24 November 1911, 20 April 1912.
49   29 December 1911.
50   5 September 1911.
51   10 November 1911.
52   9 November 1911; 10 November 1911.
53   24 April 1912.
54   The key was Young's *Analytical Concordance*.
55   15 November, 13 December 1911; 14 March, 22 April, 29 April 1912.
56   28 April 1912.
57   9 November 1911; 10, 13 May, 2 June 1912.
58   Syriac was a semitic language related to biblical Aramaic, and used in parts of the early Church.
59   J.R. Wilford, *Southern Cross and Evening Star* (London: Martini, 1950): 108–73; J.E. Welch, 'A Pilgrim on God's High Road: Canon Wilford in New Zealand'. Canterbury University MA thesis, 2006.
60   Diary: 6 May 1914.
61   Wiggins/Glen interview, ¶4.
62   Schroder, cit. Rathgen: 144.
63   Welch: 82–83; Wilford: 146–47.
64   Diary: 30 April, 19, 20 June, 2 July, 8 July 1924.
65   30 April 1924.
66   MW, ¶44.
67   Diary: 6 April–20 July 1924.
68   E.g. 6 April 1924: Rev. 21:3; 20 April: 1 Peter 1:3; 4 May: Heb. 4:12; 11 May: Mt. 4:4; 15 June: John 3:3.
69   Diary: e.g. 7 April, 12 July 1924.
70   2 May, 11 July, 12 July 1924.
71   12–13, 21–22 July.
72   29 June, 11 July 1924.
73   11 July 1924.
74   Diary: 20 June 1924.
75   'Newsletter', Latimer Foundation (NZ) Inc., n.d. [c.1969]; *E.C.F. Review* (November 1963); Pfankuch.
76   Pfankuch, 'The Reverend W.A. Orange'.
77   Sullivan, 'Like a Father'.
78   John Charles Ryle, *Knots Untied, Being Plain Statements on Disputed Points in Religion from an Evangelical Standpoint* (James Clarke and Co.: London, 1954. 31st edn). Wallace Marriott later owned Orange's copy.
79   Ryle: 10–13.
80   Ibid.: 19–20, also 7, 15.
81   Ibid.: 65–73, 84–93.
82   Ibid.: 16, 58.
83   Ibid.: 14.
84   Ibid.: 16, 62; also 13, 50, 58.
85   Diary: 7–8, 17, 29 July 1935; 22 April 1938.
86   Diary: 8, 10, 17, 29 July 1935.
87   Diary: 17 July 1935.
88   Diary: 18, 29 July 1935.
89   Diary: 18 July 1935.
90   Diary: 22 April 1938.
91   Piggin: 126, 131. Hammond had 'a mind like a rapier and a tongue like a whip': 131.
92   RR, ¶333.
93   MW, ¶75: 'I never heard him press for a decision, he just let Scripture loose upon us, left it free to do its own work.'
94   Not, at least, by the estimate of Graham Miller: JGM, ¶236.
95   Carson, 'Reflections': 19; Right Rev. Maurice Goodall, interview, 22 November 2001 (hereafter MG), ¶11. Brethren dispensational teaching divided God's dealings with humanity into up to eight different 'dispensations' in the past, present and future.
96   Diary: 7 July 1935.
97   Ibid. His diary once approvingly uses the term of someone else, probably in the (earlier) sense of that person's resistance to liberalism: 17 July 1935.
98   RT, ¶68–71; RT, ¶91–93.
99   Diary: (excluding references to the EU) e.g. 9, 14, 17, 18, 29 July 1935; 22 April 1938 (twice); 26 April 1938 (four times); 11 May 1938; 14 July 1938 (twice).

100 In 1938 he spent time in Britain with IVF leaders, spoke at a CICCU house party, and enthusiastically attended the Keswick Convention as part of a CIM group. Diary: 14–17 July 1938.
101 MW, ¶54; Williams, 'Passing'.
102 Pfankuch, 'Orange'.
103 Rathgen: 90–118.
104 Carson interview, August 1994, cit. Clark: 33.
105 The north side is the left of the church when seen from the rear of the church. The 1830s Oxford Movement reintroduced the practice of facing east, with back to the congregation, but that was generally resisted in New Zealand until the early twentieth century. After the *New Zealand Prayer Book* was introduced (1989), it became normal for Anglican ministers to stand behind the table and face the congregation.
106 A stole, a coloured scarf, is a symbol of priesthood. Low Church people opposed their reintroduction. For most ex-Sydney clergy, stoles were 'anathema': Rev. Wallace Marriott, interview, 29 September 2001 (hereafter WM), ¶70; MB, ¶69, 112. Evangelical ministers in Nelson, Sydney and England would normally wear black scarf, academic hood, surplice and cassock: RMG, ¶20.
107 MW, ¶52. Such practices included elevation of the consecrated elements, candles before images, prayers for the dead, use of the term 'Mass', wafers, prostrations during the Creed, the adoration of a crucifix (Rathgen: 75–78, 84, 110–14). Orange softened in his views in his latter years, when a Precentor at the cathedral, and sometimes attended and preached at St Michael's, an Anglo-Catholic stronghold.
108 Diary: 26 April 1938.
109 E.g. Betteridge (MB, ¶113), Marriott (WM, ¶72).
110 MW, ¶57; RT, ¶79. Teulon told Glen: 'If you don't wear a stole, you will not be ordained. Do you want to ruin your ministry before it's started, over this little piece of coloured rag?' (RMG, ¶22).
111 Thompson, interview by Glen. [c.1990]: ¶2.
112 MW, ¶53.
113 Ibid.
114 Anon., ¶50.
115 Diary: 20–24 October 1924.
116 Diary: 3, 19, 22, 25 May 1924; 17 June 1924; 7 July 1935.
117 Diary: 7 July 1935.
118 R.C. Nicholson to Lineham, 23 October 1973.
119 One of them also embarrassed his fellow evangelicals with his exaggerated fervency and his awkwardness in personal evangelism. People on a tram would change seats to get away from him.
120 1951–56.
121 Carson believed Orange had a 'persecution complex' and that most persecution of evangelicals was imaginary: interview by Lineham, n.d. [c. 1973]; Pfankuch/Lineham interview, n.d. [c.1973].
122 W.A. Orange to Guy Nicholson, 1 February 1950.
123 RT, ¶197.
124 Martin Sullivan, *Watch How You Go* (London: Hodder & Stoughton, 1975): 117, 124–25.
125 MB, ¶142–52; RT, ¶342; cf. Manwaring: 54. Orange, whose father was alcoholic, found alcohol 'loathsome' (Diary: 21 September 1914). But he was not teetotal (25 July 1935, 25 June 1938).
126 MB, ¶111.
127 Clark: 6.
128 Carson/Glen interview, ¶13; Carson: 20.
129 Diary: 6 March 1938.
130 18 April 1938.
131 VM, ¶2; *Year Book for the Diocesan Year* 1929, 1930, 1935, 1936, 1939, 1940, 1941, 1945.
132 RT, ¶100.
133 Ibid., ¶43.
134 Wiggins, in conversation, 1999; RT,

¶38–41.
135 MB, ¶197. Similarly Thompson/Glen interview: ¶8: Orange showed him 'the power of the Word'.
136 Sullivan: 125.
137 Lineham, 'Evangelical Witness': 15.
138 Diary: 7 July 1935.
139 MB, ¶21; GL, ¶4.
140 MB, ¶29; Aiken closely followed Orange's style: 'It got to the stage where we would say, "shut your eyes and you won't know whether it's Canon Orange or Dave Aiken"'(HT, ¶17).
141 JGM, ¶236.
142 Diary: 11 July 1938, 8 July 1935, 14 July 1938.
143 H.F. Ault, *The Nelson Narrative: The Story of the Church of England in the Diocese of Nelson, New Zealand 1858 to 1958* (Nelson: Standing Committee of the Diocese of Nelson, 1958); R. Bester (ed.), *Harvest of Grace: Essays in Celebration of 150 Years of Mission in the Anglican Diocese of Nelson* (Nelson: Standing Committee of the Diocese of Nelson, 2010).
144 Canon William F. Wilkens, interview, 1 August 2005 (hereafter WW), ¶4, 7. Haultain was at All Saints' (1932–39), Kimberley at the Church of the Nativity (1929–39).
145 Orange diary entry: 22 April 1938.
146 The Venerable Paul Kirkham, interview, 15 November 2001 (hereafter PK), ¶4; letter, 18 March 2002.
147 Ault: 156; WW, ¶2. In 2005, Wilkens could recall a Hilliard sermon he heard in 1934.
148 Loane: 134–35.
149 They were often those without university degrees who were unable to secure ordination in Sydney.
150 Keith Aubrey (1940), at Collingwood then Greymouth (1947–56). PK, ¶5; Rev. John Greenslade, interview, 21 November 2001 (hereafter JG), ¶8; WW, ¶27, 29; Rev. Guy Nicholson, interview, December 2001 (hereafter GN), ¶65.
151 Keith Cole, *Sincerity My Guide: A Biography of the Right Reverend P.W. Stephenson* ([Melbourne]: Church Missionary Historical Publications Trust, 1970); Susan Ledingham, 'Percival William Stephenson: Bishop of Nelson, 1940–1953', in Bester (ed.): 132–54.
152 PK, ¶6, ¶8; Ault: 161; WW, ¶3;
153 Cole: 114–15.
154 Kenneth Gregory, *Stretching Out Continually: A History of the New Zealand Church Missionary Society 1892–1972* (Christchurch: Kenneth Gregory with the authorisation of the NZCMS, n.d.): 129–31.
155 Morrell: 218–19, quoting *Yearbook of the Diocese of Nelson*, 1946: 28. The proposal did not proceed until the 1960s, and meanwhile College House and Selwyn College continued as ministry training centres.
156 E.g. Charles Haskell, Herbie Rowe, John and Rex Ford, John Meadowcroft, Owen Kimberley.
157 Ven. F.J. Ford, interview, 15 November 2001 (hereafter JF), ¶21.
158 Rev. Canon John Meadowcroft, interview, 1 November 2001 (hereafter JM), ¶11–16; WW, ¶12; JF, ¶19.
159 JM, ¶11. Similarly JF, ¶11–12.
160 WW, ¶11.

Chapter Four: The IVF and a New Evangelical Generation

1 Basil Williams to [K.] Moore, 10 May 1932, TSCF A2c/001. R.F. Judson to Williams, 25 May 1932, TSCF A2c/002; A.W. Morton to Williams, 31 May 1932, TSCF A2c/003.
2 T.F. Haughley and A.W. Morton to the executives of [the] EUs, 30 July 1935, TSCF A2c/006.; AUCEU executive to the executives of [the] EUs, 9 September 1935, TSCF A2c/008.
3 Woods later pioneered the IVF in the US, and in 1947 became general secretary of the new International

4 Fellowship of Evangelical Students. Orr, an international evangelist, arrived late in the weekend from the Ngaruawahia Convention, where he believed he had experienced a revival. J. Edwin Orr, *All Your Need: 10,000 Miles of Miracle Through Australia and New Zealand* (London: Marshall Morgan and Scott, 1936): 37. The Bulletin referred to 'others' but did not list Orr by name as a speaker, which suggests the IVF had reservations about his revivalist style.
5 JGM, ¶163.
6 A Presbyterian, Morton later studied at Moore College, was ordained into the Anglican Church, took a DPhil at Oxford, and became Dean of St Andrew's Cathedral (Sydney).
7 Williams was ordained in New Zealand but moved to Australia and worked with IVF and SU.
8 All four of the 1936 EU presidents became ministers and at some stage moved to Australia (ADMNH 1: 72).
9 Lex Miller, 'Editorial: the Evangelical Unions. The witness in the colleges', *The Student* (June 1936): 1–2, TSCF B4.
10 ADMNH 1: 84; RR, ¶343.
11 MW, ¶35.
12 IVFEU (NZ), *N.Z. Varsity Papers No. 2: The Inter-Varsity Fellowship of Evangelical Unions (N.Z.): A Sketch of Its Origins, Doctrine and Practice: A Booklet for Officers and Members* (Wellington: Executive Committee of the (NZ), n.d. [c.1940]).
13 IVFEU. *Principles of Co-operation* (London: n.d.). Also: J.N.D. Anderson, 'The Problem of Union with Other Religious Organisations', in *N.Z. Varsity Papers No. 2*: 18–20.
14 [IVF] Advisory Committee, *Evangelical Belief: The Official Interpretation of the Doctrinal Basis of the IVF* (London: the Inter-Varsity Fellowship of Evangelical Unions, n.d. [1935]).
15 Ibid: 5.
16 Ibid.: 7–9. The analogy given was the combination of divinity and humanity in the person of Jesus.
17 Ibid.: 9–11.
18 Ibid.: 10.
19 Ibid.: 23.
20 Ibid.: 24–25.
21 In the 1935 edition, books recommended included works by Griffith Thomas, R.A. Torrey, C.H. Hodge, A.A. Hodge, James Orr, Gresham Machen, W.G.T. Shedd, James Denney, H.E. Guillebaud, G.T. Manley. The dated nature of those sources (and the still weak state of evangelical scholarship) was tacitly acknowledged when it was admitted that many of them were out of print: 34. IVF itself had not long begun publishing. Bibliographies in later editions reflected the growing body of postwar evangelical biblical scholarship.
22 Hammond, *In Understanding Be Men*: 22, 24–40.
23 Frank Houghton (ed.), *The Quiet Time* (London: Inter-Varsity Fellowship of Evangelical Unions, 1933).
24 G.T. Manley (ed.), *Search the Scriptures* (London: IVF, 1934).
25 H.E. Guillebaud, *Why the Cross?* (London: IVF, 1937).
26 RR, ¶186. Lamont, Professor of Practical Theology at New College, Edinburgh, and Moderator of the General Assembly (Church of Scotland, 1936), wrote *Christ and the World of Thought* (Edinburgh: T & T Clark, 1934).
27 A. Rendle Short, *The Bible and Modern Research*, 2nd edn (London: Marshall Morgan & Scott, n.d.).
28 'I now surrender myself to Thee to be filled with Thy Holy Spirit that I may, from to-day, live a life of Sacrifice.'
29 Howard Guinness, *Sacrifice: A Challenge to Christian Youth* (London: IVF, 1936); e-mail, Dr John Hitchen, 14 July 2008.
30 E.g. IVF Booklet No. 1 and No. 7.
31 *N.Z. Varsity Papers No. 2*, largely the

work of Graham Miller.
32. Basil F.C. Atkinson, *Valiant in Fight: A Review of the Christian Conflict* (London: IVF, 1937).
33. Pfankuch/Lineham interview.
34. [IVF] Gen. Sec. [Cliff Cocker] to the Editor, *Methodist Times*, Auckland, 24 July 1945, TSCF N7/74.
35. E.g. Christchurch, 1937; Auckland, 1938; Dunedin, 1939; Wellington, 1940; Christchurch, 1941.
36. Foulkes memoirs: 13.
37. Roxburgh: conversation, 2 November 1999.
38. MF, ¶16.
39. Wisdom, ordained in 1933, served with CMS in the 1930s and succeeded Orange in Sumner.
40. *NZ Inter-Varsity News Bulletin* (October 1937).
41. JGM, ¶783–84.
42. JGM, ¶238.
43. ADMNH 1: 95.
44. Ibid.: 93, 98. Memorial Minute, in IVFEU (NZ), 'Annual Report by the General Secretary on behalf of the Executive Committee', [1957]. Cocker died suddenly, in 1956.
45. Orange diary, 18 April 1938.
46. 'Notes of Discussion between O.U.E.U. and S.C.M. (at request of S.C.M.) re Co-operation in the University, 14 March 1938', TSCF N7/62.
47. 'Confidential. Notes of Conference with General Secretary of SCM on 11 February 1938 in SCM Headquarters', TSCF N7/62.
48. 'IVF work in New Zealand', with letter [from Cocker?] to Bruce [Harris], 28 August 1950, TSCF H1/22.
49. 'The Aim of the TSPU of the IVF', n.d., TSCF I1/033.
50. Others: Stan Nicholls, Aubrey Lowden (AUCEU), commencing 1935; Reg Judson (AUCEU), Rod McKenzie (VUCEU), 1937; Jack Johnston (AUCEU), Jack Smith (OUEU), 1939; Bill Milligan (OUEU), Ernie Walsh (BTI graduate) 1940; Bill Moore (OUEU), Russell Kenward (VUCEU), 1941; Bill Wallace (1942); Jack Scarrow (1943).
51. RR, ¶401, 404.
52. In 1939 there were seven TSPU members, out of a total of forty-one ordinands.
53. JGM, ¶165; RR, ¶419.
54. GMY, ¶218; RR, ¶406.
55. HT, ¶12.
56. Dickie: 13, 324, 327; GMY, ¶231; Collie: 202. Dickie rejected substitutionary atonement.
57. RR, ¶409; corroboration in W.G.K Moore to Geoffrey King, 22 August 1995, cit. King: n.18, 337. In *The Organism of Christian Truth*, Dickie stated that his own position was intended as a mediating one between fundamentalism and modernism: 8.
58. GMY, ¶232. This incident probably reflected Dickie's hostility to pacifism and to Germany (see King: 295, 126), rather than unqualified support for the EU or its doctrine.
59. Dickie: 312–13; ADMNH 1: 104–05.
60. GMY, ¶225, 226, 234–45; RR, ¶127.
61. RR, ¶480.
62. RR, ¶401; GMY, ¶243. See also OA201, Minutes of a Special General Meeting of the Theological Hall Students Union, 17 March 1943, THSU Minute Book 1932–43, cit. David Scott Clark, 'Our Interests and Christ: The Christian Existentialism of Helmut Rex' (PhD thesis, University of Otago, 2003): 92; Minutes of a Special General Meeting of the THSU, 26 March 1943.
63. E.g. GMY, ¶147. Evangelicals appreciated Denney's *Death of Christ* [1902] but deplored his modernist views on scripture in *Studies in Theology* [1894]: JGM, ¶146.
64. GMY, ¶203.
65. JGM, ¶146, 534. Hunter later handed Miller a copy of Denney's *Studies in Theology*, urging him to read the chapter on Scripture.
66. JGM, ¶367–68, 374.
67. JGM, ¶367.
68. JGM, ¶378, ¶368.

69   JGM, ¶516.
70   JGM, ¶370. Boettner had read Miller's bulletins in the *Calvin Forum* and sent him a free copy.
71   JGM, ¶371, ¶816. Miller received books from some of those authors after acting as a pallbearer, with three other like-minded students, at the funeral of P.B. Fraser.
72   'You know what Calvin thinks of apologetics. What's the use of apologetics, when you have the *testimonium Spiritus Sancti*?': JGM, ¶377.
73   JGM, ¶552.
74   Geering, later principal of the Presbyterian Theological College, became a well known advocate, in New Zealand, for the radical secular theology promoted by J.A.T. Robinson and others.
75   Miller was strongly influenced by Roland Allen's *Missionary Methods, St Paul's or Ours?* (London: World Dominion, 1912) and *The Spontaneous Expansion of the Church and the Causes Which Hinder It* (London: World Dominion, 1927). Others who were similarly influenced included Roxburgh (in India) and Norman Perry (among Māori).
76   JGM, ¶552.
77   JGM, ¶536–37, 542, 551.
78   RR, ¶133, 118.
79   E.g. JGM, ¶515; RR, ¶491.
80   GMY, ¶212; RR, ¶390.
81   RR, ¶391. Note also 'The Aims of the TSPU of the IVF', n.d., TSCF Il/033.
82   E.g. RR, ¶388.
83   RR, ¶379, 384–85.
84   RR, ¶383.
85   GMY, ¶207; RR, ¶382, 384, 387.
86   GMY, ¶205, 209; RR, ¶375; JGM ¶515, 522, 530.
87   JGM, ¶521.
88   MW, ¶31; RT, 35, 172–82, 214–17.
89   RMG, ¶81. Also Carson/Glen interview, ¶4, 12, 14.
90   RT, ¶171.
91   RT, ¶37.
92   Ibid., ¶163, 167.
93   MW, ¶38.
94   Ibid.
95   The TSPU had thirty-two members by the end of 1941, including ten at Baptist College, seven at Knox, six at Trinity Methodist, five at College House and one at the Congregational College. By 1943, the TSPU had forty-three members. IVFEU(NZ) TSPU, n.d., TSCF Il/048.
96   The EMF in 1944 had thirty-nine members: 'List of Graduate Fellowship Members', 30 October 1944, TSCF J1/056. Many eligible ministers had not yet joined: R.S. Miller to Malcolm [Buist], 21 July 1944, TSCF Jl/027.
97   By 1944, 235 had joined the IVF Graduate Fellowship, including 139 teachers: 'List of Graduate Fellowship Members', 30 October 1944, TSCF J1/056.

Chapter Five: Anglican Evangelicals 1945–55

1   *Outlook* (20 May 1942): 9.
2   E.g. Rt. Rev. F.O. Hulme-Moir, 'Discovery and Communication', *ECF Review* (August 1959): 4.
3   As noted in e.g. Breward, *A History of the Churches of Australasia*: 302–03.
4   Barry Gustafson, 'The National Governments and Social Change (1949–1972)', in Keith Sinclair (ed.), *The Oxford Illustrated History of New Zealand* (Auckland: Oxford University Press, 1990): 267–68; Belich: *Paradise Reforged*, 297.
5   Callum G. Brown, *The Death of Christian Britain: Understanding Secularisation, 1800–2000* (London & New York: Routledge, 2001). Brown saw the 1950s as a 'deeply old-fashioned era' in which 'religion mattered and mattered deeply': 6–7. He claimed a 'strengthening piety' in Britain in the period 1945–60.
6   VM, ¶22; Canon R.E. and Mrs Helen Coulthard, interview, 19 April 2006 (hereafter REC), ¶12; GL, ¶9.
7   GL, ¶22; VM, ¶18, 21.

8   JM, ¶27.
9   Ordinands: Lester Pfankuch, Bruce Beattie, Bob Hughes, Hugh Thomson; later ordinands: Graham Lamont, John Meadowcroft, Wallace Marriott, Robert Glen, Gerald Clark (GL, ¶13). Others: Keith Mitchell, Margaret Cummings, Hope and Shirley Greenwood, Helen Marriott, Monica Morris, Vera Mott, David Powell, John Powell, Peter Rawley, Hedley Thomas, Pam Scott, Murray Wilson, Crellin Dingwall (WM, ¶13).
10 WM, ¶10.
11 E.g. JM, ¶27.
12 GL, ¶22.
13 Because of the confidentiality required, Tanner was unable to explain his actions, which were misinterpreted by some as evidence of doctrinal unreliability.
14 GL, ¶79; WM, ¶20.
15 Neil G. Lancaster, *Our Hope for Years to Come: St Martin's Parish Spreydon 1909-1984* [Christchurch: Parish of Spreydon, 1984]: 21–22, 25.
16 GL, ¶24.
17 RT, ¶35 (Reena Thompson).
18 GL, ¶24.
19 GL, ¶24; Anon., ¶16; Roger Thompson, *This is the Victory. The Church – Dormant or Militant. Some Memoirs of a Kiwi 'Sin-Buster'* (Christchurch: privately published, 1995): 21.
20 GL, ¶24: Graham Lamont, Helen Marriott, John and David Powell, Pamela Scott, Colleen Prince, Peter Rawley, Jimmy Simpson; Wallace Marriott, Ian Nelson, John Meadowcroft, Gerald Clark, five Bruhn sisters (Helen, Esther, Marie, Margaret, May), David Bremner, Ailsa Murphy, Sally Hodgson.
21 E.g. Brian Carrell, Jill Morrison, Runa Brandon, Noelene and Shirley Sandford (GL, ¶24; BC, ¶80).
22 Lancaster: 28.
23 Ibid.: 26.
24 RT, ¶81–89.
25 RMG, ¶67.
26 Lancaster: 30.
27 BRC, ¶6, 10, 13.
28 Ibid., ¶13; cf. HT, ¶17.
29 BRC, ¶15.
30 Untitled St Martin's BC Reunion booklet, n.a., n.d.: 18–20.
31 Lancaster: 27.
32 JM, ¶33.
33 BRC, ¶146.
34 In the morning services the standard Anglican hymnbook was used, *Hymns Ancient and Modern*, WM, ¶45. At Sumner, Orange had also used a set of Keswick hymnbooks, later purchased by Ian Bourne: the Ven. Ian G. Bourne, interview, November 2001 (hereafter IGB), ¶74.
35 St Martin's BC Reunion Booklet: 18–19.
36 JM, ¶33; RT, ¶246.
37 RT, ¶126–30; *Victory*: 23.
38 Anon., ¶19.
39 Ibid., ¶248.
40 Ibid., ¶18–19.
41 RT, ¶90–93; likewise MB, ¶32.
42 RT, ¶22.
43 Ibid., ¶100. Also ¶98–99; similarly, MB, ¶34–35, 40.
44 RT, ¶376.
45 Ibid., ¶232–38, 227–30, 381.
46 BRC, ¶144.
47 JM, ¶32.
48 Ibid; BRC, ¶331–37; JG, ¶11; RMG, ¶67.
49 *Victory*: 2–4.
50 E.g. Thompson to Lamont, 21 September 1965; ibid., 19 October 1965.
51 *Victory*: 1.
52 Ibid.: 12.
53 BRC, ¶19.
54 JG, ¶41.
55 'We never touched the stuff, in fact you never really saw it. Beer was the only alcohol that was really available. Beer was not considered appropriate.' (MB, ¶147; also ¶148–51).
56 BRC, ¶32–46.
57 E.g. Carl F.H. Henry, *The Uneasy Conscience of Modern Fundamentalism* (Grand Rapids:

Eerdmans, 1947): 19; 84–89.
58 Thompson, *Victory*: 23–25.
59 E.g. Jean Ross, *A Short History of the Parish of Riccarton–St James, 1906–1999* (Parish of Riccarton–St James: 1999): 11.
60 Lancaster: 23.
61 BRC, ¶268, 280.
62 RT, ¶77.
63 HT, ¶91; JG, ¶11.
64 RMG, ¶68.
65 Thompson 'always felt the bishop [Alwyn Warren] was trying to entrap him': name withheld.
66 HT, ¶128.
67 RT, ¶195. Thompson estimated the proportion of 'liberals' in the Synod in the 1960s as 80 per cent, and the number of 'Anglo-Catholics' as 10 per cent: ibid., ¶199; cf. BRC, ¶306.
68 RT, ¶187.
69 Ibid., ¶186.
70 E.g. GL, ¶26; BRC, ¶48–54.
71 E.g. BRC, ¶202. Through EU Carrell became aware of C.S. Lewis: 'I remember him helping me through some intellectual problems ... with some of the questions I heard my SCM friends raise'.
72 JM, ¶40.
73 Anglican evangelicals did, however, use the Keswick hymnbook and read reports of Keswick in the UK (WM, ¶43). Orange himself had enthusiastically attended Keswick in England and spoke at several Keswick Conventions in New Zealand (diary: 18 April 1938, 15–17 July 1938).
74 JM, ¶92.
75 Lancaster: 30.
76 *Year Book for the Diocesan Year*, 1960.
77 RT, ¶159.
78 Four hundred of those were inside and 600 outside.
79 Evangelicals believed it was the unstated policy of the Diocese not to allow an evangelical succession where 'they could get away with it' (WM, ¶16).
80 John Meadowcroft, 'Roger Thompson: An Appreciation': 9.
81 List drawn up from information provided by several informants, plus St Martin's BC Reunion Booklet: 20.
82 E.g. Edna Brooker (CMS – Northern Australia), Ronalda Connor (OMF – Malaysia), Ian Foster (CMS – East Africa), Alison Moore (East Africa), Phillipa Reaney (Northern Australia), Wallace Searle (Andes Evangelical Mission – Bolivia and Peru), Elaine Smith (East Africa), Elizabeth Smith (Malaysia and Singapore), Catherine Sellman (East Africa), Anne Scott (OMF – Taiwan).
83 1992 BC Reunion Booklet: 21.
84 1992 BC Reunion Booklet: 4–17.
85 RMG, ¶80; RT, ¶383; JG, ¶53; Rosemary R. Troughton, interview, 20 April 2006 (hereafter RRT): ¶2, 19.
86 RRT, ¶1, 5.
87 Tribute from Les Burgess (Woolston Parish), in 'With Thanks to God for the Life of Harry Thomson', *CMS News* (September 1987): 1; RRT, ¶8–12.
88 RRT, ¶7.
89 RRT, ¶3–4; RMG, ¶80.
90 RRT, ¶22–23, 6–8.
91 Thomson's ministry nevertheless produced such protégés as Tony Andrews, later Dean of Cairo.
92 Gregory: 134.
93 E.g. RMG, ¶35; JG, ¶53. For previous liberal evangelical trends in the international CMS movement, Orange diary: 22 April, 14 July 1938; Bebbington, *Evangelicalism*: 218.
94 Mott to Bayley, 2 June 2003.
95 VM, ¶18. BRC, ¶65, 69–70.
96 VM, ¶18.
97 E.g. Rev. Dale Oldham, interview, 24 April 2003 (hereafter DO), ¶42.
98 Gregory, 135; Rev. John Hewlett, interview, 9 April 2003 (hereafter JH), ¶30.
99 Ian Grant Bourne, 'A Life Observed', typescript, n.d.: 109.
100 Gregory: 210.
101 Ibid.: 143.
102 There was an understanding that Moore would recommend to

Nelson some of its less academic students: Hammond to Stephenson, 22 February 1950, Former Clerical Employees, Box 5, Archives, Anglican Centre, Nelson (hereafter NFCE) Box 5; Loane to Stephenson, April 17 1953, ibid.
103 JM, ¶130; Ledingham, in Bester (ed.): 144.
104 F, ¶28; Anon., ¶255.
105 The first two arrived in 1948, and the others in 1949, 1951 and 1954. Marriott trained at Moore.
106 They studied for an LTh through the NZ Anglican Board of Theological Studies, which had a liberal approach they did not appreciate: JM, ¶68.
107 Year Book and Summary of Proceedings of the Third Session of the Thirty-Fourth Synod of the Diocese of Nelson, New Zealand, held at Nelson, 4th September 1950 (Nelson, NZ: R.W. Stiles & Co., printers, [1950]).
108 WW, ¶10.
109 WW, ¶15–18.
110 JM, ¶24.
111 JM, ¶24, 26, 41–42.
112 JF, ¶15, 29, 33.
113 JG, ¶7.
114 JG, ¶10.
115 Ibid., ¶14.
116 JF, ¶48.
117 D.S. Edmiston, 'A Journey Together. Doug and Jane's Story'. Unpublished personal memoirs, typescript, n.d.: 58; Peter Butt, 'Doers of the Word': History of St James' Anglican Church, Lower Hutt, 1849–1978. Wellington: St James' Parish, [1978]: 40.
118 Leader of the Opposition, 1950–57; Prime Minister, 1957–60.
119 IGB, ¶30; Rev. David Pickering, interview, November 2001 (hereafter DP), ¶19; telephone conversation (hereafter DP/Tel.), 20 January 2006.
120 Canon D.S. (Doug) Edmiston, interview, November 2001 (hereafter DE), ¶27.
121 Bourne: 102.
122 Edmiston: 67; Bourne: 102. Bretton required his curates to be at Matins at 7 am every day, and was 'devastating' when he told them off: IGB, ¶34.
123 IGB, ¶32.
124 31 October 1956. Bourne: 111.
125 W.F. Bretton MA, Dean of Nelson, NZ, The A.B.C. of Our Religion ([Nelson]: n.p., 1958 [reprint]).
126 Bourne: 85; IGB, ¶36.
127 IGB, ¶38.
128 Someone nicknamed them 'Bretton's Buttons', but that was not in common usage: DP/Tel; JG, ¶49.
129 IGB, ¶16.
130 Other evangelical influences on Bourne included leaders from Christchurch at BC camps, Harvey Teulon and British missioner Canon Bryan Green.
131 Bourne: 123; IGB, ¶39.
132 Bourne: 122.
133 IGB, ¶113.
134 IGB, ¶69.
135 DE, ¶22, 24.
136 Ibid., ¶26, 44.
137 Ibid., ¶27–28, 43.
138 IGB, ¶41; DE, ¶32.
139 DP, ¶19, 33, 34, 36, 37, 39, 70, 80.
140 DP, ¶41.
141 DP, ¶45. Pickering greatly admired Thompson, but not uncritically: DP, ¶51, 53, 57.
142 DP, ¶71–73.
143 Alan Nichols, 'Penman, David John', in Dickey (ed.): 299–301; Alan Nichols, David Penman: Bridge-builder, Peacemaker, Fighter for Social Justice (Sutherland, NSW: Albatross Books, 1991).
144 Thompson attributed the original idea to Basil Williams: 'A Tribute,' Latimer (August 1966): 39.
145 VM, ¶20.
146 Ibid.
147 Latimer Magazine 26 (August 1966).
148 Editorial, Report of the 2nd Annual Conference, Tyndale House, Easter 1947, ECF, Latimer archives.
149 HT, ¶124.
150 E.g. Latimer Magazine 23 (August 1965).

151 HT, ¶126; MB, ¶147.
152 WM, ¶168.
153 Ibid.
154 [A.S. Wright] to A.R. Miller, 2 July 1951, Latimer.
155 Statement of Receipts and Payments for the year ended 31 March 1948, ECF, Latimer (the newsletters themselves may not be extant).
156 Editorial, Report of the Second Annual Conference: 3, ECF, Latimer.
157 Ibid., 11–12, 14–15.
158 IGB, ¶108.
159 J.T. Tomlinson, *The Reformation Settlement*; A.E. Barnes-Lawrence, *The Holy Communion: Its Institution, Purpose and Privilege* (London: Longmans, Green and Co, 1920) and *A Churchman and his Church* (London: Longman and Co, 1917); 'Books and Pamphlets that Every Churchman Should Read', Report of the Second Annual Conference, ECF.
160 E.g. DE, ¶28, 32.
161 MG, ¶25–26.
162 Bourne: 50; Anon., ¶31.
163 IGB, ¶21; Bourne: 50; Anon., ¶31.
164 BRC, ¶453; GL, ¶31; MG, ¶33.
165 Sullivan was principal from 1950 to 1958. After he was appointed dean in 1951, Peaston was appointed as master to do most of the teaching and day-to-day college leadership (Morrell: 219).
166 Sullivan: 117; GL, ¶31.
167 IGB, ¶23.
168 MG, ¶38.
169 IGB, ¶25.
170 JF, ¶29–30.
171 MG, ¶36.
172 MG, ¶35.
173 GL, ¶31.
174 WM, ¶169–70. The word 'irenic' (meaning peaceable) is derived from the Greek word in the New Testament for 'peace', and was used by many evangelical ministers.
175 Pfankuch/Lineham interview.
176 GL, ¶31.
177 E.g. MG, ¶35; Anon., ¶33.
178 BRC, ¶454.
179 BRC, ¶448–49.
180 GL, ¶31. The TSF had earlier been called the Theological Students' Prayer Union.
181 GL, ¶31; BRC, ¶477; IGB, ¶21; MG, ¶39; Anon., ¶36–37.

Chapter Six: Presbyterian Evangelicals 1945–55

1 James Veitch, '1961–1990. Towards the Church for a New Era,' in *Presbyterians in Aotearoa*: 144.
2 Rev. John McKinlay, interview, August 2001 (hereafter JBM), ¶127.
3 1915–1981. See [Margaret J. Miller], *Robert Strang Miller: A Tribute by his Family* (Victoria: privately published, 1983).
4 He also had contact with East African churches and missions affected by revival.
5 *Misi Gete – John Geddie, Pioneer Missionary to the New Hebrides* (Launceston: Presbyterian Church of Tasmania, 1975).
6 Rev. Dr Simon Rae, interview, 11 September 2001 (hereafter SR), ¶6.
7 1917–1988.
8 1921–1996.
9 1961–77.
10 1918–1985.
11 JGM, ¶461: 'Don Kirkby, when we rescued him for the evangelical cause, was teetering on the edge of joining Ian Dixon's party. They were wanting to get Don … We took him to a Rotorua Convention, he got renewed and could see what the potential was for his parish at Dargaville.'
12 R.I. Hall, J.K. Fairburn, D.A. Kirkby, 'Gisborne Has Been Thrilled', *Outlook* (20 September 1955): 8–9.
13 In 1956, for instance, he was a missioner in the University of Melbourne. *Outlook* (21 February 1956): 19.
14 D.A. Kirkby to John ____, 3 October 1956.

15 *Proceedings*, 1956: 239a.
16 See: (1) In-house treatments: R.S. Miller, 'Recalling the First Meeting', *EP* (November 1960): 3–4; J.G. Miller, 'Joy Cometh in the Morning', *EP* (January 1961): 3–4; Les Gosling, *To Keep the Faith. The Westminster Fellowship's Forty Years* (Manurewa: WF, 1990). Gosling's booklet is at points idiosyncratic. (2) James Veitch: 'Fundamentalism and the Presbyterian Experience', in Gilling (ed.): 24–45 (Veitch claimed the WF had 'linkages' with fundamentalism, on account of WF ministers' belief in the 1910 'fundamentals' and their affinity with the Princeton theology). (3) Brief references: Davidson: 125–26, 165; Davidson, 'Depression, War, New Life', in *Presbyterians in Aotearoa*: 142; Breward, *Australasia*: 319; Roxborogh, in Emilsen (ed.): 320.
17 J.M. Bates, *A Manual of Doctrine* (Christchurch and Dunedin: Presbyterian Bookroom, 1950): 55–56, 100, 90–93, 95, 99–100.
18 'Announcing the Westminster Fellowship'. Pamphlet and application for membership, n.d. [1950].
19 Ibid.
20 Murray: 86–87; Barclay: 50.
21 JGM, ¶455; J.G. Miller to G.M. Yule, n.d., 2. Hutchinson (*Iron in Our Blood*) makes much of later links between the Westminster Society and the WF, but gives little information on the former.
22 Minutes of 'special meeting of those interested in the exposition and maintenance of the Principles of the Reformed Faith', 28 March 1950: Minute Book of The Westminster Fellowship, 1950–61.
23 Minutes of the Fifth Annual Meeting, 29 March 1955. D.F. Wright, 'National Church Association', in Nigel M. Cameron et al. (eds), *Dictionary of Scottish Church History and Theology*: 619.
24 Miller to Yule, n.d., 2.
25 R. Miller, 'Some Thoughts Prompted by the Centenary of Father's Birth'. Typescript, 8 November 1978: 2.
26 JGM, ¶322. Note Stewart Gill, 'Preserving the Presbyterians: Links Between Canadian and Victorian Anti-Union Force in the 1920s,' *Lucas* 29 (June 2001): 39–59.
27 *Proceedings* (1947): 77–78.
28 C.L. Gosling, 'The Origins of the Westminster Fellowship', *EP* (November–December 1964): 723.
29 JGM, ¶322.
30 *TM*, 61–62.
31 See e.g. Graham Miller et al., 'Reasons For Dissent to the decision of the Assembly on Clause 2 of the Deliverance of the Church Union Committee', *Proceedings* (1954): 62–64.
32 Gosling, 'The Origins': 723–24.
33 JGM, ¶874–75.
34 R. Miller: 3; Les Gosling, *To Keep the Faith. The Westminster Fellowship's Forty Years* (Manurewa: Westminster Fellowship, 1990): 5.
35 GMY, ¶499.
36 Gosling, 'The Origins': 725.
37 GMY, ¶502.
38 Asked about the principal dynamics beyond the foundation of the WF, Graham Miller immediately expounded the story of the resistance to Church Union: JGM, ¶320. When he came home on furlough in 1949 and saw a card about the WF proposal on the mantelpiece of his mother's home in Caversham, she told him 'That's because of this last vote on Church Union': JGM, ¶325.
39 J.G. Miller to G.M. Yule, n.d.
40 R. Miller: 4. Miller used those words to describe the published family tribute to his father, not the WF. The emphasis was his.
41 GMY, ¶498.
42 E.g. [Margaret Miller]: 45.
43 GMY, ¶498.
44 Hugh Reid, 'The Worship of the Reformers', *EP* (April 1952): 4. Reid (1905–1984), a Glasgow BTI

graduate, was received into PCNZ ministry from Scotland in 1948.
45 J.G. Miller to G.M.Yule, n.d.; T.P. McEvoy, 'When the Candles Burn High the Gospel Burns Low', *EP* (July 1963): 223.
46 GMY, ¶503.
47 C.L. Gosling, 'Ten Years of Progress', *EP* (November 1960): 4–5.
48 Gosling: 5.
49 JGM, ¶325.
50 Ibid., ¶337.
51 Ibid., ¶336; G. Morrison Yule, 'In Retrospect', *EP* (November 1960): 6–8.
52 Minutes of 'special meeting of those interested in the exposition and maintenance of the Principles of the Reformed Faith', 28 March 1950: Minute Book of The Westminster Fellowship, 1950–1961; JGM, ¶338; R.S. Miller, 'Recalling the First Meeting', *EP* (November 1960): 3–4; J.G. Miller, 'Joy Cometh in the Morning', *EP* (January 1961): 3–4.
53 Revs C.L Gosling, R.S. Miller, E.C. Walsh, W.H.D. Warin, J.G. Miller, W.J. Wallace, W.G. Moore, G.M. Yule, G.P. Mitchell, E.L. Kirkby, A.C. Webster, T. Cuttle, D.N. McKenzie; Messrs A.S. McKenzie, J.S. Campbell, A. Snedden, J.D.S. Moore, R.[W.] Lange, H.A. Smith, S.W. Perry, J.P. Every, G.A. McLean, H.W. Troughton, J. Sharkie, I. Grant, D.A. Kirkby, C.A. Wilson, A.D. Finlayson, A.D. Paisley, A.S. Munro, W.A. Best, G.A. McKenzie, W.O. Mitchell, R.W. Kirkby; apologies from Revs D.R. Allen, J.G. Loan, F.B. Barton, and Messrs N. Smith, J. Marshall, J.A. Howarth.
54 'Come let us to the Lord our God with contrite hearts return'; 2 Timothy 3.
55 'Doctrine,' handwritten notes for speech; also Miller's later comments, ADMNH 7:21a.
56 JGM, ¶388; WF Executive Minutes, 28 March 1950.
57 Other executive members included Rob Miller and Messrs A.J. Howarth (Maori Hill), A.J. Kerr (Gore) and J.D.S. Moore (divinity student).
58 J.G. Miller, 'Joy Cometh in the Morning', *EP* (January 1961): 3–4.
59 Ibid.
60 Anon., ¶165.
61 *EP* (November 1950): 2.
62 Gosling, 'Why an Evangelical Fellowship of Presbyterians?', *EP* (November 1950): 1 (emphasis added). Gosling's analysis made no concessions to Church of Scotland sources for the PCNZ, and none to the theological modernism which had since swept Free Church and Church of Scotland alike.
63 In Reformation times, 'evangelical' implied an emphasis on New Testament doctrines of salvation, and could simply mean 'non-Catholic'; later, the emphasis was more on conversion and evangelism.
64 [Gosling], 'Editorial: What is an Evangelical Presbyterian?', *EP* (April 1951): 1.
65 Cf. Mark A. Noll and Cassandra Niemczyk, 'Evangelicals and the Consciously Reformed', in Dayton and Johnston (eds): 204–21.
66 [Gosling], 'Catholicism', *EP* (September 1951): 1.
67 Gosling: 5, 23–24.
68 LW, ¶366; also Wilson, letter, 8 September 1999: 'people could not for ever be dressed in 17th C[entury] waistcoats.'
69 Cf. James Veitch, 'Mapping Theological Contours', *Forum* (October 1984): 3–9.
70 GMY, ¶501.
71 E.g. [Ivan Moses?] to Ian ____, March 1946, TSCF N7/77. Chapter One was reprinted in full in an early EP. *EP* (September 1951): 2–3.
72 Ibid. '… from our [IVF] point of view it [the Confession] could not be better' but most Presbyterian ministers and elders, despite subscribing to the Confession, 'have never heard' of it.
73 J.G. Miller, 'Joy', *EP* (January 1961): 3–4.

74 JGM, ¶340.
75 JGM, ¶451 'I barely remember Calvin's name being mentioned, the whole time I was in Knox … Dr Dickie was a Schleiermacher man.' In the 1930s, nevertheless, some younger PCNZ theologians such as Bates and Steele had developed an interest in Calvin through their interest in Barth.
76 E.g. Samuel McCay was 'on principle' never a member of the the WF: 'It was sufficient so far as I was concerned to be a minister of the church, and a member of Presbytery, and, on occasion, of the General Assembly': Rev. Samuel McCay, interview, 12 April 2001 (hereafter SM), ¶65.
77 GMY, ¶310; RR, ¶51; Gosling: 8.
78 JGM, ¶122.
79 C.L. Gosling, 'The Origins of the Westminster Fellowship,' *EP* (November–December 1964): 728.
80 E.g. George Whitefield, Ebenezer Erskine.
81 'Editorial', *EP* (April 1951): 1.
82 Gosling, 'The Origins'.
83 [A.G. Gunn?], 'What is the Westminster Fellowship?' *EP* (September 1963): 260–61.
84 Gilling, 'Contending for the Faith. The "Contender" and Militant Fundamentalism in Mid-Twentieth Century New Zealand', in Gilling (ed.), *'Be Ye Separate'*.
85 'What's the Difference? Why the International Council of Christian Churches is Opposed to the World Council of Churches,' pamphlet distributed by the Bible Union of Australia, n.d., Gosling papers, 396/18, Presbyterian Research Centre.
86 C.F. Henry, 'Theology, Evangelism, Ecumenism', *Christianity Today* (20 January 1988): 23 (cit. Marsden, *Reforming Fundamentalism*: 164).
87 'What's the Difference?'
88 Support for the ICCC in New Zealand appears mainly to have been from the Reformed Church and some Brethren: Gilling, 'Contending': 49–50, 60.
89 JGM, ¶127.
90 JGM, ¶327. 'Here was a dissident voice, with a reason', and the ICCC looked like a 'useful ally'.
91 Ibid., ¶127.
92 'The Scriptures of the Old and New Testament, which are the Word of God.'
93 The word 'contained' in the PCNZ formula reflects the wording of 'Answer to Question 2', *Shorter Catechism*. In the context of the other Westminster documents, Miller understood the words 'contained in' to mean 'comprised of': ibid., ¶154. 'There can be absolutely no [other] view of the meaning of the word "contained" in the Shorter Catechism, in view of the formulations of the Larger Catechism and the Confession,' ibid., ¶154. See 'Answer to Question 3', *Larger Catechism* ('the holy scriptures of the Old and New Testament are the word of God'); *Westminster Confession* 1:II ('under the name of Holy Scripture, or the Word of God written, are now contained all the Books of the Old and New Testaments'); *Westminster Confession* 1:IV ('The authority of the holy scripture, for which it ought to be believed and obeyed, dependeth not upon the testimony of any man or church, but wholly upon God … the author thereof; and therefore to be received, because it is the word of God.'). A late sixteenth-century Scottish confession used the words *quidquid continetur* ['whatever is contained']. See also R.S. Miller, 'The Bible IS the Word of God', *EP* (July 1963): 213–19.
94 JGM, ¶157.
95 JGM, ¶152.
96 Ibid.
97 ADMNH 5: 80; JGM, ¶129.
98 JGM, ¶148.
99 Ibid., ¶159.
100 Ibid., ¶150: 'There was not a native

person who did not get the message.'
101 JGM, ¶599.
102 Gosling: 8.
103 JGM, ¶130–32. Miller faced about forty people, including the Missions Committee and several other prominent churchmen. 'They went for me, from the very beginning.' Miller's position was saved when he revealed that, with Stan Murray (secretary of the Missions Committee) present, there had been an agreement that he would defer to the Missions Committee in 1948, but would be free to bring an amendment in 1949.
104 JGM, ¶721, 728.
105 Ibid., ¶329, 334, 727. Scarrow, minister at Howick, left after his session clerk was featured in the newspaper for winning a lottery. When Scarrow asked him to resign he complained to Presbytery, which upheld the complaint: ibid., ¶330.
106 JGM, ¶728. Miller commented on the UEC's several congregations: 'one by one they petered out ... It was like a divine warning, that this is an evil thing ... God withdrew his hand.'
107 Ibid., ¶729.
108 GMY, ¶444.
109 JGM, ¶724.
110 Robert Wuthnow: 'Fundamentalists thought of apostasy within the churches as monolithic, pervasive, and sufficiently extensive to have spoiled the entire apple barrel. Evangelicals thought apostasy was mainly limited to denominational bureaucrats and professors at liberal seminaries,' cit. Gilling, 'Contending': 59–60.
111 GMY, ¶442–43.
112 Ibid., ¶505–06.
113 JGM, ¶512.
114 Minute Book of the Westminster Fellowship, 1950–61: 20 September 1955.
115 Ibid.: 15 May 1956. The minute survives, but not the letters.
116 Ibid.: 5 August 1957.
117 ADMNH, vol. 5, 88.
118 Gosling: 6.
119 *EP* (September 1951): 1.
120 J.G. Miller, 'Joy', *EP* (January 1961): 3–4.
121 Gosling: 7.
122 April 1951, WF Executive Minutes.
123 RR, ¶224. Barton (1888–1957) had been minister at St Stephen's, Ponsonby (1921–35), then St Andrew's, Gore. Yule saw him as 'very evangelistic and evangelical' (GMY: ¶40).
124 Gosling: 8, 11.
125 WF Executive Minute Book, e.g. 10 April 1951, 25 March 1952.
126 20 September 1955, WF Executive Minutes.
127 List of Charges and Stations, *Proceedings*, 1956: vii–xxvii (total excludes Home Missionaries and retired).
128 Gosling: 9, 11.
129 *EP* (November 1950): 1.
130 'All-Scotland Crusade, 1955', *EP* (December 1955): 36.
131 Annual Report, 1954, WF Executive Minute Book 1950–1961.
132 17 April 1956, WF Executive Minutes.
133 Third Annual Report, 1953, WF Executive Minute Book 1950–1961.
134 GMY, ¶302.
135 Ibid., ¶275.
136 GMY, ¶277–79, 498–500; JGM, ¶593–94. Influential churchmen in the 1940s–50s included J.D. Smith, C.J. Tocker, R.G. McDowall, D.M. Hercus, M.W. Wilson, R.S. Watson, J.D. Salmond, J.M. Bates.
137 GMY, ¶289; also SM, ¶124.
138 GMY, ¶276.
139 GMY, ¶283–84. Yule recalled a [1948] incident involving Gosling when the Moderator (Tocker) 'objected to something. They stood face to face, eyeballing each other. Tocker was demanding that he either withdraw or get down, and commanded him to resume his seat. Tocker was unfair.'
140 Name withheld, ¶103.

141 GMY, ¶283, ¶275.
142 I.G. Marquand, 'The Presbyterian New Life Movement. A Case Study in Church Growth' (MTh thesis, University of Otago, 1977).
143 GMY, ¶321.
144 Ibid., ¶354.
145 JGM, ¶756.
146 Interview, Sir Norman Perry, 29 April 2001.
147 GMY, ¶315, 317.
148 Perry interview.
149 Steele, the son of Rev. John Steele, had formerly been a journalist and travelling secretary for the PBCM. Memorial Minute, *Proceedings*, 1962: 20–21.
150 GMY, ¶316; JGM, ¶182.
151 See e.g. New Life Visitation Mission Card, Presbyterian Archives, NL8, 11.
152 Marquand: 94, 96, 101.
153 See e.g. Stewardship Card, Presbyterian Archives, NL1.
154 See e.g. Tuakau Parish, *The Call to Christian Stewardship*. Some parishes appeared more inclined to see 'stewardship' as simply a programme to get people supporting the church financially, as a gentler equivalent of the methods of the Wells Fundraising Organisation being used in some Anglican and Methodist churches. See e.g. St Andrew's Presbyterian Church, Palmerston North, *Combined Funds Canvass* (1956).

Chapter Seven: EU/IVF and the Postwar Evangelical Resurgence

1 E.M. Blaiklock to Robert Withycombe, October 21 [1970], TSCF A 3b/12.
2 Auckland, Victoria and Canterbury were not called universities until 1961.
3 Ibid. Massey EU, established in 1937, had been in recess but was re-established in 1949: *The NZ Inter-Varsity News Bulletin* (October 1937): 11.
4 'IVF work'. Bruce Nicholls (ex-AUCEU) was president in the lead-up to affiliation in 1949.
5 'Report on the Re-Forming of the Massey College EU', March 1949, initial illegible, TSCF B5/002.
6 John Brinsley, 'Window on the World', *EP* (March 1964): 457–67; TSCF A1a.
7 Knox College, Church House (Christchurch), Baptist College, Trinity College.
8 'IVF work'.
9 Robert Stewart, Gordon Lawrence and W.A. Hutchinson to W.E.D. Davies, 20 October 1960, TSCF N2/053.
10 'Massey Agricultural College EU'.
11 Sullivan: 116–17.
12 Robert Glen anecdote.
13 These included Lester Pfankuch (1949), Maurice Goodall (1950), Robert Glen (1951), Graham Lamont (1952), Robin Currie (1953), Brian Carrell (1954), Murray Pickering (1955), John Croucher (1956), Graeme Robinson (1958), David Kibblewhite (1960), Phil Thomas (1962), Howard Nicholson (1965): RMG, ¶11.
14 'Evangelical Witness': 58. Lewis Wilson (a Presbyterian) was president in 1947–48.
15 GL, ¶26; 'Evangelical Witness': 42.
16 'Evangelical Witness': 42–43.
17 JG, ¶10.
18 SM, ¶15.
19 Ibid., ¶21.
20 John Brinsley, 'Window on the World,' *EP* (March 1964): 457–67; the actual membership in 1965 was 120: administration form, TSCF A1a.
21 From 1961, Victoria University of Wellington.
22 Sullivan: 112–15. Note also 'A statement of the NCC Chaplaincy Advisory Board on the nature and function of the chaplaincy at Victoria, with special reference to its relationship with the intended appointment of an Anglican Chaplain', J.H. Ross, Chairman,

30 June 1963, TSCF N2/065; 'In NZ the Universities have shared in the general tendency to regard educational institutions as purely (and even aggressively) secular. This has probably been more marked at Victoria than elsewhere in New Zealand.'
23 VUCEU Annual Report, 31 August 1945, TSCF B1/074.
24 VUCEU Annual Report, September 1956, TSCF B2/037.
25 NCC Chaplaincy Advisory Board report, J.H. Ross. There were also 25 in the Anglican Society.
26 Administrative return, TSCF A1a.
27 'Tour of the New Zealand Colleges by the Rev. Thomas Miller, M.A.' [1945], TSCF C5/2.
28 H. Guinness 'Report on New Zealand', 12 August 1955, TSCF C5/7.
29 AUCEU Annual Report, 31 August 1951, TSCF B1/079.
30 KO, ¶18; Bruce Harris to Kaye [Johnston], 18 August 1958, TSCF B1/093. In SU and Crusader circles, Pettit would not agree to any shared communion service at conferences or at the Crusader Council if it was proposed they be presided over by anyone (especially by Anglican ministers).
31 E.M. Blaiklock, 'The Religious Situation in New Zealand', *Reaper* (July 1958): 162–63.
32 Dr Bruce Harris, letter, 30 May 2001.
33 Brian [Jenkins] to Warner [Hutchinson], 15 April 1959.
34 AUEU, 33rd Annual Report [1960], TSCF B1/105.
35 DW, ¶11 (Wood was EU treasurer and had to contest student union funding for EU on the basis of numbers); cf. 1965 administrative return, giving figures of 112 signed-up members and 270 on the mailing list, TSCF A1a.
36 John Brinsley, 'Window on the World', *EP* (March 1964): 457–67.
37 DW, ¶7, 35. Black was later principal at Inglewood High School, where he tragically lost his life at the hands of a pupil. Other evangelicals on the Westlake staff in the early 1960s included Brian Wood, David Wood, John Rimmer, Peter Blackburn, Hugh Willis.
38 Barry Gustafson to W. [Hutchinson], 15 September 1959, TSCF B1/101.
39 W.A. Hutchinson to B. Gustafson, 21 September 1959, TSCF B1/102.
40 Massey Agricultural College EU, typescript history, c.1964, TSCF B5/001.
41 1959 Annual Report, Massey Agricultural College EU, ibid.
42 'God of the Atom', 'Voice of the Deep', 'God of Creation' and 'Dust or Destiny': AUCEU Annual Report, 31 August 1951, TSCF B1/079.
43 'Can a Thinking Man be a Christian?' [mission flier], TSCF C5/7.
44 *Cruse* 2 (1968).
45 Denis Fountain [circular letter, VUWEU], n.d., TSCF B2/11.
46 In each case the date of the first edition is given.
47 A. Rendle Short, *Modern Discovery and the Bible* (London: IVF, 1949).
48 F.F. Bruce, *Are the New Testament Documents Reliable?* (London: IVF, 1943). For Bruce, see F.F. Bruce, *In Retrospect: Remembrance of Things Past* (London: Pickering and Inglis, 1980).
49 O. Hallesby, *Why I Am a Christian* (London: IVF, 1950).
50 R.V.G. Tasker, *The Narrow Way* (London: IVF, 1952).
51 Douglas Johnson, *The Christian and His Bible* (London: IVF, 1953).
52 J.C. Pollock, *The Cambridge Seven* (London: IVF, 1955). In about 1965, Pettit provided funds for every EU executive member in New Zealand to be given a copy of the book: Rev. Dr W.J. Roxborogh, interview, 17 April 2003 (hereafter WJR), ¶10.
53 Francis Davidson (ed.), *The New Bible Commentary* (London: IVF, 1953).
54 Frank Morison, *Who Moved the*

55 E.g. BRC, ¶202–06; NSC, ¶108.
56 D. Martyn Lloyd Jones, *Authority* (London: IVF, 1958). Note also his *Truth Unchanged, Unchanging* (London: James Clarke, 1951).
57 John R.W. Stott, *Basic Christianity* (London: IVF, 1958).
58 Timothy Dudley-Smith, *John Stott: A Comprehensive Bibliography* (Downers Grove: IVP, 1995).
59 J.I. Packer, '*Fundamentalism' and the Word of God: Some Evangelical Principles* (London: IVF, 1958). Alister McGrath, *To Know and Serve God: A Biography of James I. Packer* (London: Hodder & Stoughton, 1997).
60 Michael Ramsay, 'The Menace of Fundamentalism,' *Bishoprick* (February 1956); Gabriel Hebert, *Fundamentalism and the Church of God* (London: SCM, 1957).
61 Packer: 14, 24.
62 Ibid.: 24, 29.
63 Ibid.: 29.
64 Ibid.: 20–23, 38–40, 170, 178–81.
65 A. Donald MacLeod, *C. Stacey Woods and the Evangelical Rediscovery of the University* (Downers Grove: IVP, 2007): 167; McGrath: 86.
66 WJR, ¶9; DW, ¶10; Neil C. Munro, interview, 23 May 2001, ¶143; 'The IVF and the SCM in New Zealand,' typescript, TSCF N7/30. [c.1960].
67 Michael Griffiths, *Encouraging One Another* (London: IVP, 1955); *Consistent Christianity* (London: IVF, 1960); *Christian Assurance* (London: IVF, 1962); *Take My Life* (London: IVF, 1967).
68 Michael Green, *Choose Freedom* (London: IVF, 1965); *Man Alive!* (London: IVF, 1967); *Runaway World* (London: IVP, 1968).
69 Francis A. Schaeffer, *Death in the City: The Relevance of the Message of the Bible to the Twentieth Century World* (Chicago: IVP, 1968); *Escape from Reason* (London: IVP, 1968).
70 J.D. Douglas, F.F. Bruce, J.I. Packer, R.V.G. Tasker, D.J. Wiseman (eds), *The New Bible Dictionary* (Leicester: IVF, 1962). New Zealand contributors to the volume were E.M. Blaiklock, B.F. Harris, R.J. Thompson, F. Foulkes, E.A. Judge.
71 J.I. Packer, *Evangelism and the Sovereignty of God* (London: IVF, 1961).
72 MB, ¶25.
73 MB, ¶26.
74 Malcolm, 'Jubilee Address', [1986], TSCF archives.
75 E.g. see SR, ¶19–21, 29–31, 34.
76 Malcolm, 'Jubilee Address'.
77 Presidential Address [1952, E.M. Blaiklock], TSCF A1/107. The address was later published as E.M. Blaiklock, *Sanity, Confidence and Scholarship* ([Wellington]: [IVF (NZ)], n.d. [c. 1952]).
78 Blaiklock to John [McInnes], 3 November [1972], TSCF A3b/17.
79 Likewise Blaiklock, 'The Task of Educated Leadership: The Presidential Address at the I.V.F. Conference, 1962,' NZIVF Christian Codex 4: 5–6.
80 E.M. Blaiklock to Cliff Cocker, February 3 [1952], TSCF C5.
81 The IVF leadership replied sympathetically (Cliff Cocker to EMB, 20 February 1952, TSCF C5), but over the next few years numerous Guinness missions went ahead.
82 E.g. letterhead to 'Mission to the University of Otago,' OUEU, June 1952, TSCF C5: Rev. A.W. Armstrong; Rt. Rev. F.B. Barton BA; Prof. Blaiklock MA DLitt; J.S. Burt LLM; Rev. A. Clifford MSc; T.C. Cocker BCom; H.R. Fountain MCom; Dr J.M. Laird MB ChB; Rev. J.G. Miller LLB BD; Rev. M.G. Milmine MA; H.R. Minn MA BD; E.A. Missen MA; Rev. Canon Orange BA; Dr W.H. Pettit MBE MB ChB; G.E. Rowe LLB.

83 'Names and addresses of those helped and desiring further contact with Dr Guinness', with 'Mission to the University of Otago,' OUEU, June 1952, TSCF C5.
84 Notes from Graham Lamont [CCEU president] on CUC and OU missions by Rev. Dr H.W. Guinness [1952], TSCF C5.
85 Brian Carrell/Peter Lineham interview, n.d.
86 TSCF C5/7.
87 Miscellaneous newspaper cuttings re H. Guinness 1955 mission to VUC, TSCF C5/7.
88 H. Guinness, 'Report on New Zealand,' 12 August 1955, TSCF C5/7.
89 'Introducing David Stewart', leaflet [1952], TSCF C5.
90 Jubilee Address. Stewart himself was 'very disappointed' with the mission: Stewart to Prayer Companions, [1952] TSCF C5.
91 Stewart ended the Baptist and Brethren domination of BTI (in part by adding Anglican and Presbyterian lecturers), changed BTI's name, and continued the move into degree-level programmes.
92 Massey Agricultural College EU, TSCF B5/001. An atypical EU mission was that at Auckland Teachers' Training College in 1959 with the American group, the Nixon Musical Messengers.
93 'IVF work in New Zealand'. Document attached to letter [Cocker?] to Bruce [Harris], 28 August 1950, TSCF H1/22.
94 Sasse was lecturer in Systematic Theology at Immanuel Theological Seminary, Adelaide (United Evangelical Lutheran Church of Australia). Andersen was at the University of Sydney, Ramm was Professor of Systematic Theology at California Baptist Theological Seminary, and Runia was a professor at the Reformed Theological College at Geelong, Australia.
95 But Dr Masumi Toyatome (1961), who taught New Testament in the International Christian University of Tokyo, took a strongly spiritual, 'existential' approach, deliberately avoiding intellectual defence of the faith.
96 GL, ¶27.
97 Confidential memorandum from the General Secretary, IVF of EUs (NZ), to the Governing Council 13 November 1961. A10/003.
98 Hutchinson, 'Thoughts on the Doctrine of Scripture,' *NZIVF Christian Codex* III (Wellington: IVF(NZ), [1962]): 4–7.
99 'The IVF and the SCM in New Zealand,' typescript, TSCF N7/30. [c.1960]; SR ¶24, 27–28.
100 Hutchinson, 'The Spirit of Evangelicalism,' *Broadsheet* (August 1962): 1–3; 'Christ is Lord,' *Broadsheet*, (November 1958): 1–2; 'The Christian's Social Responsibilities,' *Broadshee*t (August 1960): 1.
101 SR, ¶28; JBM, ¶68.
102 BTD, ¶7; Mark Hutchinson, 'Professing History: An Interview with Rev. Professor Ian Breward, 10 July 1991', *Lucas* 12 (December 1991): 54–71 (59).
103 DW, ¶26.
104 JGM, ¶839.
105 Confidential memorandum from the General Secretary, IVF of EUs (NZ), to the Governing Council 13 November 1961, TSCF A10/003.
106 Jubilee Address [Wilf Malcolm, 1986].
107 Ibid.
108 Jubilee Address.
109 Ibid. Malcolm's comment may in part reflect the 1980s context, when the pressures from American fundamentalism had increased, and when more conservative American-based student movements were becoming established in New Zealand.
110 See e.g. *SCM Handbook* [1967]: IV, 1; 'The IVF and SCM in New Zealand.

A Brief History and Examination of the Movement', n.d., TSCF N7/30.
111 *NZSCM. Handbook for Committee Members*, 1959: 1, 35–36, 39, 41–42; *SCM Handbook* (Typescript [1967]): IV, 1; Berry Ch. 3: 1–3, 9, 11.
112 Bates, 'Memorandum'.
113 'The Two Varsity Unions', General Secretary to the Editor, *Methodist Times*, Auckland, 24 July 1945, TSCF N7/74.
114 [Moses?] to Ian ____, March 1946, TSCF N7/77.
115 [Buist] to Ivan [Moses], n.d., TSCF N7/82.
116 Ibid; Buist to Arnold Turner, 1 May 1946, TSCF B4.
117 [Buist] to [Moses], n.d., TSCF N7/82.
118 'The IVF and the SCM in New Zealand,' typescript [c.1960], TSCF N7/30.
119 [Buist] to [Moses], TSCF N7/82.
120 MB, ¶24.
121 [Moses?] to Ian ____, March 1946, TSCF N7/77.
122 'The Two Varsity Unions,' Gen. Sec. to the Editor, *Methodist Times*, Auckland, 24 July 1945, TSCF N7/74.
123 E.g [Buist] to Ivan [Moses], n.d., TSCF N7/82.
124 *SCM Handbook* (Typescript [1967]): L.B.7. (d).
125 E.g. [Arnold Turner] to Malcolm [Buist], 6 May 1946, TSCF B4.
126 E.g. Cocker to to Bill ____, 4 May 1948, TSCF B4.
127 Wilf Malcolm to Gerald Court, 30 September 1965, TSCF N2/068.
128 Ibid.
129 Hutchinson to the Rt. Rev. F.O. Hulme-Moir, 10 November 1960, TSCF N2/055.
130 See e.g. Hutchinson to the Rt. Rev. F.O. Hulme-Moir, 10 November 1960, TSCF N2/055.
131 R.A. Stewart, G. Lawrence and W.A. Hutchinson to W.E.D. Davies, 20 October 1960, N2/053.
132 Rev. Dr Donald O. Soper, 'The Inter-Varsity Fellowship', *Methodist Times*, 22 January 1955.
133 J.G. Miller to Cocker, 9 February 1955, TSCF K3/1.
134 37 Hackthorne Rd, Cashmere.
135 Orange to Fountain, 11 June 1947, TSCF N12/23. Ibid.
136 Moses to Buist, 18 December 1947, TSCF N12/29. Deane often stayed with Miller, did not agree with Orange's typology, and – a Baptist – he struggled to understand Orange's Anglican world: Fountain/Glen interview, ¶31.
137 Cocker to Secretary CET, 4 February 1948, TSCF N12/35.
138 Blaiklock to Cocker, 8 November 1948, TSCF N12/55.
139 Cocker to Fountain, TSCF N12/76c.
140 Burt to Cocker, n.d. [December 1948], with TSCF N12/73.
141 E.g. Minn to Cocker, 15 December 1948, TSCF N12/72; Pettit to Cocker, 6 May 1949, TSCF N12/76.
142 Cocker to Fountain, 31 May 1949, N12/77. Several conciliatory resolutions were passed.
143 Cocker to Fountain, 31 May 1941, TSCF N12/77; W.A. Bascard to Cocker, 20 June 1949, TSCF N12/83; Cocker to Fountain, 21 June 1949, TSCF N12/81; also Cocker to Blaiklock, 13 June 1949, TSCF N12/78; ibid., 6 July 1949, TSCF N12/84.
144 Fountain to Cocker, 3 March 1950, TSCF N12/90. Tyndale House itself was eventually sold. The CET invested the money and continued to fund Christian work, including the IVF.
145 Oliver H. Donnell to Cocker, 24 May 1950, TSCF N1/14.
146 J. Elwin Wright [Executive Secretary of the Commission on International Relations of the National Association of Evangelicals] to Bernard G. Holmes, 10 June, 1950, TSCF N1/4.
147 [Cocker] to Donnell, 21 July 1950, TSCF N1/4.
148 [Cocker] to Woods, 21 July 1950, TSCF N1/4.

149 Woods to Williams, Cocker and White, 20 September 1950, TSCF N1/4.
150 The scriptures were described not as 'inerrant' but as 'infallible'. The statement steered clear of any particular millennialist position and simply asserted Christ's 'personal return in power and glory'.
151 Donnell to Cocker, 14 July 1950, TSCF N1/4.
152 The GF was renamed the Christian Graduates' Fellowship in 1956.
153 Milmine to Buist, 23 November 1944, TSCF J17/6.
154 [Doris Weir] to Buist, 28 May 1946, J1/051. The *Bulletin* was replaced in 1956 by *Broadsheet*.
155 GF Secretary [Buist] memorandum to EMF members, 3 May 1945. Other committee members were Harry Thomson (Anglican), Ayson Clifford (Baptist), Warren Green (Methodist).
156 Cited in Milmine to Buist, 14 September 1943, TSCF J17/2 (underlining changed to italics).
157 Buist to Ivan [Moses], 20 August 1946, J1/058. Also [Doris Weir] to Buist, 28 May 1946, J1/051; Milmine to Buist, 2 November 1944, J1/17.
158 E.g. [Milmine] to Buist, 24 April 1947, TSCF J17/23; Gosling to Buist, 12 May 1948, TSCF J17/27; R.S. Miller to John ____, 9 October 1956, TSCF (no ref.); [Gosling] to Milmine, 15 March 1946, Gosling papers, 396/18.
159 E.g. a list of EMF members (27 June 1945) was annotated 'what can we get them to do?'
160 Buist to Milmine, 5 February 1946, TSCF J17/18; Gosling to Buist, 10 April 1946, J17/21.
161 Membership list, Graduates' Fellowship, October 1946, TSCF J1/061.
162 In contrast, the Teachers' Fellowship numbered 220 and attracted ninety to its conference.
163 'IVF work'.

164 Gosling to Milmine, 15 March 1946, Gosling papers 396/18.
165 [C.L. Gosling], EMF President's Report, 7 May 1946, Gosling papers 396/18; Gosling to Milmine, 15 March 1946.
166 EMF [mailing list], 25 January 1956, TSCF J17/40. A few were not in parish ministry, e.g. Blaiklock, Funnell (CIM), Deane (BTI).
167 Betteridge to Eric [Dunlop], 4 October 1954, J17/34a.
168 Betteridge to Eric [Dunlop], 2 July 1957, J17/36.
169 Goodall to [Dunlop], 30 October 1957, J17/38.
170 Minutes of Wellington Executive Committee of the CGF, 13 April 1960, TSCF J2.
171 'Memorandum regarding proposed termination of activities of Evangelical Ministers' Fellowship', 29 March 1960, TSCF J17/41.
172 'IVF work'.
173 From a Brethren family, Harris had been AUCEU president in 1942. After postgraduate study in the UK he taught classics at Auckland University under Blaiklock. He was an elder at Somervell Presbyterian and on the BTI Board. He left New Zealand in 1969 for a position at Macquarie University (Sydney).
174 'The CGF' [circular], 17 June 1957, TSCF J1/092.
175 Win Lewis to ____, 20 January 1956, J1/084.
176 Minutes of a meeting of the CGF Executive Committee, 7 October 1961, TSCF J2; Minutes of the CGF Business meeting, 6 September 1962, TSCF J2.
177 In 1949, for instance, preceding the IVF conference, ninety teachers attended the TCF conference.
178 Circular letter on IVF letterhead, Assoc. Professor B.F. Harris, 7 April 1965, TSCF J1/103.
179 'Possible list for initial circulation', Bruce Harris to Wilf [Malcolm], 21

April 1965, TSCF J1/104.
180 Minutes of inaugural meeting, 26 June 1965, TFNZ, TSCF J1/106; Clive [Sage] to Wilf [Malcolm], 6 September 1966, TSCF J1/107.
181 'Mission to the University of Otago', OUEU, June 1952, TSCF C5; Maurice Andrew, *Set in a Long Place. A Life from North to South* (Christchurch: Hazard Press, 1999): 166; Allan K. Davidson, *Selwyn's Legacy*: 300.
182 'Massey Agricultural College EU'.
183 RR, ¶433-41.
184 D.G. Shaw, 'The Westminster Fellowship Should Think Again', *Forum* (June 1962): 12-16.
185 JG, ¶73-76.
186 Muriel Porter, 'Ian Breward. An Australasian Life', in Emilsen (eds): 9-23.
187 Very Rev. Dr Ian Breward, interview, 2002 (hereafter IB), ¶19.
188 Mark Hutchinson, 'Professing History: An Interview with Rev. Professor Ian Breward, 10 July 1991,' *Lucas* 12 (December 1991): 54-71.
189 SM, ¶56-58, 66, 77.
190 SR, ¶19-21, 29-31, 34. Rae was also influenced by Catholic and Russian Orthodox writers.
191 E.g. Greenslade, ¶15, 19, 37, 41, 44, 72, 74-76.
192 E.g. 'Speaking in Tongues', Memo. No. 22, to Members of IVFC Staff, Charles H. Troutman, 2 April 1963, TSCF A3b/37. The archives give evidence that the issue became acute for IVF from 1970.
193 By about 1970, support for the SCM collapsed. It retained about fifteen to twenty members in each of its four university branches (Berry, Ch. 4: 5). The same happened internationally, as discussed in Boyd: 98-155.
194 Blaiklock to Robert Withycombe, October 21 [1970], TSCF A 3b/12.
195 'The relationship of the EUs to the Protestant Churches.' Adopted by the IVF General Committee, 16-17 January 1964.

Chapter Eight: Anglican Evangelicalism Expands, 1956-65

1 J.I. Packer, 'Theological Challenge to Evangelicalism Today,' *E.C.F. Review* (August 1961).
2 In 1965 Thompson returned to Christchurch, to the parish of St John's Latimer Square, where he developed a strong evangelistic ministry among social misfits and homeless people.
3 As a lay preacher at Bryndwr he had also been under the tutelage of Teulon: HT, ¶128.
4 Bourne: 36; Anon., ¶17; RRT, ¶29.
5 JG, ¶61.
6 MG, ¶67.
7 *St Stephen's Review* (November 1959).
8 VM, ¶13.
9 *Parish of Shirley, 1912-1987* (Christchurch [Shirley Anglican Parish], n.d. [1987]): 17.
10 *St Stephen's Review* e.g. (October 1959).
11 Ibid. (August 1952): 1, 3, 9 (September 1956).
12 Ibid. (August 1956).
13 VM, ¶15.
14 BR, ¶12.
15 MG, ¶74.
16 BR, ¶7.
17 *Year Book*: 1959, 1960, 1965.
18 Ross and Pauline Elliott and Eric Baigent joined CMS. Phil Thomas began training at Ridley.
19 Goodall was replaced by R.E. Coulthard (1967-78).
20 GL, ¶38, 73-74.
21 GL, ¶71.
22 GL, ¶60. The books he refers to were both published by IVP, in 1967 and 1965 respectively.
23 *Year Book for the Diocesan Year*, 1965.
24 E.g. Alan Stott, Ken and Ian McClelland, David Powell, Edwin Close, Bert Riseley, John Smith, Connie Carrell, Elaine Cooper. Assistants: Clarice Greenslade (youth worker), Harry Funnell, Gerald Tisch.
25 GL, ¶74.

26   RT, ¶373–76. Thompson did not use the label 'fundamentalist' of himself.
27   RT, ¶234.
28   GL, ¶44.
29   GL, ¶42, 76.
30   BRC, ¶19.
31   GL, ¶38, 82.
32   In relation to the US, Ahlstrom dubs the period 1960–75 'the traumatic years'.
33   See e.g. Callum G. Brown, *The Death of Christian Britain: Understanding Secularisation, 1800–2000* (London & New York: Routledge, 2001): 175–80; Belich, *Paradise Reforged*: 506–11; David Hilliard, 'The Religious Crisis of the 1960s: The Experience of the Australian Churches', *Journal of Religious History* (June 1967): 209–27.
34   In the late 1960s, Lamont took leave to do postgraduate study (1967–68) in Durham.
35   REC, ¶2, 310–11.
36   List of ECF Clergy, Christchurch, Latimer; *E.C.F. Review* (August 1959): 10.
37   Belfast-Styx (1963–66), then Woolston.
38   Highfield, Riccarton and (1964) Avonhead.
39   Bryndwr (1964).
40   Burnside.
41   JG, ¶63.
42   MG, ¶53; REC, ¶27.
43   MG, ¶53.
44   Lancaster: 26.
45   Ibid.: 24.
46   *St Stephen's Review* (May 1959); MG, ¶67.
47   BRC, ¶101–16. The parish was St Matthew's, in the suburb of St Alban's.
48   MG, ¶66.
49   GL, ¶36.
50   DO, ¶28.
51   BR, ¶3–5.
52   Robinson did theological study at Ridley College and a PhD in London. He was later dean of the Christchurch branch of BCNZ.
53   DO, ¶28.
54   Later a missionary in North Africa, vicar of Sumner, and bishop of Nelson (1990–2006).
55   Later a leader and staff member of the ECF.
56   Later vicar of All Saints' Nelson, Dean of Cairo, and General Secretary of NZCMS.
57   Later ordained in Britain, CMS missionary in East Africa and vicar of Shirley.
58   BR, ¶10.
59   JM, ¶51; BW, ¶49; PK, ¶7.
60   Edmiston: 112; JF, ¶26; PK, ¶7; JH, ¶41; DP, ¶85.
61   Catriona Williamson, 'Francis Oag Hulme-Moir: Bishop of Nelson, 1954–1964', in Bester (ed.): 157–90.
62   MB, ¶46; Hulme-Moir to R.G. Nicholson, 22 August 1962, NFCE Box 5.
63   Hulme-Moir to Wallace Marriott, 10 March 1961, NFCE Box 6.
64   DP, ¶85.
65   *The Witness* (1 February 1965).
66   JH, ¶41.
67   BW, ¶69.
68   E.g. 1 April 1958; 1 November 1958.
69   JH, ¶35; BW, ¶49. Others included Bill Gregory, David Davis, Bill Burchill, Donald Wilson.
70   JH, ¶41.
71   JH, ¶28.
72   JH, ¶29–30.
73   JH, ¶37.
74   JH, ¶38.
75   B. Cox and M. Oatway were New Zealanders, the others Australian.
76   Bretton, Dyer, Ken Gregory, G. Hill.
77   Classifications on the basis of ECF list and comments by Wilkens, J. Ford et al.
78   E.g. *Witness* (1 September 1959): 10; (1 April 1959): 4; (1 May 1959): 14; (1 June 1960): 5.
79   H.F. Ault, 'Memories of Ardmore, 1959', *Witness* (1 June 1959): 6–7.
80   *Witness* (1 April 1959): 4; (1 February 1964).
81   E.g. Malcolm Oatway, 'The Billy Graham Crusade – and After', *Witness*, 1 May 1959: 11–13.

82 Bretton could be dismissive and outspoken and considered some of the Moore-trained clergy too narrow: David Pickering, telephone conversation, 20 January 2006.
83 MB, ¶46; BW, ¶79.
84 JF, ¶39; name withheld, ¶71; MB, ¶46.
85 Anon., ¶49.
86 BW, ¶71.
87 Anon., ¶49; JF, ¶39.
88 C.W. Haskell, *A Sinner in Sind* (Wellington: [The Author], 1957).
89 WM, ¶122; also Edmiston, 171.
90 Taylor was at Masterton then Martinborough (1960–64); Bourne was at Eketahuna (1958–65).
91 Edmiston: 118–19.
92 For morning services, he chose his biblical passage from the lectionary.
93 DE, ¶48; also ¶46.
94 Edmiston: 92–93, 185.
95 Ibid.: 236.
96 DE, ¶41.
97 Edmiston: 107.
98 DE, ¶35.
99 DE, ¶31. McKay, from Sydney, was a lecturer in Greek.
100 DE, ¶31.
101 E.g. IGB, ¶78.
102 Edmiston: 110.
103 Gregory: 215.
104 *St Matthew's Anglican Church Dunedin* (n.d., no publisher): no pagination.
105 WM, ¶17; MB, ¶97.
106 WM, ¶17.
107 MB, ¶98.
108 Joyce Carswell, email, 4 July 2008.
109 MB, ¶99.
110 MB, ¶100.
111 MB, ¶93, 95.
112 MB, ¶102.
113 1965–71, 1971–80, 1980–89.
114 Parishioners who later became evangelical leaders included Laurie Becroft (Scripture Union) and John McInnes (TSCF). Many became missionaries.
115 MF, ¶12, ¶15; Francis Foulkes, personal memoirs: 14.
116 KO, ¶23, ¶27.
117 The group included Revs Frank Willis (St Andrew's Epsom), Harry Funnell (CIM), and Lawley Brown (missioner to seamen). Marjorie Foulkes, attending from 1941 to 1950, listed some other attendees: Ted Fawcett, Donald and Peggy Skegg, Ted Coulthard, Herbert Minn, Warren Mason, Alfred Williams, John Pybus, Hereward Ludbrooke, and Mesdames Falcon, Brooke, Howe (MF, ¶27).
118 MF, ¶23; KO, ¶11–12.
119 A.S. Wright, ECF circular letter, 1 August 1949, Latimer.
120 GN, ¶8, 13, 17, 19–20, 24, 28–29, 34, 48–50, 68, 85–86.
121 Gowing, originally from the Sydney Diocese, had previously served in the Nelson and Dunedin Dioceses: GN, ¶33. Nicholson considered Gowing a covert evangelical. In the late 1960s, Gowing refused David Aiken permission to start an Auckland branch of ECF: GN, ¶80.
122 GN, ¶35–36; ¶42.
123 S. Clark to Nicholson, 4 December 1956.
124 E.g. Peter Skegg.
125 GN, ¶38, 64, 81.
126 E.g. Ian Nelson (1971–81).
127 The only other ECF members in the upper North Island in this period were Rev. R.C. Firebrace at Te Awamutu and Canon W.T. Huata at Te Kuiti. Firebrace, an older man (b.1899), had been in ministry in Britain and in Sydney. Lamont, arriving in Hamilton in 1970, felt that there was only one overtly evangelical minister there at that time: Canon Tony Clarke, the Māori Missioner (GL, ¶111).
128 Programme, ECF Dominion Conference, 1959.
129 See Hulme-Moir, 'The Authority of the Word of God', *E.C.F. Review* (October 1959): 3–6.
130 Minutes of the first meeting of the Christchurch Committee of the Evangelical Churchmen's Fellowship, 15 September 1961. Present:

Thompson, Carson, Morris, Goodall, Lamont, H. Harper, A. Scott, H. Thomas, R. Mauger, A. Wright, J. Lewis and (by invitation) H.R. Fountain.

131 Minutes of the third meeting of the Christchurch Committee of the Evangelical Churchmen's Fellowship, 2 March 1961.

132 [Goodall] to Archeacon ___, 1 July 1963.

133 *E.C.F. Review, Quarterly Journal of the ECF (NZ)*, 1959–63. From June 1963, the *Latimer Magazine*.

134 R.F.N. Thompson, Editorial, 'Via Evangelica', *E.C.F. Review* (November 1959). In the same sentence, he began the word 'Evangelical' in both upper and lower case.

135 Thompson understood that doctrine as: 'the right of direct access to the Father through Christ and that there is no need of any intermediary'.

136 The Protestant principle of individual faith and conscience in the light of Scripture (as in Acts 17:10–11, 1 Cor. 10:15, 1 John 2:27).

137 Thompson, Editorial, 'Our Purpose – our Heritage', *E.C.F. Review* (August 1959): 2–3.

138 Thompson, Editorial, 'Our Past and Purpose', ibid. (January 1960): 1–2.

139 Thompson, 'Our Purpose': 1.

140 Ian Munro, 'The Christian and Amusements', ibid. (February 1961).

141 'The Roman Church and the Common Market', ibid. (February 1962).

142 E.g. J.I. Packer, 'Theological Challenge to Evangelicalism Today', ibid. (August 1961).

143 Thompson, 'Church Unity and World Peace', ibid. (February 1962).

144 Thompson, 'Articles or Obstacles', ibid. (June 1962); 'Regarding Authority', ibid. (August 1962).

145 Thompson, Editorial, 'Just Between Us', *Latimer Magazine, Quarterly Journal of the ECF* (NZ) (June 1963). Thompson appeared to be dependent on the work of Dyson Hague, *Through The Prayer Book*.

146 Thompson, 'Articles or obstacles'.

147 E.g. 'Book Notes', ibid. (August 1961). *The Church of England Newspaper* represented 'progressive evangelicalism', and from June 1963 was 'highly recommended' on the inside cover of the *Latimer Magazine*.

148 'Book Notes', *E.C.F. Review* (August 1961).

149 Except, in August 1962, notes of Orange's eulogy at H.W. Funnell's funeral. Orange was known to be very wary of appearing in print.

150 J.I. Packer, 'Theological Challenge to Evangelicalism Today', *E.C.F. Review* (August 1961).

151 Thompson, 'The Need Today', *Latimer Magazine* 18 (November1963.)

152 The Navigators emphasised memorising scripture as a basis of evangelism and discipleship.

153 Joe Simmonds, email, 15 January 2006; GL, ¶46; RRT, ¶34. Laugeson also spent time in Presbyterian and Brethren contexts.

154 GL, ¶46.

155 BRC, ¶496–500, 520–25.

156 BRC, ¶496.

157 *Latimer Magazine* 20 (July 1964).

158 Minutes of the Fifth Meeting of the Christchurch Committee of the Evangelical Churchmen's Fellowship, 27 July 1962.

159 John R. Brinsley to Wright, 28 December 1961.

160 Hulme-Moir to Goodall, 7 May 1962; Goodall to A.G. Gunn, 7 August 1962. The bishop worried that Anglican beliefs and practices might be compromised by people of other denominations, and the ECF would receive 'a great deal of unhappy criticism' within the Anglican Church.

161 Memo from H.P. Hanna (Evangelical Alliance, Canterbury) to Council members, copy in ECF archives dated 29 October 1963; Goodall to L. Becroft, 19 August 1965; Thompson

to Lamont, 21 September 1965.
162 Goodall to D.G. Stewart, 3 June 1965.
163 EFAC circular, October 1961.
164 First Report to Members, Latimer Foundation (NZ) Inc.
165 Packer to Goodall, 14 December 1961.
166 Meeting of the Latimer Foundation, 5 November 1962.
167 In this period, the latter was known as 'Christchurch College'.
168 Pfankuch/Lineham interview.
169 GL, ¶42.
170 GL, ¶43.
171 'ECF Branch News,' *Latimer Magazine* 21 (February 1965); GL, ¶42.
172 E.g. GL, ¶51.
173 GL, ¶88.
174 Minutes of the third meeting of the Christchurch Committee of the Evangelical Churchmen's Fellowship, 2 March 1961.
175 *Latimer Magazine, Quarterly Journal of the ECF* (NZ) (hereafter *Latimer*) (June 1963).
176 *Latimer* (September 1963).
177 *Latimer* (November 1963). Goodall became editor in 1966: ibid. (March 1966).
178 M.S.B. [Betteridge], 'Modern Morality,' *Latimer* (July 1964).
179 Dale Oldham, 'First Impressions,' *Latimer* (June 1966); 'Baptism and speaking in Tongues', ibid.
180 'In as much', *Latimer* (March 1966); 'Inasmuch, Christian Social Responsibility in 20th Century America', ibid. (June 1966); 'Book Review: Michael Green's 'Called to Serve', ibid.
181 *Latimer* (December 1970).
182 E.g. Thompson, Editorial, 'Just Between Us', *Latimer* (June 1963).
183 'ECF Branch News', *Latimer* (February 1965); [G.S. Lamont], 'The Principle of Prayer Book Revision', *E.C.F. Review* 10 (November 1961).
184 E.g. G.S. Lamont , 'The Revised Communion Service', *Latimer* (August 1966).
185 GL, ¶90.
186 L.C. Wards, 'Intercommunion', *Latimer* (May 1965).
187 IGB, ¶104.
188 GL, ¶91–92.
189 GL, ¶91.
190 Roger Thompson, 'Editorial: Church Union or Intercommunion?' *Latimer* (September 1963). His reasons were: denominational divisions do not preclude 'inner fundamental unity'; denominations arose out of conscience and conviction; union will lead to doctrinal compromise; union will give too much power to a small hierarchy; union will provoke further splits; union will not produce greater faith among unbelievers.
191 Ian Bourne, 'Ecumenism', *E.C.F. Review* (August 1959): 7–9. The editor [Thompson] added a note: 'Some of our readers may differ from the views propounded in the above article'. G.S. Lamont, 'Thoughts on the Biblical Basis of Church Union', *Latimer* (June 1966).
192 B.R. C[arrell], 'Church Union and a Country Parish', *Latimer* (April 1964).
193 'Editorial Note', *Latimer* (April 1964).
194 [Carrell], 'Church Union and a Country Parish'; Lamont, 'Thoughts on the Biblical Basis of Church Union'.
195 'ECF Branch News,' *Latimer* (February 1965).
196 E.g. *Latimer* (August 1965): a review by John Wenham of J.I. Packer (ed.), *All in Each Place. Towards Reunion in England* (Abingdon Berks: Marcham Manor, 1965); also: 'The Rev. John Stott Speaks on Church Union', ibid.
197 Several scenarios were discussed: an evangelical 'fellowship' involving IVF, a 'federation' of autonomous churches, and an 'Organic Union of Evangelical Ch[urche]s': 'JGM's final summing up', ECF archives.
198 GL, ¶52.
199 Carrell to Lamont, 5 October 1965.
200 'Meeting of the Clerical Members of the Christchurch Branch of the ECF', 11 October 1965. Note also: Executive

Committee statement: Guiding Principles in Church Union', *Latimer* (August 1966).
201 Lamont, draft letter to WF, n.d.; Carrell to Lamont, 16 October 1965.
202 IGB, ¶75–76. Carrell was also on the Prayer Book Commission.
203 BRC, ¶424–25; GL, ¶85.
204 GL, ¶83–87.
205 GL, ¶42, 89, 101. See e.g. R.A. Carson, 'The Resurrection', *Latimer* (June 1966); 'Editorial', ibid. 27 (November 1966).

Chapter Nine: Presbyterian Evangelicalism Expands, 1956–65

1 JGM, ¶851.
2 GMY, ¶23, 17–19. Miller's immediate predecessor was W.R. (Robin) Lapsley.
3 JGM, ¶578–79; ADMNH 1:53. Fraser tried to dissuade the parish's Board of Nomination, noting Miller's opposition to church union and his enthusiasm for CE.
4 In 1990, Miller was a senior (retired) leader of the Presbyterian Church of Australia, which was moving towards prohibiting the ordination of women. Through 'a flash of mercy from God', he independently concluded that Acts 2:16–21 is a primary mandate for the ministry of women, and that the apparent vetoes of 1 Cor. 14 and the Pastoral Epistles should be seen as 'an unresolved antinomy of revelation'. The ordination of women thus 'became a crusade' for him: JGM, ¶683–86.
5 JGM, ¶792; Papakura Presbyterian Church, 'February 1963 Services'.
6 E.g. Papakura Presbyterian Church, 'September Services' [1953].
7 JGM, ¶792.
8 ADMNH 7:9.
9 Rev. Dr John R. Brinsley, interview, November 2001 (hereafter JRB), ¶41; similarly LW, ¶378.
10 ADMNH 7:7. Duncan visited New Zealand in 1958.
11 JGM, ¶792.
12 L.R. Garlick, Board of Managers Report, 98th Annual Report, Papakura–Hunua–Paparimu Presbyterian Church, 1953.
13 Proceedings, 1953: 256a; 1957: 278a; Annual Reports, 1953 and 1958.
14 WJR, ¶15. The vice-principal of Ardmore Teachers' College, A.J. (Archie) Campbell, was session clerk, and the principal, A.J. Hayr, was a guest preacher.
15 ADMNH 7:45.
16 Axioms quoted in 'July 1964 Services'.
17 E.g. Ian Kemp, Beryl Howie, Muri Thompson, Barbara Good, Mary Milner, W. Searle.
18 'March 1964 Services'; 'February 1963 Services'; ADMNH 7:29.
19 Mr and Mrs Jim Gordon went to manage the Maori Boys' Farm (Te Whaiti), Mesdames Watson and Stoddard to hostel work, Miss A. Turchi to the Synod offices, and Bruce Howie as a carpenter.
20 JGM, ¶794.
21 ADMNH 7:8; JGM, ¶806.
22 Papakura Presbyterian Church, 'June Services' [1959]; 'September Services' [1959].
23 J.G. Miller, letter, 'The Crusade', *Forum* (May 1959): 8–9.
24 J. Graham Miller, 'Billy Graham in Auckland', *EP* (July 1959): 3–4.
25 ADMNH 7:32.
26 JGM, ¶806; *Proceedings*, 1958: 281a; 1959: 260a; 1960: 275a; 1962: 294a.
27 JGM, ¶573, 797.
28 'March Services', 1964.
29 ADMNH 7:31.
30 JGM, ¶218–19. This was in 1954.
31 JGM, ¶209.
32 [Colin Becroft] to A.M. Derham, 5 December 1957; BTD, ¶12.
33 E.g. Otahuhu, 1955; Marton, 1962.
34 Arthur G. Gunn, 'Editorial', *EP* (May 1962): 2
35 ADMNH 7:9.
36 ADMNH 7:32.
37 *Keswick Week* 1963: 11–15, 33–38, 57–61, 85–93, 113–20, 130–33. A

year later, Blaiklock became another New Zealand speaker at Keswick: Blaiklock (*Keswick Week* 1964: 11–15, 35–40, 59–65, 87–92, 111–17).
38 E.g. Belgrave Heights, 1958, 1961, 1965; Katoomba, 1959–60; India, 1961.
39 JGM, ¶263–75. Miller's 'very deep misgivings' were that 'we are complete in Christ … How can I then tell the people that there is some additional bonus, blessing, anointing … that they need to have?' It is not clear to what extent Miller may have been influenced in this period by critique of Keswick theology in Britain by Lloyd-Jones, Packer, and Kevan: see e.g. J.I. Packer, '"Keswick" and the Reformed Doctrine of Sanctification', *Evangelical Quarterly* (July 1955): 153–67. Packer dismissed Keswick's teaching as unbiblical, 'Pelagian' in making sanctification dependent upon natural human will, and 'delusive' in its goal of 'complete' victory over sin.
40 Collated in Graham Miller, *The Treasury of His Promises* (Edinburgh: Banner of Truth Trust, 1986).
41 Angus Ross to Miller, 1 October 1959 (cit. ADMNH: 7).
42 'Farewell to Respected Evangelical Leader', *Challenge Weekly* (20 November 1965): 6; JGM, ¶560–70.
43 Someone who greatly respected Miller but was later ambivalent about some aspects of Miller's conservatism was John Roxborogh, who attended First Church while at Ardmore Engineering School. He was converted as Miller preached through Romans, was encouraged into ministry and missionary service by Miller, did a PhD on Thomas Chalmers, and pursued an academic career in the history of mission. WJR: ¶15–16, 23, 29, 31, 91.
44 JGM, ¶291.
45 'Farewell to Respected Evangelical Leader', *Challenge Weekly* (20 November 1965): 6–7.
46 J.N. Smith, 'Graham Miller', *Outlook* (5 February 1966): 31. For aspects of Miller in Australia, see Hutchinson: 369–70.
47 D. Kirkby, 'Present Minister Tells of His Call to the Church', *Challenge Weekly* (12 October 1968): 7. Kirkby's predecessor, F.E.H. Paton (1940–57), had strong spiritual emphases. Also: [B.R. Hyland (ed.)], *Centennial History of the Presbyterian Church in Pukekohe 1868–1968* (Pukekohe: St James' Presbyterian Church, 1968): 8, 11, 20.
48 IB, ¶52.
49 JBM, ¶32.
50 *Proceedings*, 1962: 294a; St James' Presbyterian Church, Pukekohe, 'Annual Reports', 1962.
51 *Proceedings*, 1962: 291a–97a.
52 JBM, ¶32.
53 E.g. *Proceedings*, 1958: 281a.
54 *Centennial History*, 53.
55 Ibid., 53; Donald A. Kirkby, 'Racial Problems in Pukekohe: What are the Churches Doing About Them?', *Outlook* (25 March 1959): 6–7.
56 JBM, ¶34.
57 Ibid.
58 'Presbyterian Church Celebrates Its Centennial', *Challenge Weekly* (12 October 1968): 5.
59 Notes, Jewel Palmer, 15 June 2007.
60 E.g. Shep Noon Fong.
61 Robin Farnsworth (WBT), Robert and Sadie Elphick (CLTC), Claud Johnstone (WEC), Jeanette Grimmer (Middle East Christian Outreach), Colin Wylie (Borneo Evangelical Mission).
62 E.g. *The Story of the St James' World Missionary Fellowship. A Congregation's Pilgrimage in Faith*, 1967.
63 'Expanding Church Becomes Missionary Base', *Challenge Weekly* (12 October 1968): 8–9.
64 Kirkby was influenced by Rev. Neville Horn, who visited St James' in 1963, and by 'faith' principles as outlined in such pamphlets as Oswald J. Smith's

65 *How God Taught Me to Give. The Story*: 13–14.
66 JBM, ¶37.
67 LW, ¶366.
68 D.A. Kirkby to John ____, 3 October 1956.
69 JGM, ¶756; LW, ¶403.
70 *Centennial History*: 54. After Belgrave Heights, he considered an invitation to become principal of Melbourne Bible Institute, but declined: JGM, ¶757.
71 E.g. the NZ Council of the Scripture Union, CSSM, and Crusader Movement.
72 The Committee on Ministry Recruitment.
73 Three informants (names withheld).
74 J.T. Gunn (Sen.), 1875–1919. The older Gunn had died during Arthur Gunn's childhood.
75 Both Miller and Yule described Gunn as 'brilliant' JGM, ¶762; GMY, ¶529. Also Elley (RDE, ¶247) and Breward: 'Arthur Gunn had a very keen mind, there is no doubt about that. If he had had a post-graduate theological education, he had the intellect to have been a pretty formidable teacher of the Church': IB, ¶41.
76 Gunn to to J.D. Salmond, 4 May 1948.
77 E.g. Gunn to Watson, 18 December 1946; convener to Gunn, 13 January 1947; Gunn to Watson, 6 May 1947, 28 July 1947, 5 October 1947, 18 November 1947; to J.D. Salmond, 4 May 1948.
78 *Outlook* (21 February 1956): 18.
79 Sefton Campbell conducted a teaching mission at First Church: 'I was impressed at his faithfulness to the Word'. Miller claimed Campbell retained some 'inhibitions' inherited from the Theological Hall: he was 'still getting out of his grave clothes' (JGM, ¶801).
80 Alan and Muriel Lipscombe, interview, 26 March 2007 (hereafter AL), ¶7, 15, 25.
81 JRB, ¶138.
82 AL, ¶11, 18.
83 *Proceedings*, 1959: 260a.
84 *Proceedings*, 1958–65.
85 AL, ¶17.
86 D.A. Kirkby, 'Church-based Evangelism is Best. An Appraisal of Mass Evangelisms and Local Church Evangelism', *EP* (September 1962): 15.
87 JRB, ¶139.
88 JRB, ¶138, 141.
89 1916–2001.
90 John Lewis Wilson Memoirs, September 1993 (unpublished typescript): 8–9, 11; LW, ¶45–46, 56.
91 LW, ¶61–63, 99.
92 1948–51.
93 1952–54. Wilson: 12, 16; LW, ¶76, 135–36, 143, 141, 158.
94 Ibid., ¶96.
95 LW, ¶101–12, 112–13, 121–22, 127. Wilson's reaction to Gunn's tone probably grew stronger in the light of late twentieth-century concerns about fundamentalist militancy.
96 LW, ¶366, 368–70.
97 Ibid., ¶123, 429.
98 Ibid., ¶284–93.
99 JRB, ¶99.
100 Tributes to Wilson were posted on 'NZPres@GodZone.net.nz', 24–25 April 2001.
101 Ken Irwin, ibid.
102 LW, ¶210, 95; Wilson Memoirs: 21–23. Others agreed his gifts were underutilised (NZPres, 25 April 2001).
103 Because of ill health Wilson did not complete his thesis, and in 1967 returned to New Zealand, to Mosgiel.
104 JRB, ¶29.
105 Ibid; *Proceedings*, 1962: 294a; 1965: 320a; 1967: 314a.
106 JRB, ¶30.
107 JRB, ¶43.
108 JRB, ¶31, 87–88.
109 JRB, ¶1–2.
110 JRB, ¶5.
111 JRB, ¶9.
112 JRB, ¶10–13.
113 JRB, ¶52, 54.
114 JRB, ¶54, 56.
115 JRB, ¶56.
116 JRB, ¶117–18.

117 JRB, ¶122.
118 JRB, ¶98, 99, 123, 126.
119 JRB, ¶100–02.
120 Woods had entered the ministry from St James' Pukekohe, in the time of Kirkby.
121 *Proceedings,* 1960: 275a.
122 Rex. W. Lange, 'From Plough to Pulpit' (unpublished typescript, 1995): 73. The parish was already evangelical in spirit: it had a strong men's prayer meeting and previous ministers included Ian Grant and Geordie Yule (locum).
123 Ibid.: 73–76; *Proceedings,* 1959: 260a; 1960: 275a; 1962: 294a.
124 BTD, ¶9; 'From Plough to Pulpit': 50–54.
125 GMY, ¶274; JBM, ¶128. Both cited an alleged anti-evangelical comment by the Presbytery clerk, H.O. Bowman.
126 Watt came from Scotland in 1949. His ministry at Mt Eden began an evangelical succession there.
127 Blaikie (1923–1975) went to Mangere in 1964 and to Greyfriars (Mt Eden) in 1971.
128 See Marilyn Lewis, *Forrest Hill Presbyterian: 40 Years of Memories* (Auckland: Forrest Hill Presbyterian Church, 2002).
129 Gosling Papers relating to Island Bay, Presbyterian Research Centre 396/18.
130 R.D. Elley came in 1960, as a hospital chaplain. Elley thought there may have been two other ministers with evangelical sympathies, but neither of them was active in WF: RDE, ¶143.
131 Rev. Wynford Davies, interview, September 2001 (hereafter WD), ¶78. Davies was later minister at Wyndham, Greyfriars, St Andrew's Invercargill and Glendowie. From 1970–77 he left the Presbyterian Church because of the Geering controversy. There are numerous references to Davies in Geraint D. Fielder, *'Excuse Me, Mr Davies – Hallelujah!' Evangelical Student Witness in Wales, 1923–1983* (Leicester: IVP, 1983).

132 1963–78. See Memorial Minute, Alexander Stuart Munro, *Proceedings,* 2000: 32–33. See also Michael A. Reid, 'But By My Spirit: A History of the Charismatic Renewal in Christchurch, 1960–1985' (PhD thesis, University of Canterbury, 2003): 185. Munro was not himself a charismatic.
133 The EANZ, inspired by the British movement, was constituted in 1966, after the period addressed by this book. It primarily grew out of a Christchurch initiative. Other key leaders were Anglicans J.E. Davies and Harry Thomson. The other constituent bodies were the Evangelical Alliance (Auckland) and the Evangelical Fellowship of Otago. See: Constitution, EANZ, September 1966, TSCF N1/11.
134 McKenzie: 78–87. By this time, St Stephen's was declining. It had lost much of its population base. Evangelical divinity students at St Stephen's at that time included Kenneth Calvert, Neal Whimp, Ralph Penno, Ernest Task, Max Garrity.
135 Troughton had been Chaplain at Featherston Prisoner of War Camp working with Japanese prisoners. He helped quell a riot and some converted to Christianity. Michiharu Shinyu, *Beyond Death and Dishonour: One Japanese at War in New Zealand* (Auckland: Castle Publishing, 2001); *Proceedings,* 1986: 152–53.
136 E.R. (Rowland) Harries (1911–2004) was the son of E.R. (Evan) Harries (see Chapter One). The younger Harries had also been shaped by Crusaders, BTI and missionary service in the Sudan (1936–50).
137 ERH, ¶124. From 1958 to 1960, weekly attendance went from 375 to 500, and membership from 220 to 426: *Proceedings,* 1958, 282a; 1959, 261a; 1960, 277a.
138 SC, ¶270, 64, 62, 104.
139 In 1968, in the context of the Geering controversy and expected Church

Union, McKenzie resigned from the ministry: George A. McKenzie, 'Pastoral Letter to All Church Members of the Manurewa South-Takanini Presbyterian Church,' 20 November 1968.
140 Kirkby was followed by A.J. (Bert) Orange, a BTI graduate and former home missionary among Māori.
141 RDE, ¶55, 62-68, 70-71. (1) In Wellington, Elley was Chaplain of Porirua Hospital and from 1966 minister of Khandallah. (2) For Orr's account of his 1956 tour see *Evangelical Awakenings*: 162-63.
142 RDE, ¶74-76.
143 Davies, the father of Wynford Davies, also later did a locum ministry at Tuatapere-Orepuki.
144 Dunn (1909-2003) was founding chairman of the Motukarara Keswick Convention and a strong supporter of the Pounawea Convention and CE. See also: *Proceedings*, 2004: 23-24.
145 From Scotland, Reid had studied at Glasgow BTI.
146 Then at St Andrew's Invercargill, from 1963.
147 WD, ¶106.
148 Later, he established such a convention in Tasmania.
149 To St Andrew's, Launceston. Later, he was Professor of Church History (1978-81) at the Theological College of the Presbyterian Church of Victoria.
150 One possible exception was Sefton Campbell at First Church Invercargill (1960-66). He was a moderate evangelical and not obviously identified with the WF.
151 [John Brinsley] to G.I. Williamson, 8 July 1963. The figures were 100 out of c. 370.
152 8th Annual Report, 1958, WF Executive Minute Book.
153 E.g. in 1957, at Invercargill, Gore, Christchurch and Waimate.
154 Ibid.: 30 September 1957.
155 *Immortality*; *The Reformed Doctrine of Predestination*; *Studies in Theology*.
156 WF Executive Minutes: 4 August 1958.
157 Ibid.: 1 February 1960; *Reaper* (1 January 1960): 402-03 (403). The others were prosperity, controversy and compromise. He attributed Calvinism's 'lamentable revival' to Barth.
158 8th Annual Report, 1958, WF Executive Minute Book.
159 E.g. B.B. Warfield, 'The Alien Righteousness', *EP* (March 1959): 4-5.
160 E.g. P.B. Fraser, 'Abraham Kuyper', *EP* (November 1958): 7-8.
161 E.g. N.R. Sheat, 'Confident Christianity', *EP* (September 1957): 10-12.
162 E.g. *Bulwark* [Scottish Reformation Society], *Southern Presbyterian Journal* [US], *Presbyterian Record* [Canada], *Monthly Record of the Free Church of Scotland*, *Irish Evangelical* [Belfast], *Blue Banner Faith and Life* [US], *Evangelical Action* [Melbourne], *Presbyterian Guardian* [Philadelphia], *Evangelical Magazine* [London, from J.I. Packer], *Reformation Review* [Amsterdam], *Bible League Quarterly* [London], *Our Banner* [Sydney].
163 E.g. J.A. Froude, 'Calvinism', *EP* (July 1959): 12-14; James Green, 'The Distinctive Teachings of Presbyterianism', *EP* (May 1961): 5-11; Henry Cooke, 'What is Scriptural Presbyterianism?' *EP* (July 1957): 25-27; John Johnston, 'The Substance of the Reformed Faith', *EP* (January 1961): 7-9.
164 C.L. Gosling, 'The Covenant of Grace', *EP* (March 1959): 6-8; C.L. Gosling, 'Studies in the Shorter Catechism', *EP* (September 1959): 10-12.
165 E.g. William Fitch, 'Evangelicalism', *EP* (September 1961): 17-19.
166 J.A. Mitchell, 'J.C. Ryle: Evangelical Anglican', *EP* (January 1958).
167 E.g. David Hogg, 'Sunday Observance', *EP* (November 1957): 2-5; Robert A. Hoggard, 'The Truth About Gambling', *EP* (July 1961): 22-27; W.R. Lawrence, 'A Policeman's

Views on Temperance', *EP* (November 1957): 12–13; Ian Munro, 'The Christian and Amusements', *EP* (January 1961): 29–32.
168 J. Hutchison, 'How Near Is the Lord's Return?' *EP* (March 1959): 19–20.
169 E.g. Edward J. Young, 'Letters to a High School Student on Science and Evolution', *EP* (July 1957): 31–33.
170 R.S. Miller, 'Current Comment,' *EP* (March 1956): 49–50; J. Graham Miller, 'Billy Graham in Auckland', *EP* (July 1959): 3–4; 'Book List', *EP* (July 1961): 33–35.
171 Ivan M. Moses, 'Fundamentalism and the Word of God', *EP* (September 1958): 25–26.
172 Poon, an Australian Chinese minister working among New Zealand Chinese people, held a BA and BD and it is highly likely he had an IVF background.
173 Lewis (née Jones) was originally from Wales and the widow of Rev. W. Leslie Lewis (1903–1952). They had been missionaries in India. She held her BD from the University of London and was strong in Greek. Winifred Betty Lewis, 'I Remember, I Remember' (Auckland: unpublished book, 1996); Coggan: 151; Fielder: 37, 66, 69.
174 JGM, ¶393, 351.
175 WF 14th Annual Report, 30 September 1963.
176 WF 15th Annual Report, 30 September 1964.
177 WF 15th Annual Report, 22 November 1965.
178 R.S. Miller, 'The Bible IS the Word of God', *EP* (July 1963): 213–21; Hermann Sasse, 'A Binding Dogma: the Inspiration of Scripture', *EP* (January 1963): 28–33.
179 E.g. R.S. Miller, 'The Doctrine of Christ,' *EP* (January 1963): 36–42.
180 J.I. Packer, 'John Calvin', *EP* (January–February 1965): 22–30.
181 Robert Lamont, 'The Biblical Certainty of Christ's Return', *EP* (January–February 1965): 16–21.
182 I. Nelson Bell, 'The Christian Sabbath: Bulwark of a Nation', *EP* (September 1962): 38–42.
183 Evolution was not a preoccupation of New Zealand (and British) IVF-associated evangelicalism in this period. It may be that for Gunn any acceptance of evolution was beyond the pale so not worth discussing, or that Gunn was simply preoccupied with other issues. While liberals (and some evangelicals) held to theistic evolution, liberals were not conspicuously promoting such an approach, and evangelicals and liberals alike rejected atheistic evolutionism: see Ronald L. Numbers and John Stenhouse. 'Antievolutionism in the Antipodes: From Protesting Evolution to Promoting Creationism in New Zealand', *British Journal for the History of Science* 33 (September 2000): 335–50 (343–44).
184 E.g. William Still, *EP* (July–August 1964): 609–25; D.A. Kirkby, 'Church Based Evangelism is Best. An Appraisal of Mass Evangelism and Local Church Evangelism', *EP* (September 1962): 13–16; I.B. Davies, 'Revival and Its Fruit', *EP* (November–December 1964): 713–15; J.T. Gunn, 'On Making a Joyful Noise unto the Lord (Ps. 98:4)', *EP* (May 1962): 39–42; John Brinsley, 'An Interview by J.R. Brinsley with Warner Hutchinson of the Inter-Varsity Fellowship', *EP* (May 1962): 19–22; J. Graham Miller, 'Evangelical Renewal', *EP* (November 1963): 329–33; 'NZBTI', *EP* (January 1964): 425–27; J.L. Wilson, 'Second Thoughts on the New English Bible', *EP* (May 1962). 34–38.
185 Arthur G. Gunn, 'Editorial', *EP* (July 1962): 1.
186 A.J. Campbell, 'Our Youth, a Moral Crisis', *EP* (September 1962): 17–20; J. Lloyd Jones, 'The Stomach-Turning Point', *EP* (May 1963): 160–69; A.G. Gunn, 'Editorial,' *EP* (July–August 1964): 577–80; 'From The UK –

Moral Collapse', *EP* (July–August 1964): 587; A.G. Gunn, 'Sex and the Christian', *EP* (July–August 1964): 590-99.

187 E.g. A.G. Gunn, 'Window on the World', *EP* (July 1962).

188 Merrill C. Tenney, 'What is Wrong with Neo-Orthodoxy?' *EP* (July 1963): 225-27; J. Gresham Machen, 'A Plea for Honesty', *EP* (Jan-February 1966): 35-38; R.J. Blaikie, 'What is Our Gospel? A Review', *EP* (November 1963): 341-45; J.I. Packer, 'God and the Bishop of Woolwich', *EP* (November 1963): 334-40; [Gunn], 'Principal Geering's "Outlook" Article', *EP* (November–December) 1965): 333.

189 A.G. Gunn, 'What Happened to Francisco Lacueva?' *EP* XV, 1 (January–February 1965): 6.

190 Arthur G. Gunn, 'All Roads Are Now Leading to Rome', *EP* (July 1962): 6-8.

191 'Suicide? The Editor Writes to *The Outlook*', *EP* (May–June, 1965): 134.

192 Gunn, 'Review: "The Body of Christ. The New Testament Image of the Church", by Alan Cole', *EP* (July–August, 1965): 254.

193 'Suicide?' Presbyterians, he asserted, would lose 'our eldership, our simple services, our lovely Communion, our "free" prayer, our parity of the ministry, our Westminster Confession'.

194 Gunn, 'Window on the World', *EP* (March–April 1965): 70.

195 E.g. Arthur G. Gunn, 'Editorial', *EP* (July 1962): 1-3.

196 Gunn, 'Window on the World', *EP* (May. 1963): 133-44; Gunn, 'Editorial,' *EP* (September 1963): 259-64; Gunn, 'Window on the World', *EP* (September 1963): 265-70; Gunn, 'Window on the World', *EP* (September–October 1964): 647-54; [Gunn], 'Westminster Fellowship News', *EP* (January–February 1965): 4-7; Gunn, 'Window on the World', *EP* (March–April 1965): 69-77.

197 E.g. E.L. Kirkby, 'How Christian is the Roman Catholic Church?' *EP* (September 1962): 14-15; H. Farell, 'Was the Reformation Wrong?' *EP* (May–June, 1965): 154-62; Anon., 'I Married a Roman Catholic', *EP* (July–August 1965): 223-28; Wilton M. Nelson, 'Is the Roman Church Changing?' *EP* (September–October 1964): 665-72; F. Maxwell Bradshaw, 'Ecumenism Run Wild', *EP* (November 1963): 357-63; W. Stanley Mooneyham, 'Evangelicals: Divisive or Dynamic?' *EP* (May–June 1965): 138-44; Gunn, 'Just WHAT is our NCC trying to DO?' *EP* (September–October 1965): 315-18; Clyde W. Taylor, 'Evangelicals Examine Ecumenism', *EP* (November–December 1965): 334-35.

198 J.G. Miller, 'Editorial', *EP* 3 (May–June 1965): 130-32; D.A. Kirkby, 'Editorial', *EP* (Jan–February 1966): 1-4.

199 J.G. Miller, 'Window on the World', *EP* (September 1962): 5-12; John Brinsley, 'Window on the World', *EP* XV, 1 (January–February 1965): 8-16; J. Lewis Wilson, 'Window on the World', *EP* (July 1963): 199-203.

200 WF 15th Annual Report, 30 September 1964.

201 E.g. there was a 6000 reprint of *After Death What?* Minutes of the WF executive, 2 October 1964.

202 'Westminster Fellowship News,' *EP* (January–February 1966): 12.

203 JGM, ¶340.

204 J.G. Miller, 'Joy Cometh in the Morning', *EP* (January 1961): 3-4; R.S. Miller, 'Recalling the First Meeting', *EP* (November 1960): 3-4.

205 JGM, ¶343.

206 Arthur G. Gunn, *Seven Studies in Visitation Evangelism* (Manurewa: Westminster Fellowship within the Presbyterian Church of New Zealand, 1963); *Elder's Roll Book and Handbook* (Manurewa: Westminster Fellowship, 1963).

207 See e.g. '*Tell Scotland*': Strategy for

Mission (Scotland: The Church of Scotland, n.d.); D.P. Thomson, *Visitation Evangelism: Guidance for Those Engaged in House-to-House Visitation Campaigns* (Crieff Perthshire: The Author, n.d.).

208 Presbyterian Church of New Zealand, *Christ Our Life: A Communicant's Manual* (Christchurch: Presbyterian Bookroom, 1963); Minutes of the WF executive, 2 November 1962. The authors were Gunn, J.G. Miller, Kirkby, Brinsley and Wilson.

209 R.D. Elley, *I Want to Know God* (Manurewa: Westminster Fellowship, 1963); J.G. Miller, *After Death What?* (Manurewa: Westminster Fellowship, 1963).

210 M. Milmine, *How Can I Overcome Temptation?* (Manurewa: Westminster Fellowship, n.d. [1964]). and W.M. Ryburn *What Shall Be My Work?* (Manurewa: Westminster Fellowship, n.d. [1963]).

211 A.G. Gunn (ed.), *The Authority of the Bible* (Manurewa: Westminster Fellowship, 1965). The contributors were Lewis Wilson, A.C. Webster, William Still, Hermann Sasse and James I. Packer.

212 R. Strang Miller, *Our Presbyterian Faith* (Manurewa: Westminster Fellowship within the Presbyterian Church of New Zealand, 1964); cf. L.G. Geering, *What Is Our Gospel?* Faith and Order Studies, National Council of Churches in New Zealand (New Zealand: Presbyterian Bookroom, 1963).

213 R. Strang Miller, *His Day or Ours? Studies in the Biblical and Reformed Basis of the Lord's Day Observance* (Manurewa: Westminster Fellowship, 1964).

214 The titles listed were published in the years 1963–65. Others in the series were published later.

215 Donald A. Kirkby, *Book List: A Guide for the Christian Reader* (Manurewa: Westminster Fellowship, 1963).

216 Graham Miller and Arthur G. Gunn, *Evangelicals and the Ecumenical Movement* (Manurewa: Westminster Fellowship, 1964).

217 See Gunn, 'Why We Say "No" to an Act of Commitment', *EP* (November–December 1965): 324–33.

218 J. Graham Miller, *What is The Westminster Fellowship? An Explanatory Booklet Concerning the Origin, Work, Witness of the Westminster Fellowship* (Manurewa: Westminster Fellowship, n.d.).

219 A.C. Webster and G.A. Taylor, *Is Hell Empty After All? The Creeping Paralysis of Universalism* (Manurewa: Westminster Fellowship, n.d.). See A.C. Webster 'Is Hell Empty After All?' *EP* (November 1962): 31–38.

220 Arthur G. Gunn, *Sex and the Christian* (Manurewa: Westminster Fellowship within the Presbyterian Church of New Zealand, n.d.). See A.G. Gunn, 'Sex and the Christian,' *EP* (July–August 1964): 590–99.

221 A.C. Webster, *It's a Trap* (Manurewa: Westminster Fellowship, n.d.).

222 In 1958, at the instigation of R.S. Miller, the WF executive had agreed to the printing of a pamphlet by E.J. Young, *Letters on Evolution*, from the Orthodox Presbyterian Church in the US: WF Executive Minutes, October 1958. This pamphlet was not promoted by the WF executive once it was based in South Auckland.

223 D. Martyn Lloyd-Jones, *The Roman Catholic Church* (Manurewa: Westminster Fellowship, n.d.). First printed in *The Westminster Record* (May 1963).

224 Dwight H. Small, *Dancing and the Christian* (Manurewa: Westminster Fellowship, n.d. [1964]). Reprinted from *His* magazine with an introduction by Rev. Arthur G. Gunn. See Dwight Small, 'Dating With or Without Dancing,' *EP* (May 1964): 529–36. The author argued that all dancing, including ballroom dancing, communicates a 'prevalent erotic idea'. Gunn's 'Introduction' vigorously

opposed Presbyterian BC dances.
225 A.F. Olsen, *It's a Scandal* (Manurewa: Westminster Fellowship [1965]). See Alton F. Olsen, 'The Real Scandal of Protestantism,' *EP* (January 1964): 435–36. Olsen slated the 'apostasy' of liberals and ecumenists as the real scandal of Protestantism (cf. the alleged 'scandal' of denominationalism).
226 JGM, ¶749, 410. The executive was probably uncomfortable with Gunn's suggestion in the *EP* that the anti-ecumenical leaflet was 'Ideal for distribution at church union meetings': 'The WF … List of publications just released,' *EP* (November–December 1965): page following 352.
227 Minutes of the WF executive, 4 September 1964.
228 WF 15th Annual Report, 14 November 1966. Most were not successful, and 'most of them did not see the need to reply to letters' (Gosling: 15).
229 WF 13th Annual Report, 26 November 1962.
230 Minutes of the WF executive, 2 July 1965.
231 E.g. Minutes of the WF AGM, 26 November 1962; Minutes of the WF Executive, 3 December 1965.
232 'Report of the First Westminster Conference, Massey University – August 1964.'
233 JGM, ¶385.
234 Minutes of the WF executive, 2 October 1964.
235 Minutes of a Special Meeting of the WF executive, 16 October 1964. In 1965, the Glenfield Bethel Trust was established.
236 Mrs W.B. Lewis, for instance, had known Lloyd-Jones in Wales, as had Wynford Davies. Graham Miller made contact in Britain with Lloyd-Jones, who told Miller he 'read every word' of the *EP* (ADMNH: 27). The WF also corresponded with T.F. Torrance and Karl Barth. Torrance made comments which Graham Miller used in a 1962 Assembly debate, but Barth wrote back that he was 'too busy' to assist: Minutes of the WF executive, 7 September 1962.
237 Minutes of the WF executive, 1 May 1964.
238 Ibid., 2 February 1962. The tapes were prepared by Mrs Sydney Brinsley.
239 'Victorian Newsletter,' *EP* (January 1961): 13–15. Swanton, minister of Hawthorne Presbyterian Church (1940–68) had studied under Barth and in 1942 founded the *Reformed Theological Review*. He was a principal leader in the reviving of Calvinist theology in Australia (Piggin: 135).
240 Victoria: F. Maxwell Bradshaw; New South Wales: T.P. McEvoy; Queensland: D.C. Blake; Western Australia: Andrew Priddle; Tasmania: Bruce Adams. See e.g. *EP* (November–December 1964).
241 Minutes of the WF executive, 28 February 1964; 2 October 1964.
242 WF 15th Annual Report, 30 September 1964. Those and similar meetings, the links with the Westminster Society, and the subsequent role in Australia of Graham Miller are noted in Hutchinson, with the suggestion that the *EP* provided a rallying point for Australian 'evangelical activists' and the 'mutual reinforcement of evangelical Presbyterian identity': 371.
243 Minutes of the WF executive, 7 February 1964.
244 WF 15th Annual Report, 22 November 1965.
245 That connection was not nearly so apparent, though, to most other members of the executive.
246 Minutes of the WF executive, 7 August 1964; ibid., 4 September 1964.
247 Minutes of the WF executive, 6 August 1965.
248 E.g. Clyde W. Taylor, 'Evangelicals Examine Ecumenism,' *EP* (November–December 1965): 334–35.
249 The Reformed Churches of New

Zealand related to *De Gereformeerde Kerken in Nederland*.
250 See e.g. Report of the Committee on Doctrine, *Proceedings* (1956): 104a–06a.
251 A.G. Gunn, 'Editorial', *EP* (March 1964): 452.
252 E.g. G.I. Williamson to John [Brinsley], 3 July 1963; 'Mangere Reformed Church', attached card.
253 E.g. [John Brinsley] to G.I. Williamson, 8 July 1963.
254 See J. Graham Miller, 'The Ecumenical Movement – Threat or Blessing?' in Graham Miller and Arthur G. Gunn, *Evangelicals and the Ecumenical Movement* (Manurewa: Westminster Fellowship, 1964): 1–13. Lloyd-Jones' work was *The Basis of Christian Unity: An Exposition of John 17 and Ephesians 4* (London: IVF, 1962).
255 Miller felt Gunn was schismatic 'at heart': JGM, ¶771.
256 Minutes of the WF executive, 6 April 1962; 4 May 1962. The statement also noted that WF members were 'not required to share these views'.
257 Gunn, 'Why We Say "No" to an Act of Commitment', *EP* (November–December 1965): 324–33.
258 J.G. Miller, 'Editorial', *EP* (May–June 1965): 130–32. Miller argued that 'the reformed ideal of the church is the most catholic of all; the High Church the most exclusive and bigoted'.
259 See e.g. [Gunn], 'Westminster Fellowship News', *EP* (Jan–February) 1966: 17; A.G. Gunn, 'A Positive Approach to the Ecumenical Movement', in Miller and Gunn: 14–26.
260 J. Graham Miller, 'The Ecumenical Movement', in ibid.: 1–13.
261 Ibid.: 11–12; JGM, ¶849.
262 Minutes of the WF Special Meeting, 30 August 1965.
263 Minutes of the WF executive, 1 October 1965.
264 WF 15th Annual Report, 22 November 1965.
265 Miller, 'The Ecumenical Movement', in Miller and Gunn: 7.
266 Miller felt Lloyd-Jones' position was biblically and historically 'untenable' (ADMNH: 27).
267 Minutes of the WF executive, 7 June 1963; JB, ¶110.
268 Minutes of the WF executive, 5 July 1963.
269 Ibid.: 2 October 1964.
270 Ibid.: 5 June 1964.
271 Jan Van Royen, 'A Party Within The Church', *Forum* (June 1962): 10–11.
272 Donald G. Shaw, 'The Westminster Fellowship Should Think Again', *Forum* (June 1962): 12–16.
273 LW, ¶146. The accusations would have stung Wilson, who was a particularly irenic member of the WF, but was personally criticised in Shaw's article.
274 Ross Miller, 'Westminster Fellowship,' *Forum* (August 1962): 15–16. The editor then closed the correspondence, and later printed a mild response from Gunn: Arthur G. Dunn [sic], 'The Westminster Fellowship', *Forum* (September 1962): 11–12.
275 ADMNH: 33.
276 [Gunn], 'Westminster Fellowship News', *EP* (Jan–February) 1966: 12, 14–15.
277 Ian Purdie to J.D. Salmond, 18 May 1962, 9A/110, Theological Hall Committee Secretary's Papers (J.D. Salmond), 96/15/77, Presbyterian Research Centre.
278 L. Barbour and B. Spence to the *EP* [October 1964].
279 JB, ¶68. There had been an 'unbroken succession' of liberal or moderate moderators since 1951 (Barton): JGM, ¶584.
280 E.g. Minutes of the WF executive, 5 October 1962. A meeting was held at Island Bay prior to the 1962 Assembly in Wellington.
281 SC, ¶247, 118.
282 JGM, ¶835.
283 IB, ¶41.
284 GMY, ¶282; SM, ¶124.
285 SM, ¶124.

286 SM, ¶63.
287 RDE, ¶134. The moderator was John Allan.
288 ERH, ¶182. Lewis Wilson recalled someone muttering as Miller went forward to speak, 'There go the Wee Frees again': LW, ¶384.
289 GMY, ¶282.
290 ERH, ¶182. However, Elley thought Miller could be 'astringent' and therefore polarising: RDE, 244.
291 SC, ¶118, 225.
292 WD, ¶143–44. The ministers on the ship were identifiable because of their clerical collars, but he did not know them. They asked him his impressions of Assembly.
293 ERH, ¶285.
294 GMY, ¶516; JGM, ¶349: Gosling could be 'a bit cranky' and 'that was often an asset in the Assembly. He would get up and give somebody a great thumping, it would clear the air. I have seen him put J.D. Smith in his place … Gossy got up, and he exploded in a good Irish display of wrath … It was very good. He did that several times … He always got away with it. They knew it was his temperament.'
295 JGM, ¶410.
296 *Proceedings* (1965): 63. JGM, ¶412: Jim Gunn (brother of Arthur) 'stumped forward and said, "Moderator, we are brethren here, we are not going to have this division", and there was a sudden relaxation of bitterness, and that overture [sic] was thrown out'. In a conciliatory move, Miller then offered to recommend to the WF executive that the WF name be changed. The WF executive rejected his proposal.
297 *Proceedings* (1965): 32. The key motion evangelicals rejected was that 'The Faith We Affirm Together' was a 'sufficient statement of the historic Christian Faith'.
298 Ibid.: 309a–10a, 33–34. The amendment was moved by Fraser and Somerville.
299 JGM, ¶491.
300 RDE, ¶136.
301 E.g. Donald Elley, Lewis Wilson. Elley claimed he always tried hard to maintain friendships across the theological divide: RDE, ¶149. Notwithstanding that, in his interview he conveyed a pervasive sense of having experienced polarisation and marginalisation.
302 JGM, ¶609.
303 Neville Glasgow to the editor and members of the Editorial Board, 18 July 1962.
304 Neville Glasgow to John [Brinsley], 18 July 1962.
305 Minutes of the WF executive, 1 May 1964; probably the 'very hostile' letter from J.D.S. Moore recalled decades later by Yule: GMY, ¶28.
306 Minutes of the WF Executive, 3 September 1965. The wording is that of the minutes, not the actual letter.
307 (1) 'That the Church is heading back to Rome is an emotional catch-cry that only relieves people from facing the issues properly.' (2) 'Very early in my ministry I became convinced of the folly of mere anti-Catholic and anti-liberal propaganda of the type that is the regular fare of "the Contender", and has sometimes appeared in the "Evangelical Presbyterian". This ultimately plays merely into the hands of the enemy … At best it is like running up and throwing a brick through the kitchen window of your wealthy rival. It only irritates.' (3) 'The purpose of the paper [the *EP*] was not polemics or heresy hunting.' C.L Gosling, 'The Origins of the Westminster Fellowship', *EP* (November–December 1964): 723-24, 727.
308 GMY, ¶530–32; JGM, ¶747. Miller recalled only one actual confrontation with Gunn, after he told Gunn there should be no more articles in the *EP* by Grahame Kerr (of Australia), whose writing Miller considered unnecessarily provocative. Gunn rang with his resignation but changed his

mind overnight: JGM, ¶748.
309 Minutes of the WF executive, 3 September 1965.
310 'Editorial', *EP* (January–February 1966): 3.
311 Concerns about the views of Geering, principal of the Theological Hall, were first discussed at the WF executive late in 1965: Minutes of the WF executive, 1 October 1965.
312 The 1966 Conference was faced with the apparent promotion of schism by Grahame Kerr, a conference speaker who later founded the Presbyterian Reformed Church of Australia; Gosling rose to oppose him, probably mindful of how Stott had publicly refuted separatist views expressed by Lloyd-Jones: JGM, ¶771–74.
313 A.G. Dunn, G.R. Hughes, J. McKinlay, J.C. Calvert, S.H. Rae, E.L. Brown, G. McInnes, B.T. Doig, R.B. Rofe, D.M. Fergus, R.M. Yule to the Secretary, WF executive, with copies sent to to all executive members, members of the Editorial Board, and to the chairmen of regional committees, 6 July 1966. Minutes of the WF executive, 5 August 1966. In response, the new WF chairman met with evangelicals at the Hall. The executive also ruled that all material in the *EP* must be approved by the Editorial Board: Minutes of the WF executive, 30 September 1966.
314 The letter invited, inter alia, discussion of 'Ecumenism and the Evangelical Doctrine of the Church'. Many years later, Rob Yule reflected that the primary reason he was unable to support the WF wholeheartedly was its 'failure to grasp that Christian unity is a biblical mandate': email, 17 August 2007.
315 Rob Yule, son of WF stalwart Morrison Yule and nephew of the Miller brothers, was among them. He suggested he was influenced by Ronald Nash, *The New Evangelicalism* (Grand Rapids: Zondervan, [1963]): email, 17 August 2007. For Simon Rae, the issues (as he recalled) were the WF's anti-Catholicism, its opposition to church union, its doctrinaire views on secondary matters, and what seemed a failure to engage with contemporary theological issues: SR, ¶41. Breward suggested (IB, ¶59): 'They were very unhappy about Arthur's highly polemical stance. They were uneasy about the way in which the Westminster Fellowship did not connect with contemporary theological debates that they had to wrestle with in the Hall ... They felt that there was a huge job to be done, and that the Westminster Fellowship was worthy but not in touch with where they wanted to be. The issues of how you dealt with biblical exegesis, how you dealt with the issues raised by Barth and Bultmann, how you dealt with the philosophical and scientific critics of Christianity.'
316 Minutes of the WF executive, 2 September 1966.

Conclusion

1 W.A. Hutchinson to B. Gustafson, 21 September 1959, TSCF B1/102.
2 Piggin, 'Towards a Bicentennial History of Australian Evangelicalism', *Journal of Religious History* 15, 1 (June 1988): 20–37.
3 Steve Bruce, *Firm in the Faith* (Brookfield, Vermont: Gower, 1984): 80–81, 82–84, 86–87; cf. Boyd: 149–50.
4 JGM, ¶161.

Glossary

Anglo-Catholicism A High Church Anglican movement claiming a Catholic (rather than Protestant) identity for the Church of England

biblicism An emphasis on the authority and use of the scriptures

Charismatic movement A late twentieth-century, crossdenominational movement which focused on the ministry of the Holy Spirit, especially spiritual gifts (1 Corinthians 12–14), and on prayer, praise and ministry by all

church union The merger of church denominations

confessionalism An emphasis on the classic Protestant confessions of faith, such as the Thirty-Nine Articles and the Westminster Confession

ecumenism A twentieth-century movement dedicated to bringing about unity among different Christian denominations and Church union

evangelicalism A movement combining such emphases as salvation by faith, the centrality of the Cross, spiritual rebirth, a high view of the scriptures, ongoing experience of God, personal piety, evangelism and missionary work

fundamentalism A conservative, anti-modernist movement in America, emerging in the 1920s, with such tendencies as a militant attitude, separatism, anti-intellectualism, literalistic biblical interpretation, anti-evolutionism, premillennialism and social conservatism

High Church Any catholicising tendency in the Church of England, exalting for example episcopacy, priesthood, sacraments, pre-Reformation ceremony

liberalism and modernism Broad and closely related movements accepting sceptical views of the Bible's historicity, rejecting traditional Christian doctrines, and (in theological contexts) encouraging accommodations with science and modern thinking

Low Church An emphasis on the Church of England being Protestant, and on plain liturgy in keeping (in the period of this book) with the 1662 Book of Common Prayer

Pentecostalism A movement that emerged in the early twentieth century (and often formed new churches and denominations), emphasising baptism in the Holy

Spirit and the restoration of supernatural spiritual gifts especially speaking in tongues, prophecy and healing

premillennialism An eschatological (end-times) schema anticipating the rapture and tribulation prior to the second coming and millennium, and pessimistic about events preceding the end of the age

Protestantism The stream of Christianity deriving from the sixteenth-century schism with Catholicism and emphasising salvation by faith, scriptural authority, the preaching and reading of the Bible, non-ritualistic worship and individual conscience

revivalism Working for the spiritual revival of church and society through intensive campaigns of prayer and evangelistic meetings

ritualism An Anglican High Church movement emphasising ritual, e.g. incense, vestments, bells, candles, sign of the Cross

tractarianism The 1830s Tractarian Movement (or Oxford Movement) claiming an 'apostolic' basis for Anglican ordination and sacraments

Select Bibliography

A Primary Sources

1 Unpublished

(a) Archival Collections: Organisations

Anglican Diocese of Christchurch archives. The Anglican Centre, Christchurch. Sumner Parish Minute Book, 1927–60; Shirley Parish Newsletter Clippings, 1965–72 and Vestry Minutes, 1951–57; *Year Books for the Diocesan Year.*

Anglican Diocese of Nelson archives. The Anglican Centre, Nelson. Former Clerical Employees; *Year Book and Summary of Proceedings,* 1950–65.

Latimer Fellowship archives, Latimer Fellowship Office, CMS House, Christchurch. Miscellaneous records; correspondence; ECF Conference Programmes; Minute Book of the Christchurch Committee of the ECF, 1961–65; ECF Executive Minutes, 1965–70.

Presbyterian Research Centre, Dunedin. CE Otago Union 91/44/1-14; 3/199; Gosling, Rev. C.L., folders relating to EMF, CE, Island Bay Parish, IVF. 396/18; Theological Hall student files, 1930–47; Ministers' Register, www.archives.Presbyterian.org.nz.

Scripture Union (NZ) archives, records of SU, CSSM and the Crusader Movement of New Zealand, Wellington, now in the NZ Evangelical Archive of Christianity, Deane Memorial Library, Laidlaw College, Auckland. Gen. Sec. Correspondence (B.C. Lumsden, C.K. and L.G. Becroft); miscellaneous.

TSCF archives, records of IVFEU(NZ), now in the NZ Evangelical Archive of Christianity, Deane Memorial Library. Extensive archives, c.1925–75, e.g. correspondence, papers of Gen. Secretaries, Chairmen, Presidents, Vice-Presidents; folders relating to early history of EUs; folders relating to relationships with the SCM; reports and correspondence from travelling secretaries; university missions; statistical returns and lists of executive members from EUs; folders relating to TSPU, GCF, EMF, GCF, TCF, Tyndale Fellowship, Cashmere Evangelical Trust, EANZ, NCC chaplaincies, SU, YFC; [OU] EU President's Log; IVF(NZ) handbooks; miscellaneous unfiled

conference fliers, reports, leaflets, magazines, newsletters, newspaper and magazine cuttings.
Westminster Fellowship. Records now in Presbyterian Archives Research Centre, Dunedin.
Annual Reports, 1950–1965; Minute Books, 1950–61, 1962–66.

(b) Private Papers
Bayley, Dr Andrew, Nelson, relating to Rev. Harry Thomson.
Brinsley, Rev. Dr J., relating to Church Union and the WF.
Chamberlin family, Ponui Island, Camp Visitor Books, 1932–75.
Miller, Rev. Dr J.G., Wangaratta, miscellaneous papers.
Mott, Vera, Christchurch, relating to NZCMS and the League of Youth.
Nicholson, Rev. Guy, Whangaparaoa, miscellaneous.

(c) Diaries
Orange, W.A., 1909–1914; 1924–1938. Latimer Fellowship, Christchurch.

(d) Memoirs
Bourne, Ian Grant. 'A Life Observed.' Typescript, n.d.
Edmiston, D.S. 'A Journey Together. Doug and Jane's Story'. Typescript, n.d.
Foulkes, Francis. 'The Richness of Life. Recalling the Past'. Typescript, n.d.
Gray, H.B. 'The Fire of God'. Typescript, Scotland, n.d. [1932].
Gray, J.L. 'Memoirs of James Lundie Gray'. Typescript, n.d.
Lange, Rex Watt. 'From Plough to Pulpit'. Typescript, Queenstown, 1997.
Lewis, J.L. 'John Lewis Wilson Memoirs'. Typescript, 1993.
Lewis, Winifred Betty. 'I Remember, I Remember'. Unpublished book, Auckland, 1996.
Miller, J.G. 'A Day's March Nearer Home'. Typescript, Wangaratta (Australia), n.d.

(e) Sermons
Thomas Miller. Miscellaneous undated ms. sermon notes, held by J.G. Miller.
Orange, W.A., miscellaneous ms. notes and summaries by hearers.

(f) Questionnaires
Balchin, Rev. J.; Clark, Rev. S.; Davies, Rev. W.; Elley, Rev. R.D.; Galloway, Rev. I.A.; Gunn, Rev. J.T.; Harries, Rev. E.R.; Howie, Dr B.; MacGregor, Rev. I.; McCay, Rev. S.; McKinlay, Rev. J.B.; Miller, Rev. Dr J.G; Palmer, Rev. A.; Roxburgh, Rev. R.; Sage, Rev. D.; Thompson, Rev. R.; Wilson, Rev. J.L.; Wilson, Rev. W.; Yule. Rev. G.M.

(g) Correspondence
Carrell, Right Rev. B.; Carswell, Joyce; Coulthard, Canon R.E.; Greenslade, Rev. J.; Greenwood, Rev. H.; Harris, Dr B.; Hews, M.; Hitchen, Dr John; Kirkham, Ven. P.; Marriott, Rev. W.; Miller, Rev. Dr J.G.; Pickering, Rev. D.; Singleton, P.; Thompson, Rev. R.; Tracey, C.; Simmonds, J.; Troughton, Dr D.; Wiggins, Right Rev. M.; Wilson, Rev. J.L.

(h) Other
'Clergy List, Province of New Zealand 1913–1937. Extracted from the Proceedings of the General Synod.' Unpublished compilation, Kinder Library.

2 Oral History

(a) Oral history interviews

Anonymous; Betteridge, Rev. M.; Breward, Very Rev. Dr I.; Brinsley, Rev. Dr J.R.; Bourne, Ven. I.; Carrell, Right Rev. B.; Clark, Rev. S.; Coulthard, Canon R.E; Davies, Rev. W.; Doig, Rev. B.T.; Edmiston, Canon D.S.; Elley, Rev. R.D.; Fitzpatrick, Dr C.; Ford, Ven. J.; Foulkes, M.; Glen, Rev. R.M.; Goodall, Right Rev. M.; Greenslade, Rev. J.; Harries, Rev. E.R.; Hewlett, Rev. J.O.; Kirkham, Ven. P.; Lamont, Rev. G.; Lipscombe, A. and M.; Marriott, Rev. W.; McCay, Rev. S.; McKinlay, Rev. J.B.; Meadowcroft, Rev. J.; Miller, Rev. Dr J.G.; Milmine, F.; Mott, V.; Nicholson, Rev. G.; Oldham, Rev. D.; O'Sullivan, K.; Perry, Sir N.; Pickering, Rev. D.; Rae, Rev. Dr S.; Robinson, Rev. Dr Bob; Roxborogh, Rev. Dr W. J.; Roxburgh, Rev. R.; Sage, Rev. D.; Simmonds, J.; Stott, Rev. Dr J.W.R.; Teulon, Rev. A.H.; Thompson, Rev. F.N.R.; Wiggins, Right Rev. M.; Wilkens, Canon W.F.; Wilson, Canon J.; Wilson, Rev. J. L.; Wood, D.; Yule, Rev. G.M.

(b) Notes or tapes of interviews conducted by others

Notes of interviews by P.J. Lineham of Ven. R.A. Carson and Rev. L. Pfankuch, c.1973.

Taped interviews by R.M Glen of Ven. R.A Carson, R. Fountain, Rev. R.Thompson, c.1990.

3 Published

(a) Books

Allen, Roland. *Missionary Methods, St. Paul's or Ours?* London: World Dominion Press, 1912.

Atkinson, Basil F.C. *Valiant in Fight: A Review of the Christian Conflict.* London: IVF, 1947.

Bates, J.M. *A Manual of Doctrine.* Christchurch and Dunedin: Presbyterian Bookroom, 1950.

Blaiklock. E.M. *Between the Morning and the Afternoon: The Story of a Pupil–Teacher.* Palmerston North: Dunmore, 1980.

———. *The Bible and I.* Minneapolis: Bethany, 1983.

———. *No Mists Above: An Examination of Christian Belief in God.* Auckland: Institute Press, n.d. [1949].

Bretton, W.F. *The A.B.C. of Our Religion.* [Nelson]: n.p., [1958].

Bruce, F.F. *The New Testament Documents: Are They Reliable?* Leicester: IVF, 1960. First published 1943.

Dickie, John. *The Organism of Christian Truth: A Modern Positive Dogmatic.* London: James Clarke and Company, n.d. [1931].

Dixon, W. Gray. *The Romance of the Catholic Presbyterian Church.* Wangaratta: Shoestring Press, 1990. First published 1930.

Fraser, P.B. *A Brief Statement of the Reformed Faith.* Dunedin: Stanton Bros, 1932.

Guinness, Howard. *Journey Among Students.* Sydney: Anglican Information Office, 1978.

———. *Sacrifice: A Challenge to Christian Youth.* London: IVF, 1936.

———. *The Sanity of Faith.* Sydney Australia: Omega, 1950.

Hallesby, O. *Prayer.* London: IVF, 1948.

Hammond, T.C. *In Understanding Be Men: A Handbook on Christian Doctrine for Non-Theological Students.* London: IVF, 1936.

_____. *What Is An Evangelical?* Beecroft, NSW: Evangelical Tracts and Publications, 1959.

Henry, Carl F.H. *The Uneasy Conscience of Modern Fundamentalism.* Grand Rapids: Eerdmans, 1947.

Houghton, Frank (ed.). *The Quiet Time.* London: IVF, 1933.

Inter-Varsity Fellowship of Evangelical Unions. *Evangelical Belief: The Official Interpretation of the Doctrinal Basis of the I.V.F.* Compiled by the Advisory Committee. London: Inter-Varsity Papers, n.d. [1935].

Inter-Varsity Fellowship of Evangelical Unions (NZ). *N.Z. Inter-Varsity Papers No. 1: Organic Evolution: The Theory Critically Examined. The Argument for the Negative in Students' Debate, Otago University on the Subject 'That the Weight of Evidence Supports the Theory of Evolution'.* Wellington: published for IVFEU (NZ) by A.H. and A.W. Reed, 1940.

Inter-Varsity Fellowship of Evangelical Unions (N.Z). *N.Z. Inter-Varsity Papers No. 2: The Inter-Varsity Fellowship of Evangelical Unions (N.Z.): A Sketch of its Origins, Doctrine and Practice. A Booklet for Officers and Members.* Wellington: Executive Committee of the IVFEU (N.Z), n.d. [c.1940].

Inter-Varsity Fellowship of Evangelical Unions. *Principles of Co-operation.* London: IVFEU, n.d.

Inter-Varsity Fellowship of New Zealand. *New Zealand Inter-Varsity Fellowship Handbook.* Wellington: IVFEU (NZ), 1949.

Lloyd-Jones, D. Martyn. *Maintaining the Evangelical Faith Today.* London: IVF, 1952.

Machen, J. Gresham. *Christianity and Liberalism.* New York: MacMillan, 1934.

Manley G.T. and H.W. Oldham. *Search the Scriptures: A Three Year Bible Study Course.* London: IVF, 1960. 4th ed.

Miller, J. Graham and Arthur G. Gunn. *Evangelicals and the Ecumenical Movement.* Manurewa: Westminster Fellowship, 1964.

New Zealand Student Christian Movement. Handbook for Committee Members. [Wellington]: NZSCM, 1959.

Packer, J.I. *'Fundamentalism' and the Word of God: Some Evangelical Principles.* London: Inter-Varsity Fellowship, 1958.

Presbyterian Church of New Zealand, *Christ Our Life: A Communicant's Manual.* Christchurch: Presbyterian Bookroom, 1963.

Ryle, John Charles. *Knots Untied, Being Plain Statements on Disputed Points in Religion from an Evangelical Standpoint.* James Clarke and Co: London, 1954. 31st Edition. First published 1871.

Sanders, J. Oswald. *The Divine Art of Soul-Winning.* London: Picketing & Inglis, 1937.

Short, A. Rendle. *Modern Discovery and the Bible.* London: IVF, 1949.

_____. *Why Believe?* London: IVF, 1955.

Stott, John W.R. *Basic Christianity.* London: IVF, 1958.

Thompson, Roger. *God has Spoken the Words of Life.* Christchurch: privately published 1997.

_____. *This Is the Victory: The Church – Dormant or Militant. Some Memoirs of a Kiwi 'Sin-Buster'.* Christchurch: privately published, 1995.

(b) Denominational Year Books and Published Proceedings
Church of the Province of New Zealand. Clerical Directory. Christchurch. 1944–91.
Presbyterian Church of New Zealand. Year Book. 1904–65.
Proceedings of the General Assembly of the Presbyterian Church of (Aotearoa) New Zealand. 1904–2006 (from 1967, memorial minutes only).

(c) Periodicals, Newspapers and Newsletters
Biblical Recorder. May–June 1932.
Broadsheet. 1960–68.
Challenge Weekly. 20 November 1965; 23 July 1966; 6 August 1966; 12 October 1968.
Christchurch Press. 2 June 1973.
Craccum. 24 March 1938; 20 April 1959.
CSSM. June, July 1931; April, July 1932; August 1933; April, May, December 1934; May 1936; April 1937; March, June 1939.
ECF Review: Quarterly Journal of the ECF (NZ). 1959–63.
Evangelical Presbyterian. 1955–2007 .
Evening Star. 12 April 1929.
First Church Papakura. Parish Newsletter. 1953–65.
For Ministers Only. 1949–1975.
Forum. 1958–1985.
Graduates' Bulletin. March 1948
IVFEU TSPU circular. April 1939.
Keswick Week. 1958–67.
Latimer Magazine. 1963–65.
Methodist Times. 22 January 1955.
Messenger. May 1944.
Nelson Evening Mail. 19 September 1962.
New Zealand CMS League of Youth (Christchurch Branch), Newsletter. July 1954.
New Zealand CMS News. June 1961.
New Zealand Inter-Varsity News Bulletin. 1936–37.
New Zealand Inter-Varsity Supplement. July 1939.
Otago Daily Times. 13 April 1929; 9 June 1938; November 1965.
Outlook. 1916–67.
Reaper. 1927–29, 1934–35, 1957–59.
Southland Times. February 1943.
St Stephen's Review. 1956–59.
Terminal Magazine of the Inter-Varsity Fellowship of Evangelical Unions. 1931.
Witness. 1958–65.

(d) Leaflets, Pamphlets and Tracts
Assembly Life and Work Committee. New Life Evangelism, n.d.
Blaiklock, E.M. Sanity, Confidence and Scholarship. [Wellington]: [IVF (NZ)], n.d. [c. 1952].
CMS League of Youth [pledge, n.d.].
The Evangelical Churchmen's Fellowship. To Inform, to Inspire and to Witness, n.d.
Gunn, A.G. Why We Say 'No' to an Act of Commitment. Manurewa: Westminster Fellowship, 1965.
Hutchinson, Warner A. 'Thoughts on the Doctrine of Scripture'. NZIVF Christian Codex III (Wellington: IVF(NZ), [1962]).
Introducing the Student Christian Movement. [Wellington]: NZSCM, n.d.
Kirkby, Donald A. Book List: A Guide for the Christian Reader. Manurewa: Westminster Fellowship, 1963.
Laidlaw, R.A. The Reason Why. Auckland: Institute Printing and Publishing Society, n.d.
Miller, J. Graham. What is The Westminster Fellowship? An Explanatory Booklet Concerning

the Origin, Work, Witness of the Westminster Fellowship. Manurewa: Westminster Fellowship, n.d. [c. 1965].

New Zealand Bible Training Institute. *Prospectus*, n.d. [1930s].

New Zealand Presbyterian Bible Class Union. *The New Zealand Presbyterian Bible Class Union: Member's Guide*. Wellington, n.d.

The Presbyterian Church of New Zealand. *The Way to Union. An Explanation of the Results of the Negotiations for Union Between the Congregational, Methodist, and Presbyterian Churches*. 1947.

Small, Dwight H. *Dancing and the Christian*. Reprint of an article from *His* magazine, with an introduction by Arthur G. Gunn. Manurewa: Westminster Fellowship, n.d. [1964].

St Andrew's Presbyterian Church, Palmerston North. *Combined Funds Canvass*. 1956.

St James' Presbyterian Church, Pukekohe. *The Story of the St James' World Missionary Fellowship. A Congregation's Pilgrimage in Faith*. 1967.

Tuakau [Presbyterian] Parish. *The Call to Christian Stewardship*. n.d.

Westminster Fellowship. *'As We See It'. A Study of the Plan for Union*. n.d.

Westminster Fellowship. *Ten Reasons Against the Present Church Union Proposals*. 1965.

B Secondary Sources

1 Books

(a) New Zealand

All Saints' Church, Sumner Centennial. *Parish of Sumner/Redcliffs*. No publisher, n.d.

Ault, H.F. *The Nelson Narrative: The Story of the Church of England in the Diocese of Nelson, New Zealand 1858 to 1958*. Nelson: The Standing Committee of the Diocese of Nelson, 1958.

Berry, Christine. *The New Zealand Student Christian Movement, 1896–1996. A Centennial History*. Christchurch: Student Christian Movement of Aotearoa, 1998.

Bester, R. (ed.). *Harvest of Grace. Essays in Celebration of 150 Years of Mission in the Anglican Diocese of Nelson*. Nelson: Diocese of Nelson, 2010.

Biggs, Don and Lawrie Becroft (eds). *The Ponui Story. Celebrating 75 years of Scripture Union Camping*. Wellington: Scripture Union New Zealand, 2006.

Blamires, E.P. *Youth Movement: The Story of the Rise and Development of the Christian Youth Movement in the Churches of New Zealand – As Seen by a Methodist*. Auckland: Forward Books and Wesley Historical Society, 1952.

Breward, Ian. *Grace and Truth. A History of the Theological Hall, Knox College, Dunedin, 1876–1975*. Dunedin: Theological Education Committee, Presbyterian Church of New Zealand, 1975.

_____. *Religion in New Zealand Society*. [Dunedin]: Presbyterian Historical Society of New Zealand, 1979.

Brown, Colin. *Forty Years On: A History of the National Council of Churches in New Zealand, 1941–1981*. Christchurch: National Council of Churches, 1981.

Centenary, 1857–1957. St John the Evangelist, Woolston. [Christchurch], [Woolston Parish], n.d.

Davidson, A.K. *Christianity in Aotearoa. A History of Church and Society in New Zealand*, 3rd edn. Wellington: Education for Ministry, 2004.

_____. *Pioneers, Protestors and Pluralism. Exploring Presbyterian Identity.* Wellington: Presbyterian Church of New Zealand, 1989.

_____. *Pious Energy: Presbyterian Personalities and Perspectives.* Wellington: Presbyterian Church of New Zealand, 1989.

_____. *Selwyn's Legacy: The College of St. John the Evangelist: Te Waimate and Auckland, 1843–1992.* Auckland: The College of Saint John the Evangelist, 1993.

_____ (ed.). *Living Legacy. A History of the Anglican Diocese of Auckland.* Auckland: Anglican Diocese of Auckland, 2011.

Dickson, John. *History of the Presbyterian Church of New Zealand.* Dunedin: J. Wilkie & Co, 1899.

Donovan, Peter (ed.). *Religions of the New Zealanders.* Palmerston North: Dunmore Press, 1990.

Emilsen, Susan and W. Willam (eds). *Mapping the Landscape. Essays in Australian and New Zealand Christianity. Festschrift in Honour of Professor Ian Breward.* New York: Peter Lang, 2000.

Evans, Robert and Roy McKenzie. *Evangelical Revivals in New Zealand. A History of Evangelical Revivals in New Zealand, and an Outline of Some Basic Principles of Revivals.* Paihia: Colcom Press, 1999.

Gilling, Bryan D. (ed.). *'Be Ye Separate': Fundamentalism and the New Zealand Experience.* Waikato Studies in Religion III. Hamilton: University of Waikato and Colcom Press, 1992.

Gosling, Les. *To Keep the Faith: The Westminster Fellowship's Forty Years.* Auckland: Westminster Fellowship, 1990.

Habets, Myk and Tim Meadowcroft (eds). *Gospel, Truth and Interpretation: Evangelical Identity in Aotearoa New Zealand.* Auckland: Archer Press, 2011.

Haworth, Geoffrey M.R. *Marching as to War? The Anglican Church in New Zealand During World War II.* Christchurch. Wily Publications, 2008.

Hunter, Ian. *Robert Laidlaw: Man for our Time.* Auckland: Castle Publishing, 1999.

Hutchinson, W. and C. Wilson. *Let the People Rejoice. The Story of the Billy Graham Crusades in New Zealand.* Wellington: Crusader Bookroom Society, 1959.

Jackson, H.R. *Churches and People in Australia and New Zealand, 1860–1930.* Wellington: Allen and Unwin, 1987.

Lancaster, Neil G. *Our Hope for Years to Come: St Martin's Parish Spreydon 1909–1984* [Christchurch: Parish of Spreydon, 1984].

Lewis, Marilyn. *Forrest Hill Presbyterian. 40 Years of Memories.* Auckland: Forrest Hill Presbyterian Church, 2002.

Lineham, Peter J. *No Ordinary Union. The Story of the Scripture Union, Children's Special Service Mission and Crusader Movement of New Zealand 1880–1980.* Wellington: Scripture Union in New Zealand, 1980.

_____. *There We Found Brethren: A History of Assemblies of Brethren in New Zealand.* Palmerston North: Gospel Publishing House, 1977.

McEldowney, Dennis (ed.). *Presbyterians in Aotearoa*. Wellington: the Presbyterian Church of New Zealand, 1990.

McKean, John. *The Church in a Special Colony. A History of the Presbyterian Synod of Otago and Southland, 1866-1991*. Dunedin: Synod of Otago and Southland, Presbyterian Church of Aotearoa New Zealand, 1994.

Matheson, Peter. *From Scotland with Aroha. Exploring our Presbyterian Heritage*. Wellington: Presbyterian Church of New Zealand, 1988.

[Miller, J.G., R.S. and T.F.]. *Thomas Miller, M.A.: A Family Tribute by His Sons*. Christchurch: Presbyterian Bookroom, 1949.

Orange, Claudia (ed.). *The Dictionary of New Zealand Biography* 3 (1996), 4 (1998), 5 (2000): Auckland University Press; Wellington: Department of Internal Affairs, 1998.

Parish of Shirley, 1912-1987. [Christchurch]: [Shirley Anglican Parish], n.d. [1987].

Pratt, Douglas (ed.). *'Rescue the Perishing': Comparative Perspectives on Evangelism and Revivalism*. Auckland: College Communications, 1989.

Rae, Simon. *Towards a New Century. St. Stephen's - Leith Valley 1971-1996*. Dunedin: St Stephen's Presbyterian Church, 1996.

Reid Martin, Margaret et al., *A Deep Flowing Stream: New Zealand Women and their Churches, 1893-1993*. Auckland: Christian Research Association, 1993.

Salmond, J.D. *By Love Serve. The Story of the Deaconesses of the Presbyterian Church of New Zealand*. Christchurch: Presbyterian Bookroom, 1962.

Sanders, J. Oswald. *Expanding Horizons: The Jubilee History of the New Zealand Bible Training Institute*. Auckland: Institute Press, 1971.

Scott, Harold. *A Pioneering Ministry: Presbyterian Home Missionaries in New Zealand, 1862-1964*. Wellington: Presbyterian Church of New Zealand, 1983.

Shaw, Trevor. *E. M. Blaiklock: A Christian Scholar*. London: Hodder Stoughton, 1986.

Stenhouse, John and Jane Thomson (eds). *Building God's Own Country: Historical Essays on Religions in New Zealand*. University of Otago Press, Dunedin, 2004.

St Matthew's Anglican Church Dunedin. n.d.

Sutherland, Martin. *Conflict & Connection: Baptist Identity in New Zealand*. Auckland: Archer Press, 2011.

Thomson, John S. *Light in Darkness. The Story of Andrew M. Johnston 'The Blind Evangelist'*. Gore: Gore Publishing Co, 1975.

Troughton, Geoffrey. *New Zealand Jesus. Social and Religious Transformations of an Image. 1890-1940*. Bern: Peter Lang, 2011.

Turner, Harold. *The Laughter of Providence. Stories from a Life on the Margins*. Auckland: Deep Sight Trust, 2001.

[Untitled] St. Martin's Bible Class Reunion Booklet. [Christchurch, 1992].

(b) Other

Barclay, O. *Evangelicalism in Britain, 1935-1990*. Leicester: IVP, 1997.

Bebbington, D.W. *Evangelicalism in*

Modern Britain: A History from the 1730s to the 1980s. London: Unwin Hyman, 1989.

———. The Dominance of Evangelicalism: The Age of Spurgeon and Moody. Nottingham: InterVarsity, 2005. Vol. 3 (1840s–1890s) of the IVP's 'A History of Evangelicalism' series, David W. Bebbington and Mark A. Noll (eds).

Boyd, Robin. The Witness of the Student Christian Movement: 'Church Ahead of Church'. Hindmarsh, SA: ATF Press, 2007.

Breward, Ian. A History of the Churches of Australasia. Oxford: Oxford University Press, 2001.

Brown, Callum G. The Death of Christian Britain: Understanding Secularisation, 1800–2000. London & New York: Routledge, 2001.

Bruce, F.F. In Retrospect: Remembrance of Things Past. London: Pickering and Inglis, 1980.

Bruce, Steve. Firm in the Faith. Brookfield, Vermont: Gower, 1984.

Calver, Clive and Rob Warner. Together We Stand. London: Hodder and Stoughton, 1996.

Cameron, Nigel M. de S., David F. Wright, David C. Lachman, and Donald E. Meek (eds). Dictionary of Scottish Church History and Theology. Edinburgh: T&T Clark, 1993.

Carpenter, Joel. Revive Us Again: The Reawakening of American Fundamentalism. Oxford: Oxford University Press, 1992.

Catherwood, Christopher. Five Evangelical Leaders: John Stott, Martyn Lloyd-Jones, Francis Schaeffer, James I. Packer, Billy Graham. Wheaton: Harold Shaw Publishers, 1985.

Coggan, F. D. (ed.). Christ and the Colleges: A History of the Inter-Varsity Fellowship of Evangelical Unions. London: IVF, 1934.

Coleman, Richard J. Issues of Theological Conflict: Evangelicals and Liberals. Grand Rapids: Eerdmans, 1972.

Crockford's Clerical Dictionary. A Reference Book of the Established Church of England and of the Other Churches in Communion with the See of Canterbury, 1949–50. London: Oxford University Press, 1950.

Dayton, Donald W. and Robert K. Johnston (eds). The Variety of American Evangelicalism. Knoxville: University of Tennessee, 1991.

Dickey, Brian (ed.). Australian Evangelical Dictionary of Biography. NSW: Evangelical History Association, 1994.

Dudley-Smith, Timothy. John Stott: A Global Ministry. Leicester: IVP, 2001.

Ellingsen, Mark. The Evangelical Movement: Growth, Impact, Controversy, Dialog [sic]. Minneapolis: Augsburg Publishing House, 1988.

Emilsen, Susan and W. Willam (eds). Mapping the Landscape. Essays in Australian and New Zealand Christianity. Festschrift in Honour of Professor Ian Breward. New York: Peter Lang, 2000.

Gordon, James M. Evangelical Spirituality: From the Wesleys to John Stott. London: SPCK, 1991.

Graham, Billy. Just as I Am: The Autobiography of Billy Graham. London: Harper Collins, 1998.

Harris, Harriet A. Fundamentalism and Evangelicals. Oxford: Clarendon Press, 1998.

Hart, D.G. *Deconstructing Evangelicalism: Conservative Protestantism in the Age of Billy Graham*. Grand Rapids: Baker Academic, 2004.

Hutchinson, Mark and Stuart Piggin (eds). *Reviving Australia: Essays on the History and Experience of Revival and Revivalism in Australian Christianity*. NSW: Centre for the Study of Australian Christianity, 1994.

Hunt, K. and G. *For Christ and the University: The Story of the InterVarsity Christian Fellowship of the U.S.A., 1940-1990*. Downers Grove: IVP, 1991.

Hutchinson, Mark. *Iron in our Blood: A History of the Presbyterian Church in New South Wales, 1788-2001*. Sydney: Ferguson Publications and the Centre for the Study of Australian Christianity, 2001.

Johnson, D. *Contending for Faith: A History of the Evangelical Movement in the Universities and Colleges*. Leicester: IVP, 1979.

Judd, Stephen and Kenneth Cable. *Sydney Anglicans: A History of the Diocese*. Sydney: Anglican Information Office, 1987.

Kelley, Dean M. *Why Conservative Churches are Growing: A Study in Sociology of Religion*. New York: Harper & Row, 1972.

King, John C. (ed.). *Evangelicals Today*. Guildford and London: Lutterworth Press, 1973.

Laird, Dr John. *No Mere Chance*. London: Hodder and Stoughton, 1987.

Lewis, Donald M. *Christianity Reborn: The Global Expansion of Evangelicalism in the Twentieth Century*. Grand Rapids: Eerdmans, 2004.

Loane, Marcus L. *Archbishop Mowll: The Biography of Howard West Kilvinton Mowll Archbishop of Australia and Primate of Australia*. London: Hodder and Stoughton, 1960.

MacLeod, A. Donald. *C. Stacey Woods and the Evangelical Rediscovery of the University*. Downers Grove: IVP, 2007.

Manwaring, Randle. *From Controversy to Co-existence: Evangelicals in the Church of England, 1914-1980*. Cambridge: Cambridge University Press, 1985.

Malcolm, Charles W. *Twelve Hours in the Day: The Life and Work of the Rev. Lionel B. Fletcher D.D.* London and Edinburgh: Marshall, Morgan and Scott, 1956.

Marsden, G. *Evangelicalism and Modern America*. Grand Rapids: Eerdmans, 1984.

Marsden, George M. *Understanding Fundamentalism and Evangelicalism*. Grand Rapids: Eerdmans, 1991.

McGrath, Alister E. *A Passion for Truth: The Intellectual Coherence of Evangelicalism*. Leicester: Apollos, 1996.

_____. *To Know and Serve God: A Biography of James I. Packer*. London: Hodder & Stoughton, 1997.

[Miller, Margaret J.]. *Robert Strang Miller: A Tribute by his Family*. Victoria, Australia: privately published, 1983.

Nash, Ronald H. (ed.). *Evangelical Renewal in the Mainline Churches*. Westchester, Illinois: Crossway Books, 1987.

Noll, Mark A. *The Princeton Theology 1812-1921: Scripture, Science, and Theological Method from Archibald Alexander to Benjamin Breckinridge Warfield*. Grand Rapids: Baker Book House, 1983.

_____. *The Rise of Evangelicalism: The Age of Edwards, Whitefield and the Wesleys*. Downers Grove and Leicester: IVP, 2004. Vol. 1 (1730s–1790s) of the IVP series 'A History of Evangelicalism', David W. Bebbington and Mark A. Noll (eds).

Noll, Mark A., David W. Bebbington, and George A. Rawlyk (eds). *Evangelicalism: Comparative Studies of Popular Protestantism in North America, the British Isles and Beyond, 1700–1990*. Oxford: Oxford University Press, 1994.

Orr, J. Edwin. *All Your Need: 10,000 Miles of Miracle Through Australia and New Zealand*. London: Marshall Morgan and Scott, 1936.

Piggin, Stuart. *Evangelical Christianity in Australia: Spirit, Word and World*. Melbourne: Oxford University Press, 1996.

Poole-Connor, E.J. *Evangelicalism in England*. London: Messrs Hutchinson & Co, 1965.

Pollock, J.C. *The Keswick Story. The Authorised History of the Keswick Convention*. London: Hodder and Stoughton, 1964.

Randall, Ian M. *Educating Evangelicalism. The Origins, Development and Impact of London Bible College*. Carlisle: Paternoster Pres, 2000.

_____. *Evangelical Experiences: A Study in the Spirituality of English Evangelicalism, 1918–1939*. Carlisle: Paternoster Press, 1999.

_____. *What a Friend We Have in Jesus: The Evangelical Tradition*. Maryknoll, NY: Orbis, 2005.

Rawlyk, George A. (ed.). *Aspects of the Canadian Evangelical Experience*. Montreal: McGill-Queens University Press, 1997.

Rawlyk, George A. and Noll, Mark A. (eds). *Amazing Grace. Evangelicalism in Australia, Britain, Canada, and the United States*. Grand Rapids, Michigan: Baker, 1993.

Rosell, Garth (ed.). *The Evangelical Landscape: Essays on the American Evangelical Tradition*. Grand Rapids: Baker, 1996.

Stackhouse, John G., Jnr. *Canadian Evangelicalism in the Twentieth Century: An Introduction to its Character*. Toronto: University of Toronto Press, 1993.

Stenhouse, John and G.A. Wood (ed.). *Christianity, Modernity and Culture. New Perspectives on New Zealand History*. Adelaide: Australian Theological Forum, 2005.

Stone, Jon R. *On the Boundaries of American Evangelicalism*. New York: St. Martin's Press, 1997.

Stonehouse, Ned B. *J. Gresham Machen: A Biographical Memoir*. Edinburgh: Banner of Truth, 1987.

Sullivan, Martin. *Watch How You Go*. London: Hodder & Stoughton, 1975.

Symondson, Anthony (ed.). *The Victorian Crisis of Faith*. London: SPCK and Victorian Society, 1970.

Sweeney, Douglas A. *The American Evangelical Story: A History of the Movement*. Grand Rapids: Baker Academic, 2005.

Tatlow, Tissington. *The Story of the Student Christian Movement of Great Britain and Ireland*. London: SCM, 1933.

Thomas, C.R. (ed.). *Evangelism and the Reformed Faith, and Other Essays Commemorating the Ministry of J. Graham Miller*. Christian Education Committee of the Presbyterian Church of Australia, 1980.

Tidball, Derek. *Who are the Evangelicals? Tracing the Roots of Modern Movements*. London: Marshall Pickering, 1994.

Warner, Rob. *Reinventing English Evangelicalism, 1966–2001: A Theological and Sociological Study.* Milton Keynes: Paternoster, 2007.

Wolffe, John. *The Expansion of Evangelicalism: The Age of Wilberforce, More, Chalmers and Finney.* Nottingham: IVP, 2006. vol. 2 (1790s–1840s) of the IVP series 'A History of Evangelicalism', David W. Bebbington and Mark A. Noll (eds).

2 Articles

(a) New Zealand

Breward, Ian. 'Religion and New Zealand Society'. *New Zealand Journal of History* 13, 2 (1979): 138–48.

Brown, Colin. 'Christianity: Mainline Denominations to the 1960s', in Peter Donovan (ed.). *Religions of the New Zealanders.* Palmerston North: Dunmore Press, 2nd edn, 1996: 58–74.

Carson, R.A. 'Some Reflections on the Life of W. A. Orange'. *Latimer* 111 (August 1992): 19–22.

Davidson, Allan K. 'A Protesting Presbyterian: The Reverend P.B. Fraser and New Zealand Presbyterianism, 1892–1940'. *Journal of Religious History* 14, 2 (December 1986): 193–217.

Gilling, Bryan D. '"Almost Persuaded Now to Believe": Gospel Songs in New Zealand Evangelical Theology and Practice'. *Journal of Religious History* 19, 1 (June 1995): 92–110.

_____. 'Back to the Simplicities of Religion: The 1959 Billy Graham Crusade in New Zealand and its Precursors'. *The Journal of Religious History* 17, 2 (December 1992): 222–34.

Jackson, Hugh. 'Churchgoing in Nineteenth-Century New Zealand'. *New Zealand Journal of History* 17, 1 (April 1983): 43–59.

Lange, Stuart. 'The Role of the Evangelical Unions and Inter-Varsity Fellowship in Defining Evangelical Identity in Mid-Twentieth Century New Zealand', in Myk Habets and Tim Meadowcroft (eds). *Gospel, Truth and Interpretation: Evangelical Identity in Aotearoa New Zealand.* Auckland: Archer Press, 2011.

_____. 'Spirit and Reason: Canon Orange and Professor Blaiklock as Contrasting Exemplars of Evangelical Identity in Mid-Twentieth Century New Zealand', in Myk Habets and Tim Meadowcroft (eds). *Gospel, Truth and Interpretation: Evangelical Identity in Aotearoa New Zealand.* Auckland: Archer Press, 2011.

_____. 'Westminster Fellowship Evangelicals and the History of Presbyterianism in New Zealand', in Geoffrey Troughton and Hugh Morrison (eds). *The Spirit of the Past: Essays on Christianity in New Zealand History.* Wellington: Victoria University Press, 2011.

Lineham, Peter J. 'Finding a Space for Evangelicalism: Evangelical Youth Movements in New Zealand', in W.J. Shiels and Diana Wood (eds). *Voluntary Religion.* Oxford: Basil Blackwell, 1986: 477–94.

Meadowcroft, John. 'Roger Thompson: An Appreciation'. *Latimer Focus* 10 (March 2003): 9–10.

Oliver, W.H. 'Christianity among the New Zealanders.' *Landfall* 20 (1966): 4–20.

Pfankuch, L.E. 'The Reverend W.A. Orange, Vicar of Sumner 1930–

1945', in *All Saints Church, Sumner Centennial. Parish of Sumner/Redcliffs*. No publisher: n.d.

Simpson, J.M.R. 'Joseph W. Kemp: Prime Interpreter of American Fundamentalism in New Zealand in the 1920s', in Douglas Pratt (ed.). *'Rescue the Perishing': Comparative Perspectives on Evangelism and Revivalism,* Waikato Studies in Religion I. Auckland: College Communications, 1989: 23–42.

Stenhouse, John. '"The Wretched Gorilla Damnification of Humanity": The "Battle" between Science and Religion over Evolution in Nineteenth-Century New Zealand'. *New Zealand Journal of History* 18 (1984): 143–62.

Stoop, Graham C. 'Continuity and Change: Reflections on the Theological History of the Bible College of New Zealand'. *Reaper* 74, 3 (1992): 16–18.

Veitch, James. 'A Controversy Revisited: 1966–1970 and All That!' *Forum*, 37, 3 (April 1984): 3–8.

(b) Other

Bebbington, D.W. 'Evangelical Christianity and Romanticism'. *Crux* XXVI, 1 (1990): 9–15.

———. 'Evangelicalism in its Settings: The British and American Movements Since 1940', in Mark A. Noll, David W. Bebbington and George A. Rawlyk (eds). *Evangelicalism: Comparative Studies of Popular Protestantism in North America, the British Isles and Beyond, 1700–1990*. Oxford: Oxford University Press, 1994: 365–88.

———. 'Evangelicalism in Modern Scotland'. *Scottish Bulletin of Evangelical Theology* 9 (1991): 4–12.

———. 'Under the Southern Cross: Connecting North and South in Evangelical Scholarship'. *Lucas: An Evangelical History Review* 23/24 (June/December 1997–78): 121–40.

Dickey, Brian. 'Christianity in Australia: Does Being An Evangelical Matter?' *Lucas: An Evangelical History Review* 17 (June 1994): 5–18.

Goodhew, David. 'The Rise of the Cambridge Inter-Collegiate Christian Union, 1910–1970'. *Journal of Religious History* 54, 1 (January 2003): 62–88.

Hilliard, David. 'The Religious Crisis of the 1960s: The Experience of the Australian Churches'. *Journal of Religious History* 21, 2 (June 1967): 209–27.

Holmes, Stephen R. 'British (and European) Evangelical Theologies', in Timothy Larsen and Daniel J. Treier (eds). *The Cambridge Companion to Evangelical Theology*. Cambridge: Cambridge University Press, 2007: 241–58.

Hutchinson, Mark. 'Professing History II: An Interview with Professor Edwin Judge, 12 September 1990'. *Lucas: An Evangelical History Review* 11 (April 1991): 29–41.

———. 'Professing History III: An Interview with Professor Bruce Harris, 27 October 1990'. *Lucas: An Evangelical History Review* 10 (December 1990): 27–34.

———. 'Professing History: An Interview with Rev. Professor Ian Breward, 10 July 1991'. *Lucas: An Evangelical History Review* 12 (December 1991): 54–71.

Lange, Stuart. 'Orange Pips and the Evangelical Churchmen's Fellowship 1945–1972'. *Churchman* 125, 3 (2011): 201–14.

Larsen, Timothy. 'Defining and Locating Evangelicalism', in Timothy Larsen and Daniel J. Treier (eds). *The Cambridge Companion to Evangelical Theology.* Cambridge: Cambridge University Press, 2007: 1-14.

Lawton, Bill. 'The Winter of our Days: The Anglican Diocese of Sydney, 1950-1960.' *Lucas: An Evangelical History Review* (July 1990): 11-32.

Marsden, George. 'Fundamentalism as an American Phenomenon: A Comparison with English Evangelicalism.' *Church History* 46 (June 1977): 215-32.

Noll, Mark A. 'Evangelicalism at its Best,' in Mark A. Noll and Ronald H. Thiemann. *Where Shall my Wond'ring Soul Begin? The Landscape of Evangelical Piety and Thought.* Grand Rapids: Eerdmans, 2000: 1-27.

Numbers, Ronald L. and John Stenhouse. 'Antievolutionism in the Antipodes: From Protesting Evolution to Promoting Creationism in New Zealand.' *British Journal for the History of Science* 33 (September 2000): 335-50.

Packer, J.I. '"Keswick" and the Reformed Doctrine of Sanctification.' *Evangelical Quarterly* XXVII, 3 (July 1955): 153-67.

Parker, D. 'Evangelicalism in Australia According to Stuart Piggin: A Response'. *Lucas: An Evangelical History Review* 21/2 (June/December 1996): 115-22.

Piggin, Stuart. 'Billy Graham in Australia, 1959. Was it Revival?' *Lucas: An Evangelical History Review* 6 (October 1989): 2-33.

_____. 'Introduction: The Reflex Impact of Missions on Australian Christianity', in Mark Hutchinson and Geoff Treloar (eds). *This Gospel Shall be Preached: Essays on the Australian Contribution to World Mission.* Sydney: Centre for the Study of Australian Christianity, 1998: 7-26.

_____. 'The American and British Contributions to Evangelicalism in Australia,' in M.A. Noll, G.A. Rawlyk and D.W. Bebbington (eds). *Evangelicalism: Comparative Studies of Popular Protestantism in North America, the British Isles and Beyond, 1700-1990.* Oxford: Oxford University Press, 1994.

Sandeen, E.R. 'The Princeton Theology. One Source of Biblical Literalism in American Protestantism'. *Church History* XXXI, 3 (September 1962), 307-32.

Sewell, Keith W. 'Christian Historiographical Methodology: Some Foundational Considerations'. *Lucas: An Evangelical History Review* 15 (June 1993): 1-13.

Smith, Timothy L. 'The Evangelical Kaleidoscope and the Call to Christian Unity'. *Christian Scholar's Review* 15, 2 (1986): 125-40.

Stackhouse, John G., Jnr., 'The Emergence of a Fellowship: Canadian Evangelicalism in the Twentieth Century'. *Church History* 60 (June 1991): 247-62.

_____. 'The Historiography of Canadian Evangelicalism: A Time to Reflect.' *Church History* 64, 4 (December 1995): 627-34.

Sweeney, D.A. 'The Essential Evangelicalism Dialectic: The Historiography of the Early Neo-Evangelical Movement and the Observer-Participant Dilemma'.

Church History 60, 1 (March 1991): 70–84.

Sweet, Leonard I. 'Wise as Serpents, Innocent as Doves: The New Evangelical Historiography'. *Journal of the American Academy of Religion* 56 (1988): 397–416.

Wright, David F. 'James Barr on "Fundamentalism": A Review Article'. *Themelios* 3, 3 (1978).

3 Unpublished Papers, Theses and Dissertations

Carrell, Brian. 'Evangelical Anglicans and the Canterbury Settlement'. A paper presented to the Latimer Fellowship in Christchurch, 13 October 2000.

Clark, Jeremy. 'The Evangelical Ministry of William A. Orange, 1930–1945'. Auckland Consortium of Theological Education BTh Research Essay in Church History, Melbourne College of Divinity, 1995.

Garing, Maureen Nola, 'Four Square for Christ. The Presbyterian Bible Class Movement, 1902–1972: Its Background, its Rise, its Influence and its Decline'. MA thesis, Victoria University of Wellington, 1985.

Gilling, Bryan Dudley. 'Retelling the Old, Old Story: A Study of Six Mass Evangelistic Missions in Twentieth Century New Zealand'. DPhil thesis, University of Waikato, 1990.

Ireton, Douglas E. 'O Lord How Long? A Revival Movement in New Zealand, 1920–1933'. MA thesis, Massey University, 1985.

King, Geoffrey. 'Organising Christian Truth: An Investigation of the Life and Work of John Dickie'. PhD thesis, University of Otago, 1998.

Lineham, Peter J. 'Evangelical Witness at Canterbury University: A History of the EU/CU 1930–1974'. Paper, TSCF archives, 1974.

Marquand, I.G. 'The Presbyterian New Life Movement. A Case Study in Church Growth'. MTh thesis, University of Otago, 1977.

Pound, Geoffrey R. 'Rev. Joseph William Kemp and the Auckland Baptist Tabernacle, 1920–1933'. MA research essay, University of Auckland, 1978.

Rathgen, David G.S. 'The Church in New Zealand 1890–1920, with Special Reference to W.A. Orange'. Joint Board of Theological Studies Licentiate of Theology thesis, 1969.

Rogers, Owen. 'The New Zealand Presbyterian New Life Movement'. University of Otago BD dissertation, 1990.

Simpson, Jane Mary Ramsay. 'Joseph W. Kemp and the Impact of American Fundamentalism in New Zealand'. BA (Hons) directed study, University of Waikato, 1987.

Veitch, James. 'Nothing Will Ever be the Same Again! New Zealand Presbyterians in Conflict September 1965–November 1967'. Australian College of Theology DTh thesis, 1999.

Index

Adams, Graham 182
Addison, Mavis 50
Aiken, David 59, 68, 82, 101, 103, 167
All Saints' (Nelson) 98, 158, 160
Allan, John 79
Allan, Patricia (née Robinson) 94
Allen, D.R. 189
Allen, Roland 125, 240 n.75
Alexander hymns 19, 46
American Council of Christian Churches 13, 118
Andersen, W.A. 136
Andrews, Tony 156
Anglican Church: Ryle's views 63; Sydney 16, 49, 63–64, 65, 66, 69, 76, 97, 98, 157, 158, 159, 160, 164, 209; *see also* Anglo-Catholicism
Anglican Church in New Zealand and evangelicals: to 1945 17, 57–71; 1945–55 87–106; 1956–65 150–75; since 1965 213, 214; Auckland Diocese 96, 163–65, 175, 207, 213; Book of Common Prayer 63, 65, 82, 166, 167, 172, 174; and Brethren 60, 61, 62, 65, 209; and charismatic renewal movement 214; Christchurch Diocese 89–95, 98–99, 127, 143, 150–57, 159, 165, 173, 175, 206, 207, 209, 210; and Church Missionary Society 95–97; and church union 194, 200; and Crusader movement 54–55; different strands and emphases 208; and Evangelical Ministers' Fellowship 145, 146; and Evangelical Unions 44, 48–49, 50; generational differences 170–75; 208; High Church 17, 61, 63, 66, 93, 101, 162, 163, 164, 168, 200; intercommunion 172–73, 200; interdenominationalism 32, 75–76, 173; and Inter-Varsity Fellowship 75, 76; Low Church 17, 65, 66, 69, 70, 82, 92, 98, 102, 110, 158, 159, 160, 162, 209; Nelson Diocese 17, 30, 59, 65, 66, 68, 69–71, 76, 96, 97–99, 103–04, 127, 150, 157–60, 164, 165, 175, 207, 209, 213; St Matthews (Dunedin) 162–63, 165, 175, 207; Thirty-Nine Articles 63, 65, 73, 101–02, 167; and Tyndale Fellowship 147; Wellington Diocese 96, 99–101, 104, 160–62, 207; *see also* College House; Evangelical Churchmen's Fellowship; St John's College; and names of individual churches and people, particularly Orange and Thompson.
Anglican Evangelical Fellowship 76, 106
Anglo-Catholicism 14, 62, 65, 66, 69, 82, 92, 105, 162, 194, 236 n.107
anti-intellectualism 13, 28, 53, 80, 132, 138, 141, 207
Ardmore Teachers' College 178, 179–80
Christian Union 126, 136, 180
Arminianism 115
Armstrong, George W. 147
Atkinson, Basil 75
Auckland University (College) Evangelical Union (AUEU, AUCEU) 46, 49–50, 53, 72, 129–30, 135–36, 142, 164
Australia (and Australians, Sydney, Melbourne) 16, 17, 34, 42, 49, 54, 59, 6364, 65, 66, 69, 70, 72, 76, 81, 97, 98,

Index **289**

101, 103, 109, 129, 135, 136, 146, 147, 157, 158, 159, 160, 163, 167, 181, 182, 184, 198, 209, 241 n.6, 242 n.82, 262 n.121, 264 n.162; *see also* Moore College and Ridley College

Baptist churches and people 19, 32, 33, 44, 49, 50, 60, 75, 76, 119, 127, 129, 130, 136, 143, 145, 146, 164, 209, 213, 214
Baptist College 147
Barber, Laurie 147
Barrett, Bob 151
Barrett, Dennis 159
Barth, Karl 20, 33, 47, 77, 138, 268 n.236
Barton, Frazer 122
Bates, J.M. 87, 109
Beattie, Bruce 94, 95, 159
Bebbington, David 12, 14
Becroft, Colin 50, 55, 103, 127, 137, 142, 164
Betteridge, Maurice 59, 68, 94, 97, 105, 146, 153, 154, 162–63, 167, 188
Bible: authority and primacy 12, 13, 27–28, 37, 39, 44, 45, 51, 62, 74, 80, 101, 109, 113, 114, 118, 119, 121, 132, 139, 165, 166, 167, 168, 173; critical views 18, 19, 28, 39, 74, 80, 109; and Evangelical Unions 45, 46, 48, 51, 52; inerrancy or infallibility 13, 14, 15, 27, 44, 45, 53, 72, 73, 79, 81, 91, 105, 113, 114, 115; Orange's teaching 57, 58–59, 61, 62, 65, 68, 95, 206; personal and family reading 18, 26, 31, 196; study 31, 43, 46, 48, 73, 74, 96, 157, 158, 162, 163, 178–79, 183, 193, 196, 208; Thompson's teaching 89–90; translations 194
Bible Class: and Crusader movement 54, 57; William Orange's BC (Christchurch) 54, 57, 58, 60, 65, 67, 68, 88, 95, 96, 141–42, 157, 164, 206; and Graham Lamont (Spreydon) 152; Thomas Miller's BC (Dunedin) 29–30; and St Matthew's Dunedin 162–63; Roger Thompson's BC (Spreydon) 89–90, 92, 94, 95, 159, 242 n.82; and Harry Thomson's BC (Spreydon) 96; in Nelson Diocese 70, 157–58; and South Auckland evangelical Presbyterians 179, 183, 187, 188; *see also* Presbyterian Bible Class Movement
Bible Leagues 102
Bible Presbyterian Church 118

Bible Society of Otago and Southland 30, 162
Bible Training Institute (BTI) *see* New Zealand Bible Training Institute.
Biblical Recorder 26
biblicism 12, 16, 27
Billy Graham Crusades 14, 115, 123, 164; New Zealand (1959) 16, 21, 94, 129, 144, 155–56, 159, 161, 164, 165, 167, 179–80, 183, 187, 188, 190, 191, 209, 210
Birch, A.E. 44
Bissett, John 19, 33, 34, 39, 40, 78
Black, A.S. (Alex) 130, 254 n.37
Blaikie, Robert 189, 263 n.127
Blaiklock, E.M. 33–34, 36, 43, 44, 49, 52, 53, 59, 77, 129, 133–34, 142, 143, 147, 148, 149, 153, 182, 189, 192, 208, 210
Boettner, Loraine 80, 192
Bounds, E.M. 63
Bourne, I.G. (Ian) 64, 100, 105, 160, 174
Boys' Brigade 179
Brethren *see* Open Brethren.
Bretton, W.F. (Bill) 99, 157–58, 160, 165; protégés 99–101, 104, 159
Breward, Ian 147–48
Brinsley, John 187–88, 193, 197, 199
Brown, Cree 42, 43, 44, 78, 210
Bruce, F.F. 131, 132, 147
Brunner, Emil 47, 138
BTI *see* New Zealand Bible Training Institute.
Buist, Malcolm 137, 139–40
Burgess, Les 95, 168
Burt, David 55
Bythell, Frank 97
Bythell, Noel 159

Cairns, Ian 147
Calvin and Calvinism 20, 27, 29, 33, 64, 80, 115, 116, 123, 177, 181, 182, 190, 192, 193–94
Cambridge Conventions 33
Cambridge Inter-Collegiate Christian Union (CICCU) 14, 15, 42, 49, 66, 73, 74, 75, 128
Campbell, Ken 183
Campbell, Sefton 185, 262 n.79
Canterbury University (College) Evangelical Union (CUEU, CUCEU) 46, 48–49, 127–28, 135, 137, 140, 147

Carlisle, D.B. Forde 118, 120
Carrell, Brian 94, 106, 153, 163, 171, 172, 174
Carson, R.A. (Dick) 59, 82, 154
Cashmere Evangelical Trust 141, 142
Challenge Weekly 182
Chamberlin, Fred and Gertrude 55
Champion, Eric 69
charismatic (renewal) movement 214
Children's Special Service Mission (CSSM) 55, 56, 57, 60, 76, 93, 95, 127, 169, 173, 190
China Inland Mission (CIM) 16, 17, 30, 63, 157, 185, 209
Christian Beacon 118
Christian Century 167
Christian Endeavour (CE) 18, 26, 27, 29, 30, 31–32, 93, 107, 145, 179, 180, 187, 188, 225 n.71
Christian Graduates Fellowship (CGF) 146–47
Christian Business Men's Association 185
Christian Union(s) 43, 45, 126
Christianity Today 167, 174, 207
Church Missionary Society (CMS) 17, 59, 69, 94, 142, 150, 157, 159, 161, 163; and Anglican evangelical expansion 95–97, 104; and Evangelical Churchmen's Fellowship 169; League of Youth 96, 97, 100, 151, 156–57, 158; Spring Schools 95, 96, 100, 103, 157, 162
Church of Christ (Life and Advent) 32, 49, 75, 76
Church of England *see* Anglican Church
Church of England Newspaper 167, 171
church union 27, 30, 38–39, 110–12, 117, 102, 123, 153, 167, 171, 172, 173–74, 187, 188, 214–15; and Westminster Fellowship 174, 192, 194, 196, 199–200, 201, 202, 203, 205; *see also* ecumenical movement
Church Union Committee 182, 199
Church Worship Society 112
Churchman 167
Clark, Colin 94
Clark, Dallas 191
Clark, Gerald 94, 154
Clark, Stephen (Steve) 55, 190
Clarke, R. 193
Cocker, Cliff 50, 56, 76–77, 137, 143, 239 n.44
Cold War 14, 87, 88, 144
Cole, Alan 128

College House 68, 78, 82–83, 88, 98, 99, 100, 104–06, 127, 153
confessionalism (Reformed) 20, 37, 40
Congregational(ist) people and churches 19, 32, 34, 49, 109, 137, 145
Connell, Pat 183
Contender 121, 198
conversion(s) 12, 20, 26, 62, 64, 90, 98, 135, 136, 151, 152, 156, 164, 179, 186, 187, 190, 206
Coulthard, R.E. (Ted) 153, 154
Cox, Bernard 94, 101, 159
Cross, Jim 127
Crusader Council 72, 143
Crusader movement 54–56, 106, 111, 115, 143, 145, 151; Auckland 164, 179, 186; and Bretton 99; camps 54–55, 60, 93, 127, 287; and Evangelical Churchmen's Fellowship 169; and Evangelical Unions 54, 55, 57, 126, 127, 130, 147; influence on future evangelical ministers 54–55, 67, 68, 88, 93, 96, 97, 100, 147, 152, 153, 188, 190, 205; interdenominationalism 76, 127, 129, 173, 207; and Laird 49, 56; lead by youth 156; and Thomas Miller 30; and Tyndale House 141, 142; and Scripture Union 233 n.109
Curson-Siggers, W. 162

dances and dancing 20, 29, 30, 31, 46, 67, 89, 92, 95, 153, 158, 160, 167, 180–81, 193
Davie, A.D. (Arch) 189
Davies, I.B. (Ivor) 191
Davies, Wynford 136, 190, 203, 263 n.131
Day, Jean 50
Deaconess College 183
Deane, John 46, 129, 136, 142, 143
Denney, James 37, 80
Dental Nurses' EUs 126
Dickie, John 18, 35, 37–39, 79, 80, 116
Doctrinal Basis (IVF) 44–45, 51–52, 54, 73, 113, 114, 133, 139, 140, 141, 144
Don, B.W. 154
Donnell, A. 44
Douglas, J.D. 197
Duff, Alexander 192
Duncan, George B. 178
Dunn, Cliff 191
Dyason, E.E. 189
Dyer, James 97

Index   291

Eaton, Derek 156
ecumenical movement 30, 118, 120, 121, 143, 167, 194, 195, 197, 199, 201, 202, 214-15; *see also* church union; National Council of Churches; World Council of Churches
Edmiston, Doug 100, 161, 162, 165
Edridge, Peter 94
Elley, R. D. (Don) 125, 136, 191, 196, 264 n.141
Elliott, J Kennedy 18, 27
Elliott, Howard 26
Elliott, Ross 151
empirical rationalism 15
eschatology 15, 193, 196, 224 n.44
Evangelical Alliance(s) 102
Evangelical Alliance of New Zealand 169, 182, 190
Evangelical Belief 73-74, 81
Evangelical Bible League of Otago 30, 44
Evangelical Churchmen's Fellowship (ECF) 101-04, 112, 142, 145, 146, 207, 208, 210; 1956-65 165-70; Auckland 164; Christchurch 153-54; and church union 173, 174; conferences 100, 103-04, 158, 162, 165; Dunedin 162; *E.C.F. Review* 166-68, 171; *Latimer Magazine* 103, 171-72, 211; as lay movement 168-69; Nelson 159; and Thompson 103, 161, 166-67, 168, 171, 172; Wellington 160-62; and wider evangelical nexus 169; younger evangelicals 97, 171, 175
Evangelical Fellowship in the Anglican Communion (EFAC) 170
Evangelical Ministers' Fellowship (EMF) 144-46, 240 n.96
Evangelical Presbyterian 107, 114, 123-24, 125, 186, 192-95, 198, 200, 202, 204-05
Evangelical Quarterly 28, 80
Evangelical Students Fellowship 44, 46
Evangelical Unions, New Zealand: Auckland 164, 179; beginnings 42-46, 210; and Bretton 99; conservatism 51-54, 66, 149; and Crusader movement 54, 55, 57, 126, 127, 130, 147; emphases on reason and evidence 130-35; and fundamentalism 50-54; and Graham Miller 121, 138, 181, 209; and Hume-Moir 157; influence on future evangelical ministers 78-83, 97, 98, 100, 102-03, 104-06, 107, 147-48, 152, 153, 156, 188, 189, 191, 193, 202, 205, 206, 207; interdenominationalism 127, 130, 173, 207; and Inter-Varsity Fellowship 42-43, 44, 72, 74, 76, 131-33; missions 48, 53, 77, 108, 134, 135-37, 147; and Orange 12, 42, 44, 49, 52, 57, 60, 65, 66, 68-69, 75, 76, 77, 88, 127, 137, 208; post-Second World War growth 126-49; and Presbyterian Church 48, 49, 108, 109, 111, 112, 113, 122, 127, 193, 202; regional distinctives 48-50; role in identity of New Zealand evangelicalism 11-12, 27, 42, 50, 54, 56, 67, 70, 83, 104, 149, 204, 206, 207; and Stephenson 69; and Student Christian Movement 43, 44, 45-48, 52, 53, 56, 77-78, 79, 111, 117, 119, 128, 136, 138, 140-41, 202, 207, 210; and Thomas Miller 30, 32, 40, 41, 42, 44, 48, 52, 129, 206; and Thompson 91, 93; and Tyndale House 142; and university chaplains 140-41; *see also* Inter-Varsity Fellowship of Evangelical Unions (New Zealand); and names of individual EUs
evangelicanism: Australia 16, 198, 209; Britain 14-15, 28, 42-43, 50, 51, 52, 56, 62, 63, 75, 88, 102, 144, 167, 170, 174-75, 207, 208-09; Canada 16; definitions 12; origin of term 12; United States 13-14, 15, 28, 50, 52, 88, 143-44, 207, 209
evangelicanism in New Zealand 15, 16-21, 206-11; defining moments 210-11; influential people 210; interdenominationalism 30-36, 75-76, 93, 188, 207, 209-10; since 1965 212-15; *see also* Anglican Church in New Zealand; Inter-Varsity Fellowship of Evangelical Unions (New Zealand); Presbyterian Church of (Aotearoa) New Zealand; and organisational names beginning Evangelical …
evangelism 12, 30, 34-35, 36, 47, 53, 97, 108, 135-37, 158, 184, 194, 196, 208, 236 n.119; *see also* Billy Graham crusades
Everill, R.T. 164
evolution 13, 14, 15, 28, 52, 53, 91, 130, 193, 194, 271 n.183
existentialism 148
expository preaching 26, 29, 32, 52, 55, 58, 62, 63, 68, 89-90, 95-96, 99, 103, 107,

129, 136, 150, 151, 161, 162, 177–78, 181, 182, 197, 206, 214

Fact and Faith Films 130
Far East Broadcasting Company 197
First Church Otago (Dunedin) 25, 26, 40, 43, 48, 113
First Church (Papakura) 176–82, 185, 186
Fitzpatrick, Dennis 182
Fitzpatrick, N.C. (Norrie) 193, 197
Fleming, Ian 41
Fletcher, Lionel 19, 30, 31, 34, 188, 189, 209
Flewellen, J.J. 154
Ford, John 97, 98, 105
Forum 201
Fosdick, H.E. 19, 20, 48
Foulkes, Francis 50, 75
Foulkes, Llewellyn 163
Fountain, K.H. (Howell) 44, 49, 76, 127
Fountain, Russell 60, 127
Fountain, Wyn 55
Fraser, Ian 177
Fraser, P.B. 18, 26, 38, 39, 40, 116, 192, 222 n.64
Free Church 18, 27, 48, 111, 114, 192, 193
Freeland, R. 193
fundamentalism 13, 15, 28, 56, 75, 79, 91, 113, 137, 152, 188, 207; and Evangelical Unions 50–54; '*Fundamentalism' and the Word of God* 131; and separatism 13, 53, 118, 120, 121, 143, 144; and Westminster Fellowship 117–22, 197, 199
Funnell, Harry 60, 72, 94, 103, 154, 155, 167

Gaudin, Bill 94
Geering controversy 120, 174, 175, 204, 213
Geering, Lloyd 79, 80–81, 120, 147, 203
General Assembly *see under* Presbyterian Church of (Aotearoa) New Zealand
Gibb, James 25
Girls' Brigade 179
Girling, Russell 97
Girling, W. 97
Glen, Robert 59, 94, 151, 345
Goodall, Maurice 59, 76, 106, 146, 150–52, 154, 167, 171, 172, 174, 210
Gosling, Les 59, 78, 111, 112, 113, 114, 117, 123, 144, 189–90, 198, 203, 204, 270 n.307

Gowing, E.A. (Eric) 97, 164
Graduates' Fellowship (GF) 73, 144, 145, 146–47
Graham, Billy 13, 14, 121, 131, 161, 169, 193, 207, 209; *see also* Billy Graham Crusades
Graham, John 189
Grant, Donald 43
Grant, Ian 189
Gray, H.B. 18
Gray, J.L. 19, 144
Green, Michael 132, 172
Green, S.S. (Samuel) 188, 193, 203
Greenslade, John 94, 98, 147, 154
Greenwood, Hope 59
Greenwood, Shirley 59
Gregory, Kenneth 97, 98, 162, 165
Greig, Fred 94
Griffith, Thomas 98
Griffiths, Michael 132
Guillebaud, H.E. 74
Guinness, Howard 42, 43, 44, 46, 54, 55, 74, 126, 127–28, 134, 135–36, 147, 209, 210
Gunn, Arthur 125, 174, 184–86, 193–95, 196, 197, 198, 199, 200, 201, 202–03, 204, 210, 262 n.75
Gunn, James (Jim) 184, 189

Hallesby, O. 131
Hamblett, W.A. 48, 162
Hammond, R.B.S. 64
Hammond, T.C. 53, 59, 64, 74, 77, 79, 103, 164, 166
Harries, Evan R. 19, 20, 33, 39, 40, 44, 222 n.80
Harries, E. Rowland 55, 190, 204
Harringay Crusade 14, 164
Harris, Bruce 106, 146, 147, 148
Harris, Neville 183
Harris, Rod 183
Hart, Roland 129
Haskell, Charles 160, 165, 167
Haultain, Donald 69
Hayford, Jack 178
Henry, Carl 13, 118
Herriot, Miss 44
Hewlett, John 151, 158
Hilliard. W.G. 69
Hobbs, Pierce 182
Hodge, A.A. 27, 37, 80, 192
Hornblow, Edgar 164
Horwell, A.D. (Arthur) 125

Index 293

Howie, Hallam 43, 48
Hughes, Bob 97, 98, 159
Hughes, Graham 182
Hull, George 97
Hulme-Moir, Dorothy 157
Hulme-Moir, Frank 99, 157, 158, 160, 165, 167
Hume, F.A. 191
Hunter, S.F. 39, 79, 80
Hunter, Sit Thomas 128
Hutchinson, Warner 133, 137–38, 148, 171, 206

Ilam School of Engineering EU 126
In Understanding Be Men (Hammond) 53, 64, 74, 77, 81, 131
inerrancy or infallibility *see under* Bible
intellectual bases of Christian faith 13, 64, 65, 105, 152, 175, 177, 208; Evangelical Unions/Inter-Varsity Fellowship 52–53, 56, 74, 93, 131, 132, 134, 135, 136–37, 138, 140, 141, 148, 152, 153, 171, 206; Student Christian Movement 48, 132; *see also* anti-intellectualism
International Council of Christian Churches (ICCC) 118–19, 120, 121, 143, 198, 207, 210
Inter-Varsity Fellowship (IVF): Doctrinal Basis 44–45, 51–52, 54, 73, 113, 114, 133, 139, 140, 141, 144; establishment 14; graduate movements 146; and ICCC 118; publications 14, 73–74, 80, 81, 131–32, 133, 193; role in shaping evangelicalism 14–15, 16, 193
Inter-Varsity Fellowship of Evangelical Unions (New Zealand) (IVF(NZ)): British flavour 72–75; conferences 75–76, 77, 93, 100, 121, 137, 141, 142, 144, 164, 165, 181; conservatism 52, 131, 139, 149, 199, 207, 211; different strands and emphases 207–08; emphases on reason and evidence 130–35; establishment 72–73, 210; and Evangelical Churchmen's Fellowship 169; and Evangelical Unions 42–43, 44, 72, 74, 76, 131–33; and evangelical unity 75–77, 207; and ferment of 1960s 148; graduates 146–48; and Graham Miller 121, 138, 181; and Hume-Moir 157; influence on future evangelical ministers 78–83, 107, 205, 206, 207; interdenominationalism 75–77, 127, 129, 130, 173, 205, 207; internal conflict 141–43; and Laird 56; and Methodist Church 141; Nelson Diocese 159; network of people shaping people 137–38; and Orange 58–59, 60, 64, 68–69, 77, 208; post-Second World War growth 126–49, 213; and Presbyterian Church 75, 76, 108, 112, 113, 115, 116, 122, 123, 193; and recruits for Church Missionary Society 97; renamed Tertiary Students' Christian Fellowship 213; and Thomas Miller 30; and St Martin's, Spreydon 93; and Student Christian Movement 44–45, 72, 73, 74, 77–78, 138–41, 202, 211; sub-sections 73; and United States evangelicals 143–44; *see also* Evangelical Unions, New Zealand
Inter-Varsity Missionary Fellowship 73
Irvine, A.G. 18

Jack, David 183
Jansen, Guy 128
Johnson, Douglas 123
Johnson, John 41
Johnston, A.H. 160, 162
Johnston, Andrew 19, 33, 36, 191
Johnston, Douglas 69
Johnston, Kaye 161
Jolly, Isaac 18, 20, 37, 39, 40
Jones, Gwilym 189
Judge, Edwin 59

Keals, Ian 182
Kemp, Ian 50, 55, 129, 137
Kemp, Joseph 19, 35, 129, 189
Kennedy, C.A. 18
Kenward, Russell 49, 189
Keswick hymnbook 46, 90, 226 n.76, 241 n.34
Keswick and Keswick-type conventions 16, 32–34, 93, 108, 159, 164, 165, 178, 181, 193, 194, 198, 209
Keswick movement 14, 17, 145, 169, 191, 207, 226 n.82
Kimberley, O.J. 69, 70
King, Leo 164
Kirkby, D.A. (Donald) 76, 108, 115, 125, 182–84, 193, 196, 197, 198, 204, 209, 210, 244 n.11
Kirkby, E.L. (Ted) 76, 108, 189, 191

Kirkby, R.W. (Rob) 76, 108, 193
Kirkham, Paul 69, 157, 158, 160
Knots Untied (Ryle) 63, 103
Knox College 185, 202; *see also* Theological Hall

Laidlaw, R.A. (Robert) 44, 49, 129, 182, 185, 189, 230 n.20
Laird, John 41, 49, 50, 52, 54, 55, 56, 72, 75, 186, 190, 205, 210
Lamont, Daniel 74
Lamont, Graham 59, 68, 94, 104–05, 106, 137, 151, 152–53, 154, 165, 167, 171, 172, 173, 174, 175
Lange, R.W. (Rex) 188–89
Langrell, Gordon 94
Latimer Foundation (NZ) 170
Latimer House 168, 169, 170
Latimer Magazine 103, 171–72, 211
Latimer Society 147
Laugeson, Don 168, 169
Lay Institute for Evangelism 164
League of Youth (NZCMS) 96, 97, 100, 151, 156–57, 158
Lewis, C.S. 14, 131
Lewis, W.B. (Winifred) 147, 193, 196, 265 n.173
liberal evangelical movement 14, 79, 105
liberalism 21, 65, 67, 91, 134, 143, 211; and Anglican Church 19, 82, 89, 93, 98, 101, 102, 105, 106, 129, 166, 168; Australia 16, 17; Britain 14, 131, 141; EUs/IVF 51, 66, 80, 132; and Presbyterian Church 19, 20, 26–27, 37, 38, 39, 79, 81, 107, 109, 110, 111, 115, 118, 121, 123, 174, 177, 186, 194, 199; and rationalism 134; and Student Christian Movement 42, 43, 79, 139, 207; United States 13
Lincoln College EU 46, 126
Linton, Jim 78
Lloyd-Jones, D. Martyn 109, 131, 190, 196, 199, 200, 268 n.236
Loane, Marcus 64, 76
Loveridge, Barry 159
Lowden, A.H. (Aubrey) 189
Lowe, Bob 127
Luther, Martin 27

MacGregor, I.D. (Ian) 190
MacGregor, Margaret 56
Machell, Bernard 70, 158, 159, 167
Machen, J. Gresham 28, 80, 109, 175, 192

Major, H.D.A. 14
Malcolm, Wilf 128–29, 136, 137–38
Maori Evangelical Fellowship 179
Marriott, Wallace 59, 94, 96, 97, 151, 154, 163
Martin, Vine 55
Massey Agricultural College EU 46, 126, 136, 147, 148
Masters, Roy 182
Mathieson, Don 101, 128
Mathieson, Sally (née Gentry) 101
Matiu, Tia 179
Mauger, Ron 168
McCay, Samuel 128, 148
McCheyne, Robert Murray 63
McEvoy, T.P. 109
McInnes, Garth 182
McIntire, Carl 13, 118–19, 120, 143
McKay, Ken 161
McKenzie, Alistair 182
McKenzie, D.N. 38
McKenzie, G.A. (George) 41, 191
McKenzie, R.G. (Rod) 190
McKenzie, R.H. (Roy) 41, 108, 191
McKinlay, John 183
McLean, G.A. 191
McLellan, Ian 94
McMillan, Cushla (née Brereton) 94
McMillan, Ian 41
McNab, John 110
Meadowcroft, John 59, 90, 94, 97, 98, 154, 163
Melanesian Mission 92
Methodist people and church(es) 26, 75, 76, 110, 141, 145, 147, 201, 213
Methodist Revival Fellowship 169, 174
Methodist Times 141
Mid-New Zealand Convention, Renwick 191
Miller, Flora 81
Miller, Jean 31
Miller, J.G. (Graham) 40, 68–69, 80–81, 106, 176–82, 210; and Australia 198, 209; and ICCC 119, 120, 121, 210; and IVF/EU 48, 72, 76–77, 78, 121, 138, 181, 209; in New Hebrides 108, 119–20, 177, 179, 180; influence on evangelical ministers 188, 191; and New Life Movement 125; and Westminster Fellowship 112–13, 116, 122, 181, 182, 193, 196, 198, 199–200, 202, 203, 204, 210; and women's ordination 260 n.4
Miller, L.B. 141, 142, 142

Index 295

Miller, Marion (née Strang) 26, 29, 31
Miller, R.S. (Rob) 40, 48, 72, 76, 106, 107, 109, 111, 113, 123, 191, 192, 193, 196, 198, 203, 264 n.149
Miller, Thomas 25–27, 72, 80, 120; controversies and dissent 26, 36–40, 110, 111; evangelical legacy 40–41, 112, 117, 178, 205, 210; and Evangelical Unions 12, 30, 32, 40, 41, 42, 44, 48, 52, 129, 206; evangelicalism 12, 27–30, 75, 112, 114, 210; and interdenominational evangelical nexus 30–36
Milligan, W.J. (Bill) 41, 191
Milmine, M.G. (Mervyn) 34, 48, 78, 120, 144, 191, 193, 196
Minn, H.R. 48, 52, 80, 142, 148
Mitchell, J.A. 190
Mitchell, Keith 94
Modern Churchmen's Union 14, 102
modernism 17, 18, 19, 20, 21, 28, 35, 43, 45, 51, 52, 53, 61, 74, 79, 118, 129, 140, 194, 199, 207, 208
Moody, D.L. 18
Moody Bible Institute 130
Moore College (Sydney) 17, 64, 66, 69, 97, 101, 103, 157, 158
Moore, J.D.S. (Jim) 41, 107–08, 191
Moore, W.G. (Bill) 41, 191
Morgan, Campbell 15
Morris, Leon 132, 168
Morris, Les 150, 151, 154, 156
Morton, Archie 49, 72
Moses, Ivan 50, 121, 127, 137
Moses, Ruth 137
Mott, Vera 59, 101
Mowll, Howard 63–64, 69
Munro, A.S. (Alex) 108, 190
Murphy, M. 193
Murray, A.A. 120
Murray, J.S. 201
Murray, Don 182
Murray, Graeme 183

Nash, Walter 99
National Association of Evangelicals (NAE) 13, 121, 143–44, 198, 207
National Church Association in the Church of Scotland 109
National Council of Churches 99, 120, 140–41, 156, 159, 173, 194, 214
Navigators 168, 169
Neale, George 38
Nelson, Ian 94, 159

neo-evangelical movement 13–14, 92, 118, 120, 121, 143, 144, 174
neo-orthodoxy 21, 47, 137, 138, 194
neo-Pentecostalism *see* Pentecostalism
New Life Movement 124–25, 178, 184, 187, 249 n.154
new morality 148, 153, 194
New Zealand Bible Training Institute (NZBTI/BTI) 19, 33, 35–36, 41, 49, 108, 125, 129, 136, 143, 147, 164, 169, 182, 183, 185, 186, 189, 190, 194, 207
Ngaruawahia Easter Conventions 33, 179, 181, 191
Nicholls, Bruce 137
Nicholls, Stan 189
Nicholson, Bob 54, 59, 70, 82, 159
Nicholson, Guy 164–65
Nicholson, W.P. 30, 34–35, 53, 226 n.104–05, 227 n.113
Northern Ireland Evangelical Group 197
North Shore Teachers' College EU 126
Norton, Ed 182
Nurses' Christian Fellowship (NCF) 97, 126

Oatway, Malcolm 101, 158, 159
Ockenga, Harold 13, 143
Oldham, Dale 156
Olsen, A.F. 196–97
Open Air Campaigners (OAC) 164
Open Brethren: and Anglican evangelicals 60, 61, 62, 65, 143, 209; and Baptists 209; biblicist character 213; and Christian Endeavour 32; and conventions 33; and Crusader movement 55, 56; and EUs/IVF 42, 44, 48, 49, 52–53, 127, 129, 130; and Inter-Varsity Fellowship 75, 76, 138; and Tyndale Fellowship 147; and Tyndale House 141
Orange Pips 57, 59, 63, 64, 66, 67, 68, 69, 70, 82, 89, 94, 97, 98, 99, 101, 103, 104, 105, 151, 154, 159, 162, 163, 206
Orange, W.A. (William) 57–60; Bible Class 54, 57, 58, 60, 65, 67, 68, 88, 95, 96, 141–42, 157, 164, 206, 236 n.1, 236 n.6, 237 n.20; and Brethren 60; and Bretton 99; and Crusader movement 54; and Evangelical Churchmen's Fellowship 101, 102, 103, 153, 165, 168, 170; evangelical faith 60–67, 143, 164; and Evangelical Unions/IVF 12, 42, 44, 49, 52, 57, 60, 65, 66,

68–69, 75, 76, 77, 88, 127, 137, 208; impact 67–69, 75, 82, 83, 95, 96, 98, 101, 112, 127, 150, 171, 175, 178, 186 (*see also* Orange Pips, above); key leader of Anglican evangelicalism 12, 57, 75, 210; and Miller 141–42; and Nelson Diocese 69–71; and Thompson 59, 68, 82, 89–90, 91, 92, 101
Orr, Edwin 72, 128, 191, 238 n.4
O'Sullivan, Kevin 50, 54, 55, 137, 161
Otago Evangelical Bible League 119
Otago University Evangelical Union (OUEU) 45, 46, 47, 48, 51, 77, 78, 107, 128, 135, 147, 184, 210
Outlook 19–20, 26–27, 32, 33, 35, 36–37, 38–40, 48, 181, 182, 198, 199–200
Overseas Christian Fellowships 126
Overseas Missions Committee 182
Oxford Movement *see* Tractarianism

Packer, J.I. 12, 131–32, 166, 168, 170, 192
Paltridge, Henry 94
Papesch, Elinor 183
Parr, Stephen 68, 82, 83
Peaston, Monroe 105
Penman, David 101
Pentecostalism 134, 148, 214
Perry, Norman 125
Pettit, William 43, 44, 49, 56, 72, 76, 129, 142
Pfankuch, Lester 59, 94, 98, 105–06, 151, 154, 172
Pickering, David 94, 100–01, 158, 159
pietism 12, 33, 39, 108, 192, 208
Piggin, Stuart 16, 211
Pinwill, Andy 88
Ponui Island Crusader camps 54–55
Poolman, Reg 189
Poon, John 193
Pounawea Conventions 30, 32–34, 113, 181, 191
Powell, David 156
prayer 18, 20, 25, 26, 28, 31, 32, 43, 46, 57, 62–63, 77, 95, 100, 107, 112, 114, 179, 206
Prayer Book (Anglican) 63, 65, 82, 166, 167, 172, 174
predestination 19, 80
premillennialism 28
Prendergast, Rose 98
Presbyterian Bible Class Movement 18, 19, 26, 32, 78, 81, 107, 116, 124, 125
Easter Camps 181, 184, 187, 191, 226

n.55; and Thomas Miller 29–30 South Auckland 179, 183, 187, 188
Presbyterian Church of America 118
Presbyterian Church of (Aotearoa) New Zealand (PCNZ, PCANZ) and evangelicals: to 1945 17–20, 25–41; 1945–55 107–25; 1956–65 176–205; since 1965 213; Auckland (1956–65) 189; charismatic renewal movement 214; Christchurch (1956–65) 190; different evangelical strands and emphases 208; Dunedin 190, 204 (*see also* St Stephen's Presbyterian Church); and Evangelical Ministers' Fellowship 145, 146; and Evangelical Unions 48, 49, 108, 109, 111, 112, 113, 122, 123, 127, 193, 202; General Assembly 27, 30, 37, 38, 39–40, 110, 122, 124, 125, 176, 186, 201, 202, 203–04, 213; and interdenominationalism 32, 35–36, 111, 115, 182; and Inter-Varsity Fellowship 75, 76, 108, 112, 113, 115, 116, 122, 193, 202; Missions Committee 119, 120, 121; provincial New Zealand 190–92; South Auckland 176–89, 193, 202, 203, 207, 210–11; and Student Christian Movement 109, 111, 117, 202; and Tyndale Fellowship 147; Wellington (1956–65) 189–90; *see also* Theological Hall; Westminster Confession; Westminster Fellowship; and names of individual churches and people, particularly Thomas Miller and Graham Miller.
Presbyterian Church of Canada 195
Presbyterian Church League 110, 111, 112
Presbyterian Church of the New Hebrides 108, 119–20, 177, 179, 180
Presbyterian Church, United States 118
Presbyterian Māori Synod 179
Princeton theology 18, 27, 37
Pritchard, John 182
Protestant Political Association 26
Protestant Reformation Society 102, 197
Purchas, Elizabeth 151
Puritanism 12, 75, 80, 192
Pyatt, W.A. 173

Rae, Simon 148, 278 n.315
Ralph, Bruce 182
Ralph, Ken 137, 182

Index 297

Ramm, Bernard 136
Reaper 35, 129
reason 74, 89, 130–35, 166
Reeves, Paul 164
Reformation 12, 27, 63, 64, 65, 75, 101, 109, 110, 112, 114, 115, 123, 139, 167, 192, 194
Reformed Churches of New Zealand 113, 114, 120, 122, 198–99
Reformed theology 33, 64, 73, 107, 108, 109, 111, 113, 114–16, 168, 170, 178, 179, 199, 200, 203, 208
Reid, Gordon 41
Reid, Hugh 191
revivals: New Zealand 18, 20; Scotland (1859) 18
revivalism 12, 16, 17, 19, 29, 33, 34, 40, 47, 53, 64, 108, 159, 194, 208, 209
Rex, Helmut 80
Ridley College (Melbourne) 59, 101, 103, 163
ritualism 11, 17, 61, 66, 112
Robertson, Winifred 56
Robinson, Bob 156
Robinson, J.A.T. 175, 194
Rolleston, A.E. 154
Romanism 110, 112, 194–95, 199, 200, 202
Rosser, Stan 163
Roundhill, Ken 137, 142
Roxborogh, John 266n.43
Roxburgh, Irvine 147
Roxburgh, Rymall 34, 41, 78, 81
Runia, Klaas 136
Russell Street Bible Class 26
Ryburn, W.M. 196
Ryle, J.C. 63, 80, 98, 103, 168, 192

Sabbatarianism 18, 193, 196
Sadlier, W.C. 69
Sage, David 41, 189, 193
Salmond, J.D. 41
Salvation Army 19, 26, 32
Sanders, J.O. (Oswald) 33, 35–36, 49, 168
Sankey hymns 19, 26, 46
Sasse, Hermann 136
Scarlet, J.S. 190
Scarrow, Jack 120, 252 n.105
Schaeffer, Francis 132
Schoneveld, Bert 183
Schurr, Geoffrey 151
Scott, Archie 168–69
Scottish Common Sense philosophy 15
Scottish Reformation Society 198

Scripture Union (SU) 95, 97, 127, 141, 169, 181, 186, 190, 207
Scroggie, Graham 15, 62
Second blessing theology 33, 261 n.39
Second Coming 28, 45, 52, 64, 65, 194; *see also* eschatology
secular theology 147, 148, 194, 213
separatism 102, 115, 199, 200, 205; American fundamentalism 13, 53, 120, 121, 143, 144; and EUs/IVF 53–54, 75, 207; Orange 67; McIntire and ICCC 118–19, 120, 143, 198; and Reformed Church 199; Thompson 92–93; and Westminster Fellowship 115, 199–200
Shaw, Donald 147
Sheat, Norman 191
Shedd, W.G.T. 80
Sheldon, Lance 151
Shields, T.T. 119
Short, Rendle 74, 131
Simeon, Charles 63, 65, 166, 168
Simkin, W.J. 96, 163, 164
Simmons, Joe 168
Smith, Gordon 72
Smith, J.N.A. (Jack) 34, 187, 190
Somerville, Jack 34
Somerville, Ray 100, 161, 162, 165
Soper, Donald 141, 195
Spargo, George 94, 159
Spurgeon, Charles 25, 27, 62
St Aidan's (Bryndwr) 150, 153, 154, 156
St Andrew's (Epsom) 164
St Andrew's (Hoon Hay) 94, 152, 155
St Andrew's Presbyterian Church (Manurewa) 184–86
St James' (Lower Hutt) 99, 100, 101
St James' (Lower Riccarton) 88–89, 152, 241 n.9
St James' Presbyterian Church (Pukekohe) 19, 182–84, 185
St John's College 69–70, 82, 147, 164
St John's (Latimer Square, Christchurch) 60, 154
St John's (Woolston) 95, 150, 154, 156, 168
St John's Presbyterian Church (Papatoetoe) 185
St Martin's (Spreydon) 89–95, 98, 100, 104–05, 150, 151, 152–53, 154, 155, 156, 159, 210
St Matthew's (Dunedin) 162–63, 188
St Stephen's (Shirley) 150–52, 154, 155, 156
St Stephen's Presbyterian Church

(Dunedin) 25, 29–30, 31, 32, 33, 36, 40, 41, 107, 112, 147, 188, 201, 269 n.134
St Timothy's (Burnside) 154
Stanton, Graham 163
Steele, J.V.T. (Tom) 33, 34, 39–40, 125
Stening, George 60
Stephens, Frank 137
Stephenson, P.W. 69–70, 97, 99, 103
Stevely, Alan 48
stewardship campaigns 125, 151
Stewart, David 136, 209
Stott, John 12, 14, 128, 131, 168, 169, 170, 178, 200, 209
Strahan, Thomas 182
Strang, Marion *see* Miller, Marion (née Strang)
Street, Jennie 31
Student Bible League 43, 44
Student Christian Movement (SCM) 14, 20, 26, 42, 43, 233 n.48; decline in membership 127, 128, 129, 195, 213; and Evangelical Unions 43, 44, 45–48, 52, 53, 56, 77–78, 79, 111, 117, 119, 128, 136, 138, 140–41, 202, 207, 210; and Inter-Varsity Fellowship 44–45, 72, 73, 74, 77–78, 138–41, 202, 211; and Presbyterian evangelicals 18, 109, 111, 117, 202; reading material 132; Theological Hall students 78–79
Student Life 213
substitutionary atonement 26, 37, 38, 45, 73, 74, 80, 109, 139, 140, 166
Sullivan, Martin 59, 63, 67, 105–06, 128, 151
Sunday School 29, 60, 89, 93, 95, 100, 107, 152, 158, 161, 179, 187
Sutton, P.E. 160
Swanton, Robert 198

Tanner, Carl 88–89
Tasker, R.V.G. 132
Taylor, David 105
Taylor, Hudson 63, 92
Taylor, R.J. 160
Taylor, Ron 94
Teacher's Christian Fellowship 147
Teachers' Prayer Fellowship 73
temperance movement 26, 193
Temple, W.P. (Bill) 125, 189
Tertiary Students' Christian Fellowship (TSCF) 213; *see also* Inter-Varsity Fellowship of Evangelical Unions (New Zealand)

Teulon, Harvey 59, 82, 153, 154
Theological Hall, Knox College, Dunedin 18, 26, 35, 37, 41, 48, 78–82, 83, 115, 116, 128, 147, 181, 184, 186, 188, 204–05
Theological Students' Fellowships (TSF) 106, 126, 147
Theological Students' Prayer Union (TSPU) 73, 79, 240 n.95
Thirty-Nine Articles 63, 65, 73, 101–02, 167
Thomas, Griffith 98
Thomas, Hedley 60, 168
Thomas, Phil 151, 156
Thompson, H.F. 193
Thompson, Muri 182
Thompson, R.J. 127
Thompson, Reena 90, 98
Thompson, R.F.N. (Roger) 89–95, 150, 152–53, 159, 210; and Crusader Movement 54; and church union 173; and Evangelical Churchmen's Fellowship 103, 161, 166–67, 168, 171, 172; and Evangelical Unions 127; and Graham Miller 76; influence 94–95, 97, 98, 100–01, 104, 105, 150, 151, 162; and Orange 59, 68, 82, 89–90, 91, 92, 101; evangelical conservatism 170–72
Thomson, Andrew 192, 195
Thomson, G.I. 193
Thomson, Harry 48, 59, 68, 76, 82, 95, 127, 150, 151, 154, 162, 210; and Church Missionary Society 95–97, 104
Thomson, Hugh 97, 154
Thomson, Ian 187
Tonks, Colin 94, 153
Torrey, R.A. 16, 18
Tovey, Peter 59, 154
Toyatome, Masumi 252 n.95
Tractarianism 17, 166, 173, 196
Tripp, Dick 94, 153
Troughton, Hessel 190, 263 n.135
Turner, Arnold 50
Tutt, Kelvin 158
Tweedie, Bert 189
Tyndale Fellowship 147
Tyndale House (Christchurch) 88, 141–42, 165, 170

'The Underground' (Anglican group, Auckland) 164
United Evangelical Church 120
United Maori Mission 179

United Presbyterian Church 111
University of Waikato EU 126

Valiant in Fight 75
Veitch, James 147
Victoria University (College) EU (VUCEU, VUEU) 46, 50, 107, 108, 128–29, 130, 135, 136, 139

Wallace, Bill 40, 191
Walsh, Ernie 189
Wardlaw, R.J. 193
Wards, Laurie 94
Warfield, B.B. 27, 80, 175, 192
Warin, Wyvern 110
Warner, Peter 128
Warren, Alwyn 66, 151, 173
Watt, Douglas 189
Webster, A.C. (Cliff) 108, 189, 191, 196
Wellington Teachers' College EU 136
Wells, R.H. 190
Wells Organisation 92, 151, 161
Wesley, John 25, 27
Wesleyans 31, 75; *see also* Methodist people and church(es)
Westminster Confession 18, 73, 102, 111, 113, 115–16, 117, 123, 184, 186, 188; and Scripture 247 n.93
Westminster Theological Seminary 109
Westminster Fellowship (WF): late 1950s 192–93; 1960s 193–205, 210–11; anti-modernism 208; beginnings 109–12, 112–14, 145, 210, 246 n.53; and church union 174, 192, 194, 196, 199–200, 201, 202, 203, 205; early years 122; evangelical and reformed emphases 114–16, 198–99, 200, 203, 207; and Evangelical Churchmen's Fellowship 169; evangelical critique 204–05; and Evangelical Ministers' Fellowship 146; *Evangelical Presbyterian* and other publications 107, 114, 123–24, 125, 186, 192–97, 198, 200, 201, 202, 203, 204–05; and fundamentalism 117–22, 197, 199; and Graham Miller 112–13, 116, 122, 181, 182, 193, 196, 198, 199–200, 202, 203, 204, 210; international connections 197–98; and IVF 76; and Moore 108; opposition to 201–04; Presbyterian ministers' involvement 185, 186–87, 189, 190, 191, 192, 193, 195, 203; Presbyterian views 116–17, 188, 191; and Reformed Churches of New Zealand 198–99; and Rob Miller 107
Weston, Brian 183
West-Watson, Campbell 66
Wiggins, Max 51, 54, 59, 82–83, 151, 154
Wilberforce, William 63
Wilford, J.R. 62
Wilkens, W.F. (Bill) 97, 98
Williams, A.E. 182
Williams, Basil 54, 59, 68, 72, 76, 77, 82, 134
Williams, Donald 159
Willitts, Marcus 182
Wilson, Challis 127, 189, 190
Wilson, Lewis 115, 127, 142, 186, 193, 199, 203
Wilson, Tom 189
Wisdom, Walter 76, 88, 154
Withers, J.T. 151
Witness 157, 159
Woods, Stacey 69, 72, 143
Woods, Tom 183, 188, 189
World Council of Churches (WCC) 118, 120, 143, 195
World Evangelical Alliance 144
Wright, Alf 168

Yolland, H. 49
Young Men's Christian Association (YMCA) 18, 125
Youth for Christ (YFC) 143, 144
Youth with a Mission 184
Yule, G.M (George, Geordie) 176–77
Yule, G.M. (Morrison, Morris) 33, 34, 40, 78, 111, 113, 120, 121, 189, 193
Yule, R.M. (Rob) 271 n.313, 271 n.315